W9-BRZ-255

19.95

HISTORY OF EDUCATION AND CULTURE IN AMERICA

HISTORY OF EDUCATION AND CULTURE IN AMERICA

H. Warren Button

State University of New York at Buffalo

Eugene F. Provenzo, Jr.

University of Miami

Prentice-Hall, Inc., Englewood Cliffs, New Jersey 07632

142598

Library of Congress Cataloging in Publication Data

Button, H. Warren.
   History of education and culture in America.

   Bibliography
   Includes index.
   1. Education—United States—History.   2. United
States—History.   I. Provenzo, Eugene F.   II. Title.
LA205.B86   1983   370'.973   82-12388
ISBN 0-13-390237-4

Editorial/production supervision:
   Maureen Connelly
Cover design: Ray Lundgren
Manufacturing buyers: Edmund W. Leone
   and Ron Chapman

© 1983 by Prentice-Hall, Inc., Englewood Cliffs, N.J. 07632

All rights reserved. No part of this book
may be reproduced in any form or
by any means without permission in writing
from the publisher.

Printed in the United States of America

10 9 8 7 6 5 4

ISBN   0-13-390237-4

Prentice-Hall International, Inc., *London*
Prentice-Hall of Australia Pty. Limited, *Sydney*
Prentice-Hall Canada, Inc., *Toronto*
Prentice-Hall of India Private Limited, *New Delhi*
Prentice-Hall of Japan, Inc., *Tokyo*
Prentice-Hall of Southeast Asia Pte Ltd., *Singapore*
Whitehall Books Limited, *Wellington, New Zealand*
Editora Prentice-Hall do Brasil Ltda., *Rio de Janeiro*

To Raymond E. Callahan

CONTENTS

x   Contents

ACKNOWLEDGMENTS

Our first obligation is to our students collectively, who provided the impetus for this book. Among them we are especially obligated to Phyllis McGruder Chase, Truman Beckley Brown, Concepcion Garcia, Thomas A. Michalski (whose knowledge of Buffalo Polonia we have employed), Gary N. McCloskey, William Bonds Thomas (who later saw the manuscript in near-final form), and Chokesui Ahagon. We have been aided by several graduate assistants, especially John G. Ramsay and Elizabeth Graham. Our colleagues have also been most helpful, especially Maxine Seller, who read the manuscript in its entirety, and Gail P. Kelly, Robert S. Harnack, and Melvin J. Tucker, who reviewed portions of it. Special thanks also go to William E. Eaton, Donald R. Warren, Wayne Urban, Arthur Wirth, and Robert Kottkamp. Our wives, Lee and Asterie, read carefully, criticized constructively, vastly encouraged, and showed the greatest of forbearance. The flaws and errors of this book are our own.

The authors' volume entitled *Sources for The History of American Education and Culture* is available from The University Press of America, Washington, D.C.

H. Warren Button
Eugene F. Provenzo, Jr.

INTRODUCTION*

This work focuses on the relationship between education and American culture. While it deals mainly with the history of the public schools, it also attempts to understand less formal means of education. We do not assume that the schools have been the sole, or even the most important, source of learning in our culture. For example, schools are not, nor have they ever been, as important as the family in the educational process. In the education of many people they have often been less important than religion or even apprenticeship. In our own era, schools seem to play a less important role than television in the education of many people.**

We assume that our readers are primarily interested in schools and their history. Many will be teachers or prospective teachers. Our emphasis will therefore be on schools and the people who have taught and learned there. We hope to present students, teachers, and administrators, as well as others who have been involved with schooling, as real people coping with the problems of living in a complex and changing culture. While much that we will present will be abstract, the

---

* The introduction is an adaptation by the authors of H. Warren Button's paper, "Creating More Usable Pasts: History in the Study of Education," *Educational Researcher*, VIII (May, 1979), pp. 3-9. Republished with the permission of the American Educational Research Association.

** For citations, see "Bibliography, Sources, and Notes," pp. 343-367. The last three words of each quotation are given, followed by its source.

people we will discuss have been and are more than merely abstractions of thought or belief.

Texts on the history of American education have traditionally focused on the public schools to the exclusion of nearly any other subject. The public school was seen as the agency or institution that led to most of what was admirable in American life—a society that was open, but orderly; a society that was safe from revolution, and a society in all respects equitable and just.

The traditional historical interpretation of American education has been one focusing on the perfection of the schools—the story of their foreordained, inevitable, and successive triumphs. The schools spread from their beginnings to every territory and state. They spread to include high schools and public colleges and universities. They spread downward, providing kindergarten for young children, and even nurseries for still younger children. More and more the schools provided learning that had previously come from the home, or from an apprenticeship. The schools taught morals and values. They taught occupational skills. They taught appreciation of the arts, and fear of tobacco, alcohol, and other drugs.

The most important of the traditional educational historians was Ellwood P. Cubberley of Stanford University, whose *Public Education in the United States* (1919) stayed in print for thirty years and was read and studied by generations of prospective teachers. Some earlier historians had written in the same spirit, and for decades books about the history of education were patterned after Cubberley's. A few books in this tradition are still in use—for instance, S. Alexander Rippa's *Education in a Free Society* (1980). R. Freeman Butt's *Public Education in the United States* (1978) seems in many ways to be a return to this earlier tradition.

Much of the information that the traditional educational historians have amassed is still useful and illuminating. We dispute many of their interpretations, however. That the growth and shaping of the public schools was inevitable is an argument that we do not necessarily agree with. We understand the beginnings of that convention in the history of American education. It was written in times when most American historians dealt with something like the inevitable destiny of the United States—a destiny closely linked to the belief in progress. The historical imperative, the inevitability of progress, was a part of Hegel's philosophy and for fifty years was the most prominent assumption in American education. However, to understand it is not necessarily to accept it.

The Cubberley tradition of history of education was reconsidered and largely supplanted in the 1960s. Bernard Bailyn, prominent historian of colonial America, was one of the first and most influential critics. *Education*, he argued, was properly defined as the sum of everything intended to enculturate child, youth, and adult—family, church, newspaper, and so on. Among those institutions intended to enculturate, schools—especially colonial schools—were a small part of the pattern and process. Bailyn's advice was in some ways awkward to accept. It entailed a complete redefinition of a subfield of history. More exactly, it abolished the accepted definition. History of education was cultural history and social history; all of history but "with politics left out." It was a prospect that opened bright possibilities for educational historians. It was also life in a *ganzfeld*, a world without cues and direction.

The second critic of the 1960s was Lawrence A. Cremin. (Cremin as historian has many strengths: The most unusual of them is the ability to reconsider, and to change his mind.) *In The Wonderful World of Ellwood Cubberley* (1965), a critique and bibliographic essay, his formulation of the history of education was that it should be a history of "institutions" that have educated including not only schools, but also families, churches, libraries, publishers, newspapers, television, and so on. These institutions were to be seen in the context of the society of their time. Educational historians underwent a completely new way of looking at their subject.

Several new historians of education brought to the history of education new political orientations. Cubberley had been sure that all had been for the best. By the 1960s, some had no such certainty. First, Raymond E. Callahan brought to the history of education the old radical conviction that in a great many ways schools had worked out badly, that reform was an imperative. Callahan's *Education and the Cult of Efficiency* (1962) was dedicated to George S. Counts, who of course had been one of the pioneer radical sociologists of education.

One of the most prominent historians of education in the 1960s and 1970s has been Michael B. Katz, who has been categorically certain that in a great many ways schools have worked out badly. He has perhaps been as sure in his conviction as Cubberley had been in his. Katz's contributions to history of education in works such as *The Irony of Early School Reform* (1968) and *Class, Bureaucracy, and the Schools* (1971) have been devoted to why schools did and do support existing class structure because of their formal, hierarchical, bureaucratic, unyielding nature.

Katz is among the most distinguished of the new wave of educational historians loosely known as *Revisionists*. While we agree with much that revisionist history has to say about American educational history, we also disagree with certain of its assumptions. Revisionist history often has about it the air of predestination, of inevitability, of certain evolution. If in traditional history there was unwavering progress toward perfection, in revisionist history there is often the assumption of certain disintegration and decay, of schools as institutions that can only grow more and more exploitative, more and more repressive, more and more an impediment to change.

Bailyn changed the field of educational history by extending its boundaries. Katz and the revisionists changed educational history by introducing political and social philosophy into the field. Other changes, somewhat quieter, but perhaps even more important, have now begun in the methodology of educational history. While old techniques are still valid, new research methodologies have the potential to reorient the field. Historians in general, and educational historians in particular, are beginning to discover the usefulness of the computer and empirical approaches to historical research. Content analysis, a particular interest of one of the authors, is just beginning to come into use, as is the analysis of visual and photographic data related to education. Such methods encourage the pursuit of what may be termed "history from the bottom up"—a grass-roots history. In this sense, the more traditional intellectual history that has dominated much of the writing in the field is being supplemented by a new type of history. Much of the content of our text reflects some of these new directions.

History of education is a hybrid specialty, as are the sociology of education and educational psychology. As they do, it comes from a parent that is a "pure" discipline. Unlike sociology of education and educational psychology, history of education comes from a pure discipline that is one of the humanities. The grand strategies of all empirical inquiry, all inquiry about the real palpable world whether in the physical sciences, the social sciences, or history, are much the same. What may be unique, however, to a particular field of inquiry are its tactical approaches. History has its own tactics, conventions, and canons of research. It answers in its own way the analogues of the empiricists' questions about reliability and validity. History lives with its uncertainties, just as the social sciences live with probabilistic findings.

While, like the social scientist, the historian is often interested in widely applicable findings and theory, the historian is more often interested in the particular or unique event, the specific era, the set of closely interrelated events.

History, or specifically, the history of education, is not, except in a certain philosophic sense, the past. History is a description and interpretation of the past. It is history in this sense that can be useful. As historians, however, we feel that history should be more than merely useful. Part of the discipline of studying the past is literary. In the United States, the first great historians—Irving, Prescott, Bancroft—were interested as much in form as in content. History should also be of value simply because the lives of people in the past—their actions and deeds, their motives and meanings—are intrinsically interesting.

For improving education, we believe that history can explain something of the present, how we have gotten where we are. It can generate hypotheses that account for the schools' obstinate, perverse, adamantine resistance to change. History can lead to the formulation of general laws—in this context, concerning schools, schooling, and education.

History can inform. Probably more than in any other aspect of education's history, there has been informative work on the history of school administration. It seems clear that school administrations' use of management standards for efficiency and business procedures was initially the result of outside pressures and influences, rather than an organic part of schools, schooling, or the process of education. It is strongly argued that the development of the typical city school administrative bureaucratic hierarchy was not inevitable, and that there were real alternatives to it—far less constraining alternatives. These historians' conclusions have become part of the general literature of school administration.

History can describe. It is often more valuable when it explains. As historians, we strongly feel that the results of historical research in education are useful but must be used in their own ways. History has limits, because it cannot provide the degree of certainty that comes from testing hypotheses in empirical research. History, instead, has its own strength: wide perspectives, long views, rich sources, and rich data. History is not solely utilitarian; it could not be and should not be. But history has been and should be used to improve education.

Since education is always in a cultural context, the history of education should also be within that context. In four general sections we have sketched events, developments, and moods that have been important in our culture—in Colonial times, in the first century of independence, in the times of Progressive reforms, and since the beginning of the Depression. Without that background an account of the history of education is far less meaningful.

HISTORY
OF EDUCATION
AND CULTURE
IN AMERICA

PART ONE
BEGINNINGS

Education and schools are part of a wider culture and society. Therefore the history of education, or even the history of schools only, must be written against the background of a more general history. Since the roots of American education are English, this brief description begins with England and follows the growth and change of the colonies until the time of the American Revolution.

The sixteenth century was a time of change for Europe. The New World and voyages to the East had yielded rich and splendid cargoes of gold and silver, silk, and spices. The revival of trade circulated the new wealth throughout Europe. Intellectual riches resulted from the rediscovery and continued reexamination of texts and manuscripts from classical Rome and Greece. It was the time of the Renaissance, the rebirth or reawakening of the traditions of classical culture. The scholars known as *humanists* who led this revival saw themselves as taking up the pursuit of knowledge where barbarians had interrupted Classical authors a thousand years before. Other men looked at the decadent Church and protested. They became Protestants. The Church, they said, had to return to its essentials, to its original simplicity. Imperatively, the teachings of the Bible were to be followed in the Church. The Church's accumulations of a thousand years—the elaborate ceremonials and rituals, its riches and worldliness—were to be discarded. Protestantism was, of course, a cause to which men dedicated their lives and for which some suffered death. While there were many Protestant sects in England in the 1600s, the most important single group there at that time was the Puritans, whose purpose was to purify the Church of England—not to replace it.

In England, with the death of Elizabeth I in 1603, an age of exuberance was coming to an end. A great age of seamanship and discovery, typified by the explorer Sir Francis Drake, was over. The splendid flowering of English literature and drama, at its height in William Shakespeare's plays, was also coming to an end. The 1600s in England were less colorful than the Elizabethan era, less remarkable for art than for science, and most remarkable for religious disputes and revolution inspired by religion. By 1600, the middle class was, as a result of peace, prosperity, and trade, much more numerous than it had previously been and had an increased influence in politics. The middle-class merchants and craftsmen and landowners accumulated wealth and, as Puritans, power enough by the 1640s to challenge—and execute—a king.

When Columbus searched for a shorter way to the Far East, his voyage joined together the fates and futures of Europe and the Americas. In South and Central America the Spanish found empires to conquer and riches to loot. For them the land farther north was less promising. There were no gold mines or riches to seize. The eastern shoreline of North America stretched for 2,000 miles and more, northward and eastward. It was indented and broken in many places by river mouths and other safe harbors. The climate was temperate in most places. The Native Americans, misnamed *Indians*, belonged to hundreds of tribes with almost as many different languages. In general, they had little in common with one another and did not unite in order to resist the settlement of their lands by the early colonists. The existence of numerous rivers and harbors, of a moderate climate, and natives unorganized for resistance, made North America splendid for colonization, if not for immediate exploitation. The Atlantic seaboard, a narrow strip along bays and navigable rivers, was the location of the first settlements. It was also the area in which nearly all settlers lived until after the Revolution.

The establishment of the colonies followed a fairly general pattern. The first step was the organization of a *company*, a group of adventurers or investors. It was desirable, if not absolutely necessary, to have a charter—a license to occupy a part of the land. An expedition was organized and ships contracted. The voyage itself was hazardous and trying—the Pilgrims' six-week passage from old England to New England, for example, was not long by the standards of the times. In the early colonies there were "starving years," the interval between arrival and the harvesting of food enough for survival. Only after these stages could a colony prosper and grow. There were always risks and often failures, especially for the earliest colonies. It is to be understood that there were exceptions to the general pattern of settlement. Plymouth Colony was established in a place where the Pilgrims did not have charter rights to settle. Rhode Island and Connecticut were begun without sea voyage, by men and women who came by land from Massachusetts. There was no "starving time," or famine, in Boston.

Many different motives underlaid the establishment of the colonies. No colony was begun for a single reason. Some colonies were established strictly for trade and profit. Other colonies, most notably Massachusetts, were founded by individuals who hoped to establish godly and perfect societies, religious utopias based upon their interpretation of the Bible. Still other colonies were intended to serve as refuges for those persecuted for their religious faith. Nearly all the colonists expected to better themselves in material ways. Some expected riches.

Virginia is a good example of a colony founded in hopes of profit. The London Company was incorporated to colonize. Stock was sold. A board of directors was named. A charter from the king was secured for colonization along the southern Atlantic coast and west to the "South Sea." The expedition was organized in London—badly organized, as it turned out. The leaders were ineffectual, the men "disordered persons ... profane ... riotous ... diseased ... crazed ..." (also sick, starved, regimented, and seeking a new life). During their twenty-week voyage in 1606-07, sixteen of the 120 men died, and only fifty-three lived through the first winter. The colony survived largely because of the leadership of Captain John Smith; corn was planted, and peace made with the Indians. Contrary to initial hopes, there was no gold to be found. The "South Sea" remained undiscovered. Trade with the Indians was not very profitable, and in addition they resisted Christianization and sometimes bloodily and violently attacked the colonists. It would be several years before the Virginia colony was secure and before the planting of tobacco would lead to more general prosperity.

By 1648, there were 15,000 settlers on small farms along the branching bays of eastern, tidewater, Virginia. Gardening and farming, hunting and fishing provided plentiful food. Most of the land was forest. Houses were still small, and planters worked their corn and tobacco fields with their "servants," men and women who had indentured themselves—or contracted—to work five years, more or less, to pay for their ocean crossing. Only a few Blacks had been brought over, and there were no slavery laws in Virginia during its first fifty years. These would come later. The early Virginians were members of the Church of England, but Puritan in sentiment. Churches were built soon after the settlers arrived; church attendance was required, and idleness, gambling, and working on Sundays were forbidden. The impressive plantation houses of Virginia would not be built until the 1700s, but the founders of some of Virginia's most famed families, Byrd, Lee, and Carter for instance, were already in the process of establishing themselves.

Massachusetts was the most important colony of god-seeking utopians, although the settlers also hoped for prosperity. Indeed, they held that "stewardship," the accumulation and care of wealth was in itself a sign of grace. Unlike the Virginians, they came in part because the English government in the 1630s frowned increasingly upon Puritan beliefs.

The most important group of Puritan settlers arrived in 1630. Under the leadership of Governor John Winthrop they brought with them their company's charter and were its officers, as well as the leaders of the colony's government. More than a thousand men, women, and children arrived aboard seventeen ships. Boston and seven other towns were established.

In spite of Winthrop's hopes and plans, Boston did not remain a "city of

God," if it ever was. Perhaps the hopes and lives of the Puritans are most fairly represented by the smaller towns. Dedham, a few miles south of Boston, serves as an example. The founding families of Dedham had come from a number of places in England; they had found that they shared a common faith. The town was founded in 1636, at which time a government made up of the settlers was formed. House lots around a square, a *common*, were allocated, and outlying fields assigned in proportion to the size and wealth of families. After long discussion and prayer, the congregation agreed to a church "covenant" and a minister was recruited. Disputes were to be settled as among brothers. There are virtually no instances from this period of the prosecution of court trials or suits. To live in Dedham was to live in a godly place. It was to live in peace and tranquility, in families, houses, and a village such as those known in England. For forty years Dedham in a modest way was a working utopia.

In Boston many of those who came were "strangers," not members of the Puritan Congregational Churches. Often Puritans' sons and daughters failed to have the experience of being born again, a condition for church membership. Before 1700 the better-off merchants were accumulating more wealth. The poor remained poor. Concern had developed over the increasing number of unmarried mothers. There had been an attempt to open a brothel in the city. Even more distressful, those in control of Boston found themselves threatened by those with democratic tendencies. The Puritan hopes of a religious utopia had failed. Bostonians were interested in trade and other matters as well as in the church. Even at the expense of utopianism, they were prudent men and women, intent on living by the laws of England so as to protect their charter and rights. Successful "stewardship" increased the difference between rich and poor. (A famous historian has said that America has been the *dis*proving ground of utopias. But Americans have always had a fondness for utopias, from John Winthrop's to Timothy Leary's, and since.)

Pennsylvania is representative of the colonies established as refuge. Its founder, William Penn, was a devout Quaker, or Friend, and a firm believer in freedom in Christian worship. The Quakers were the most extreme Protestant group to emerge from the late 1600s. For them, repentance and truth was dependent upon the individual. The church was not necessary for salvation. Penn himself had been imprisoned several times in England. Quakers there were prohibited from holding office and even from attending universities. Penn's colony was to be a refuge for not only the Quakers, but also for the members of other faiths.

Pennsylvania's charter was secured from the king of England as payment for the king's debt to Penn's father. Pennsylvania's *Frame of Government* explicitly provided for freedom of worship. Philadelphia ("City of Friends") was established in 1682. The Quakers welcomed to the city many German Mennonites, also religious refugees. Except for the New York Dutch, the Mennonites were the first large non-English-speaking group in the colonies. Pennsylvania land was fertile and cheap, and although established late, became one of the largest and most prosperous of the English colonies.

The other colonies were in some ways like Virginia, Massachusetts, and Pennsylvania. Like the Virginians, Marylanders sought profit from the raising of tobacco. Carolinians later had the same goal and raised rice and indigo. Rhode Island, Connecticut, and later New Hampshire were offshoots of Puritan Massachu- ♦ setts. Maryland, settled earlier, had been in part intended as a haven for Catholics. Georgia, last of the original thirteen colonies to be settled, was also to be a refuge, though for people who were poor rather than discriminated against on grounds of religion.

In the 160 years before independence, feelings about religion weakened, and churches of many kinds appeared in most of the colonies. In the middle 1700s religious enthusiasm grew during the "Great Awakening," which was partly a reaction to *rationalism*, the cold and impersonal scientific logic that was gaining support.

In those hundred and sixty years the colonies' population grew to 3 million. Puritans and planters and Quakers were joined by tens of thousands of German Protestants and Scotch-Irish Presbyterians, as well as by growing numbers of Blacks. There were at least a few men and women from every kingdom in Christendom. Prosperous port cities, like the smaller cities in England, developed, although nearly everyone (nineteen out of twenty) still lived on farms or in villages.

In some colonies, growth after the first years was natural. Families were larger, especially beginning in the later 1700s. Fewer babies died. Individuals lived longer. Once the hazards of the sea crossings were overcome, the colonies had a "healthy clime" as compared with England. Pennsylvania and the other colonies grew by immigration also. The Germans continued to come, and Mennonites and members of many sects established communities of their own. The Presbyterian "Scotch-Irish" of northern Ireland were driven from their homes by failures of crops, by English trade and manufacturing restrictions, and by poverty. There were unwelcome English restrictions upon Presbyterian churches.

Many of Pennsylvania's immigrants came as contract laborers, *indentured servants*. Most indentured themselves because they had no money to pay for the sea crossing, but the signing of indentures seems to have been common because a "master" could give guidance in one's first years in the New World. Before 1776, the population of Pennsylvania had spilled southwestward, into the Shenandoah Valley of Virginia and onto the Piedmont—the uplands—of the Carolinas, and even into northeastern Georgia.

In the tidewater South the need for workers led to importing indentured servants. Those who brought indentured servants were granted land as an added incentive, fifty acres for each servant. By the middle 1700s, indentured servants were harder to obtain. More slaves were introduced into the colonies. Most had been kidnapped or bought from villages in West Africa. Blacks were first introduced into America at Jamestown in 1619, but it was only later that the English-speaking American colonies became an important market for slaves. (There would be slaves, though in smaller numbers, in all the other colonies.)

Long before 1776, differences in wealth and power in the colonies increased. To have wealth was to gain wealth, of course. Some New England merchants who had come from London, or had relatives there, had credit. In Virginia the cost of a plantation also came from the profits of importing goods and exporting tobacco.

Other plantations were bought from the earnings of doctors and lawyers, and occasionally of ministers—*parsons.* Sometimes marriage to a rich widow provided capital. In the 1700s, a few families in Virginia were "well-off," though not nearly as rich as the richest Englishmen. They owned handsome houses, shares in ships, iron furnaces and forges, and sometimes thousands and tens of thousands of acres of land. While much forested land was kept in reserve to replace worn-out fields, other land was bought for investment or speculation. The sons of wealthy planters, automatically entitled to special consideration because of their families, were "aristocrats."

Yet, wealth was not the norm. Most colonists in the North and South were of the "middling sort." In most instances they were farmers, but they also were skilled and semiskilled workers, and their families. The social structures of the colonies were relatively open. Although most families did not, it was possible for the poor to become rich. For the Pepperells of Maine, two generations was needed, as was the case for the Byrds of Virginia. Accumulation of wealth was possible within one's own lifetime. One early Massachusetts governor, Sir William Phips, for example, had started life as an orphan and shepherd. What most often happened was that a former indentured servant became the owner of a farm, or the son of a "middling" sea captain or small trader became a merchant. Downward movement came less often. For the slave, of course, there was only the smallest mobility at most, from field hand to plantation craftsman. Being freed was rare.

What men wrote in the 1600s often seems strange now. It is confusing to read their writings with sprinklings of references to the Bible and now-forgotten authors and Latin quotations. In contrast, what was written in the later 1700s now often seems clearer, more straightforward and modern, to our minds perhaps more logical. We understand with less difficulty what a John Adams or a Thomas Jefferson or a Benjamin Franklin said. Their language is plain to us. The "provincials," those who lived in the colonies in the fifty years or so before the Revolution, were practical persons. They were materialistic—as many of us are—and wanted to better themselves and to own more. Provincial Americans belonged to any of a number of churches, or none. They were not much interested in an idea that seemed to have no immediate use. They were violently anti-Catholic and suspicious of "Papists." To Englishmen, Protestant since the reign of Henry VIII, "Papists" were the enemy. They were prejudiced against Jews, though those prejudices were weaker than they had been, and weaker than they would become. Blacks were despised. The provincial Americans could wait for rewards. "A penny saved is a penny earned," Ben Franklin wrote.

Society and culture in America would change. Not all the colonists in 1776 saw themselves as Americans. Some saw themselves as loyal Englishmen away from home. Others thought of themselves as "Bay Staters," Virginians, or whatever, and would for long to come. Still, the pattern of society, culture, and nation had been set. Chapter 1 describes schooling and education during roughly the first hundred years—the Colonial era. Chapter 2 deals with Provincial America until the time of the Revolution.

CHAPTER ONE
EUROPEAN AND
COLONIAL SOURCES

Although the early colonization of North America was also undertaken by the Spanish, French, Dutch, and even the Swedes, the English settlers played decisive roles in laying the foundations for American culture and education. Yet the English settlers were also European in their traditions and outlook. This being the case, it is in the context of a wider European cultural heritage and tradition that an analysis of American education must begin.

The development of preuniversity schooling had been somewhat erratic in England during the Middle Ages. Most schools were connected with cathedrals, although some were under the control of church organizations. The schools were intended primarily for the education of the clergy. (*Clerical* now has two meanings, "office work" and "of the clergy." The meanings were once identical.) Schools were generally subject to the supervision and control of the Church, which not only licensed the school masters, but also dictated methods of instruction and the subject matter to be taught.

Elementary schooling in England during the fifteenth century was provided by a number of arrangements. Typically a child would learn his ABCs from the local priest, or in an elementary "reading" school that was either independent or combined with a Latin grammar school. Other opportunities for elementary learning were provided by the Song Schools, usually attached to a cathedral or church, which had as their purpose training boys as choristers. In addition to musical training, students of the Song Schools were taught reading and writing, and occasionally the rudiments of Latin.

The Latin grammar schools were not, as our modern use of "grammar" implies, elementary schools. Instead, they had as their purpose the teaching of Latin grammar and language. Their origin lay in the educational principles of Classical Antiquity. The schools were almost entirely dependent upon Ancient Roman texts as the basis for their curriculum. Students memorized grammatical rules and examples from the works of Ancient authors such as Donatus and Priscian, or from Medieval grammarians such as Alexander de Villedieu. Once they had obtained a reasonable command of the rudiments of Latin grammar, the students would then proceed to read introductory texts, such as Aesop's *Fables* and the *Disticha* of Cato, which was a collection of maxims in verse. They read also the work of more advanced Latin authors such as the poet Terence, the rhetorician Cicero, Ovid, Virgil, and the historian Sallust. Early Christian authors such as Prudentius and Boethius were also frequently read.

Significantly, the students attending the Latin grammar schools did not read complete works, but only extracts taken from various authors. Instruction was exclusively oral. Typically, the master would read examples aloud from a handwritten manuscript. After explaining its content, he would have the students repeat the information with him. Most learning was therefore based upon recitation. Speaking the language was emphasized as much as reading and writing it.

In general, the Latin grammar schools in medieval England, as well as on the Continent, were limited in the instruction they provided. Most of the learning in these schools was of a practical nature. Although examples for instruction were based primarily upon the works of ancient authors, the Latin that was taught was of a practical sort, closely linked with the vernacular, for use in the church and for other formal purposes. Little attention or appreciation was given to subtleties and sophistication of Latin as a language.

Despite dependence upon ancient sources, medieval grammar schools largely rejected the cultures and traditions of antiquity. Greek, which had been a particularly important subject in ancient schools, was totally neglected as a subject of study in the medieval grammar schools. The adoption and use of classical Latin authors was subordinated by the church to sacred learning.

By the beginning of the sixteenth century, a number of remarkable changes were overtaking the Latin grammar schools in England. The introduction of printing was just beginning to make its impact felt during the 1480s and 1490s. In 1483, for example, John Anwykll, a master at the Magdalen College School, published a grammar and later a phrase book with excerpts from Terence translated into English. By approximately 1500, John Holt had published the elementary instructional text *Lac Puerorum*, which included woodcuts intended to help the student learn declensions. A number of other important factors led to change in schools. The work of the English and continental humanists was particularly important. The humanist movement dated back to the thirteenth century and the work of Francesco Petrarch (1304-1374) and others. Renaissance humanists advocated the

FIGURE 1-1   Allegorical representation of the progress of education from the 1508 Basel edition of *Margarita Philosophica* of Gregory de Reisch. The youth, having mastered his hornbook, advances towards the temple of knowledge. Wisdom holds the key to the temple, in which are included authors such as Donatus, Priscan, Aristotle, and Boethius. Reprinted in Elwood P. Cubberley, *Syllabus of Lectures on History of Education* (New York: Macmillan, 1902), p. 85.

revival of ancient classical literature and education. They felt that learning and education provided the key to human affairs.

In defining their philosophy and purpose, the humanists spurned the utilitarian Latin of the Middle Ages, and instead adopted as a model the elegance of Cicero and other authors of the Augustan age. Under the humanists the study of ancient Greek revived and with it the reexamination of the work of ancient Greek authors, particularly Plato and Aristotle. In England, the attempt to revive classical texts and methods of instruction was led by the humanist scholars William Grocyn, John Colet, Desiderius Erasmus, and Thomas More. Excepting More, each of these men had studied on the Continent, and each of them was thoroughly imbued with the philosophical ideas and beliefs of antiquity.

While the humanists were interested in the philosophies and literature of the ancients, they were at the same time Christians and concerned with the reform of the church. In England, John Colet and others strongly criticized the corruption of the English clergy and called for the return to a simpler form of apostolic Christianity. On the Continent, Dutch-born Desiderius Erasmus emphasized the duty of parents to provide their children with a proper Christian education. Both Colet and Erasmus, and many others as well, felt that only through the careful study and reinterpretation of ancient Christian texts could the true intent and purpose of the church fathers be understood, and in turn be fulfilled. At the same time, the study of classical Roman authors would provide models of language and citizenship.

The principal source of guidance for the humanists in reviving the educational philosophy of the ancients was the Roman rhetorician Quintilian's work, the *Instituto Oratoria*, from the middle of the fourth century. Quintilian's purpose was to outline the training necessary to produce an educated citizen. During the Middle Ages, the work was only available in a very fragmented form. It was rediscovered in its entirety, in 1416, by the Florentine humanist Poggio. The *Institutio* was used extensively by the humanists during the first half of the sixteenth century to define the philosophy and curriculum of the English and continental Latin grammar schools.

In their use of the educational methods outlined by Quintilian, the humanists were attempting to recreate the pedagogical system of the ancient Romans. They created something quite different. What they brought about was a new synthesis, one which combined the educational theories of the ancients with the educational practices of the later Middle Ages and the early Renaissance.

The Renaissance English Latin grammar school traces its origins to the Cathedral School at St. Paul's in London. In the twelfth century a school was founded in conjunction with the cathedral. By the beginning of the Renaissance, however, it was no longer in existence. The school was refounded in 1509 by John Colet. Instead of placing the school under the control of the cathedral, Colet and his supporters established as lay trustee the London guild of mercers (cloth merchants). When he established the school, Colet was neither concerned with educating the clergy nor the nobility, nor with sons of members of the guilds. Schooling was to be for the sons of the general citizenry.

In 1512, Colet appointed William Lily as his first master. With Erasmus, Lily was largely responsible for drawing up the curriculum of the school. The spirit of this curriculum and the school in general is clearly outlined in the statutes for the school written by Colet in 1518. Under "What Shall Be Taught," Colet wrote that he hoped that the students would always be taught

... in good literature both Latin and Greek, and good authors such as have the very Roman elegance joined with wisdom, especially Christian authors that wrote their wisdom with clean and chaster Latin either in verse or in prose, for my intent is by this school specially to increase knowledge and worshipping of God and Our Lord Christ Jesus and good Christian life and manners in the children.

Unfortunately, the original curriculum from St. Paul's does not survive. William Lily, in his *Carmen de Morbuis*, which he prefixed to his Latin grammar, mentioned that Virgil, Terence, and Cicero were the most important authors to be read by the schoolboys. A subsequent curriculum outlined by Cardinal Woolsey in 1528 for his school at Ipswich, England and almost surely derived from the course of study at St. Paul's, was based exclusively on pagan authors. In the third form* Aesop and Terence were to be read, in the fourth form Virgil, in the fifth form Cicero, in the sixth form Sallust or Caesar, in the seventh form Horace and Ovid, and in the eighth form a general selection of ancients. Essentially the same curriculum could be seen in other English grammar schools during the late sixteenth and early seventeenth centuries.

Authors read in conjunction with the humanist curriculum, and included in the Renaissance grammar schools, were not much different from those studied during the Middle Ages. Humanists made their most important departure from the medieval educational tradition by developing authoritative texts, as well as fully reestablishing the Classical curriculum in its entirety—in particular the study of Greek.

English and continental humanists also created much that was new. Erasmus formulated a series of elementary exercises in Latin during the late 1490s, while he was a theology student. In its earliest version, the work consisted of simple idioms, phrases, and examples of dialogue. Expanded during his first trip to England, these exercises were eventually published in 1518 under the title of *Colloquies*. With his other major pedagogical works, *De Copia* and *Adages*, the *Colloquies* represented the continuation of the classical Latin tradition infused with the spirit of the Renaissance humanists. This spirit survived the English Reformation. When the appropriation of church property by Henry VIII ended support for church-operated Latin grammar schools, new schools supported by cities, guilds, private gifts, and inheritances took their place.

The spirit of the Renaissance also revitalized Oxford and Cambridge Universities, offshoots of the University of Paris, which had originally been founded in the thirteenth century. Erasmus, the greatest of the humanists, visited Colet at Oxford and taught at Cambridge. English universities were centers of "puritanism," which attempted to reform the Church of England. Puritanism was strong in Cambridge, and strongest in its Emanuel College.

Form in Latin grammar schools meant "class" or "grade," The usage may have come from an older meaning of form, bench.

The importance of the work of the humanists for the development of education in early colonial America was not only that they shaped the education of many of the original settlers. They also provided important models that would be used in the establishment of colonial schools. Puritanism was important in a different way, in that it led to a concern for religion and salvation which also shaped the lives of the first Americans. Yet, despite the fact that the early settlers brought with them much of the European and English school tradition, as well as religious conviction, the new land worked important changes—ones that would bring about a new synthesis and ultimately a distinctively American culture and system of education.

COLONIAL BEGINNINGS

Colonial children received their first education at home, as American children still do. The church played a far greater part in the child's education than churches generally do now. The most important part of vocational training was by apprenticeship. A child who went to school went to any variety of them. Schools in the colonies appeared early: "reading"or primary schools; for boys, "Latin grammar," special purpose, secondary schools; and in New England, Harvard College. Although settlers of New England were more interested than those of some other colonies in schooling for their children, we cannot assume that all New Englanders were well schooled, or that no southerner was.

There is much we do not know about colonial education. Records have been lost or destroyed, or they never existed. Some parts of colonial education have not been studied in detail. There are many variations in colonial American education, ones highly different from our own experiences; it is only in the last hundred years that American schools have been organized into a single pattern. Any generalizations we can make here about colonial education will have many exceptions. The reader must see the history of colonial education as tentative, more tentative than most history. One additional caution should be noted: Teachers' and prospective teachers' first professional concern in education is with the schools. But schools were clearly not the first concern of the colonials. One of the more useful general conclusions from the history of education is that schooling has continuously and vastly increased in scope and function during the last 350 years.

Underlying any type of education are the assumptions of the parent or teacher about the nature of children and the type of education that is appropriate for them. Such beliefs play a critical role in shaping the educational system and schooling. The range of views of children in colonial America is shown in the following verses. The first was written by Anne Bradstreet, poet in Massachusetts in the mid-1600s. The second, somewhat earlier, is by the father of John Winthrop on the birth of his son:

Stained by birth from Adam's sinful fact,
Thence I began to sin as soon as act:
A perverse will, a love of what's forbid,
A serpent's sting in pleasing face lay hid.

Welcome sweet babe thou are unto thy parents dear
Whose hearts thou hast filled with joy, as well
　　　that doth appear.

Bradstreet and Winthrop's parents were Puritans. Bradstreet wrote as a Calvinist, as some Puritans were from the time of the colonies' establishment. For one of that "authoritarian temperament," Philip Greven has written that

". . . family government was authoritarian and rigorously repressive. Parental authority was absolute, and exercised without check or control. . . . Obedience and submission were the only acceptable responses for children."

This was the temperament which followed logically from the views of John Calvin. Calvin, who was a Swiss reformer and theologian of the mid-1500s, had most convincingly preached that mankind, including babies and children, were damned and depraved, stained by the original sin of Adam. As the *New England Primer* put it, "In Adam's Fall/We sinned all."

But other parents were, as Winthrop's father had been, "authoritative" rather than "authoritarian." They were, as Greven has written, ". . . respectful toward legitimate and essential authority within the family, yet aware of the need to limit the exercise of authority within certain established boundaries." Children were

FIGURE 1-2   Facing pages from a 1777 edition of *The New England Primer* **printed by Edward Draper in Boston.**

Words of five Syllables.

A-bo-mi-na-ble	ad-mi-ra-ti-on
Be-ne-dic-ti-on	be-ne-fi-ci-al
Ce-le-bra-ti-on	con-fo-la-ti-on
De-cla-ra-ti-on	de-di-ca-ti-on
E-du-ca-ti-on	ex-hor-ta-ti-on
For-ni-ca-ti-on	fer-men-ta-ti-on
Ge-ne-ra-ti-on	ge-ne-ro-fi-ty

Words of fix Syllables.

A-bo-mi-na-ti-on	Gra-ti-fi-ca-ti-on
Be-ne-fi-ci-al-ly	Hu-mi-li-a-ti-on
Con-ti-nu-a-ti-on	I-ma-gi-na-ti-on
De-ter-mi-na-ti-on	Mor-ti-fi-ca-ti-on
E-di-fi-ca-ti-on	Pu-ri-fi-ca-ti-on
Fa-mi-li-a-ri-ty	Qua-li-fi-ca-ti-on

A Leffon for Children.

Pray to God.	Call no ill names.
Love God.	Ufe no ill words.
Fear God.	Tell no lies.
Serve God.	Hate Lies.
Take not God's	Speak the Truth.
Name in vain.	Spend your Time well.
Do not Swear.	Love your School.
Do not Steal.	Mind your Book.
Cheat not in your play.	Strive to learn.
Play not with bad boys.	Be not a Dunce.

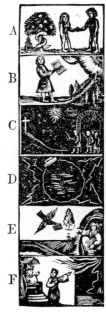

A　In A D A M's Fall
　　We finned all.

B　Heaven to find,
　　The Bible Mind.

C　Chrift crucify'd
　　For finners dy'd.

D　The Deluge drown'd
　　The Earth around.

E　E L I J A H hid
　　By Ravens fed.

F　The judgment made
　　F E L I X afraid.

reasoned with, not ordered about. They were to be treated leniently if possible. They were to be loved and were seen as being essentially good.

Bradstreet and Winthrop demonstrated the extremes; the way most parents felt was probably somewhere in between. Bradstreet, in another mood, wrote tenderly of her own children. What the "real" nature of the child is would often be discussed in the times that would follow. (Greven has also written about a third temperament and of education for the "genteel," which will appear later in this book.)

Most of what children learn during their first years is from their parents and families. We learn our native language that way, as well as motives and habits. This is what sociologists call "primary socialization." How we have been socialized depends upon the customs and beliefs, the personalities and temperaments of our parents. Beyond Greven's work we have incomplete information about primary socialization in colonial families. We know that in some ways it was quite different from the socialization that recent generations have experienced. Greven points out that babyhood, or at least its outward signs, lasted longer then; boys and girls alike wore babies' clothes, long dresses and aprons, until they were five or six. At the same time, adulthood came sooner after childhood; there was not the long period in between that we call adolescence. We can be sure, too, that children became familiar with death sooner then than children now. The colonists multiplied and were healthier than the English, but one infant in four or one in five died. Perhaps because the probability of a baby's death was too great to risk much love, parents may have somewhat withheld love from young children.

It has been thought that colonial families were "extended" families and that children and their parents shared their home with grandparents, uncles, aunts, and other relatives, and often with servants. However, several recent studies have shown that this was not usually true, and that most households were "nuclear," consisting of only father, mother, and children. In Plymouth Colony and Bristol, Rhode Island, there were most often families of parents and four children, and probably families elsewhere were roughly the same size then; later there would be more children. In one important way childhood was different from that of our own time, since children then were an economic help instead of an economic burden. Even a small child could help in the garden or the kitchen.

Beyond infancy and primary socialization, children learned by helping in kitchens, gardens, fields, and orchards. Cows were to be milked and pastured, pigs fattened and slaughtered. Butter was churned and soap boiled, fruit dried, and meat salted and cured. Girls were taught to cook, to spin flax and wool, and to weave. Boys learned to provide food and shelter. The colonial child who learned to read was as likely to be taught reading at home as by going to school.

The Protestant churches, and particularly the New England Puritan churches—later called *Congregational Churches* because the congregation controlled them—existed primarily to teach. The central feature of the church service, Sunday morning and Sunday afternoon, was the lengthy sermon, intended to explain and to provide examples of evil and righteousness. The colonials believed that each man and woman and child was responsible for his or her own salvation, and that knowledge of the Bible and of religious principles were necessities for salvation. The largest Massachusetts churches, which employed two ministers, called the second one the *teacher*. (The word *teacher* was not often used in any other way in colonial America.) The minister or teacher was to "catechize" the children, that is, teach by asking questions for which answers were to be memorized. Each church, often each congregation, had its own catechism or statement of faith. The Church of England was less intent on this than many others, but its *Book of Common Prayer* of the mid-1700s directed that the assistant minister should

> . . . Diligently upon Sundays and Holy Days, or on some other occasions, openly in his Church, instruct or examine so many Children of his Parish, sent unto him, as he shall think convenient, in some part of this Catechism. . . .

Upon one feature of learning parents, ministers, and school masters agreed: To learn was to learn to say.

Most colonial and provincial people were farmers, but others became craftspersons. As had been the case in England, the crafts were learned by apprenticeship, by working with and for a master craftsman, by example and practice. A boy or girl was apprenticed by contract. Perhaps in return for a payment by the apprentice's family and always in return for the young person's work for several years, masters guaranteed they would teach the "art and mysteries" of their particular craft, and often guaranteed that the apprentice would be taught to read as well. The master was to feed and clothe the apprentice, and also to see that the apprentice received proper religious instruction. The master became a substitute father; one way to provide for an orphan was to apprentice, to "put out," a boy or girl. Paul Revere served an apprenticeship as a silversmith. Benjamin Franklin was apprenticed to his brother who was a printer, but ran away, a fairly common occurrence. Girls were occasionally apprenticed, to learn bonnet-making for instance, or to become more expert spinners or weavers. Even law and medicine were often learned through an arrangement something like an apprenticeship. A would-be lawyer "read" with a practicing lawyer. A physician-to-be "attended" a physician. A very few school masters served apprenticeships, although that was certainly unusual.

At school or at home the child learned to read by roughly the same process by which many of us today learn. First the letters, capital and lower case. It was more complicated then, with Roman, *Italic* and 𝔊𝔬𝔱𝔥𝔦𝔠 type faces. Then there were syllables and their sounds, in one primer *ab, ac,* and so on to *zy*. Third, there were words, short ones first, and then sentences, adages, or Bible verses. The idea of reading instruction at home is one that we are not used to now, but it was common in the 1600s and 1700s. If not at home, the child might learn at a *dame* or *reading* school, sometimes paid for by tuition, occasionally by taxes.

It has been argued that schools were established in the New England colonies to subject all children to "the creed of the Puritan sect." The statute most often quoted, and perhaps the most important, is the Massachusetts Act of 1647. Its opening paragraph reads:

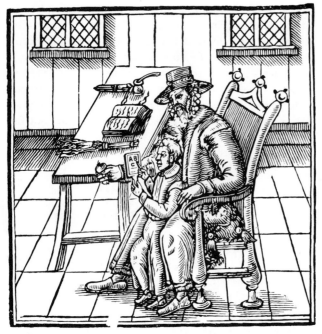

FIGURE 1-3   Title page of *Hornbye's Horn Book,* pub-
lished in London in 1622. Reprinted in Ellwood P. Cubberley,
Syllabus of Lectures on History of Education (New York:
Macmillan, 1902), p. 186.

> It being one chief project of that old deluder, Satan, to keep from the knowl-
> edge of the Scriptures, as in former times keeping them in an unknown
> tongue, so in these later times by persuading from the use of tongues, so that
> at least the true sense and meaning of the original might be clouded with false
> glosses of saint-seeming-deceivers, and that learning may not be buried in the
> graves of our forefathers in church and commonwealth, the Lord assisting our
> endeavours. . . .

The act then mandated the establishment of reading schools in all towns of fifty or
more families, and of grammar schools in towns of one hundred or more families.
The act was sometimes obeyed, sometimes flouted.

The Act may be read literally, of course. But Morison argues that the pre-
amble was written "to add a religious sanction to social obligation." This seems
more persuasive when early acts in the other colonies are considered.

New Haven, 1642: "for the better training up of the youth of this town, that
through God's blessings they may be fitted for public service thereafter, either in
church or in commonwealth. . . ."

Massachusetts, 1648, Connecticut, 1650: "Forasmuch as the good education
of children is a singular behooval and benefit to our commonwealth. . . ."

Plymouth Colony, 1677: "Forasmuch as the maintenance of good literature does tend to the advancement of the prosperity and flourishing state of societies and republics. . . ." This is not to say that the teaching of religion, of the Bible, of catechisms, was not important. But it was not the single concern, and perhaps not the most important one.

In Virginia the establishment of schools was more difficult than in New England because settlers did not live in compact settlements, but instead lived on farms and plantations spread along river banks. Still, there seem to have been reading schools there by 1640. Probably many of them were taught by part-time "school" dames and masters in their own houses. Others were taught by ministers of the Church of England.

In Philadelphia the first school master was Enoch Flower, who had had twenty years' experience teaching in England, and who was authorized to collect tuition for teaching reading, writing, and accounting. The best remembered of the earliest Pennsylvania reading masters was Francis Daniel Pastorious, a German Mennonite Protestant. As far as we know he was far from a typical reading master. He used German, Latin, and English fluently. He had earned a Ph.D. in Germany and had written several books. He was an important leader of the Pennsylvania German community, serving as a town clerk, justice of the peace, and representative to the Pennsylvania assembly. Just before 1700 he was teaching a school in the attic or loft of the Quaker meeting house in Philadelphia. Later he taught in Germantown. Judging from the *New Primer* that he wrote, he taught the letters, then syllables, then words, then reading, with other material—weights, distances—as an afterthought. The *New Primer's* mnemonic rhyme for remembering the alphabet is a good example of "authoritative" non-Calvinistic temperament, and is quite different from that in the *New England Primer:*

All Blessings Come Down Even From God; His Infinite Kindness Love & Mercy, Now, of Old & Perpetually, Quicketh Refresh and Strengthen True Upright Willing Xians & Young Zealots.

But the *New Primer* lists alphabetically eighty-odd sins, from adultery to youthful lusts.

In colonial America the intermediate school, for boys only, was the Latin Grammar School, both for general education and as preparation for college. What was to become the Boston Latin Grammar School was established in April 1635, when the town decided that "our brother Philemon Pormont, shall be entreated to become schoolmaster, for the teaching and nurturing of children with us." By 1647 eight Latin grammar schools had been established in Massachusetts, supported, as Latin grammar schools had been in England, by taxes, gifts, endowments, and tuition in varying proportions. A "free" Latin grammar school was established in New Haven in 1642, after Ezekiel Cheever, the most famous of the New England Latin masters, had taught there privately for some years. A Latin grammar school

FIGURE 1-4 A nineteenth century illustration of the Boston Latin Grammar School originally included in Barnard's *American Journal of Education* and reprinted in Ellwood P. Cubberley, *The History of Education* (Boston: Houghton Mifflin, 1920), p. 362.

was also established in Hartford in the same year. In Rhode Island a Latin grammar school had probably been established as early as 1640. In Virginia two Latin grammar schools were endowed by inheritance and established, the Symes School before 1647, and the Eaton School after 1659.

From about 1640 to 1659, there was a Catholic Latin grammar school in Maryland, for "either Protestants or Catholics," taught by Ralph Crouch, who had been a Jesuit novice and eventually became a Jesuit priest. A "large and stately mansion" probably served as Crouch's residence, student living space, and schoolroom. There were short-lived Catholic schools in New York and Maryland about 1680, but until then Crouch's school was the only Catholic Latin grammar school in the English-speaking colonies.

A Latin grammar school was established in Philadelphia in 1689. Its first master was George Keith, a friend of Governor William Penn and Quaker founder George Fox. Keith had been a tutor and a school master. A speaker, apologist, and missionary for the Quakers, or Friends, he had been imprisoned in Scotland and England for his religious beliefs half a dozen times. His assistant was Thomas Makin, who later became master of the school. Evidence seems to suggest that Makin taught arithmetic as well as Latin.*

The influence of the Classical literary and educational tradition on the curriculum of these early Latin grammar schools was great. Unfortunately, no direct complete records of what was taught survives from these early schools. There is a surviving outline of curriculum of the Boston Latin Grammar School from 1712. From it, as well as booksellers' records, personal accounts, diaries, and personal

---

*In 1733 Makin's brief obituary appeared in a Philadelphia newspaper: "On Monday Evening last, Mr. Thomas Makin fell off a wharf into the Delaware [River], and before he could be taken out again, was drowned. He was an ancient man, and formerly lived well in this city, teaching a considerable school; but of late years he was reduced to poverty." *Pennsylvania Gazette*, November 29, 1733. Quoted from Wickersham, James Pyle, *A History of Education in Pennsylvania* (Lancaster, Pa.: Inquirer, 1885) p. 43.

recollections from the later 1600s, we can reconstruct a typical curriculum for the Latin grammar schools.

Besides such works as the "accidence" or beginning Latin grammar book, there were in the first three years texts such as the *Disticha* of Cato, Corderius' *Colloquies*, and *Aesop's Fables*. In the fourth year Erasmus' *Colloquies* and Ovid's *de Tristibus* were studied, and the reading of *Aesop's Fables* continued. In the fifth year Erasmus' *Colloquies* was completed and Ovid's *Metamorpheses* begun. Numerous other Latin authors were studied in the sixth and seventh years, and the students were introduced to Greek. There is no evidence that study of a catechism was part of the Boston Latin School curriculum, but it certainly was a part of curricula elsewhere in New England.

Essentially, what was studied in the Boston Latin Grammar School was the same curriculum as that studied in the English Renaissance grammar schools such as St. Paul's, which John Colet had reformed 130 years before. Boston Latin's long-time master, Ezekiel Cheever, had also attended St. Paul's.

That the Latin grammar school curriculum had not changed in more than a century seems paradoxical. Although religion was the primary concern of the Puritans, it was not a first concern at Boston Latin. On a new frontier, certainly, there was more useful knowledge than Latin. There are two solutions to the paradox. The first is to note mitigating circumstances. Latin was necessary for theology, for medicine, and for foreign correspondence, and it did provide a key to classical literary masterpieces. The second solution of the paradox seems to us to be more generally satisfactory. Schools, that argument goes, do not answer only to the social and cultural needs of the moment. Schools—masters, texts, scholars; and later, teachers, administrators, and school boards—are in themselves social institutions, with customs and conventionalities of their own. They may have not, for good or bad, answered to the felt needs of the moment. We shall see again and again the seeming contradiction between curricula and social needs.

We know about a few Latin grammar schoolmasters: About Elijah Corlet, because his small stone schoolhouse was in Cambridge, Massachusetts, and served as a preparatory school for Harvard; about Ezekiel Cheever, whose extraordinarily long career seemed at his death and afterward a splendid example of devotion to the teaching of young scholars in Boston. Of most masters we know nothing at all.

Master Elijah Corlet (1610-1687) had been a student at Oxford. His reputation as master was already good in 1643, when an early favorable report, *New England's First Fruits*, said that his school was

> ... a fair [faultless] *Grammar* school for the training up of young scholars, and fitting them for *Academic Learning*, that ... they may be received into the College.... Master *Corlet* is the master, who has very well proved himself for his abilities [,] dexterity, painstaking in teaching of youth under him.

Elijah Corlet's scholars were ambitious boys and youths of Cambridge. A number of boys from other New England towns were sent to Cambridge to benefit from Master Corlet's instruction. Corlet's school prepared thirty of Harvard's graduates, a quarter of the total, in the mid-1600s. Corlet was supported—probably rather badly—by tuition, some paid in farm products; gifts, occasional grudging payments from the town, and a grant of land. He was one of the longest-lived, best-known, and presumably most capable of the Latin masters.

Ezekiel Cheever (1614-1708) had at the time of his death been a New England schoolmaster for seventy-one years. Born in London, son of a shopkeeper selling cloth (or, some say, a spinner), he had attended St. Paul's school, which John Colet had reformed more than a hundred years before. Cheever studied at Emanuel College, Cambridge, the favorite college of the English Puritans.

He had come to New England in 1637, perhaps on the same ship as Corlet. Cheever taught at New Haven, at first in his house and then as master of the "free" school there. In 1649 he became the master of the endowed Latin grammar school at Ipswich in northeastern Massachusetts; when Anne Bradstreet's family moved on, one of her sons stayed behind to study with Cheever. One of Cheever's own sons subsequently played a small part in the witchcraft trials in nearby Salem. In 1660, Cheever moved to Charlestown, and in 1671, to Boston, where he was master of the Latin Grammar School for the thirty-seven years remaining before his death. Like Corlet, Cheever was an ideal—and idealized—colonial master, a master for a long career instead of merely in passing; diligent; industrious; dedicated; regular in attendance (colonial schools were open six days a week year around); godly. Unlike Corlet, Cheever was well paid. One of the most prominent ministers of New England said at one point that "Tis Corlet's pains, and Cheever's, we must own. / That thou, New England, art not Sycthia [barbaric] grown." Many others have agreed.

The earliest masters of the smaller towns were a varied group. In Dedham, sixteen miles south of Boston, there were nine masters between 1644 and 1672, teaching English, writing, Latin grammar, and arithmetic to boys. One started to teach at twenty, another at sixty. Four had attended college. One, Michael Metcalfe, had been trained as a weaver's apprentice in England before being forced into exile. "Enemies conspired against me to take away my life, and sometimes, to avoid their hands, my wife did hide me in the roof of the house, covering me with straw." (Eight Metcalfes taught in Dedham in the following 250 years.) Two of the masters later became ministers; one stayed on as a respected farmer. The first masters of New Haven, Dorchester, and even Boston showed the same range of education and, usually, the same brief service as masters.

The peak of formal schooling in the colonies in the 1600s was Harvard College. It was patterned upon European colleges, in particular upon Emanuel College, Cambridge University. In turn Harvard has been a model for many colleges and universities in America.

Harvard was established in 1636, only a year after the establishment of the Boston Latin Grammar School. The Massachusetts legislature voted Ł 400 for a college. It was established at Newtowne, which was speedily renamed Cambridge. The following fall John Harvard, a recently arrived Puritan minister, died, leaving half his estate and all his library to the college, which was then named in his honor.

The establishment of such an institution was a remarkable accomplishment for people struggling to establish themselves in a primitive land. Yet it was an act consistent with the intellectual ambitions of the Puritans, and also with their experience. By 1640, 135 graduates and former university students had come to New England. As historian Lawrence A. Cremin wrote a few years ago, ". . . higher learning had been a salient feature of the puritan experience in England, and it remained so in New England."

The first reason for Harvard's establishment was to provide education for the ministry. As *New England's First Fruits* (1643) put it:

> After God had carried us safe to *New England*, and we had built our houses, provided necessaries for our livelihood, reared convenient places for God's worship, and settled the civil government; One of the next things we longed for, and looked after was to advance *Learning* and perpetuate it to posterity; dreading to become an illiterate ministry to the Churches, when our present ministry shall lie in the dust.

But the preparation of ministers was not the only purpose of Harvard. If half of its graduates in the 1600s became ministers, half did not, and many had no intention of becoming ministers. The Harvard charter of 1650 said the purpose of the college was "the advancement of all good literature, arts, and sciences." The curriculum did not emphasize the study of divinity.

In the summer of 1638, Harvard's first president, Nathaniel Eaton, taught Harvard's first classes. Eaton, who had studied at Cambridge University and in Holland, seemed well qualified. But the students (who lived in the college from the beginning) were served moldy bread, spoiled beef—or no beef—and sour beer—or no beer. Students were whipped, and Eaton was dismissed when it was charged that he had beaten his assistant with a walnut club "big enough to have killed a horse." Classes were suspended.

In 1640, Henry Dunster was named president. He was thirty-one then and had just arrived in New England. He had graduated from Cambridge, then had been a school master and *curate*, or assistant minister. Until 1643 he taught all the classes. At that time, two "tutors" were appointed to help him. For fourteen years he delivered lectures, and raised money for the new college. He also managed a printing press that his wife had inherited. When he resigned in 1654, after disagreements with students and with Harvard's board of overseers, college customs and rules had been established, and Harvard would continue.

When Dunster was president of Harvard, three years were required for a degree. To be admitted, a student was required to be able to read, write, speak, and understand Latin. Teaching was in Latin. A basic knowledge of Greek was also required. Students studied logic, rhetoric, ethics, physics, metaphysics, and Hebrew on Saturday morning. The study of divinity was via catechisms.

The enrollment of Harvard was between twenty and fifty. The average age of new students was less than sixteen; they were ranked in class according to their scholarship.* Students were the sons of fathers of the better sort; colony officials, physicians, large land owners, or ministers. Craftsmen's sons sometimes attended; although a few scholarships were available, there were almost no sons of small farmers. Students' surviving notebooks and personal libraries show that the reading of some of them went far beyond textbooks, and that there were pranks and riots, no doubt entertaining.

This, then, was the general pattern of schooling in the 1600s: reading learned at home or in a reading school; for a few boys there was as long as six or seven years of study in a Latin grammar school; and for a very few, college study at Harvard. But the general pattern was often violated. Some boys, and a few girls, learned from parents, masters, or tutors what other boys learned in Latin grammar schools. Some children never learned to read at all, since school attendance was not compulsory and parents did not or could not instruct them. Some Latin grammar schools also accepted reading pupils. At the end of the 1600s, some boys were sent to "writing" school. By the early 1700s, others studied in schools in Boston that were conducted by masters who were paid tuition and who taught a welter of subjects: mathematics (for surveying or navigation), French, Greek, and even needlepoint and fencing. Newspaper advertisements published in Boston from the beginning of the eighteenth century include many announcements of masters teaching bookkeeping, surveying, navigation, and languages for commerce.

Aside from the variations in schooling in the English-speaking colonies, there were also Dutch, German, and even Swedish and French schools. The Dutch schools, of course, were in New Netherland, which had been established in 1624 by the Dutch West India Company as a fur trading post and supply base for Dutch traders. The first reading school opened in New Amsterdam (New York City) in 1638. By 1664, when New Netherland was surrendered to the English and became New York, there were eleven reading schools in the colony. A Latin school was operated for a year or two. Schooling in New Netherland resembled schooling in New England but there were important differences. Schools in New Netherland were established by and under the control of the Dutch West India Company, which paid masters. Masters were selected and licensed by a committee in Holland, comprised of the Amsterdam Dutch Reformed Church ministers. The reading master in New Netherland was to assist the minister. One master's contract called for him to clean the church, ring the church bell, read parts of the Sunday church services and substitute for the minister in his absence, teach the catechism, serve as the church messenger, and dig the graves.

The first New Amsterdam reading master was Adam Roelansen, whose life and teaching in New Amsterdam have been carefully investigated. His was not a particularly inspiring life. He was named as defendant in at least three civil suits, and was charged with slander and attempted rape; he was convicted of the latter.

In Pennsylvania, schools were generally established by churches. German churches established German schools, but most of their growth was in the 1700s

*Not until the 1700s were class rankings based upon the social eminence of students' families. The practice was abandoned in 1770.

and we will return to them. New Sweden, in the valley of the Delaware River, may have had a reading school. If so, it was closed in 1655, when the Dutch took over New Sweden as the English would take over New Netherland. An attempt to revive the Swedish schools in the early 1700s was not successful. Among the New Netherlanders were French Huguenots. Their schools were, naturally, taught in French.

One of the purposes of the first English colonists had been to Christianize the Indians. The Royal Charter for Virginia began with an expression of concern for Christianizing Indians who "as yet live in darkness and miserable ignorance of the true knowledge and worship of God." English hopes of Christianizing and "civilizing" were far from the interest of most Indians. In 1622, "Henrico College" was being built for the instruction of Indians and a "rector" had been named. Then, in a large-scale and well-planned attack, the Indians butchered the workers and their families. A report to the Virginia Company in London said that "the way of conquering them is much more easy than that of civilizing them and Christianizing them." For 200 years Indians would be taught so that their souls might be saved.

About the Indians themselves it is difficult to generalize. Indian cultures varied enormously. There were both warlike and peaceful tribes; tribes quick to accept change, and tribes quick to reject it; and differences in values and in social organization, which were as great. There were hundreds of tribes and nearly as many languages. Far westward, Spanish soldiers and priests were already conquering the land and beginning the Christianization and subjugation of Indians there. Indians who were to be converted needed to know the Bible (and so needed to read) or the Mass. To be within reach of the Protestant meeting hall or the Catholic chapel or church, it was necessary for Indians to be sedentary farmers rather than nomadic hunters. For some Indians a change in religion meant the dismemberment of their culture; it is said that the Pueblo Revolt against the Spaniards in 1680 (successful for eighteen years) resulted from that realization. Beyond conversion, missionaries also had cultural preferences. Spaniards tried to recreate medieval monastery life, with servants, gardens, and farms. New England missionaries favored recreated New England towns.

The most famous Puritan missionary to the Indians, John Eliot, said he found it "most necessary to carry on civility with religion." Being a good Christian was reading the Bible, farming instead of hunting, living in a village, attending church, and wearing cloth instead of skin clothes. Eliot spent forty-four years as minister of a church in Roxbury, Massachusetts and in preaching to the local Algonquin Indians. He translated catechisms, the psalms, and finally the Bible into the local Indian language. A few Indians heard Eliot's sermons in their language and became Christians. At Natick, adjacent to Dedham, an Indian village was established. Homes and a meeting house were built; the meeting house also housed the school for reading, of English as well as the Algonquin language. Thirteen other "praying Indian" villages were established with Eliot's help, and with financial support of the first missionary society in England, the New England Society for the Propagation of the Gospel. On Nantucket Island, off the coast of Massachusetts, three generations of the Mayhew family were also missionaries to the Indians. There were others, of course. John Cheever, Ezekiel's son, was for twenty-three years missionary to the Indians of Plymouth Colony. There is no record of his success.

The Indian boys New England missionaries hoped to train as ministers were sent to Elijah Corlet's Latin grammar school in Cambridge, and if they lived, to Harvard. As students they progressed well enough. At the commencement of 1659, Harvard's president said they "gave good satisfaction . . . considering their growth in the Latin tongue." But the Indian scholars died of consumption and "hectic fevers" thought (correctly enough) to have been brought about by the changes in their diet, clothing, and way of life. (Indians, it seems reasonable to say after 300 years of experience in their schooling, do not do well outside the context of their tribal culture, unless they have fully accepted, and been fully accepted by, American culture. But the death rates were appalling.) Of the twenty Indian boys sent to Master Corlet, two survived to complete the work for their bachelor's degrees at Harvard. One, Joel Iacoomis, suffered a grim fate. Before commencement he visited his relatives, and while returning to Cambridge he was shipwrecked on Nantucket Island. He was drowned or, it was said, he was "murdered by some wicked Indians."

CONCLUSION

Education in colonial America does not clearly demonstrate the origins of American public schools, as historians once thought. It does, however, provide a basis for making several informative generalizations about education.

Considering American Indians and missionaries, one might begin to see that it would be difficult for missionaries, even if they wanted to, to change religion without changing schooling, or to change religion without changing a culture. The experience of the Indians in Elijah Corlet's school and at Harvard might illustrate one of the hazards of removing children or youths from their native environments and cultures simply for the sake of schooling.

More widely, one might see that some societies and cultures, such as those of the colonies, operate and survive well enough without extensive systems of schooling. More schooling may—but possibly may not—be necessary in a highly technological culture.

The schools of colonial America had limited purposes and small numbers of pupils. The balance of this text about the history of American education will address many matters, but always with increasing responsibilities assigned to the schools, and increased time spent in schooling and the resources used for it.

Schools do not automatically shape themselves to the needs of a society, nor do they teach everything they are intended to teach. Schools are partly independent organizations, following their own customs and conventions. The "paradox" separating what a school teaches and what a society appears to need is a consequence of the partial independence of schools. The colonial masters had roles very much different from those of present teachers. *Teach* was a verb and not a noun.

In colonial America there was every possible precedent for financing schools, all that had been employed in England—tuition, tax, gift, endowment, and land rent, singly or in any combination. Patterns of control varied as greatly. Schools were controlled by town meetings, by trustees or *feoffes*, by committees, by those paying tuitions, or by the masters themselves. The analysis of control is complicated because the colonials did not make the same clear distinction we make between "public" and "private." They spoke of "free" schools, but sometimes meant that admission to them was "free" in that any qualified student could attend, and sometimes to mean that the schools were free, without charge, for students whose parents could not afford to pay.

The schools of the colonials might have served as precedents for anything—or nothing.

CHAPTER TWO
CULTURE AND
SCHOOLING BEFORE
THE REVOLUTION

In the 1600s, colonists most often thought and acted like Englishmen or other Europeans away from home. The social and cultural history of the colonies in the 1600s is largely the history of the transportation of a culture and society, and of schools.

In the 1700s, until the eve of the Revolution, those who lived in what would become the United States still thought of themselves as loyally English, but no longer as Englishmen away from home. They lived in one of the parts of England, in its transoceanic "provinces," as other Englishmen lived in Kent or Cornwall. The provincials' way of speech, thought, and behavior were already distinctive. The social and cultural history of America in the 1700s is largely a history of a transmuted, changed society and culture, and of its schools.

Schools changed with their environment, often lagging behind, but occasionally leading the changes. Growing cities, because of the variety of their residents and simply because of their size, made available to parents living therein a number of schools to choose from. In the middle colonies, particularly in Pennsylvania, the convention of many church-related schools, together with the many churches, led to diversity of schools. However, because of distances, there were fewer choices for any one child's schooling. In New England, schooling tended to be more practical. District schools and traveling schools added to convenience but had their educational drawbacks. Nevertheless, literacy was more general. In Virginia and in the rest of the South, self-supported masters and Church of England ministers operated schools, and there were tutors and an occasional "governess." School learning seemed to increase there also. In provincial America, a new and American school, the academy, made its appearance. Although few slaves and Blacks were taught to read, a few schools demonstrated that they should be taught. During the same time several new colleges were established, usually for religious reasons.

The period of provincial America ended with the Revolution, which had primarily political purposes and, as immediate outcomes, little more than political effects.

BECOMING AMERICA

The stately neoclassic houses built by the well-off in the 1700s are among our most prized public landmarks. Their graceful mahogany or walnut furniture and marvelously simple silverware are museum pieces. They preserve the appearance of a part of life in the 1700s, but not the parts important to us here and not the practical parts of life.

Perhaps the American practicality, the search for solutions to everyday problems, came from living in a new environment with new problems. Whether because of their environment or not, the provincial Americans wanted and needed practical answers immediately. A tale by Benjamin Franklin demonstrates the concern and response: A militia chaplain told Franklin the men would not attend prayer meetings. Franklin, more than usually modest because he was not a praying man, had a suggestion. "It is perhaps below the dignity of your profession to act as steward of the rum; but if you were only to distribute it out after prayers, you would have them all about you." Franklin said that "never were prayers more generally and punctually attended."

Practicality was a state of mind. Rationalism was a way of thought. It was based on the belief that truth, often "Self-evident truth," could only be discovered from that which was seen or experienced, and must be developed by rational analysis. Rationalism was an extension of scholarly humanism. It was—and is—the basis of scientific thought. Among the scientists of provincial America was Benjamin Franklin, inventor of the lightning rod and Franklin stove. (Franklin comes to mind in every connection. He was almost the spirit of provincial America.) In a way John Bartram, Franklin's friend, was as typical. He collected plants from Florida to the Ohio Valley to Nova Scotia. He was a "naturalist" or "natural philosopher" who observed, collected, and classified, rather than experimented.

In political thought American rationalism took a turn backward, away from the English royalist arguments of the 1700s and back to the 1600s, the English period of the Glorious Revolution, when "republican" thought had been strongest in England. The English Whigs who sympathized with American Revolutionaries were in an important way reactionary. In provincial political matters the most highly thought-of philosopher was John Locke (1632-1704) who, in his *Treatises on Government*, had argued that government was a "social contract." To this line of thought John Adams and Thomas Jefferson adhered, no matter how strong their disagreements on many other matters:

> We hold these truths to be self-evident, that all men are created equal; that they are endowed by their creator with certain inalienable rights; that among these are life, liberty, and the pursuit of happiness. . . .

The number of provincial Americans grew from 250,000 in 1700 to 3 million at the beginning of the Revolution. There were many immigrants, but families were larger, too. As Franklin noted, provincial American men and women married younger, because it was not too difficult to support a family. Families were larger than they are today because children were most often an economic asset, and because brides were usually younger. The Biblical advice to "be fruitful and multiply" was followed. The effect upon family life has not, as far as we know, been studied. A provincial woman commented in her diary: "I have often thought that women who live to get over the time of child-bearing . . . experience more comfort and satisfaction than at any other period of their lives."

Most provincial Americans were of the "middling sort," and others of the "better sort." By the mid-1700s there were in America social graduations and social class structures. Compared with Europe then or with the United States in the 1800s, there were only a few rich and a few poor, but their numbers had increased. Since a community, or indeed an entire province, could accumulate wealth, most families in it could become more prosperous. As well as can be judged, this was the general pattern. The indentured servant or other immigrant could and very often did become a farm owner. The son of a middling sort of merchant sometimes became wealthy. But it is necessary to add quickly that in the older and more heavily farmed areas there was less mobility, and that people became poorer more often than wealthier.

There were few Africans in the colonies of the 1600s. The colonists had brought with them from Europe their racial prejudices, but until the late 1600s slavery had not been institutionalized, which is to say that laws had not been enacted until then to protect slaves' owners. In the middle and late 1700s, it was more and more difficult for planters in the South to get indentured servants from Europe. Therefore, with reluctance, they purchased slaves. The black population of the United States had reached a half million by 1776.

In Virginia and in Maryland, an aristocracy, a class made up of people whose high social position had been determined by the circumstances of their birth or marriage, had taken shape. The most prominent Virginia families—for instance, the Carters, the Smiths, and the Byrds—were rich by American standards. Their social position could not be rivaled. There were many Virginian planters, merchants, and craftsmen of the middling sort, but the aristocrats set the tone and, largely, ruled. A similar but somewhat later aristocracy appeared in South Carolina. The large

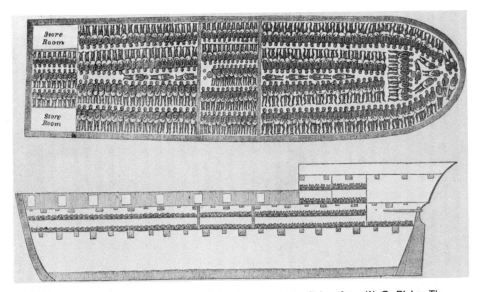

FIGURE 2-1 Illustration showing the decks of a slave ship. Taken from W. O. Blake, *The History of Slavery and the Slave Trade, Ancient and Modern* (Columbus, Ohio: Printed by H. Miller, 1862), pp. 304-305.

landowners of New York had aristocratic position in their society. In Boston, and to a lesser extent in the other large seaport cities, there were merchant aristocrats.

There had always been violations of the old Puritan standards, both because Puritans had human weaknesses and because many of the colonists had not been Puritans. But in the mid-1700s, the old standards seemed to have been lost. Even in Boston there were far too few church pews to accommodate the Bostonians if they had all elected in a given Sunday to go to church, which of course they did not. In the cities there were taverns, brothels, and theaters. Some merchants were more interested in profits than in salvation. Perhaps the cities in part reflected the easy moral codes of England at the time.

On the frontier, behavior was largely unrestricted by social conventions; even where it had been strongest, the moral codes were breaking down. In New England there were still two-hour-long Sabbath sermons and the old droning psalms, but many had fallen away to other churches, and most did not belong to any church. There were many signs of this falling away. For example, babies born less than nine months after marriage had once been rare and scandalous, but, by the mid-1700s, became commonplace. When one New Englander, recently a bride, gave birth to a child seven and a half months after marriage, her church refused even to censure her. Bundling—sleeping fully clothed in the same bed by an engaged couple—was not a completely innocuous custom by former Puritan standards of behavior, but the old social norms had faded.

The Puritan faith was also being supplanted. The Church of England had established a congregation in Boston in 1689. Unitarian convictions—that there should be complete religious freedom, and that none of the theologies or catechisms of the conventional churches were essential to Christianity—appeared. Beyond this, even, was *deism*, the belief in a God who had created the universe and the natural laws that governed it but who would not intervene. "God the great clockmaker," a phrase stated somewhat irreverently, indicated a vision of God that originated from a scientific view.

Before 1750, there had been a revolution, or a counterrevolution, in religion. It seemed to be a reaction against the commonplace abandonment of the old faith and morality, against the increasing instability of society, and against rationalism, deism and worldliness, and the broadening and dilution of old faiths. Called the *Great Awakening*, it spread through all the major denominations. In New England its strongest spokesman was Jonathan Edwards, a Yale graduate and a Congregational minister. The term *Great Awakening* was, as a matter of fact, his. More than any other person, he was famed for his preaching of hellfire and damnation. For him salvation might come only through a return to strict Calvinism, with its original sin and predestination. In the Dutch Reformed Church the first awakener was Theodore Frelinghausen, a New Jersey pastor, who had come from Holland in 1714. He preached in English, contrary to the custom of his church. As did the other evangelists of the Great Awakening, he appealed by emotion, fervor aroused to encourage salvation. In his efforts he was joined a few years later by Gilbert Tennant, a Presbyterian. Another of the successful evangelical preachers was George Whitefield, who made nine tours of America between 1739 and 1771.

By 1750, the first wave of the Great Awakening was past, although there would be further instances of it in the South in the next few years, and a tide of "New Reawakening" would appear in the 1800s. Perhaps it led to feeling rather than thought in religion, and to a certain kind of equalitarianism in which all men and women were equally damned. For those converted or at least apprehensive, the Great Awakening turned religion into a central concern, a concern that would affect schooling.

PROVINCIAL SCHOOLING:
THE CITIES

Our society was shaped on the frontier, historians argue. On the other hand, the intellectual and institutional parts of our history have more often been shaped in our cities. Many of the developments of schools in the 1700s took place in the cities. The largest cities were Boston, population 16,000; Philadelphia, 13,000 and rapidly growing; and New York, 11,000. Each of the largest cities, and some not so large, offered many choices in schooling; their very size made the alternatives possible.

Patterns of schools and schooling were generally similar in the largest cities. In Philadelphia some boys studied at the Quaker Latin grammar school. At one time or another in the 1700s, schools were operated by several churches: the Church of England, German Reformed, Moravian, Lutheran, and Baptist. Most schools in the cities were, however, private, operated by their masters. A white boy in a large city could be sent to school to learn any subjects his parents thought fitting, if they could pay for it and if he could be spared from work. Even if a boy could not be spared from work or was an apprentice, there were master-operated night schools that he could attend. At its best, schooling in the largest provincial cities was purchased in a free market. An outstanding master earned twice as much as a carpenter and lived comfortably. For the pupil of parents of limited means, there were other masters whose fees were lower. For girls there were fewer possibilities even in the big cities, but many of the private schoolmasters and schoolmistresses, "school dames," accepted them at beginning schools. There were schools that would accept girls who were to study English, or Latin, or feminine and lady-like accomplishments—as examples, needlework, singing, or playing the harpsichord or spinet. Between 1740 and 1776, there are records of about 130 schoolmasters and mistresses in Philadelphia. Of course, not all of them were teaching at any one time, but there were surely others of whom there is no record. We cannot estimate the average length of a child's schooling because school and class sizes cannot be estimated. We do know that nearly all men and most women in Pennsylvania could write their names, and that there were three newspapers in Philadelphia, and libraries.

In New York and Boston there were also free markets in schooling. There were newspapers there, and they were read as eagerly as in Philadelphia. In New York the Church of England's Society for the Propagation of the Gospel operated several free schools for the poor, including one for Blacks, and the Dutch schools, by then supported by the Dutch Reformed Church, were still open. Private masters taught in Boston, too, supporting themselves by tuition. A second Latin grammar school had been established, and the town of Boston also supported three writing schools, primarily for teaching boys to write the clear legible script expected of clerks and useful to others, and arithmetic. One writing master was John Tileston, who had turned to teaching because his hand was so seriously burned when he was a child that he could only hold a pen or a penknife in it. Tileston was one of the very few masters who had been trained by apprenticeship. He would not retire until 1819, after having taught for seventy years.

PROVINCIAL SCHOOLING:
PENNSYLVANIA

In the Pennsylvania of farms and small villages there were schools established by and connected with each of the English-speaking churches. The Quakers', or Friends', schools were under the direction of the "weekly meetings," local congregations. They appointed schoolmasters and schoolmistresses to teach pupils "to read the Holy Scriptures and other English books, and to write and cast accounts

[,] so far as to understand some necessary rules of arithmetic. . . ." There were also schools of the Church of England, and of the Presbyterian Church and even the Roman Catholic Church.

The Church of England was aided in the mid-Atlantic colonies and in the South by the Society for the Propagation of the Gospel in Foreign Parts–the S.P.G. Founded in England in 1701, it established in the following seventy-five years, 170 missions and appointed eighty schoolmasters in America. One of its aims was to convert or reconvert provincials to the Church of England. (A second aim was to Christianize Indians, in which it was not successful. Its third aim, the Christianization of Blacks, will be discussed later in this text.)

The Germans in Pennsylvania were bound together by their language and their churches; a distinctive cultural minority, the Pennsylvania "Dutch" (*Deutsch* translates as German) still exist in the United States and Canada, and there are still schools of some of the Pennsylvania German denominations. The first German schools in Pennsylvania had been established by the Mennonites. The Mennonite Church splintered in Switzerland, producing several sects, including the Amish. Further divisions took place in America. There were also German Lutheran and Reformed Churches, the German Roman Catholic Church, Schweckenfelders, Dunkers, and Ephrata Hermits.* Like the English-speaking churches, the larger German churches established schools.

The first Moravians, persecuted members of a German sect that was opposed to both Catholicism and Lutheranism, came to Pennsylvania in 1740, after an earlier settlement in Georgia had failed. They believed in communal settlements, a kind of Christian socialism. They also believed in communal schools. Children were to board there. Parents were not to visit and not to send expensive gifts. The first Moravian communal school was opened in 1742 by Nicholas Ludwig, Graf (Count) Zinzendorf und Pottendorf. After Zinzendorf had returned to Europe to share his faith there, several other communal schools were established. Indians were sometimes pupils there; the Moravians saw missionary work as most important.

The best remembered of the German schoolmasters of the 1700s is Christopher Dock, who taught near Philadelphia and in small settlements, from 1718 until 1771. He was the author of *Schulordnung* (1770), on teaching. Dock was a Mennonite (though not all his pupils were) who was interested first in teaching piety, morality, and manners. Second, he taught reading, starting as usual with a rhymed alphabet. Third, he taught writing. Arithmetic in his school was perfunctory, intended as far as one can tell to help a pupil find a psalm or other Bible passage, or a hymn to be sung. Tradition says Dock died in prayer in his school at the end of a day. From the *Schulordnung*, one would conclude that Dock was a gentle teacher, nearer to Greven's description of "authoritative" than of "authoritarian." Whipping a child was only the last resort for Dock. But Calvinism and its sternness was not unknown in the German schools. By 1740, the German Reformed

---

*Cremin also mentions Labadists, New Born, New Mooners, Separatists, Zion's Brueder, Ronsdorfer, Inspired, Gichtelians, Depellians, and Mountain Men. (See Bibliography p. 348.)

Church schools were using the *New England Primer* translated almost word for word.

The Scotch-Irish lost their cultural identity soon. Their language, English, did not set them apart. Neither did their church, since there were English and Scotch Presbyterians too. More often than the Germans, they settled on the frontier, where cultural differences and church denominations were easily blurred.

The Presbyterians, whether from North Ireland or not, brought with them a concern for schooling, much like that of the Puritans nearly a century earlier. In the Presbyterian reading schools there was the usual course of study: reading, catechisms, Bible, and, as time allowed, writing and a little arithmetic. If the Scotch-Irish were settling on the raw frontier, a school might wait a little. But the schools were not far behind the frontier, occasionally not far enough. In the summer of 1764, Master Enoch Brown and nine of his pupils were killed and scalped in their schoolhouse at the foot of the Blue Ridge Mountains. A tenth was scalped but survived. One was "truant" and probably lived because of his truancy. Others were absent because of "hot weather and seasonal duties"—it was at the height of the harvest.

In Pennsylvania the parochial schools, those connected with churches, became a tradition, as did diversity in education. That tradition would long survive and, indeed, survives in some places still. Parochial schools and diversity would later postpone the establishment of public schools. Within limits this also held true for schooling in the other middle colonies, New York, New Jersey, and Delaware.

PROVINCIAL SCHOOLING: MASSACHUSETTS

There were general similarities, too, in New England schooling. Massachusetts's was as near to typical as any. A representative town is Dedham, although, of course, schooling in each New England town differed in detail. The settlements in Dedham had spread—its population had grown to 750 by 1700, and 1900 by 1765. In the first half of the 1700s, Dedham's Latin grammar school had continued, and the town employed a year-round Latin and English schoolmaster. Between 1700 and the 1750s, the Dedham masters were young men, nearly all of them Harvard graduates and awaiting calls to the ministry. Because many families moved beyond walking distance from the schoolhouse, Dedham arranged for the master to teach in various locations in the town for a few weeks at a time. This was a "traveling school," which had made its first appearance in New England before 1700, and was for a time commonplace.

In the 1750s, the traveling school was replaced by four schools, which came to be controlled by the different sections of the town. These were "district schools," locally controlled, of which much more was to be heard. Their beginning pupils studied English, and the advanced ones, Latin. Teaching in Dedham was no longer a year-round occupation, since all the Latin and English schools then met in the winter at the same time. Masters came and went more quickly. In the 1750s, only half of Dedham's masters were college graduates; in the 1760s, only a third. In the 1750s, women began to teach in Dedham, as much as a hundred years after school dames had first been employed elsewhere in New England. In Dedham, women first taught in summertime reading schools and were first paid from money bequeathed for schooling expenses. Most men who had lived in Dedham had been literate from the beginning, at least literate enough to sign their names. By 1760, only one out of five women signed by mark, an *x*.* The women of Dedham were literate far more often than formerly. At school and with the help of tutors, boys still learned Latin. Between 1760 and 1783, eighteen of Dedham's young men graduated from Harvard.

We have scraps of information about some provincial New England masters because they were later famous or because they were quaint. The letters of future president John Adams, who taught in Worchester in western Massachusetts, 1755-58, after graduating from Harvard, have been published. He wrote to friends about his pupils, sometimes annoyed, sometimes amused and fanciful. ". . . [L] ittle runt-lings, just capable of lisping A B C, and troubling the master." ". . . My little school, like the great world, is made up of prigs, politicians, devines, L.D.'s, fops, buffons, fiddlers, sycophants, fools, coxcombs, chimney-sweepers. . . ." His oldest scholars were learning Latin. During those three years Adams read, dined, and talked with the leading citizens, and learned law.

PROVINCIAL SCHOOLING:
THE SOUTH

The clergy of the Church of England, private schoolmasters, and plantation tutors played important parts in schooling in the South. The Church of England was the established (that is, tax-supported) church of the region, as the Congregational Church was in most of New England. However, there were always too few capable dedicated Church of England ministers. Their parishes were large, and they were expected to visit church members as well as conduct services. As their time and resources allowed, they were to catechize and teach. Although they normally went from catechism to Book of Common Prayer and Bible, their teaching occasionally included Latin.

Since the mid-1600s, there had been private masters in the South. At their least, they were not much better scholars than their students and were poorly paid. Devereaux Jarrett, orphaned son of a Virginia carpenter, read "indifferently" and his handwriting was a "sorry scrowl" when he began to teach at nineteen.

---

*Standards for estimating literacy have shifted from time to time, generally upward. A signature is not a good test of literacy. An otherwise illiterate person may have learned to sign his or her name. Some provincials could read but not write. Poor people do not and did not usually sign legal documents; therefore the sample was not representative. However, one study has demonstrated that if and when people sign their names, people can also read.

... [T] that I might appear more than common in a strange place, and be counted somebody, I got me an old wig, which, perhaps cast off by the master, had become the property of his slave, and from the slave it was conveyed to me. But people are not obliged, you know, to ask how I came by it. . . .

In his first year of teaching, Jarrett earned only one sixth as much as a carpenter would have. He caught malaria, but was well pleased recalling that he had been able to buy on credit two fine shirts.

From 1758 until 1773 Donald Robertson, capable and prosperous, a Scotch university man, was master of his own private school in Virginia. From his school he earned on the average Ł 90 a year, nearly twice a carpenter's wages; he also had a farm. About half his students studied English, the other half Latin, for which the tuition was twice as much. The students were boys, except for Miss Patsy Throckmorton in early 1761. (Girls did not go to private schools as a rule, but more often than not learned how to read.) Robertson had an average of thirty pupils. About half of his students were with him for a year or less, and only one in twenty for more than five years. Most of his students had learned to read before they came, and some went to other schools. The notebook of James Madison, a better student, has extensive notes on Socrates and Plato, and on Locke and more recent philosophy. It would be interesting to see the notebook of, say, Tommie Broadus, who spent six years instead of the usual two or three studying English.

The children of some middling well-off planters, as well as those of the wealthy, were tutored. It has been said that their tutors were often indentured servants, but that may have been first said in spite. One tutor, John Harrower, was an indentured servant. He had sailed and walked from the north of Scotland to the south of England without finding employment or profit, and in 1774, "reduced to the last shilling," he had signed an indenture. Landed at Fredericksburg, Virginia, his contract was sold to Colonel William Daingerfield of Belvedira plantation, and as Daingerfield's servant, he taught the colonel's three sons. "His elder son Edwin, ten years of age, entered into two syllables in the spelling book. His second son Bathurst, six years of age, in the alphabet. William, his third son, four years of age, does not know the letters." Daingerfield helped Harrower find additional tuition-paying students. The colonel was generous and friendly, although Mrs. Daingerfield disliked Harrower's Scotch way of speaking and his punishment of her children. Harrower was not well schooled, and even his spelling showed his Scotch burr. He seems to have been a thoughtful and religious man, although he was drunk with Colonel Daingerfield on Christmas Day, 1775—Harrower, because he was homesick for his wife and children, and Daingerfield, because his tenants had not paid their past-due rent.

Philip Vickers Fithian was employed in the fall of 1773 to be for a year the tutor for Colonel and Mrs. Robert Carter of Nomoni Hall, a plantation a few miles from Belvedira. The Carters were a rich aristocratic family, and the upbringing and education of their children seems representative of those of the aristocratic and wealthy. Fithian was a graduate of Princeton and was preparing to become a Presbyterian minister. (Fifthian and Harrower apparently never heard of each other.) A few weeks after his arrival Fifthian wrote to a friend:

> I began to teach his [Colonel Carter's] children on the first of November. He has two sons, and one nephew; the oldest son is turned seventeen, and is reading Sallust [a favorite Latin author] and the Greek grammar; the others are about fourteen, and in English grammar and arithmetic. He has besides five daughters which I am to teach English, the eldest is turned of fifteen, and is reading the *Spectator* [an English magazine, the standard of graceful English]; she is employed two days every week learning to play the pianoforte and harpsichord. The others are smaller, and learning to read and spell. Mr. Carter is one of the chancellors of the upper court [council, upper house, member] at Williamsburg [capital of Virginia], and possessed of as great . . . fortune as any man in Virginia. . . .

Fithian, presumably having been raised in an "authoritative" or "moderate" family, was unaccustomed to the aristocratic way of child rearing. The children of the Carters were raised by slaves (and tutors) as much as by their parents. Slave women often served as wet nurses for the children of southern aristocrats. By Fithian's standards the Carter children were "indulged"—spoiled. Schooling was cancelled or postponed for pleasure: horse races, balls and parties, cock fights, and boat races. Girls were expected to learn to play the piano and guitar, and to learn to dance with style and grace. The children of the Carters were being prepared to be gentlemen and ladies.

There were variations, naturally, in the education of aristocrats and gentility. There might be servants in the place of slaves. Occasionally there was a governess in place of a tutor; Fithian mentioned several times governess Sally Panton, recently arrived from London. Sometimes boys—and, less often, girls—were sent away to school. Occasionally a son or daughter was returned to England for school, although not as often as has been traditionally said. But in sum, the sons and daughters of aristocrats were being educated to become aristocrats.

Taking them together, the well-off, the middling, and the poorer sort of Virginians and southerners generally were better schooled than they had been a century earlier, if not quite as well schooled as New Englanders. Virginians in the oldest, eastern part of the state were generally literate. Between 1763 and 1771, in Elizabeth City County, nine white men out of ten and two out of three white women could sign their names; in the 1600s, only one woman in three had been able to write her name. Many children still learned to read at home, and apprentices learned from their masters, but in 1745, at least five men and a woman taught in the county—a master at Symes or Eaton School, the Church of England minister, and private masters or tutors. The role of the school was less important than in New England, but as in New England, men and women were better educated than a hundred years before. In Virginia and in the rest of the South, there was less schooling in the up-country frontiers, but New England and Pennsylvania had their less well schooled frontiers, too.

SCHOOLING FOR BLACKS:
THE FIRST PRECEDENTS

Nearly all the half million Blacks in America in 1776 were slaves. Few of them could read, and fewer still could write. Most of those who did learn, as poetess Phyllis Wheatley did in Boston, were taught outside schools. Schools and schooling for Blacks, when they did exist, usually resulted from efforts of churches, particularly those of the Church of England and the Quakers.

The Church of England's Society for the Propagation of the Gospel (S.P.G.) provided support for many of the Church of England efforts to Christianize Blacks and for that purpose to teach them to read. In New York City it supported the school of Elias Neau, begun in 1704. Neau taught school three nights a week, for Blacks and also for Indians and Whites. He sometimes had more than a hundred pupils. When he died in 1722, other missionaries continued his school.

The Church of England's Charleston, South Carolina, school for Blacks, established in 1743, followed a straightforward plan, according to one account. Two slaves, Harry and Andrew, were purchased. They built the schoolhouse and then were taught to teach reading, which they did for some years. The more usual plan, of course, was for a white missionary or schoolmaster to teach, as in a school founded in Philadelphia in 1743. One of the less formal schools for Blacks was established by The Reverend Jonathan Boucher, who was also rector of a parish and master of a school for better-off boys and managed his own plantation. With the support of another English society, the Associates of John Bray, he preached to, converted, and baptized slaves. To aid in Christian instruction, Boucher "set up two or three serious and sensible black men as schoolmasters to teach the children around them merely to read in their leisure hours." Perhaps that not unjustly sums up the view of the Church of England: Blacks had souls: Therefore Blacks should be converted: Therefore it would be valuable for them to read: But worldly matters were not interfered with in any way. Some slave owners wanted assurance that Christianizing their slaves would not interfere with their ownership. Laws, for instance one passed in South Carolina in 1711, insured that even if slaves had been converted to Christianity, their conditions of bondage were not in any way affected.

Colonial slave owners gave little further thought to schooling for slaves, but their learning became a crucial part of the economy of the Southern plantation. Carl Bridenbaugh's *Colonial Craftsmen* described numerous slave artisans in the later 1700s. Occupying the position of journeymen, usually having learned their craft from white craftsmen, slave artisans were plantation sawyers, carpenters, coopers, blacksmiths, farriers, and coachmen, and in the planters' houses they were cooks, maids, and even butlers. Slave artisans also worked in Charleston, South Carolina, Philadelphia, New York, and other cities. Often the slave artisan was seen by free white craftsmen as an unfair source of competition.

The Quakers, starting with their founder George Fox, found slavery morally evil. Quakers in Pennsylvania were discouraged and later forbidden to own slaves, and may have established a school for Blacks as early as 1700. Other black children were taught with white children in the Quaker schools. The best remembered and most important Quaker school for Blacks was the one founded in Philadelphia in 1770 by Anthony Benezet.

Benezet was a refugee French Protestant, as Neau was. Like Corlet and Cheever, Benezet had been a master throughout his career. Benezet had taught in Germantown (where Pastorous had taught), then in the Friend's English School (where the first master had been Enoch Flower), and had been master of a Quaker school for girls. He was a saintly man, gentle and charitable. More important, he believed that Blacks were "generously sensible, humane, and sociable, and that their capacity is as good, and as capable of improvement as that of white people." What was most important was that Anthony Benezet, with fellow Quaker John Woolman, were the first American abolitionists. The Church of England had hoped to save souls. To put it simply, Benezet and his fellow abolitionist Quakers aimed to save men and women.

An "African School" was proposed to the Quaker Monthly meeting in Philadelphia by Benezet in 1770, when he was master of a school for "indigent" (poor) girls. The proposal was approved. From 1782 until his death in 1786 after the Revolution, he was master of the Philadelphia African School. Much of his estate was willed to the school. It thrived, and the Quakers opened other "African" schools. While he was master of the African School, Benezet was one of the most determined spokesmen for abolition, speaking not only to Americans but also across the Atlantic.

AN AMERICAN SCHOOL: THE ACADEMY

Historically, the new kind of school, the academy, is associated with the name of Benjamin Franklin of Philadelphia, although it is not clear that the idea of the academy was wholly originated by him. John Milton had proposed a plan for a type of academy as early as the 1640s. Before discussing Milton's contribution, however, it is best to say what an academy was and what it would become: An *academy* was a secondary school, not usually a preparatory school for college. It was privately controlled and privately financed, by tuition and gifts, but also often by public funds. Many academies were affiliated with churches, but most were "public" in the sense that any student who could pay tuition could attend, regardless of church membership. Most academies offered a wide range of studies—some people said too wide. But even to a definition this broad, there are exceptions. A few academies offered college-level instruction. A few continued the old Latin grammar school curriculum and eventually became college preparatory schools. Some academies were controlled by a state or the national government, as West Point and Annapolis are (though, of course, they are no longer secondary schools).

In 1749, Franklin published a pamphlet, *Proposals Relating to the Education of Youth in Pennsylvania*. In the academy he proposed, youth was to be instructed in ". . . those things that are likely to be *most useful* and *most ornamental*, regard being had to the several professions for which they are intended." The charter for the academy, granted a few months later, specified that it was to teach

> . . . the Latin and Greek languages, the English tongue, grammatically and as a language, . . . French, German, and Spanish . . . history, geography, chronology, logic and rhetoric, writing, arithmetic, algebra . . . natural and mechanic philosophy [science], drawing . . . and every other useful part of learning.

It was a long way from the Latin and Greek of the Latin grammar school.

In the proposal Franklin most often cited John Milton, who had also proposed a type of academy in his *Tractate on Education* in 1644; John Locke, who had died in 1714 but was still the most often quoted philosopher in provincial America; Charles Rollin and George Turnbull, then well known; and others. At the very least, Franklin contributed a synthesis that was a good match for the provincial experience. Before briefly describing the short and unsuccessful history of Franklin's Academy of Pennsylvania, some other sources of the academies need to be examined.

The inspiration for academies in America, it has sometimes been said, was the dissenters' academies in England, schools for the education of young men not allowed to attend Cambridge or Oxford in the 1700s because they were not members in good standing of the Church of England. However, careful study has shown that there was a great deal of variety among the dissenters' academies, and so collectively they could not have had influence. If the American provincial academies were influenced by *an* English academy, the academy at Northampton may have had more influence than any other. The language of instruction there was English, and the variety of subjects taught was similar to that taught later in American academies. Master Philip Doddridge of Northampton did correspond with several Americans, but it is not clear how much he influenced them.

It has also been argued that academies followed the examples set by American Presbyterians. They established schools because it was necessary for "New Side" evangelical Presbyterians, who were very much influenced by the Great Awakening, to provide training for new ministers. It followed that the "Old Side" Presbyterians also needed to train ministers of their conviction. It is surely true that a number of Presbyterian ministers did establish schools. The most famous of them was the "Log College," which had been established in 1727 by William Tennant, father of evangelist Gilbert Tennant. The schools of the Presbyterians were called *academies* and began early in the 1700s.

Thus, it might be said that the academy was another invention of Benjamin Franklin's, or that the academies were inspired by one in England, or that the needs of the Presbyterian Church had led to the academies. Perhaps more important than any of this was the trend toward practicality in provincial American schooling. As an example, within a few years James Maury, Virginia parson-schoolmaster wrote that a student should "be chiefly employed in studies which will be useful to him in approaching the active scenes of life. . . . [He] ought to be instructed as soon as possible in the most necessary branches of useful, practical knowledge. . . ." No matter how complicated the history of the invention or introduction of the academy, it is entirely clear that it was the product of its times. Distinctly American academies would be established by the thousands in the 1800s, and would be the most important kind of American secondary school until the rise of the high school toward the end of the 1800s.

The Academy of Philadelphia opened in 1751. Although it became the ancestor of the University of Pennsylvania, Franklin thought it a failure. Its "English school" became not much more than preparation for its "Latin school," and the Latin master was in charge of the Academy.

The Academy's first English schoolmaster, David Dove, a portly and voluble man, had come to Philadelphia in 1750. His teaching in the Academy of Pennsylvania gained Franklin's approval, because he admired Dove's student's elocution. Out of school Dove was a political caricaturist and writer of pamphlets, a "sarcastic and ill-tempered doggerelizer, who was but ironically *Dove*, for his temper was that of a hawk, and his pen the beak of a falcon pouncing upon his prey." It is fitting that a caricature is the surviving picture of him. He wrote supporting Franklin and his friends, changed sides, wrote against them, and attacked both sides on one issue or another. Dove insisted on also teaching at his own private school, to the objection of the Academy's trustees, and resigned or was discharged in 1753. Thereafter he kept private schools in and near Philadelphia.

"COLLEGE ENTHUSIASM"

Harvard had been established in 1636 and, after a false start, reopened in 1640. For sixty years it was the only college in the English colonies. The second college was William and Mary in Williamsburg, the capital of colonial Virginia, and was chartered by the King in 1693. The charter cost two years of effort by Commissary (bishop's representative) James Blair. Like Harvard, its first stated purpose was to provide ministers for the colony. As did Harvard, it provided a part of the formal education of many other students. William and Mary's Latin grammar school opened in the 1690s, and its first permanent buildings were completed in 1699. Students did not graduate from the college of William and Mary until the early 1700s.

The third American college, Yale (to use the name by which it is now known) was chartered by the legislature of Connecticut in 1701. It was established because leaders of Connecticut felt the need for a college, and because conservative ministers in Massachusetts felt that Harvard was already too liberal and too much under the influence of unitarians. Yale was at Killingsworth and Saybrook,

Fter God had carried us fafe to *New-England*, and wee had builded our houfes, provided neceffaries for our liveli-hood,rear'd convenient places for Gods worfhip, and fetled the Civill Government: One of the next things we longed for, and looked after was to advance *Learning*, and perpetuate it to Pofterity; dreading to leave an illiterate Miniftery to the Churches, when our prefent Minifters fhall liein the Duft. And as wee were thinking and confulting how to effect this great Work; it pleafed God to ftir up the heart of one Mr. *Harvard* (a godly Gentleman, and a lover of Learning, there living amongft us) to give the one halfe of his Eftate (it being in all about 1700.l.) towards the erecting of a Colledge, and all his Library: after him another gave 300.l. others after them caft in more, and the publique hand of the State added the reft : the Colledge was, by common confent, appointed to be at *Cambridge*, (a place very pleafant and accommodate and is called (according to the name of the firft foun der) *Hervard Colledge.*

FIGURE 2-2   Text describing the founding of Harvard University from "New England's First Fruits, 1643" p. 12. Reprinted in *Quinquennial Catalogue of the Officers and Graduates, 1636-1920* (Cambridge, Massachusetts: Harvard University, 1922), p. 5.

Connecticut before it moved to New Haven in 1716. As Harvard had been, it was named for an early benefactor.

Frederick Rudolph, in *The American College and University*, points out the similarities among the first three colonial colleges. As had Harvard's founders, William and Mary's and Yale's founders declared that their colleges would train ministers. All three colleges were governed by their presidents and a board of outside laymen and ministers serving as trustees. The long-time English tradition had been government by faculty, but the lack of a strong and permanent faculty had made that impossible. The conventional American pattern of control of colleges is the one that was first introduced at these earliest American colleges. The first three colleges were partly supported by taxes, but the other pre-Revolutionary colleges were not.

The fourth American college, Princeton, was not chartered until forty-five years after Yale. Princeton was the first of the colleges to be founded as a result of the Great Awakening. The colleges coming out of the Great Awakening were controversial, and governmental aid could not be obtained for them. Princeton was the college of the evangelistic—"New Side"—Presbyterians, some of whose education had been at the "Log College" of William Tennant.

Within the thirty years remaining before the Revolution, five more colleges were established. To use present-day names, they were Brown, Columbia, Dartmouth, Rutgers, and the University of Pennsylvania, all the result of what Yale President Ezra Stiles called "college enthusiasm." Except for the University of

Pennsylvania, the new colleges were intended to educate ministers and other young men in the new or "reawakened" denominations. All of these colleges were small. Even Harvard and Yale had no more than 100 or 200 students.

The colleges faced contradictions that would continue after the Revolution. One of these contradictions was the need for tuition to meet expenses, and hence the need to attract as many students as possible. While the colleges could and did demand that professors and tutors be of their faith, there were no religious tests for students; the need for students made such qualifications impractical. For chartering and survival there was need for wide support. Although Eleazar Wheelock had intended Dartmouth College for Indians, in order to receive a charter and to attract donations, it was necessary that the college have a more general attractiveness and admit other students.

There was a conflict in curriculum, too. Although most of the colleges had been intended to strengthen faith, the science of the 1700s, coming more than anywhere else from the Scottish universities, was introduced into the course of study. At Yale in the mid-1700s, students studied algebra, geometry, and calculus. Copernican astronomy, which placed the sun instead of the earth at the center of the universe, was introduced. At William and Mary a professor of "natural philosophy," William Small, was appointed in 1758. There would later be a long and heated conflict between science and religion, but it did not arise as long as science was seen as evidence of God's handiwork.

At the time when academies with more practical and general courses were beginning to be established, the first professional courses were being offered in American colleges. George Wythe was professor of law at William and Mary, and his students included Thomas Jefferson. Medicine was taught at the University of Pennsylvania starting in 1765, and at Columbia (then called King's College) in 1767. Students there could study anatomy, physiology, and chemistry, as well as applied medicine.

At some of the colleges, particularly Harvard, Brown, and Columbia, students were early and loud advocates of revolution against England. At the first commencement at Brown University in 1767, for instance, there was a debate on "whether British America can under present circumstances consistent with good policy, affect to become an independent state."

THE REVOLUTION

There have been many explanations for the causes of the American Revolution. The central issue—the most important cause of the American Revolution and the one that is most crucial in determining its immediate effect—was political. The Colonists' collective political experiences had for 150 years been different from people of mother-country England. The fundamental issue underlying the Revolution was independence, freedom from what was seen as the tyranny of King George

III and Parliament. Only a few leaders wanted to change society or to redistribute wealth, as the French and Russian revolutionaries would. The immediate outcome of the Revolution was independence because most of the Revolutionary leaders had intended no more than that.

The political and ideological battles that led to the Revolution were sometimes fought in colonial assemblies and by speechmakers. But most often they were fought in newspapers and pamphlets, by writers and editors. They were effectively fought and followed with great interest because before the beginning of the Revolution most men knew how to read. Since most men and women had been taught to read in schools, the schools contributed indirectly, but nonetheless significantly, to the coming of the Revolution. Perhaps the strong pro-Revolutionary convictions on the college campuses also speeded the coming of the Revolution.

Not all Americans supported the Revolution. Perhaps one third of them favored it, one fourth of them opposed it, and the rest were onlookers. A few schools were destroyed, as Rutgers was when British Colonel Simcoe burned its building. Others were closed, as the Boston Latin School and John Tileston's writing school were. Some schools, such as Dartmouth College, continued undisturbed except for the usual wartime effects of inflation and shortages.

The Revolution wrecked lives and made careers, and divided the families of schoolmasters as well as others. The experiences of John Lovell, master of the Boston Latin School, and of his son James Lovell, usher (assistant master) at the school, are examples of schoolmasters caught up in these kinds of events.

John Lovell (1710-1784), A.B. Harvard, 1728, had been master of the Boston Latin School since 1734, as the successor of Nathaniel Williams, who had followed Ezekiel Cheever. Loyalist (Tory) students remembered him as gentle. The Revolutionaries (Whigs) remembered him as a flogging despot. A portrait of John Lovell still exists, a picture of a well-fed, smug-looking man wearing an Eastern turban, a fad of the time. One of his former students reported shuddering when he looked at the painting. John Lovell believed in loyalty—loyalty to England. When the British evacuated Boston in 1776, John Lovell went to Halifax with them as a refugee.

James Lovell had been usher of the Boston Latin School for fifteen years and a strict disciplinarian in school. He supported his wife and five sons on a modest salary of £ 60 a year and what he could earn by teaching arithmetic before school and teaching French at night. In the pockets of a Revolutionary leader killed at Bunker Hill, the British found letters implicating the younger Lovell as a revolutionary. On the strength of these letters, the British troops clapped Lovell in jail. Young Lovell shared as a prisoner his father's voyage to Nova Scotia. He was later freed as part of a prisoner exchange and became a member of the Continental Congress, a man of some political power. Old John Lovell died in Halifax, leaving behind him relics of a prosperous past, "a mahogany desk . . . a ditto tea table . . . two china punch bowls," and the household furnishings of a poor man, "one pair blankets . . . one small copper tea kettle (old)." Young Lovell, the revolutionary, lived on—a citizen and official of the new American republic.

FIGURE 2-3   Portrait of John Lovell based upon a painting by
Nathaniel Smibert. From *The Memorial History of Boston,* Vol. 2,
Justin Winsor, editor (Boston: James R. Osgood and Company,
1881), p. 401.

The last major campaign of the Revolution ended with the surrender of a
British army at Yorktown in 1781. The peace treaty was signed two years later.
Then, in the words of a patriot, it was "time to begin again."

CONCLUSION

The history of education in the colonies was at first the history of the "transit," or
transportation, of a culture across the Atlantic, and its transplanting into the
wilderness. Later, perhaps from roughly the time of Ezekiel Cheever's death in
1708, education and schooling evolved as American culture and society evolved.
As Lawrence Cremin has written, education during the provincial period was popularized. It provided an opportunity for learning that would be more easily attained,

more appropriate in subject, and more directly controlled by the public. At the same time, the role of the schools was increasing. Children learned to read in schools more often, rather than at home. Parts of the knowledge needed for trades and professions were taught increasingly in school rather than by apprenticeship.

Schools were influenced by a changing way of thought, less devout and less theological, more logical and more scientific. Some schools were also influenced by the Great Awakening, which was in part the reaction to the new rationalism. As American culture drifted toward materialism, the schools shifted, belatedly, toward a material emphasis. As America's first cities grew and became more prosperous, the varieties of education available within them grew. When schools are private enterprises, they follow the same patterns of growth and change as other small enterprises.

At the same time, the colleges affected the professions of law and medicine, making the equivalent of apprenticeship less important. Schooling also changed the social standing of the student. As Philip Fithian wrote to a friend, a college degree from Princeton was as good in Virginia—as far as social standing was concerned—as Ł 10,000.

The Revolution interrupted schooling, but did not immediately change it.

PART TWO
AGE OF THE COMMON MAN

The Corliss steam engine was the largest in the world, forty feet high, 700 tons, 2500 horsepower at thirty-six revolutions per minute. It provided power for Machinery Hall, a 1400-foot-long building, quite appropriately designed by railway engineers, which was part of the 1876 Philadelphia Centennial Exhibition Machines, at the height of the Industrial Revolution, were a most important attraction at the Centennial Exhibition. Granted, one could see there what one wished to see: machinery, paintings, Japanese bronzes and lacquerware, even a display of false teeth. Two conclusions were certain: In its first hundred years the United States had become a great power, and Americans in 1876 lived in a world in which machines had become overwhelmingly important.

The United States and its culture had changed in many ways. Values and beliefs had shifted. Socially, America was more varied and more complex, with a much larger population. The economy had grown prodigiously. The United States had been enlarged geographically, too. Its western border, which had formerly been the Mississippi River, was, by 1876, the Pacific Ocean. Ways of travel had changed. Trails had been replaced by highways and canals. Canoes and flat-bottomed barges had been replaced by steamboats. Railroads moved products and people more quickly and inexpensively. America manufactured goods instead of only selling raw materials and buying manufactured products. The American political system had changed: nearly every American man was entitled to vote. A system of schooling—tax supported, state controlled, and available for nearly every child—had been developed. Generals, explorers, businesspeople, statesmen, inventors—many, perhaps all, Americans—had contributed to progress.

It is a temptation to search for the mainspring, the driving force, for American change. There have been compelling arguments that the changes in America have come first from cultural values, social dynamics, the West and free land, efficient transportation, the American Industrial Revolution, a republican form of government, or even from distinctive American patterns of schooling. However, a search for the driving force in American history will almost certainly be unsuccessful. Progress, or change, came from interaction of all these factors.

The culture of a time and place is never uniform or monolithic; there are always dissenting views and deviant behaviors. Here, only general features can be sketched: the work ethic, the romanticism, the faiths and reformers of the time.

The "Protestant ethic"—the concept was German sociologist and historian Max Weber's—was and is a set of convictions and habits. Tomorrow is more important than today. To save is better than to spend. To be rich is to be righteous. To work is better than to rest. Your fate is in your hands, and you are responsible for it. These beliefs were not new, of course. Benjamin Franklin's *Poor Richard's Almanac* had stated them in pithy little sayings. The Protestant ethic is still important. (Critics say schools depend upon it too much, and so penalize pupils who do not share it.) The Protestant ethic seems to have been most pervasive in America in the early and mid-nineteenth century. Americans were inventors. (Abraham Lincoln patented a strange device to enable steamboats to walk over mud banks.) They looked to each person to reform himself or herself. (Solitary confinement cells in prisons were to aid the convict in doing so.) Americans were industrious. On the farm or in the shop or factory, they worked long hours, longer than before, much longer than today.

Americans of this period were, more than before or most times since, "romantics." They turned away from what seemed to them to be the limits of classical and conventional learning; in philosophy, this was a basis for *transcendentalists*, the most famous of whom was Ralph Waldo Emerson. They emphasized the virtues of the individual and the evils of society. In education romantics thought of the child as a garden plant, to be cared for and cultivated so that it would develop, grow, unfold, and bloom. For the romantics, feeling was more important than thought; grown men and women read Johann Goethe's *Sorrows of Werther* and wept at the hero's death by his own hand. It was the fate of man, or woman, to be isolated, alone; Lord Byron, poet, revolutionary, convention flouter was an influential man, a hero. Edgar Allen Poe not only wrote as a romantic but seemed to live as one.

Admiration for classical heroes and classical architecture continued and in some ways increased after the Revolution. Thomas Jefferson's architectural design for the University of Virginia was neoclassical. Admiration was reflected in place names, too: Cincinnati, Ohio; Syracuse, New York—or even Hannibal, Missouri, the setting for *The Adventures of Tom Sawyer* and boyhood home of its author, Mark Twain.

During the same time the romantics rediscovered nonclassical history, architecture, and art. One of the authors much admired and much read by Americans was Scotsman Sir Walter Scott. Many of his high romantic novels had historical, nonclassical settings. *Ivanhoe*, perhaps most loved of them, was set in medieval England. There had been a revival of Gothic architecture in England. Churches and schools and other American public buildings were built in that style in America. Many American homes were adaptations in wood, "carpenter Gothic" and "steamboat Gothic." Some survive and are cherished. American Gothic was followed by designs inspired by Italian villas, Swiss chalets, and, at the extreme, Egyptian tombs and mosques of India. There were also American romantic painters, members of the "Hudson River School," glorifiers of nature.

This was also a period of reform. Our first interest here is in school reformers and reforms, but there were other reformers and other causes. The most important of these reformers were abolitionists; their cause was to end slavery. American abolition may have had its beginnings with the efforts of schoolmaster Anthony Benezet. In 1807, Congress ended by statute the legal importation of slaves. The American Colonization Society was founded ten years later to send Blacks back to Africa; the intent was charitable (if racist); the practice, wholly impractical. Among abolitionists, William Lloyd Garrison was one of the most influential and determined abolitionist spokespersons. He established an abolitionist newspaper, the *Liberator*, in 1831. He wrote about abolition:

> On this subject I do not wish to think, or speak, or write with moderation. . . . I am in earnest—I will not equivocate—I will not excuse—and I will not retreat a single inch. And I will be heard.

The *Liberator* undertook, with some success, to convert Northerners to abolitionism. Another abolitionist, Elijah Lovejoy, was killed in Alton, Illinois, when his newspaper office was mobbed in 1837; he became the abolitionists' first martyr. One of the abolitionist heroines was Harriet Tubman, an escaped slave who aided other slaves to escape northward. Even more famous were the characters of *Uncle Tom's Cabin*, the best-selling antislavery novel that appeared in 1852. "Uncle Tom," the name of a "good darky" who "knew his place," was an insulting term a few years ago.

Most southerners, though not all of them, were antiabolitionist. Slavery was a part of the southerner's idealized way of life. Slavery was profitable in work-demanding cotton, sugar cane, and tobacco fields. In parts of the South black slaves were much more numerous than Whites. A few white refugees from Haiti settled in the South, and southerners knew of the deaths of 2,000 Whites at the hands of Black Haitian revolutionaries. Southerners were alarmed by Nat Turner's Rebellion in Virginia in 1831 and by other slave uprisings. Finally, there was John Brown's 1859 attempt at Harper's Ferry, Virginia, to start a general insurrection of slaves. After seventeen deaths Brown was captured by troops under the command of Colonel Robert E. Lee, and hanged. The abolitionists had another and greater martyr: "John Brown's body lies moldering in the grave / But his soul goes marching on. . . ."

The most important reformers of the times were the abolitionists, and those in which we are primarily interested were school reformers. It is not to be forgotten that this was the time of many reformers and would-be reforms. One of them, "temperance," which later became prohibition, was the basis for the Eighteenth Amendment. It serves as one of the best examples of ill-considered and unsuccessful reform. Some other causes have devotees still. "Women's suffrage" was devoted to securing voting, property, and other rights for women. Other projected reforms seem less important, although they have their ardent supporters now: vegetarianism, the prevention of cruelty to animals, and suppression of the use of tobacco. Dr. Sylvester Graham, an important supporter of abolition, was also a devoted vegetarian and the developer of unbolted whole wheat flour. We use his name when we speak of *Graham crackers.*

In the late 1700s, detached and logical ways of thinking about religion and about God had led to deism and to outright atheism. In the 1800s, there was renewed commitment and warmth of faith for the churches and for religion. In long-settled places there was propriety and faith, and weekly attendance at services in churches that were impressive as they could be made to be. Nearer the frontier there was less propriety. Religion and faith there were strengthened by traveling preachers, many of them Methodists, and days-long camp meetings. The society, culture, and the schools of the time must always be seen against this background.

New churches and sects appeared. Unitarianism, the faith and conviction of liberal gentlemen and ladies, began with a somewhat mystical reformulation by William Ellery Channing, initially while he was a tutor in Richmond, Virginia. Other churches and sects were further from conventionality. One group, the Millerites, believed that the end of the world would come on March 21, 1843, and made every preparation for that event. Other sects established religious utopias: the "Shakers," founded in 1774, who forbade marriage and sexual intercourse; the Oneida community, along somewhat different lines; the Amana community in Iowa. The names of the latter two are still familiar. The most nearly successful of the religious communities was, of course, Salt Lake City, established in 1847 by the Mormons.

There were also nonreligious, shorter-lived utopias. There were more than thirty "phalansteries," pre-Marxist rural communes. The most famous of them was Brook Farm, near Boston. Many prominent transcendentalists came there during its short existence. New Harmony, Indiana, established in 1825 by Robert Owen, is particularly interesting because of its socialistic principles and its Pestalozzian schools.

The United States' population grew from 5 million in 1800, to 39 million in 1870. By 1870, there were great cities. The population of New York was 800,000;

that of Philadelphia, 500,000. After an ebb tide, immigrants were flooding in again, from Ireland and Germany. Regional differences had increased. Southerners, with their "unique institution" of slavery, western farmers, and eastern city dwellers and factory workers had different views and spoke in different accents. America had become much more diverse as well as larger.

In 1800, there had been only a few Americans west of the Appalachians. By 1840, they were settling in Iowa. In 1849, the Gold Rush brought 80,000 men and some women to California, which became a state the next year. In the 1870s, homesteaders were establishing themselves in sod cabins in the Dakotas and Montana. Unsettled land, free or cheap, was the most important attraction of the West, far more important than gold. The West was the country of the common man, the location of purest democracy. The rich generally did not go west, and new western fortunes would usually take decades to accumulate. Cowboys, embattled Indians, hardrock miners, and sod-breaking farmers would become a part of America lore.

After the War of 1812, American cities resumed their rapid growth. Cities were ports then, where farm and natural products—cotton, wheat, fish, pitch pine— were gathered for shipment by sea, and where finished and tropical products—cloth, tools, guns, coffee, sugar—were sold by merchants. Shipping itself and buying and selling were the sources of merchants' growing wealth. The *transportation revolution* was a necessary preliminary to the growth of manufacturing and of inland cities. Between 1815 and the Civil War, transportation was revolutionized by the building of turnpikes, canals, railroads, and steamboats. Larger sailing ships, and later, propeller-driven iron steamships, appeared on the Atlantic Ocean. In 1861, a telegraph line replaced the pony express. Even the transportation of information had been revolutionized. Most important, freight rates declined by three-fourths or more. For the first time it was feasible to ship farm products—for instance, wheat— from the Ohio valley to the eastern seacoast. The cost of shipping manufactured products west also declined, of course.

By 1825, the cities of the Ohio and Mississippi Rivers—for instance, Cincinnati, Pittsburgh, Saint Louis—and the Great Lakes—Buffalo, Detroit, Chicago—had begun their most rapid growth. Typically, they also had industries, processing farm and raw products. Cincinnati was "Porkopolis," where hogs were slaughtered and pork cured for shipment. Pittsburgh, although like the others at first a trading city, produced iron and glassware. Buffalo was the eastern terminal of Great Lakes shipping, where wheat was unloaded from lake boats, and where much of it was milled into flour before it was shipped farther eastward.

Some other early manufacturing was located in the cities, too, because transportation was good there and workers were available, and because the cities themselves were markets. Fortunes were made in cities, or at least displayed there by the building of mansions, by elaborate furnishings for them, by the finery of wives' clothing, by an elaborate way of life. Cities were centers of cultural life. Painters and writers found patrons in the cities. The largest audiences for theatre and music were in the cities. There was not only great wealth and comparative sophistication there, but also extreme and commonplace poverty. Living costs seem low to us—in 1851, a New York City family of five could live on $10.37 a week—but wages were lower still, and being "out of work" was too common. In 1846, one person in seven in New York City was a pauper. Houses were overcrowded, airless, lightless, unsanitary. Crime and illness in the cities were distressingly commonplace. Many of the new immigrants lived there, not much more comfortably than in the old land.

Between the War of 1812 and the Civil War, 5 million immigrants came to the United States. The most common reason for coming to America was hope of economic gain. Immigrants came also because of their religious or political beliefs. About 2 million of the immigrants were from Ireland. For reasons we do not entirely understand, population had increased in Ireland, as it had in the rest of Europe. The cost of food had risen. In Ireland, farm landlords, who were greedy or at least opportunistic, evicted tenants or raised land rents. A million Irish children, women, and men starved to death when the Irish potato blight struck in the late 1840s. Irish newcomers settled in the largest seaport cities, New York, Boston, and Philadelphia. They were not welcome. They were "papists," Roman Catholics, "Clodhoppers," reputedly often drunk, surely underemployed or unemployed. The life expectancy of an Irish child born in Boston in the 1850s was six years.

Germans also immigrated in large numbers. Before the Civil War many were Protestants, troubled by interference with their churches. In 1831, 3,000 members of a Hamburg, Germany, Lutheran church came together to Buffalo. German Catholics and German Jews immigrated also. A few of the Germans were "48ers," liberal or even radical exiles avoiding the draft. Smaller numbers of immigrants came from Norway and Sweden and other European countries. Thousands of Chinese laborers were brought to the Pacific Coast. Some immigrants who were skilled workers quickly found jobs and enjoyed at least some prosperity. Many of the immigrants settled on farms in the West or became farmhands there. Others found jobs in the first mills and factories. On the West Coast, laborers recruited in China provided the heavy labor for the building of railroads. In the Lowell, Massachusetts, cotton spinning and weaving mills, Irish families replaced the first mill "operatives," girls and women from farming New England. Lowell was the first American industrial city. Water power was plentiful there, and transportation good. A number of cotton spinning and weaving mills were built there, starting in 1846.

Most of the new immigrants settled in Philadelphia, Boston, New York and other northern cities. Relatively few settled in the South. By 1860, only 500,000 immigrants lived below the Mason-Dixon line. Only New Orleans had a substantial immigrant population. By the time of the Civil War, New York, Milwaukee, St. Louis, Chicago and other big cities had foreign populations that outnumbered those of American birth.

Although the Industrial Revolution in England had been underway since at least 1750, it did not take place in the United States until much later. The process of industrialization was long and complicated. It was necessary to develop or borrow designs for the machines that would replace skilled labor—the designs for the first power looms, in Rhode Island in 1811, were more stolen than borrowed. It was necessary to provide power for the machines, first from water wheels and water turbines, later from steam engines, which provided most of the power after 1870. For factories to be profitable, it was necessary to develop at least a rudimentary management system. For manufactured goods a mass market was necessary: the transportation revolution had aided in that.

Industrialization had its price. It tended to concentrate wealth and power. Workers were exploited; working hours were long; the pay, low. It made it more difficult for skilled craftsmen to maintain themselves. It was expensive for our environment. Industrialization did result, however, in America being less dependent upon foreign manufactured products. Products generally were less expensive. A clock, after clockmaking had been industrialized, cost $2. Farming, also, had been revolutionized by machines performing tasks that men had formerly done. Productivity increased and with it, the standard of living.

Wars had social, cultural, and political consequences of their own. Even the War of 1812, embarrassing and at most indecisive, had its consequences. It led to a shift of capital from shipping to manufacturing, hurrying the American Industrial Revolution. The headlong attack by Andrew Jackson on the Indians of Florida had a consequence, easing the acquisition of Florida by the United States. The hero of the Battle of New Orleans, Andrew Jackson, became the hero of the common man and two-term President.

The Mexican War produced more glory, though its ends were more venal. Texas and the Southwest were added to American territory. Another military hero, Zachary Taylor, was elected to the Presidency.

However, no American war has had greater social consequences than the Civil War. The causes of the war, remote and immediate, have been the subject of many books. The war itself has been the subject of many more. Occasionally a school figured directly in the fighting. For instance, the southern students of Virginia Military Institute, as the "Cadet Corps," fought in the Battle of New Market. Eight student cadets were killed then. The record of the 33rd Illinois Infantry is less distinguished, but it was a school regiment. Most of its recruits were from an Illinois normal school, and the principal of the school was the regiment's colonel. In 1862, the end came to a Kirksville, Missouri academy, when a battery of field artillery galloped up and unlimbered its guns on the lawn. But those are mere details, three among many. The consequences of the war concern us here. The first human consequence was the death of hundreds of thousands of soldiers, North and South, black and white. The first social consequence was the freeing of the slaves. Abolitionists melted away, their cause triumphant. They believed that slavery was immoral and evil: Most of them did not believe that Whites and Blacks were equals or should be treated as equals. Of course, for Blacks, freedom was only the beginning. Economically, the South was devastated, and it would be the end of the century before it recovered. In the North there were new fortunes. All these would affect schools and education. Once more a military hero, U.S. Grant, became President.

In 1876, American wealth was growing fast, but the distance between the rich and the poor was greater. Businessmen had built large-scale enterprises, but it was difficult to organize worker unions. There were mansions in the cities, but also crowded, dirty, damp, airless flats in crime-ridden slums, where death rates were high. For good or for bad, city governments were often controlled by political bosses and their machines. Americans were prejudiced against Catholics, against Jews, against foreigners, and White prejudice against Blacks was still strong. In the North there had been and would be race riots. General Sheridan had repeated that "the only good Indian is a dead Indian." In the summer of the Philadelphia Exposition, 1876, General George A. Custer made his last stand at Little Big Horn. Custer, dead, was a hero. It would be a long time before white Americans would begin to feel that what Custer had attempted was wrong in principle. In 1876, there would be doubts about the honesty of the national government. General Orville Babcock, President Grant's personal secretary, was implicated in a distillers' tax avoidance deception. Secretary of War William W. Belknap resigned rather than face impeachment for selling Indian trading posts. Nevertheless, President Grant, with Emperor Dom Pedro II of Brazil and many other dignitaries, was president at the opening of the Philadelphia Centennial Exhibition.

CHAPTER THREE
SCHOOLING IN THE
NEW REPUBLIC

As a rule, successful revolutionaries have drastically changed patterns of schooling. The American Revolutionaries were an exception to the rule. They had no wish to change the schooling or the nature of their fellow citizens. They wished to preserve rather than change. Except for independence from English king and English parliament, they had no intent to change. Consequently, they made no effort to change the schools or education.

In the fifty years after the Revolution, the schools, of course, did change. The "republican spirit" appeared during the American Revolution, and during the French Revolution a few years later. The "republican spirit" led to new views of men's and women's nature, of society, of government, and of the contributions to be made by schooling. There were changes in theories about schooling. Thomas Jefferson, perhaps better known for other things, developed a social philosophy that was both representative and influential in his times, and proposals for schooling followed from it. His unsuccessful bill for the establishment of common schools in Virginia, introduced in 1779, anticipated in many ways the forms common schools would take fifty years later. The founding of the University of Virginia was his accomplishment; yet the University was only a fragment of the public school system he had originally envisioned.

During those fifty years new kinds of schools appeared. One of the new kinds of school was a Pestalozzian school, which appeared in 1825 in the short-lived utopia of New Harmony, Indiana, and is further discussed later in this chapter. Another new kind of school was the monitorial, or Lancastrian, school, which was widely popular where the poor, particularly the urban poor, were numerous, and where resources for schooling were small. The monitorial school is also discussed later in this chapter. Academies, which had first appeared before the Revolution, were established by the hundreds, and even by the thousands. Dozens of new colleges were established.

For the "common" or "district" schools, new school texts reflecting the "republican spirit," and voicing the new nationalism—but the old religious values—appeared quickly. Noah Webster's *A Grammatical Institute of the English Language, Part I*, later editions of which were to become famous as the "Blueback

FIGURE 3-1   Frontispiece and title page from Noah Webster's "Blueback Speller." Note in the frontispiece, the Ancient Greek goddess of wisdom Minerva is pointing the child towards the temple at the rear of the illustration in which are enshrined Knowledge and Wisdom.

This Spelling Book is almost universally used throughout the United States, the sale of it being *one million* copies per annum!!!

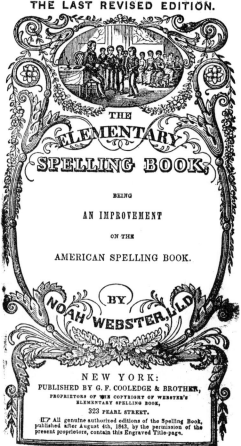

Speller," was the first published in 1783, only two years after the British surrendered. Jedidiah Morse's *Geography Made Easy* appeared the next year. Both of these texts, and others, deliberately tried to educate their readers in a political and value system that was consciously "American."

Both the development of thought and the evolution of schools required time. At the end of the Revolution not much was changed. Of course, some Loyalist masters had fled, but others resumed teaching. For Robert Proud of Philadelphia, "revolt, rebellion, and destruction, under the name and pretense of Liberty" were "popular and disagreeable objects." He spent the years of the Revolution in seclusion, but in 1780, returned as master of the Friends Latin school.

In New York, as Carl Kaestle describes it, there were still schools supported by churches. Perhaps thirty masters operated their own private for-profit schools, and there were dames' reading schools. As before the Revolution, schooling was offered in something like a free market. Parents chose what schooling seemed best from what schooling they could afford. For the poor—and in the cities the poor were becoming more numerous—there were only the church schools. Often there was no schooling at all. The monitorial schools would not appear in the cities until twenty years later.

In the South, education changed relatively little after the Revolution. John Davis, who had served in the British navy and who had learned "passable" Latin and French, spent four years, 1798-1802, traveling and teaching in the South. Not as well qualified as Philip Fithian, he lived and taught in circumstances less opulent than Fithian's. He lived with a family in their log house on a new plantation in South Carolina, and taught the family's children. At other times he was treated with disdain. Toward the end of his stay in America, he taught, very much as John Harrower had, in a school in Virginia only thirty miles from where Harrower had taught.

Even after new kinds of schools and education were appearing, older ways of schooling survived. In 1831, Abigail Mason of Salem, Massachusetts, went to Virginia to be the governess of Robert Temple's family on their plantation near Richmond. Teaching the Temple children, her life was probably not much different from that of a governess Philip Fithian had known fifty years earlier on the eve of the Revolution.

THOMAS JEFFERSON AND BENJAMIN RUSH, THEORISTS

While the decades following the Revolution saw a continued decline in the importance of the study of Latin in the schools, the basic vision of education as a moral enterprise was maintained. Noah Webster's intention was probably not much different from most educators' when he declared in the introduction to his spelling book that its purpose was to help teachers instill their students with ". . . the first rudiments of the language, some just ideas of religion, morals and domestic economy."

Undoubtedly the most important characteristic that emerged in the educational practice and thought following the Revolution was a deliberate cultural nationalism. The new nation's political and social values emphasized the worth of governments based upon the principles of a classical republican ideology. The disorder of the Revolution and the preceding colonial rule would be corrected by the proper implementation of a democratic republic, in which a virtuous citizenry through the help of government would establish a new social order.

Opinions varied during the period as to the specific characteristics that the new republic would have. Essentially what was conceived was a system of government whose strength was lodged in a largely agrarian population of independent landholders. The republican philosophy required participation in government by its landowning citizenry freed from monarchial rule. Property ownership was a critical qualification for participating in politics. Aristocrats and inherited status were largely rejected in favor of a natural leadership of talented men. Ideally, through the enactment of republican principles of government, cultural unity could be achieved—one that would provide the nation with a basis for its identity. Education was to play an important role in the establishment of this democratic republican consciousness.

Thomas Jefferson, best known of the early republican educational theorists, was born at Shadwell, Virginia, on April 13, 1743. His father, Peter, although not of a particular distinguished family, was nevertheless a member of Virginia's landed gentry. His marriage, in 1739, to Jane Randolph linked him to one of Virginia's most important families, and placed him and his children in a prominent position in local society. At the time of his death, when his son Thomas was fifteen, Peter Jefferson owned more than sixty slaves and between 7,000 and 10,000 acres of land.

Jefferson's early years were probably typical for the son of a successful Virginia planter, although the closeness of his home, Shadwell, to the frontier may have exposed him to influences that were more democratic than those of the older and more traditional tidewater region of Virginia. After having learned to read and to do basic arithmetic, Jefferson was sent at the age of nine to a school conducted by the Reverend William Douglas. Besides religious instruction, Jefferson also received training in French, Latin, and Greek.

Starting when he was fourteen, Jefferson attended a school under the direction of the Reverend James Maury. Maury was a much more sophisticated scholar than Douglas, and provided Jefferson with a thorough grounding in the Greek and Latin classics, and in contemporary literature. Maury, as has been said, was an early advocate of utilitarian schooling rather than pure classical preparation. Jefferson studied with Maury for two years, and then entered the College of William and Mary.

At William and Mary, Jefferson came largely under the influence of William Small, the single lay member of the faculty. According to Jefferson, Small was a man knowledgeable in most areas of science, of a liberal disposition and a gentleman. It was from Small that Jefferson received his first systematic introduction to science, philosophy, and social theory.

Jefferson began to read law while still a student at William and Mary, and practiced law until shortly before the outbreak of the Revolution. It was as a lawyer that he first put forward ideas about education. Asked to accept a cousin as an apprentice, Jefferson refused, explaining that he did not have the time to adequately train an apprentice. He wrote that most lawyers had a tendency to require apprentices to do their work for them, and usually did not provide them with adequate time for their studies.

Jefferson was elected to the Virginia House of Burgesses in December, 1768. His involvement in politics would continue until his death more than fifty years later. So too would his interest in education. In 1779, Jefferson put forward in the House of Burgesses a systematic plan for public education in Virginia entitled "A Bill for the More General Diffusion of Knowledge." In the bill, Jefferson outlined a system of schooling that would support his more general political and social philosophy.

According to Jefferson, a democratic society needed an educational system that would provide its citizens with the understanding and knowledge necessary for them to not only be able to pursue their own personal happiness, but also to fulfill their obligations and duties as citizens. Education would also provide the training that would allow those with unusual talents to assume roles as leaders of the culture.

Jefferson's educational bill of 1779, which was not adopted by the House of Burgesses, proposed that a natural aristocracy be identified by means of the educational system, one which would supplement rather than supersede the existing aristocracy based upon birth and wealth. Jefferson proposed to do this by means of a three-tiered school system that would provide a free general education for the entire population, but would also select and train for positions of leadership those individuals of superior intelligence and virtue.

According to his plan, Jefferson would have estabished a school program that operated in two distinct manners. For the general citizenry, a system of instruction was to be established that would provide them with three years of free schooling. Beyond basic instruction in reading, writing, and arithmetic, each individual would be provided with a general background in the principles of democratic government.

The second phase of Jefferson's educational program was to be implemented by means of a system of twenty Latin grammar schools, which were to be established throughout the Commonwealth of Virginia. Those who wished to pay the necessary tuition could send their children to these schools at their discretion. In addition, a set of examiners would visit the elementary schools throughout the commonwealth, and provide scholarships to a limited number of the community's most talented boys. As Jefferson outlined his proposal:

Of the boys thus sent in one year, trial is to be made at the grammar schools one or two years, and the best genius of the whole selected, and continued six years, best geniuses will be raked from the rubbish annually, and be instructed at the public expense, so far as the grammar schools go. At the end of six years' instruction, one half are to be discontinued (from among whom the grammar schools will probably be supplied with future masters); and the other half, who are to be chosen for the superiority of their parts and dispositions, are to be sent and continued three years in the study of such sciences as they choose, at William and Mary College. . . .

Jefferson felt his plan would provide basic instruction in reading, writing, and arithmetic for every male citizen, as well as more specialized training for those individuals of unusual ability. In addition, a basic uniform political education would be provided to the entire citizenry. Significantly, Jefferson opposed religious indoctrination on the part of the schools. He felt that in a republic individuals should not have imposed upon them any type of instruction that would be contrary to their personal religious creeds.

Although Jefferson advocated the separation of church and state, he realized that it would be virtually impossible to eliminate all religious functions from the schools. In the general education bill that he proposed to the Virginia legislature in 1817, for example, Jefferson argued that the educational system should simply be required not to threaten through compulsory religious instruction the religious freedom of any group attending the schools. According to his proposal, no religious rite or instruction could be required of a student attending the public schools, ecclesiastical figures would be excluded from administrative positions in the schools, and the establishment of a professorship of divinity would be prohibited at the University of Virginia.

To some extent Jefferson's views represented a compromise with existing religious authority and tradition. Commonly held religious holidays by the various religious groups within Virginia could be observed by both the public schools and university; religious materials and issues could be studied at the university if they were placed in a literary or philosophical context. Thus students in philosophy could study the implications underlying religious belief, or Biblical languages such as Hebrew or Greek, but not promote specific views concerning religion. Religion could be dealt with in the context of reason, but not dogmatically.

Jefferson failed to convince the members of the Virginia House of Burgesses of the need for a uniform system of public elementary schools. Cost and class interests undoubtedly encouraged its defeat. It was not until the mid-1830s that widespread support for public schools of the scope and impact Jefferson proposed was to develop throughout the United States.

Jefferson is perhaps the only major theorist to have put forward his ideas on education during the Revolution. In the decades following the Revolution, numerous other theorists presented specific proposals concerning the type of educational system that would be most suitable for the new republic. Among the most important of these theorists was Benjamin Rush.

Rush was a signer of the Declaration of Independence and early established himself as one of the leading intellectual figures of the new nation. A graduate of

Princeton, Rush was the best-known physician of his period. Having graduated from Princeton University in 1760, he had studied medicine at the College of Philadelphia and at the University of Edinburgh, which at the time was probably the most sophisticated center of political, philosophical, and social thought in Europe, as well as a major center for the study of medicine.

Rush was acutely aware of the significance of education in the promotion of the newly achieved republican system of government. As he wrote in a letter in 1786:

> We have changed our forms of government, but it remains yet to effect a change in our principles, opinions and manners so as to accommodate them to the forms of government we have adapted. This is the most difficult part of the business of the patriots and legislators of our country.

Rush argued that the educational system established during the colonial period encouraged diversity. Through the establishment of a uniform system of education—one which included the establishment of a federal or national university—Rush hoped to create an essentially homogeneous population that would be particularly well-suited to a uniform and peaceful system of government.

Unlike Jefferson, who was strongly opposed to the inclusion of religion in education, Rush felt that it should be an important subject in any system of public schools. According to him, by being exposed to the principles of Christianity, society was assured that the individual would possess those virtues that were most desirable for the citizen of a republic. Rush felt a Christian could not fail to be a good republican citizen since

> ... every precept of the Gospel indicates those degrees of humility, self-denial, and brotherly kindness which are directly opposed to the pride of monarchy and the pageantry of a court.

Rush's vision of the republic was clearly one of a Christian commonwealth.

Despite his strong religious convictions, Rush, as well as contemporaries of his such as Noah Webster and Jedidiah Morse, were strongly opposed to any foreign involvement in the education of American citizens. Their efforts in this area were clearly part of a larger movement to define and establish a national identity and tradition independent from that of Europe, and England in particular. The threat posed by the failure to establish an independent cultural identity seemed serious. In England, Lord Sheffield published a pamphlet declaring that cut off from the political and cultural influence of England, the American political experiment would fail.

Nationalists in all sections of the culture emerged in order to support the development of a specifically American consciousness. Artists such as Charles Wilson Peale began to paint works with specifically patriotic themes, while Joel Barlow composed an epic patriotic poem, *Columbiad*. They were clearly self-

THE CRISIS,,

OR THE CHANGE FROM ERROR AND MISERY, TO TRUTH AND HAPPINESS.

1832.

IF WE CANNOT YET

LET US ENDEAVOUR

RECONCILE ALL OPINIONS,

TO UNITE ALL HEARTS.

IT IS OF ALL TRUTHS THE MOST IMPORTANT, THAT THE CHARACTER OF MAN IS FORMED FOR—NOT BY HIMSELF.

Design of a Community of 2,000 Persons, founded upon a principle, commended by Plato, Lord Bacon, Sir T. More, & R. Owen.

EDITED BY
ROBERT OWEN AND ROBERT DALE OWEN.

London:
PRINTED AND PUBLISHED BY J. EAMONSON, 15, CHICHESTER PLACE,
GRAY'S INN ROAD.

STRANGE, PATERNOSTER ROW. PURKISS, OLD COMPTON STREET,
AND MAY BE HAD OF ALL BOOKSELLERS.

1833.

FIGURE 3-2 Title page from *The Crisis* edited by Robert and Dale Owen. Robert Owen's portrait is included at the top of the page. A drawing of the architectural design for a utopian community of approximately two thousand persons is included in the center of the page. Courtesy of the Library of Congress.

conscious in their nationalism. Yet despite their limitations, they represented a specific attempt to solve the problem of establishing a distinctive national identity.

ROBERT OWEN, JOSEPH NEFF
AND FRIENDS: UTOPIANS

Robert Owen was, like Jefferson, a social theorist. As they did for Jefferson, schools played an important part in his theories. Jefferson had envisioned a farming society, but Owen an industrial one. Owen was born in Wales in 1771. He was himself a successful and prosperous industrialist, manager, and partner in British cotton mills. As a reformer and utopian, he was a forerunner of the socialists.

The "infant schools" Owen established in New Lanark, Scotland, and New Harmony, Indiana, were loosely based on the work of Swiss educator Johann Heinrich Pestalozzi. Pestalozzi had been born in Zurich, Switzerland, in 1746, the son of a lower-middle-class family. Having tried careers in the ministry, the law, and farming, he gradually turned to education. Strongly influenced by the work of the French philosopher Jean Jacques Rousseau (1712-1779), Pestalozzi argued that men are born neither good nor evil, but instead are shaped by the environments in which they live. The idea of providing children with healthy and supportive environments, which would allow them to develop their personalities and characters to the fullest extent, was to be the basis of Pestalozzi's educational system.

Profoundly disturbed by the apparent disintegration of Swiss peasant society and family life taking place as a result of the rapid growth of cities and towns, Pestalozzi became concerned with reestablishing the importance of the family as a unit, and of using education as a means of developing an understanding of the world, through the use of object lessons whose applicability to real life situations would immediately be evident. Both of these ideas were developed by Pestalozzi in his book *Leonard and Gertrude*, which was first published in 1781. Written in the form of a novel, *Leonard and Gertrude* was loosely based on the story of a Swiss peasant woman's struggle to reform her alcoholic husband and educate her own children and the children of her village. Although not formally trained as a teacher, Gertrude, the heroine of the book, had an instinctive ability to instruct children. Warm and loving, she developed a curriculum for the children, which emphasized things they were already familiar with from their homes. Pestalozzi, for example, explained how the instruction Gertrude gave the children to whom she was teaching arithmetic

> ... was intimately connected with the realities of life. She taught them to count the number of steps from one end of the room to the other, and two of the rows of five panes each, in one of the windows, gave her an opportunity to unfold the decimal relations of numbers. She also made them count their threads while spinning, and the number of turns on the wheel, when they wound the yarn onto the skeins. Above all, in every occupation of life

she taught them an accurate and intelligent observation of common objects and the forces of nature.

Appealing to the senses, rather than simply to reason, Gertrude's system emphasized the natural goodness and curiosity of the child. By emphasizing the importance to the learning process of love and the idea of practical and object lessons, Pestalozzi radically departed from rigid authoritarian modes of education, emphasizing obedience and rote memorization, that were then common in Europe.

Owen first became interested in education as a means of improving the conditions of workers in his factories. Indeed, he is best known as an early socialist. Interested in further developing his investments, Owen, together with his business partners, acquired the New Lanark cotton mills in Scotland in 1799, and proceeded to develop a community around the mills, which was a model of social and industrial organization for the period.

Owen did not believe that industry should be a specialized activity separated from agriculture, but that the two should be carefully integrated. In this sense, Owen was repudiating the dichotomy between the city and the countryside that was to become a major issue in Europe and America during the nineteenth century. It was Owen's intention to establish industry in a rural setting under ideal conditions that would eventually not only lead to improved working conditions for laborers, but also lay the foundations of a new moral and social order.

Owen was particularly concerned with the welfare of children in the programs that he established at New Lanark. Child labor was widely used in factories in England during the late eighteenth and early nineteenth centuries. When Owen first arrived at New Lanark, the working conditions of children in factories horrified him. Such conditions were typical in England during the period. Robert Dale Owen, Robert Owen's son, in his autobiography recalled his experiences when he was fourteen and his father took him on a tour of various British mills.

> The facts we collected seemed to me terrible almost beyond belief. Not in exceptional cases, but as a rule, we found children of ten years old worked regularly fourteen hours a day, with but half an hour's interval for the midday meal, which was eaten in the factory. . . .In some large factories, from one-fourth to one-fifth of the children were cripples or otherwise deformed, or permanently injured by excessive toil, sometimes by brutal abuse. The younger children seldom held out more than three or four years without serious illness, often ending in death.

Robert Owen set out to eliminate conditons such as these. In doing so, education was to play a crucial role in his reforms.

Owen believed that education was the cause of most good and evil, misery and happiness found in the world. At New Lanark he radically improved working conditions for children in his factories and developed an exemplary educational program for them. His ideas concerning education were clearly rooted in the belief that individuals were primarily shaped by their environment, and that given a decent education and living conditions, "the good" would predominate. In this sense, Owen saw education as being a critically important means for achieving the reform of society.

In 1824, Owen came to the United States and purchased from a communal religious group called the Rappites 30,000 acres of land in Indiana, along the lower Wabash River. Owen's purchase included the village of Harmony. Quickly renamed New Harmony, the village became the center of a major utopian experiment. At Owen's invitation, more than 800 people settled there by the following year to create a "New Moral World" in the wilderness. Among the basic programs set up by Owen and his followers, the system of schools was undoubtedly the most successful. Owen's educational efforts at New Harmony were largely supported by the work of William Maclure and Joseph Neef.

Owen met Maclure at New Lanark in the summer of 1824. In many respects their careers closely paralleled one another. Maclure was born in Scotland in 1763. Like Owen, he had made a fortune in business and then turned to other interests. Coming to the United States during the late 1790s, Maclure began pioneer studies in the field of geology and minerology. Within a few years he established, both in the United States and in Europe, a reputation as an important scientist.

Maclure, along with his scientific interests, became concerned with education. In 1805, he visited Pestalozzi's school in Yverdon, Switzerland, and quickly became a supporter of Pestalozzi's system of education. Wishing to establish a Pestalozzian school in the United States, Maclure asked Pestalozzi to suggest someone who could set up such a program. The Swiss educator suggested Joseph Neef as a candidate. Meeting with Neef, who was then living in Paris, Maclure was impressed by him and his ideas and agreed to support him in the establishment of a Pestalozzian school in the United States.

Maclure financed Neef for two years while he learned English. Some time about 1808, a Pestalozzian school was established by Neef near Philadelphia, the first such school in the United States. After a few years the school was transferred to Delaware County, Pennsylvania, where it was eventually forced to close because of objections by the local community to Neef's atheism. Giving up teaching, Neef moved to Louisville, Kentucky, and took up farming.

Despite the failure of the school under Neef's supervision, Maclure continued to support various educational experiments. In 1819, he went to Spain and attempted to establish a school based upon the educational ideas of Pestalozzi and Philip Emanuel von Fellenberg (1771-1844), an early advocate of agricultural and trade education. In addition Maclure was involved in the support of Pestalozzian schools in Paris under the direction of Guillaume Sylvan Casmir Phiquepal d'Arusmont and Madame Marie Duclos Fretageot. The Spanish educational experiment ended in 1823, when the French army entered Spain and brought to an end the liberal Spanish rule under which Maclure had established the school. Forced to flee, Maclure made his way to Ireland and then England, and finally to Scotland and New Lanark, where he met Owen.

By then Fretageot and Phiquepal d'Arusmont had with Maclure's help transferred their activities to Philadelphia, where they operated a Pestalozzian school.

After some hesitation, Maclure agreed to go to New Harmony with Owen and direct the utopian colony's schools. Significantly, Maclure had complete control of the educational experiment. Neef, Fretageot, and Phiquepal d'Arusmont worked with him. The school opened in 1826.

In many respects the immigrant and higher schools established at New Harmony represented a continuation of the Pestalozzian programs begun by Owen at New Lanark. The schools were also a radical new beginning and anticipated many of the educational reforms that were to be proposed during the nineteenth century. One fundamental concept was that of free public education for all members of the community. Classes included both sexes. Emphasis was placed upon "object methods" of instruction. Whenever possible, visible concrete examples were presented to the children. Geometry was taught by means of a machine called a *trigonometer*, and arithmetic by a kind of abacus. Natural history was studied by direct observation, while geography was learned by having students make their own maps and globes.

Drawing and music were included as important parts of the school curriculum, as was gymnastics. Language training was provided by bringing together children of different language backgrounds to teach one another. Central to the curriculum was the program in trade education, which was the first of its type in the United States. Included in the program was instruction in engraving and printing, as well as in other manual arts.

The educational experiment at New Harmony was short lived. Almost from the start, Owen and Maclure disagreed about the school and its operation. Maclure envisaged the schools as being centers for scientific study, in which the students and their teachers would systematically pursue new fields of inquiry. Owen increasingly saw the schools as centers that would draw the members of the community together by cultivating in them similar dispositions and beliefs. By the spring of 1827, these differences were of little meaning, since the utopian experiment had come totally to an end. The schools in various forms continued for some time afterward.

Although largely a failure, the educational experiment undertaken by Maclure and Owen at New Harmony was to anticipate many of the major trends and reforms that took place in American education during the nineteenth century. The emphasis upon Pestalozzian principles of instruction, the attempt to use education as a vehicle of reforming the society, the idea of the school as a social center, as well as the emphasis upon industrial or trade education, are all issues that were to figure prominently in the educational programs and reforms of the middle and late nineteenth century.

In varying forms Pestalozzi's ideas were popularized by many individuals. In England Samuel Wilderspoon, at first a master and then agent of the London Infant School Society, did much to promote "infant schools" in England. They were for a time popular in the United States, in a not very Pestalozzian form that brings to mind today's nursery schools, and they probably served the same general functions.

ROBERT RAIKES, JOSEPH LANCASTER,
AND ANDREW BELL: CHARITY AND UTILITY

Two other new kinds of school, the Sunday school and the monitorial school, appeared. Both, but particularly the monitorial school, were important because they established or strengthened conventions of thought about schooling. Both Sunday and monitorial schools were first popular in Great Britain. England's industrial revolution was well underway. As a result, the poor in the cities had become more numerous and more conspicuous. In England, too, it was a time of political and social reform. Despite its political independence the United States had not yet achieved complete intellectual independence, and often adopted English precedents.

The Sunday school was popularized in England after 1780 by Robert Raikes, a newspaper publisher and editor in Gloucester. A rather natural development, Sunday schools had been organized by some revivalists of the Great Awakening in England and in the American colonies. Their increased popularity in England was from Raikes's efforts, as well as from greater concern for the needs of the poor. Usually the Sunday schools were in cities, although there are records of Sunday schools outside them. It was said that in 1821 there were 430,000 Sunday school pupils in England. Sunday schools eventually appeared in every American state. There were 5,000 Sunday school pupils in Boston and nearly 600 in Salem, Massachusetts. To demonstrate their learning, the Salem pupils recited Bible verses—one pupil learned 1600 of them—and gave answers to questions about the Bible. In the United States the American Sunday-School Union supported the development of Sunday schools. It also influenced the direction of their development, so that they would come to be exclusively concerned with religion, and would become the kind of Sunday school some of us or our parents remember from childhood.

The first assumption about Sunday school pupils was that they were in ignorance of Christianity and therefore in danger of damnation. The primary purpose of the Sunday school was to teach religion. In some Sunday schools the Bible was the only textbook. Teaching for salvation was already a very old idea, as was reading for salvation. Second, the Sunday schools were for poor children and teaching was a form of charity to the poor. Sunday school teachers were usually volunteers, charitable young Christians who contributed their Sundays—except for the time of church service—to good works for the poor.

Of a different nature was the monitorial or Lancastrian school first developed by Andrew Bell and Joseph Lancaster. Bell organized a prototype school in Madras, India. Lancaster's monitorial school in London was the first to gain wide attention. Later there were hot debates as to the originator of the monitorial system. In America Joseph Lancaster, Quaker schoolmaster, was far more influential than Andrew Bell, Church of England clergyman. Bell and Lancaster would be fascinating subjects for psychohistorians.

Andrew Bell (1753-1832) was a tutor in Virginia from 1774 until 1781, a contemporary of Philip Fithian. In Virginia, Bell saved Ł 350. He would always know the value of money. Back in England, he was ordained by the Church of England and in 1787 was in Madras, India. He was appointed to serve in and was paid for nine concurrent posts there, and saved Ł 3,000 a year. In 1797, after he returned to England, he wrote and published *An Experiment in Education. . .*, describing the school he had superintended in Madras. In England he spoke and wrote in behalf of his system of schooling. He again had concurrent well-paying posts. Near the end of his life he was unable to speak, whether for physical or psychological causes. Most of his fortune of Ł 250,000 ($800,000) was left, paradoxically, to support his system of schools.

Joseph Lancaster (1778-1838), son of a sieve maker, was born and grew up in Southark, a worker's part of London across the Thames River from the old city. Lancaster became a Quaker and a reformer. In 1798, he opened a school in Southark for poor boys, where pupils, "monitors," taught younger pupils. His school was admired and supported by many, including King George III. He described his system, by then fully developed, in 1805, in *Improvements in Education. . . .* Lancaster's biographer said that as a teacher Lancaster had "zeal, self-confidence, ingenuity. . . , intuitive insight into the nature of children, an ardent love for them, and rare power of managing them." Lancaster was a compelling speaker. One of his extracurricular passions was spending, as Bell's was saving. Lancaster spent his money, his schools' money, his benefactors' money. His coach drawn by four horses was a substantial extravagance. Eventually he was imprisoned for his debts. Lancaster also seems to have been a practicing sadist. This might have been suspected from the bizarre school punishments he devised: yokes, shackles, sewing boys into blankets, and pupils in baskets hauled to the ceiling. A recently published letter is persuasive.* Debts, and sadistic tendencies, drove him to America, where his "system" was already known and he was honored. He lived and organized schools in Philadelphia. When his reputation overtook him, he went to Baltimore to establish a "Lancastrian Institute" there. In 1825, he was invited to Caracas, Venezuela, by Simon Bolivar, but $20,000 for the establishment of schools somehow disappeared before the schools materialized, and Lancaster returned to the United States. In New York City, he was struck and killed by a runaway team and coach.

The central feature of the monitorial school was having pupils, serving as "monitors," teach less advanced pupils. Of course, this had been done previously (and would be done later), but not as systematically. So that monitors might instruct, it was necessary to divide lessons, and knowledge, into small bits. For example, the first step taken was to teach the beginning pupil—most often a boy— the letters of the alphabet. This was reduced to teaching first the "perpendicular" letters, **I, H, T, L. E. F, i, l.** The "triangular" letters, **A, V, W**, and so on, followed,

*H. R. deS. Honey, *Tom Brown's Universe: The Development of the English Public School in the Nineteenth Century* (New York: Quadrangle/New York Times, 1977, pp. 202-203.

and then the "circular" ones.* Pupils learned to read from wall charts or book pages, a page at a time. The pupils competed for prizes: badges, medals, candy. In that way, a monitorial school was like a mammoth never-ending spelling bee. A monitor heard the recitals. A monitor tested and promoted the pupils. A monitor took attendance.

In New York City the Free School Society, later called the Public School Society, adopted monitorial instruction. The Public School Society was a charitable, nonprofit organization, receiving state and city appropriations to provide schooling. Between 1805 and 1853, the Society would provide schooling for a half million New York City boys and girls. As Michael Katz has pointed out, the Free School Society was an example of a "corporate volunteeristic" organization, one alternative to public school organization as we know it. Corporate volunteerism in New York City provided cheap schooling, without administrative costs. Of course, with this kind of organization middle class benefactors controlled the schooling of the children of the poor. It was called "benevolent despotism" by an earlier historian.

The Public School Society adopted the monitorial system because, as John Griscom wrote, of *"1st Cheapness, 2nd, Large Number...."* Griscom, a hawk-nosed, slope-shouldered Quaker, established a successful monitorial "high school" in New York City, a combined primary, elementary, and secondary school. Monitorial schools appeared in Detroit, Springfield, Massachusetts, Saint Louis, Buffalo, and other cities. The African School of New York City also adopted the monitorial system. One third of New York City's 1,800 Black children were enrolled there.

It is worth considering assumptions, explicit and implicit, that supported the monitorial schools. As the Sunday schools were, the monitorial schools were

FIGURE 3-3   A Monitorial School in operation; from a manual published by the British and Foreign School Society. Reprinted in Paul Monroe (editor), *A Cyclopedia of Education*, Volume 4 (New York: Macmillan, 1913), pp. 296-297.

*Lancaster's schools did teach reading and writing concurrently, an exception to then usual procedures.

primarily for the children of the poor. In New York City in 1823, the cost of a year's instruction of a pupil in a monitorial school was only $1.80. As in the Sunday schools, the teaching of Christian beliefs and morals was important. Lancaster insisted that there be religious instruction and insisted that it be nondenominational. (The latter was an important disagreement with Andrew Bell, who insisted that the doctrine of the Church of England be taught.) As most monitorial schools did, the New York African school started the day with readings from the Bible.

If instruction was to be given by young and inexperienced monitors, it was necessary that what was to be learned be split into small segments. From one point of view this was (and is) logical enough. As Griscom saw it, even scientific knowledge was of unrelated facts—"pyroligneous acid" did not prevent the spread of yellow fever, iodine was helpful in the treating of goiter. From an opposing view, saying that knowledge and learning are nearly endlessly divisible is like maintaining that a cathedral is a high pile of rocks, or that a sonata is played by depressing the keys of a piano 3,000 times.

More conspicuous was the analogy of the school as machine. If, as the deists argued, God could be "the great Clock Maker," it was commendable for a school to be a "perfect machine" and for teaching to be mechanical and endlessly repetitive, as the motion of a clock pendulum was. Monitorial schooling was "a new machine of immense power, parallel and rival to...the greatest of modern acquisitions to mechanical operation." To another writer, "every boy seems to be the cog of a wheel—the whole school a perfect machine."

Beyond the analogy of the school as machine was the analogy of the school as factory. One of the Bell's supporters wrote that "the principle of schools and manufactories is the same. The grand principle ... is the division of labour applied to intellectual processes." These lines of thought were predictable enough. In one way they were efforts to develop and apply a science of education, to make schooling orderly and its outcomes logical, rational, and predictable. Before more than a few dozen Americans worked in factories, many Americans had heard of factories and anticipated them with pleasure. Teachers were sometimes referred to as *operatives*. Governor DeWitt Clinton of New York saw the monitorial school as a labor-saving machine. The machine analogy and the factory analogy would be important. As Karl Kaestle wrote a few years ago, Lancaster caught the spirit of a new technological age and applied it to the problem of mass education. Our schools have not escaped the preoccupation with classification and output that began with the monitorial movement, for we still live in an industrialized age.

By 1830, enthusiasm for monitorial schools had ebbed, although they would persist or reappear when there was not money for other forms of instruction.

DISTRICT SCHOOLS: SCHOOLBOOKS

While the new kinds of schools appeared, older kinds survived. In Massachusetts and Connecticut, state laws, though somewhat less stringent than the colonial ones, perpetuated the town and district schools. District schools were established in New

York State and in the western areas in which New Englanders settled. However, other patterns of school funding and control persisted. Even where there were district or town schools many children were sent to private ones. As late as 1825, the New York Public School Society found nearly 400 private schools in New York City. In Pennsylvania schooling continued to be primarily the responsibility of churches anxious to perpetuate and spread their theologies and faiths. Farther south, schooling was a private responsibility, and the schools were generally private.

The proprietary, or entrepreneurial, school had the simplest form of payment for and control of schooling. Alonzo Potter quotes the recollections of an early nineteenth century Kentuckian:

> The applicant for a school would draw an article of agreement, stating what branches (subjects) he was able to teach, and for what rates of compensation. The paper was passed around from house to house for signatures, and subscriptions partly payable in money and partly payable in "produce." The tuition of the children of the poor was paid customarily by the public-spirited individuals of comfortable fortune. . . .

As before the Revolution, schools were supported by every conceivable means. There were gifts and endowments, "rate-bills" or tuition tax, charges for firewood, and state "permanent funds" paying interest to the schools. In New York State there was an attempt to support public schools by lotteries.

Although the idea of establishing a federally supported university failed to be adopted in the Constitutional Convention, support for the establishment of schools at the elementary level and secondary level was provided by the Federal government through the Ordinances of 1785 and 1787. The Land Ordinance of 1785 outlined the procedures under which western frontier lands were to be surveyed. The new land was to be divided by surveyors into six-mile-square townships. Each township was divided into one-mile-square (640-acre) sections, and section 16, near the center of each township, was to be reserved for the public schools. If school lands were sold, receipts were to be invested or spent for the public schools. (New England colonials had made roughly the same provisions.) The Ordinance of 1787 confirmed this policy. "Religion, morality, and knowledge, being necessary for good government and the happiness of mankind, schools and means of education shall forever be encouraged".

The land grants to states and territories were the first federal aid to education. A very few of the Land Ordinance school lands were kept by school systems, but usually they were sold. Unfortunately, money received for them was not always used for the intended purpose. In Illinois, for example, the capital and interest from the sale of the school lands was allowed to accumulate in a school fund. During the early 1830s, the bulk of these funds, more than $100,000, was channeled by various means into programs for the building of canals and railroads. Similar actions took place in other states.

The published recollections of pupils in the first republican years are usually negative. Sixty years later Nathan Hedges remembered without pleasure attending school near Morristown, New Jersey:

The first [school there] I attended was taught by a cruel old man, by the name of Blair, usually known as "Clubber Blair." The [school] house was new, about sixteen feet square; had a writing table on one side, fast to the wall, for the larger pupils; all others were seated on benches made of slabs. The only books used in spelling and reading were Dilworth's Spelling book and the Testament. I have no recollection of an arithmetic [book] in the school. Geography and grammar were not even thought of. To spell, to write, to read in the Testament, and to work the four elementary rules of arithmetic, comprised the whole scope, aim, and object of the school. . . . I well remember that when I could not multiply by even one figure, he would give me a sum in multiplication, with four figures for a multiplier, and from day to day would pound my bare feet with his hickory club for not doing the sum correctly. He furnished no help, no instruction, no kind encouragement to a beginner, but relied on the severity of his punishment.

Hedges did concede that other district school teachers were "more qualified and more humane."

We should keep in mind that many of the recollections of those early republican schools were printed a half century later to show how much the schools had improved. It is possible, also, to find a scattering of recollections of men and women who had enjoyed attending district schools. However that may be, financial support was certainly meager. School terms were usually short. The status of teachers was low. Many district schools were open for only a few weeks during the winter. In others there was a summer term for the smaller children who were not needed on farms between planting and harvest time. Only a few schools in the cities and in the most prosperous towns still stayed open through the year. Colonial times' scattering of well-paid masters nearly disappeared, except perhaps for men teaching in the academies. Elsewhere, *master* was giving way to *teacher*, more humble, more pious, with greater hoped-for dedication, and lower wages.

Pupils in the district schools and in those similar to them provided their own schoolbooks. They used books that their families had or that their families preferred. Each pupil was heard individually, coming forward to "toe the line" painted on the school house floor and to recite. Each pupil proceeded at his or her own pace. There were no classes. The district schools were not "graded." A capable pupil could proceed without waiting, and at least in principle, a less capable pupil was spared embarrassment. On the other hand, a busy teacher with a big "school"— many pupils—might be able to devote only a few minutes daily to each child.

In general, to learn was to memorize, still. In the *American Spelling Book* there were "Familiar Lessons." This is a part of one of them:

Henry, tell me the number of days in a year. Three hundred and sixty-five.— How many weeks in a year? Fifty two.—How many days in a week? Seven— What are they called?. . .

FIGURE 3-4 A District School in Connecticut illustrated in *The Malte-Brun School Geography.* Reprinted in Clifton Johnson, *Old-Time Schools and SchoolBooks* (New York: Macmillan, 1904), p. 116.

For somewhat older pupils, Nathaniel Dwight's *System of the Geography of the World* (first edition, 1795) was in question-and-answer form from beginning to end. It could be mastered only by memorizing.

The most plentiful evidence of the content of instruction in this period is in surviving school books. School textbooks have always been important determinants of what has been taught. They were especially important when teachers were ill-prepared and emphasis was on memorization, rote learning. Hundreds of school texts were published, some in dozens of editions. They were read and studied by rich and poor, and often by the old as well as the young. Noah Webster's spelling book, first titled *A Grammatical Institute of the English Language, Part I*, was first published in 1783. In 1816, Webster claimed, probably without great exaggeration, that more than 3 million copies of his spelling book had been printed.

It is true that there are limits to discovering what was taught from what old texts said. Some subjects, most obviously writing, or penmanship, were usually taught without a printed text. Some school books were used in academies, rather than in district schools. Some books, for example *Aesop's Fables*, were used as school books although they were not so intended. At least some teachers taught mathematics from notes rather than books. Some school books were used in a variety of schools; common or district schools, academies, and private schools. But even taking into account these limits, schoolbooks determined much of the curriculum. School textbooks presented a consistent set of values and beliefs. They reached large, geographically dispersed, and culturally diverse audiences. Therefore, the texts that appeared after the Revolution were one of the beginnings of mass political and cultural education in American culture.

As before, schooling started with the teaching of reading. New editions of the *New England Primer* continued to appear, but there were changes. An engraving of King George III was retitled George Washington. The alphabet rhymes were changed. For instance, the earlier "Queen Esther comes in royal State, / To save the Jews from dismal fate" was replaced by "Queens and kings / Are gaudy things." There were many new primers, including *The Boston Primer, New York Primer, American Primer, Columbian Primer, The Evangelical Primer* (almost entirely religious in content), and *The Franklin Primer*. Lessons, as in the Colonial period, began with reading: first letters, then syllables, then words.

Next, the schools taught writing and spelling. "Correct" spelling would be far more important in the 1800s. Thomas Dilworth's *A New Guide to the English Tongue*, a British spelling, grammar, and reading book popular since the 1750s, was replaced by Noah Webster's speller, with reading lessons but without grammar. American speech, as Noah Webster maintained, was no longer identical to British speech, and American spelling should therefore be different. Originally titled *A Grammatical Institute of the English Language, Part I*, Webster's speller was later *The American Spelling Book*, and after 1829, the *Elementary Spelling Book*. Often called the "Blue-Back Speller," tens of millions of copies were sold in the 1800s and into the 1900s. An 1817 edition, after preliminaries, presented the alphabet from *a* to *z* and *&*. It proceeded wih one-syllable words, plurals, two-syllable words, and so on. It also included selections for reading. A typical selection was the fable of "The Boy that Stole Apples," taken word for word from Robert Dodsley's *Select Fables of Esop and Other Fabulists* (1761), first included by Webster in the 1787 edition of his spelling book.

Of the Boy that Stole Apples

An old Man found a rude Boy upon one of his trees stealing Apples, and desired him to come down; but the young Sauce-box told him plainly he would not. Won't you? said the old Man, then I will fetch you down, so he pulled up some tufts of Grass, and threw at him; but this only made the Youngster laugh, to think that the Old Man should pretend to beat him down from the tree with grass only.

Well, well, said the old Man, if neither words nor grass will do, I must try what virtue there is in stones; which soon made the young Chap hasten down from the tree and beg the old Man's pardon.

MORAL: If good words and gentle means will not reclaim the wicked, they must be dealt with in a more severe manner.*

Interestingly, the fable "Of the Boy that Stole Apples" was included in numerous school books published in the nineteenth century. It may have been the source of Theodore Roosevelt's famous statement concerning American foreign policy of "speaking softly and carrying a big stick."

The American Spelling Book concluded with a list of place names, ". . . The History of the THRIFTY AND UNTHRIFTY," and "A Moral Catechism" in question-and-answer form. Webster's spellers were not unusual in this respect. The *United States' Spelling Book*, widely used in the West, included the story of the New Testament and numerous maxims: "A bad life will make a bad end." Spelling books were intended to teach more than spelling. They were to teach reading and dashes of geography and grammar. More generally, they emphasized piety, morality, and patriotism.

---

*American Spelling Book was unremittingly masculine. *Boy* and *man* appear fifteen times as often as *girl*. *Woman* is not mentioned.

Many arithmetic books were in use; according to one source, at least sixty-five of them. The most popular arithmetic books seem to have been Englishman Thomas Dilworth's *The Schoolmaster's Assistant* (1773), Nicholas Pike's *New and Complete System of Arithmetic* (1788), and Nathan Daboll's *School Master's Assistant* (1800). The books began with the rudiments of arithmetic and continued through the "rule of three" (direct and inverse proportion) and square roots. To learn arithmetic was to learn "rules" for every occasion. The assumption was that pupils could read, read well. Daboll wrote that addition is "putting together of several smaller numbers of the same denomination into one larger." Pupil sometimes compiled simplified versions, presumably dictated by teachers. Arithmetic books dealt with many units of measurement: currency in cents and shillings; weight in grams and pennyweights, drams and ounces; cloth in nails and ells; distances in fathoms and hands; land in poles and roods; liquid in anchors and runlets, firkins, and hogsheads; and in dry measure, pottles and pecks. Even in arithmetic, patriotism could be reflected: "Washington was born in the year of our Lord 1732: He was 67 years old when he died: in what year of our Lord did he die?"

A greater variety of schoolbooks was needed because a greater variety of subjects was taught in common schools and in the academies. "The young masters and ladies throughout the United States" to whom Jedidiah Morse dedicated his geography books were to learn in greater detail about the United States. America's orators-to-be needed material for the practice of elocution. If history was to be taught, a history of the United States was called for, although this was a while in being developed.

Beyond the primer, reading lessons in spellers, and the Bible, reading in school was often intended to serve as preparation for elocution or public speaking. Americans spoke rather than wrote, listened rather than read. "Great Orations"— speeches in legislative halls, arguments before the bar, platform addresses, and sermons—were, as Daniel J. Boorstin has observed, the American media. Among the most successful of the early compilers of readers was Caleb Bingham, himself a professional elocutionist (and onetime usher to John Tileston, Boston writing master). About 600,000 copies of his *American Preceptor* were sold. A 1799 edition of *American Preceptor* has 228 pages and one hundred selections from speeches, the Bible, sermons, poetry, and short stories. It begins with "General Directions for Reading and Speaking" by Hugh Blair, Edinburgh professor of rhetoric. Perhaps a dozen selections were by Americans. Selections in *American Preceptor* and other reading and elocution books often dealt with conventional virtues. The anonymous editor of the *Columbian Reader* (3rd edition, 1815) wrote that "*In making selections for the following pages, an uniform preference has been given to such pieces as were calculated to instil into the minds of youth the principles of virtue and morality. . . .*" There were admonitions about the virtue or vice of disrespect, charity, forgiveness, industriousness, superstition, benevolence, generosity, argumentativeness, cheerfulness, modesty, integrity, candor, ingratitude, and liberality.

Patriotism was also an occasional topic. Bingham included an elegy to Columbia, which began

Columbia, Columbia, to glory arise;
The queen of the world and the child of the skies;
Thy genius commands thee; with rapture behold,
While ages on ages they splendors unfold.

Ten years later, a selection in Asa Lyman's *American Reader* described the death of George Washington.

Thus on the fourteenth of December, 1799, in the sixty-eighth year of his age, died the father of his country, "the man, first in war, first in peace, and first in the hearts of his fellow citizens." This event spread gloom over the country, and the tears of America proclaimed the services and virtues of the hero and sage, and exhibited a people not insensible to his worth.

The *American Preceptor* and the others were eventually overtaken in sales by a three-book series edited by Lindley Murray, a Loyalist New Yorker living in England.

As an example of often-displayed nationalism, Jedidiah Morse wrote about more recent immigrants that

The time, however, is anticipated, when all improper distinctions shall be abolished; and when all the languages, manners, customs, political and religious sentiments of the mixed mass of people which inhabit the United States, shall come to be assimilated, as that all nominal distinctions shall be lost in the general and honourable name of Americans.

Like most of the textbook writers, Morse was a New Englander, and reflected his background. "New England has a very healthy climate. It is estimated that about one in seven of the inhabitants live to the age of 70 years; about one in thirteen or fourteen to 80 years and upwards." Morse seemed to feel that slavery was an evil. Of the Virginia planters he said:

Labor is carried on almost wholly by slaves; who, in many of the countries, are much more numerous than the whites. Great numbers of the white inhabitants are thus exposed to habits of idleness, and to the manifold evils and vices which always accompany it.

Proslavery southerners, of course, objected to such passages, as well as to northern authors of schoolbooks about the South and its culture in general. In 1795, Virginia jurist St. George Tucker published a pamphlet objecting to Morse's description of the southern states. According to Tucker, not only were Morse's physical descriptions of the South inaccurate, but also his interpretations of southern life misrepresented and distorted the culture as it actually was.

Even so, Morse was not immune to the charms of parts of the South. Of Charleston, South Carolina he said:

> And in no part of America are the social blessings enjoyed more rationally and liberally, than in Charleston. Unaffected hospitality, affability, ease in manners and address, and a disposition to make their guests welcome, easy and pleased with themselves, are characteristics of the respectable people in Charleston.

There are many other geography books, nearly fifty others published before 1840. Among the more popular works were Nathaniel Dwight's *System of Geography of the World* (1795), more than 200 pages of unbroken questions and answers, a catechism of geography to read, to memorize, and to recite. J. A. Cummings's *Introduction to Ancient and Modern Geography* (1813) also included a geological section and an introduction to spherical geometry. Cummings, following the example of Oliver Goldsmith, was careful to make comparisons and show connections between countries, for instance in commerce Cummings published a short, eighty-three-page version, *First Lessons in Geography and Astronomy,* in 1818.

There were fewer schoolbooks for other subjects that were usually taught in academies rather than in common schools. *Cheever's Accidence, a Short Introduction to the Latin Tongue,* was still in use. *American Latin Grammar,* compiled by Edward Rigg, had been published by 1780, and was in its eighth edition in 1793. Science books were unusual, but *Conversations on Chemistry,* by Jane Marcet, a British author, appeared in the United States in several editions starting in 1809. A simplified and shortened version of Goldsmith's *Natural History,* edited by Mrs. M. Pilkington, was printed in Philadelphia in 1810.

Schoolbooks reflected the biases, and even the personalities, of their authors. They also reflected, more generally, the biases of the new nation's culture. They both shaped and were shaped by curriculum. For good or for bad, a national elementary curriculum was appearing. The curricula of the academies, to which we now turn, were much more varied.

ACADEMIES AND COLLEGES

The most rapidly multiplying form of school in the United States, 1781-1825, was the academy, the origins of which have been described in Chapter 2. Their speedy multiplication began after, or even during, the Revolution. Latin grammar schools were converted into academies or replaced by them. (One of the few Latin grammar schools that did survive was the Boston Latin School, the first to have been founded in the colonies.) The academies also supplanted in large part the earlier entrepreneurial or private venture schools. Academies were established in the North, the South, and the West. There were probably more than a hundred academies by 1800, and more than a thousand by 1830.

FIGURE 3-5   Illustration of a new building at Phillips Academy,
Andover, Massachusetts. From *Harper's New Monthly Magazine,*
Vol. 55, September 1877, p. 564.

The academy, ideally, was incorporated and was charted by the state. It was a legal entity under the control of its board of trustees. In general, this was the same as the legal procedure for establishment of a college. A charter testified legitimacy, and incorporation had the advantage of giving an academy a continued existence, or at least the possibility of continued existence, after the departure of a popular "preceptor," "principal," or "president." However, most academies operated without the formality of a charter. Ideally, an academy had an endowment that would produce revenue to supplement tuition, but most academies did not. Academies had a variety of names: *seminaries* for boys or girls, *institutes, collegiate institutes,* or even *colleges.* The names of individual academies ranged from resonant to rustic—*Liberty Hall* in Virginia; *Eel River Seminary* in Indiana. A few of the early academies were Latin grammar schools in all but name, and continued the traditional classical curriculum. Phillips Andover, which had opened in 1778, later offered other courses, perhaps "for the great end and real business of life," as its charter said. However, it continued the classical subjects and served as a preparatory school. More than eighty years later one of its first pupils, Josiah Quincy, wrote:

The course of studies and text-books I do not believe I can from memory exactly recapitulate; I cannot, however, be far out of the way in stating that "Cheever's Accidence" was our first book; the second, "Corderius;" the third, "Neops;" then, if I mistake not, came "Virgil.". . . .Our studies in Greek were slight and superficial . . . a thorough ability to construe the four Gospels were all required of us to enter the college. . . .

Of "methods and discipline," . . . I can only say that the former was strict and exact, and the latter severe. . . .

Other academies, most of them, were intended to be terminal institutions, serving as alternatives to college rather than as preparation for them.

The academies' pupils were young and old. At Phillips Andover, Josiah Quincy, aged six, was seated next to James Anderson, aged thirty. Many other academies had preparatory departments teaching the elementary subjects. A few academies had students studying college-level subjects. The academies were primarily schools for middle-class and well-off pupils. Samuel Phillips, Jr. was benefactor of Phillips Andover and also of Phillips Exeter Academy. At one point he wrote that ". . . certainly the happiness of such a child (a rich child) is of as great consequence as that of a poor child, his opportunity of doing good much greater." However, tutitions were within the means of middle-class parents, and some academies made loans to poor students and found them work to pay their expenses. The academy students included at least some of the poor as well as many of the middle class and some of the sons and daughters of the well-to-do.

The pre-Revolutionary precedents for secondary schooling for girls were slender indeed. Academies for girls, and academies that admitted girls as well as boys, were an important departure, following from the "republican spirit." Before 1790, there were at least four short-lived private schools for girls in New England. The course of study in Jedidiah Morse's school in New Haven appeared in a public announcement: ". . . Reading, Arithmetic, English Grammar, Geography, Composition. . . ." It might have been the course for a boys' academy except for the addition of ". . . the different branches of Needle Work," and because Latin was not offered. In 1787, John Poor established an academy in Philadelphia for ". . . instruction of young ladies in Reading, Writing, Arithmetic, English Grammar, Composition, Rhetoric, and Geography."

Miss Sarah Pierce's Litchfield Female Academy was successful and well documented. (Some students in their twenties were not "girls." A ten-year-old pupil was too young to be called a "lady.") Miss Pierce (1767-1852) was described as "a small woman, slender and fragile," "a woman of more than ordinary talent," with "fair complexion and blue eyes." It was said that in 1792, when she started to teach in Litchfield, Connecticut, she and two or three students met in the dining room of her home. After her school had grown, a schoolhouse was provided.

Her school house was a small building of only one room, probably not exceeding 30 ft. by 70, with small closets at each end, one large enough to hold a piano, the other used for bonnets and over garments. The plainest pine desks, long plank benches, a small table and an elevated teacher's chair, constituted the whole furniture.

The number of students increased to nearly 140, "females" from nearly every state and from Canada. It was said that one girl had ridden horseback 150 miles to attend. Since there were no dormitories, students boarded with approved families, as at most academies. A student neatly paraphrased the rules:

> Been neat in your chambers? Combed your hair? Cleaned your teeth? Left anything out of place? Been present at table? At family prayers? Been to bed at the proper time? Rose in season? Studied two hours without speaking? Disturbed others? Been angry? Been impolite? Told an untruth? Wasted time in school? Mis-spent the Sabbath? Read in the Scriptures?. . .

In 1833, room and board was $1.75 or $2.00 a week, perhaps higher than at most places. Tuititon that year was $6.75 a quarter, half again what it had been thirty years earlier. In 1821, students studied arithmetic, grammar, geography, history, natural science, and chemistry. Miss Pierce's brother-in-law taught writing. For extra tuition girls could study music, painting, or French. In 1835, girls between eight and fourteen who were studying French could room and board with a Mrs. Gimbrede, since "she loves young girls . . . the only way to learn to speak French well [is] to live in a French family."

The renowned law school conducted by Judge Tapping Reeve was also in Litchfield. The law students attended balls given by the academy girls, and in turn organized balls for them, sometimes in the dance hall at the tavern. Only academy students who were sixteen or older were permitted to attend the law students' balls. Nevertheless, Juliana McLachlan, "beautiful and a belle," was at fifteen the bride of a law student. There were also academy plays in which law students as well as academy students took parts. Attendance at Sunday church was required, and sermons heard there were matters of interest.

Although the course of study at Miss Pierce's school was like that at other academies, social life and recreation were, of course, quite different. The purpose of the Litchfield Female Academy was also different in a quite fundamental way. As Miss Pierce's nephew, and successor as principal, said in his farewell address:

> Our object has been, not to make learned ladies, or skillful metaphysical reasoners, or deep read scholars in physical science: there is a more useful, tho' less exalted and less brilliant station that woman must occupy, there are duties of incalculable importance that she must perform: that station is home; these duties, are the alleviation of the trials of her parents; the soothing of the labours & fatigues of her partner; & the education for time and eternity of the next generation of immortal beings. . .

The speaker was expressing the usual view of women's education. Schooling for women was to make them better daughters, wives, and mothers. It was not intended to make them the social or intellectual equals of men. However, innovationists and reformers had established that women should be educated in academies. As early as 1808, and as far off as Ste. Genivive, Missouri, an academy at least planned a "female department." Long before Miss Pierce retired in 1833, there were many academies for women, and still more admitted women as well as men. We will return to them and to the spread of academies generally.

Instruction at some colleges had been interrupted by the Revolution, of course. Yale's faculty and students had been driven from New Haven by fear of starvation. Rutgers's only building was burned by British raiders. William and Mary's building, near Yorktown, became quarters for French soldiers, who set fire to it accidentally. When college instruction was resumed, it followed the older pattern in most ways. Fascination with the French and their revolution did lead to the introduction of French in a few of the colleges.

The founding of new colleges, the "college enthusiasm," resumed after the Revolution, and by 1800, there were perhaps twenty-five colleges in the United States. Most of them were in the old Northeast, but at least half a dozen were in the South: North Carolina, Georgia, Tennessee, and Vermont established colleges and funded them in a modest sort of way. A few of the new colleges were in the West, near the frontier. Transylvania (in English, "beyond the forest") in Lexington, Kentucky, lost six of its original trustees in Indian wars.

Historians disagree as to the causes for the new colleges' establishment; piety or pride, parochialism or profit. Piety may have led to colleges; several of their presidents said their first purpose was to strengthen and extend faith, piety, and prayer. Contrarily, it has been argued that college supporters (and academy supporters, starting with Samuel Phillips, Jr.) acted to add to their status in their communities. It has been argued that colleges were established because college students would bring money with them. The issue is open, and the histories of some of the early colleges would support each of these theses. It seems to us that piety was more frequent than pride or avarice, although they were not mutually exclusive.

It was often said that the first purpose of the colleges was to preserve and strengthen morality and Christian faith, and to aid in strengthening character. As a Yale alumnus said:

> ... although I did not, perhaps, profit as much as I ought, by the strict lessons of precision and morality which I received in my Connecticut Alma Mater, yet it is impossible that a youth brought up ... under the eye of the venerable Timothy Dwight, should not have been in some degree moulded and impressed by the circumstances in which his ductile youth was passed.

College presidents were nearly always ministers, and nearly all the early colleges (including those that were state supported and called "universities") were affiliated with a church denomination. School days began and sometimes ended with prayers in the college chapel, at which attendance was required.

Boys attended colleges, too, because of the lingering tradition that a gentleman should have a "liberal" education or, less and less often, because they were to become ministers, lawyers, or physicians. A college education was not needed to teach in a district school. It was not usually preparation even for teaching in an academy. Yale, the largest of the colleges, had no more than 250 students. No more than one boy in 200 attended college, including the occasional American who studied in Europe.

Unlike the academies, the colleges usually had dormitories and "commons" (for everyone) dining halls, survivals from colonial and earlier English traditions. All the college students were male, and, except for one in hundreds, white, and no older than high school students are now. At the end of the 1700s, they considered themselves to be atheists or deists, as was then the fashion. Dartmouth and some of the new small colleges admitted poor boys and men, and so aided mobility from the farm to the pulpit. On the other hand, the colleges were the scenes of student riots, disruptions, and town and grown fights, and there is some counter-evidence suggesting that even the small old colleges did not effect longtime changes in students' values.

In 1800, there were no electives; all courses were required for graduation. The college course was primarily the classical one, to which a mathematics course, one year, once a week for an hour or so, had been added. Only a few colleges offered a course in "natural history" (roughly, general science) then, although in the next twenty years natural history courses would be added by most of the colleges, and some of them would also offer chemistry.

That colleges in the United States were so long in including more than a few snippets of science in their curricula seems strange. One of the thrusts of the Enlightenment was scientific. Before 1800, universities in Germany had professors in natural sciences, or in the segments of it that would become scientific disciplines. In 1816, nineteen of thirty-three professors at the University of Edinburgh in Scotland taught medicine or one of the sciences. Americans knew of and admired the University of Edinburgh, and more of them seem to have attended it then than any other European university.

There are several plausible reasons for the colleges' delay. The pattern of organization of the colleges, with each entering class typically taught by the same tutor for three or four years, did not lend itself to specialization. Nearly all the colleges were poor, sometimes on the brink of bankruptcy, and science professors and their expensive demonstration equipment and laboratories were beyond the colleges' means. The colleges saw themselves as just that, and not as universities. Few of them had professional schools, and none offered other graduate study. They did not support scholarship or research. Finally, industry and technology did not depend much then upon the "pure" mathematical or experimental sciences, and would not for most of another hundred years. Pure science had not much more immediate application than Latin did. Although one might have expected it to be, the objection to science was not religious. The most devout were sure that science would serve to demonstrate the handiwork and glory of God.

CONCLUSION

For many historians of education the period between the Revolution and the "Common School Revival" about forty years later has been a sort of prelude to school history, neither important nor interesting, and for some, negligible. To overlook that time is, of course, to overlook the republican educational theorist Thomas Jefferson and his contemporaries interested in education. The school in New Harmony, Indiana, was the first systematic, wholehearted application in the United States of the school theory and practice of the leading educationist of his day, Johann Pestalozzi. In a way as important, if less elegant and elevated, the monitorial schools of Joseph Lancaster and Andrew Bell strengthened the concept of the pupil as recipient of charity, and added to education the analogy of school as machine or as factory. Those, too, would have many consequences that have not ended. The organization of "common" schools into state, county, and city systems had not begun, but a tradition of elementary school curriculum was set, which in some ways still survives. The academies are of interest as an educational expression of their times, because they are the only American mode of schooling that has approached extinction, as one of the ancestors of the public high school and because, for reasons good or bad, there are at least some signs of their revival. The colleges of that time are not (fortunately) the colleges of our time, but corporately and spiritually they are ancestors of today's colleges and universities.

Theorists, romantic Pestalozzians' schools, machinelike monitorial schools, hetrodox academies, and devout and pious colleges all set the stage, making up their times and shaping our own.

CHAPTER FOUR
THE RISE OF THE
COMMON SCHOOLS

Between the 1820s and the end of the Civil War, schooling had become an increasingly important issue in American culture. By the 1830s, in industrialized states of the Northeast such as Massachusetts, New York, and Pennsylvania, wide-ranging programs had been enacted to introduce free universal public schooling at the elementary level. Known as the *Common School Movement*, this effort to provide mass popular education for all white citizens was essentially a series of state movements that rapidly spread throughout the nation. In spirit, the Common School Movement recalled Thomas Jefferson's fundamental belief that a democratic government depended upon an educated citizenry.

The causes for the emergence of the Common School Movement are extremely complex. As Lawrence Cremin and others have pointed out, the decades preceeding the 1830s saw a number of critical changes take place in American culture, which were to have a major impact on education. An increasing democratization of politics developed during the Jacksonian period. Social equality emerged as an increasingly important issue. The rise of the "Common Man" accompanied the development of a coherent nationalism.

Historians have tended to look upon the Common School Movement in extremely positive terms. The traditional wisdom has been that in their attempt to provide free universal elementary education, the common schools were important vehicles of social reform that provided opportunities for newly arrived immigrants and the poor to improve the conditions of their lives and those of their children. Lead by idealistic and humanitarian intellectuals, an enlightened working class was able to overcome the narrow interests of not only the wealthy elite population, but also the conservative religious groups within the culture.

This essentially idealistic interpretation of the origins of the Common School Movement has been seriously questioned since the late 1960s by the writings of Revisionist historians such as Clarence Karier, Joel Spring, Walter Feinberg, Michael Katz, Samuel Bowles, Herbert Gintis, and others. According to Katz, who has particularly focused on the Common School Movement in his work:

> . . . the extension and reform of education in the mid-nineteenth century were not a potpourri of democracy, rationalism and humanitarianism. They were the attempt of a coalition of the social leaders, status-anxious parents, and status hungry educators to impose educational innovations, each for their own reasons, upon a reluctant community.

Katz's research, which tends to focus on organizational and structural analysis, represents a powerful reinterpretation of the traditional role of schooling in American culture.

In this and the chapters that follow, the reader will find much explained by the Revisionist interpretations of Katz and others. Other interpretations will be drawn upon as well. Education and schooling in America presents the historian with a number of paradoxes. Beginning during the Revolution, education was seen as being a means of reforming the culture through its children. As Donald Warren has explained in his study on the United States Office of Education:

> Education, as formulated during the country's beginning years, represented a national, as over against a sectional, concern and a chance for achieving nationhood. Talk about education braved unsettling realities; it endured, not because schools fulfilled the high expectations, but inexplicably because they did not. American education, as both process and institution, has never escaped the reformist role in which it was cast in the republic's first days.

As the Revisionists have pointed out, in examining the history of American schooling, it is clear that schools have tended more often than not to reinforce and support the status quo. The schools have consistently voiced rhetoric emphasizing equality or opportunity across racial, social, and economic lines. Schooling and education clearly has not delivered all that it has promised.

This chapter examines some individuals and forces that were responsible for the emergence of the common schools. Beginning with an examination of the roles of those who taught in late eighteenth and early nineteenth century American culture, we then examine changes in attitudes toward childrearing, which took place during this period. The chapter concludes by looking at some of the forces and individuals responsible for promoting the Common School Movement in America.

THE TEACHER

Important redefinitions of attitudes and beliefs are frequently reflected in the language of a society. An example of this can be found in the increasing adoption and use of the word *teacher* during the early nineteenth century. This redefinition can provide us with important insight into changes that had been taking place in both education and American culture during this period. The use of the word *teacher* by about 1820, instead of the older one, *master*, to denote one who taught, was more than change in fashion of speech. The change of words went with a change in the nature of an occupation. It had consequences for those who taught, for the organizing of schools, and for the education of children.

(By sociological definition, an *occupation* is a role or a set of roles. To fill an occupational role, specialized knowledge and skills, of varying kinds of degrees, are required. With occupational roles are status and prestige, also in varying degrees. There are norms and expectations of behavior that go beyond the job. Odd combinations of occupation and behavior seem—are—incongruous. Farmers do not generally play Mozart, and nuns do not smoke cigars.)

Those who taught before about 1820 were nearly always called *masters*, though of course there were *school dames, governesses, tutors,* and others. The term *teacher* was seldom used. *Masters* ideally knew the classics. The classics were the content of what was to be taught and, at the same time, they determined the method of teaching. While *masters* taught beginning pupils, "abcedarians," that was not their only or primary task. The *teacher*, by contrast, was at the beginning concerned more than anything else with teaching the elementary subjects. The teacher's skill was to be in what we would call classroom management and was not expected to go beyond that. Masters were to have a commitment to teaching and for the moral and spiritual welfare of their students. Teachers were to be "consecrated," to be wholly devoted to the interests of their pupils, to be sort of lesser servants of the Lord. Lucy Larcom, later a professional writer, described in a cloying (but possibly autobiographical) verse what was wanted:

> In a dreary school-house
> A girl, young and fair,
> Spent life, strength, and beauty.—
> "She scatters live seed:
> She works in wild thought-fields,
> The starved soul to feed."

In 1838, a Pennsylvania superintendent of schools implied the difference of the out-of-school behavior of the teacher and the master:

> The profession of teaching is much elevated. Instances of bad moral character and intemperate habits, are hardly to be met with though formerly School

FIGURE 4-1   A district school teacher illustrated in the frontispiece to *The Child's Guide*, 1833. Reprinted in Clifton Johnson, *Old Time SchoolBooks* (New York: Macmillan, 1904), p. 255.

Masters, who above all others should be perfectly exemplary as a class, were not remarkable in this respect.

It is hard for us to think of a teacher who in the 1880s earned a substantial wage or who earned even fairly high status or prestige. We know of masters in the 1700s who enjoyed incomes that were substantial for the time. To repeat, Ronald Robertson in Virginia averaged Ł 90 a year in earnings from his school, nearly twice the earnings of a skilled carpenter regularly employed. In 1775, three of Boston's public school masters were paid Ł 100 and the other two, Ł 120, and probably fees. One of them was also provided with a home.

As we see it, the change from *master* and what it implied, to *teacher* came from shifts in social values and from changes in the pupils who were the masters', and then the teachers', clientele. As to the change in social values, we must return to the "republican spirit" and one facet of Revolutionary thought. After the Revolution, in keeping with the republican spirit, it appeared that learning the classics or about the classics was not important. For some—we cannot say how many—the teaching of the classics was an affront, an insult to and the exploitation of the common man. As Massachusetts tavernkeeper William Manning wrote:

> Many are so rich that they can live without Labour. Also the merchant, phisition, lawyer & devine, the philosopher and school master, the Juditial and Executive Officers, & many others who could honestly git a living with-

out bodily labours. . . . [T]hese professions naturally unite in their skems to make their callings as honourable & lucrative as possible. . . .

Specifically about school masters Manning wrote:

> . . . [T]he few are always striving to oblige us to maintain grait men with grate salleryes & to maintain Grammer Schools in every town to teach our Children a b c all which is ondly to give imploy to gentlemens sons. . . . For there is no more need of a mans haveling all the languages to teach a Child to read and write & cifer than their is for a farmer to have the marinors art to hold plow.

Manning was an extremist, but admiration for classical learning, or any school learning very far beyond the rudiments, lost much of its value as a badge of social rank and position. By 1820, when the master had become nearly obsolete and had been largely replaced by the teacher, the educational qualifications for entering the traditional professions—medicine, divinity, and law—were very much reduced. Perhaps a parallel to the disappearance of the master was that of the peruke maker. Perukes, wigs for formal occasions, which for a hundred years had been badges of official and social position, also lost favor. Basil Hall, early nineteenth century traveler and commentator, was said to have seen the disappearance of perukes as evidence of the "universal ascendency of the democratic principle in the U. S." He was entirely right.

At the same time, as classical education was less valued, primary education for a larger proportion of children was, more than it had been formerly, felt to be of value. Jefferson saw general literacy as necessary for the democracy he envisioned. Noah Webster saw schooling as an aid to stronger nationalism. The appearance of Sunday schools and infant schools and the passing enthusiasm for monitorial schools were evidence of widespread conviction of the value of schooling. As more children attended school, more poor children attended. The lower the status of the clientele, the lower the prestige of the occupation that serves it.

Most masters were replaced by teachers. Others were replaced by those who taught in academies, who had a variety of titles. One source mentions *tutors, professors, professor-principals, principal tutors, tutor governesses, instructors,* and *preceptors.* Those who taught in academies seldom called themselves *teachers.* For fifty years, until the public high schools became common, a *teacher* taught beginning pupils beginning subjects. A primary or district school teacher required less substantive knowledge. In part, the status of a profession depends upon the knowledge it employs.

The appearance of the *teacher* and the disappearance of the *master* had several effects. If less formal learning was needed by the teachers, it became seen as more appropriate, as well as cheaper, to employ women as teachers. For a hundred years or more, most teachers have been women. With required formal learning reduced and entry into teaching easy, teachers' salaries would be low during the next hundred years. With pupils coming from poor families more often than from middle-class ones, the social status of pupils tended to reduce the status of teachers, who themselves came most often from families of limited means.

Of course the title *master* lingered. Authors used it for nostalgia. Ichabod Crane in Washington Irving's "Legend of Sleepy Hollow" was a master. It was used in out-of-the-way rural places, as Edward Eggleston used it in his novel *The Hoosier Schoolmaster*. *Masters* survived in conservative Boston schools, where reformers found them difficult or impossible to change. They appeared or reappeared in prestigious private New England preparatory schools, presumably to add an air of age or Englishness. But for most practical purposes the *master* left the stage, to be replaced most often by the *teacher*.

THE AMERICAN CHILD

The early decades of the nineteenth century saw not only the emergence of new roles for the master and teacher, but also a redefinition of patterns of family life and childhood. By the beginning of the 1820s, it is clear that family organization and childrearing practices in the United States were not only significantly different from those found in the early republic, but also from those found in Western Europe. At least among white middle and upper-class families, democratic ideals and principles were not only changing the aspirations parents had for their children, but were also influencing their attitudes toward childrearing and education.

European visitors to the United States during this period had great interest in the differences in childrearing practices between their own countries and America. The French penal reformer Alexis de Tocqueville (1805-1859), for example, in the second volume of his work *Democracy in America* devoted an entire chapter to the American family. According to de Tocqueville, the American family was being radically redefined as a result of the democratic experience. The autocratic rule of the father, which characterized most European families, had been abandoned:

> In America the family, in the Roman and aristocratic signification of the word, does not exist. All that remains of it are a few vestiges in the first years of childhood, when the father exercises, without opposition, that absolute domestic authority which the feebleness of his children renders necessary and which their interest, as well as his own incontestable superiority warrents [sic].

According to de Tocqueville, as the child approached adulthood, filial obedience became more and more relaxed, and the child was encouraged to become increasingly independent.

The independence of the American child was carefully observed and commented on by European visitors to the United States. Harriet Martineau (1802-1876), an English writer and reformer visiting during the mid-1830s saw American children as being remarkably free and independent when compared with their European counterparts. Often European visitors saw this tendency towards independence on the part of the American child in a negative light. During the 1850s, Adam Gurowski complained about "the prodigality, the assumption, self-assertion and conceit" of the American child. In a similar case, a British naval officer, Captain Frederick Marrayat, described overhearing the following account between an American child and his parents in 1837:

'Johnny, my dear, come here,' says his mamma.
'I won't,' cries Johnny.
'You must my love, you are all wet, and you'll catch cold.'
'I won't,' replied Johnny.
'Come, my sweet, and I've something for you.'
'I won't.'
'Oh! Mr. _____, do, pray make Johnny come in.'
'Come in, Johnny,' says the father.
'I won't.'
'I tell you, come in directly, son—do you hear?'
'I won't,' replies the urchin, taking to his heels.
'A sturdy replublican, sir,' says his father to me smiling at the boy's resolute disobedience.

It is important to note that many of these early visitors who were highly critical of the American child were also critical of their parents and American culture in general. In reading the comments of these authors, it is clear that the assertiveness and individuality of many Americans offended the sensibilities of European observers of American culture. Materialism, restlessness, and self-centeredness are themes repeatedly raised by Europeans in discussing Americans during this period.

It was during the 1820s and 1830s that there appeared for the first time a substantial body of literature written and published in America dealing with child-rearing and child care. In 1826, for example, Dr. William Dewees, professor of midwifery at the University of Pennsylvania, published *A Treatise on the Physical and Medical Treatment of Children*. Among the earliest and most widely read works in America on pediatrics, Dewee's work reflected an increasing concern over the medical needs of children as distinguished from those of adults.

In a more popular vein were works on childrearing such as Lydia Maria Child's *The Mother's Book* (1813) and Jacob Abbott's *The Child at Home* (1833), which came into widespread use providing practical suggestions and ideas concerning the care and raising of children. Numerous themes emerge in these works and suggest that the observations and analyses of many European visitors concerning the nature of American childrearing and family organization were too simplistic. According to Robert Sunled, at least three different approaches to childrearing were evident in the child care books written during the first half of the nineteenth century. The first of these approaches could be found during the pre-Revolutionary eras and corresponded to what Philip Greven has described as an "authoritarian" approach to childrearing. The second corresponded roughly to Greven's "authoritative" approach and also clearly reflected the influence of the Enlightenment thinkers John Locke and Jean Jacques Rousseau. The third and final approach taken toward childrearing in the early nineteenth century represented what was essentially a new point of view, emphasizing the child's natural development.

The first school of thought had its origins in the Calvinist tradition of the child being born in original sin. As Theodore Dwight explained in *The Father's Book* (1834): "No child has ever been known since the earliest period of the world, destitute of an evil disposition however sweet it appears." Parents had the duty of making sure that their children were preveated from following their naturally depraved tendencies. Obedience to the demands of adults alone could insure the salvation of the child. When a child refused to follow the demands of a parent, it was felt to be critically important not to let children get their way. Sunled, for example, quotes a mother writing in *The Mother's Magazine* who explains how her sixteen-month-old daughter refused to say "dear mama" at the request of her father. Failing to get the child to change her mind, the parents then left the child alone in a room, where she screamed wildly for ten minutes. Ordered again to say "dear mama," the child refused and was whipped for her disobedience. This process was continued until finally after four hours the child submitted.

Such an example may seem extreme, but the fact that it was reported in an obviously positive light in a widely circulated magazine of the period indicates that such methods for dealing with children were probably acceptable among a significant number of parents. Physical punishment was not always necessary. Constant persuasion and the eventual breaking down of the child's will seems to have also been common.

A second widely prevalent approach to childhood seemed to be derived from the works of the English philosopher John Locke and resembled those of the French social theorist Jean Jacques Rousseau. According to them, environment played a crucial role in shaping the child. Since children were highly vulnerable to the potential corruptions of adult society, an attempt was made to keep the child as free from corruption as possible. Although the perception of the child was different from the more traditional Calvinist approach, the emphasis upon strict parental guidance and control was much the same. Essentially in the Calvinist approach the child was seen as being corrupt, while the less rigid environmentalist approach saw the child as having the potential to be corrupted.

Corruption of the child was possible in many different ways. Many of the child care books of the period warned of ruinous consequences of masturbation. Disease, insanity, and even death were commonly cited as the consequences of such activities. Rather than discovering masturbation spontaneously, it was assumed by many of the authors of the period that "respectable" children were introduced to the evils of masturbation by servants, slaves, or depraved school children. Moral virtue was associated with cleanliness. Individuals such as Dr. Dewees set forth ideal goals of having children toilet trained by the age of one month. Lack of adequate early training encouraged the child's autoerotic tendencies. As Dewees warned:

> Children should not be permitted to indulge in bed long after daylight; as its warmth, the accumulation of urine and faeces, and the exercise of the imagination, but too often leads to the precocious development of the sexual instinct.

A third and final approach to the child emphasized the need to nurture and encourage the child's natural tendencies. Parents were seen as guides who encouraged the natural potential of their children. Lydia Maria Child in *The Mother's Book*, for example, maintained that:

> Children are not so much influenced by what we say and do in particular reference to them, as by the general effect of our characters and conversation. They are in a great degree creatures of imitation. If they see a mother fond of finery, they become fond of finery; if they see her selfish, it makes them selfish, if they see her extremely anxious for the attention of wealthy people, they learn to think wealth is the only good.

Clearly the foundations of many of our modern attitudes toward childrearing can be found in this third approach expressed by Child, which emphasizes the need for parents to nurture and guide the child.

Changes in attitudes toward childrearing were closely related to changes in schooling that took place during the early phases of the Common School Movement. The feminization of the teaching profession, and the primacy of moral over intellectual instruction, suggest models based upon principles of childrearing as much as upon traditional pedagogy.

ORIGINS OF THE COMMON SCHOOLS

As new attitudes toward children and childrearing emerged during the early decades of the nineteenth century, so too did new attitudes toward education. Free public elementary education for all citizens had been an ideal of intellectuals Thomas Jefferson, Benjamin Rush, and others since the time of the Revolution. Yet by the beginning of the nineteenth century, rather than being seen as the birthright of all citizens, free schooling was more often equated with charity or pauper schools such as those established by the Free School Society of New York, the Philadelphia Society for the Free Instruction of Indigent Boys, and the Benevolent Society of the City of Baltimore for the Education of the Female Poor.

As outlined in earlier chapters, programs supporting free public education date back to the early colonial period. Although laws such as those passed in Massachusetts in 1647—requiring towns to establish elementary schools for their children—could be found in a number of the colonies, their effectiveness was extremely limited. Property taxes levied to pay for the schools, as in our own era, were extremely unpopular. Many townships lacked sufficiently large populations to be able to support a school adequately. Even if a town did have enough people living in it to properly support a school, they were often so spread out that it was difficult to establish the school in a convenient central location. Schoolmasters moving from one village to another, teaching children for a few months at a time, provided a limited solution to the problem.

As populations increased into the eighteenth century, most localities in areas such as New England established schools of their own, as they had in Dedham. Commonly referred to as *district schools*, these village or neighborhood schools were ungraded and served the needs of all of the children within the community. Technically, the term *district* referred to the division of the town for purposes of schooling. They were restricted in size to distances that children could reasonably be expected to walk to school. Control of these schools was completely maintained by the local taxpayers.

As one might expect, the quality of education depended upon local taxpayers' commitment to the schools. When they worked well, the district schools not only provided children with good basic instruction, but they also tended to draw the community together in a common purpose or activity. Citizens of the district levied taxes, appointed instructors, determined the length of the school year, maintained the schoolhouse, and acted as final arbitrators in conflicts between students and teachers. More often than not, however, citizens' commitment to the school in their district was limited. Grossly inadequate funding characterized many of these schools, eventually leading to the use of rate-bills.

The rate-bill was a device that placed an additional tax on those families who had children attending school. In effect, the rate-bill was tuition charge intended to supplement local taxes. Unfortunately, the rate-bill imposed a burden on poorer families who were unable to pay this additional tax. In rural areas, those who were so poor that they could not pay the rate for their children were also often too proud to be excused from it and to send their children to school as "charity cases." In cities, particularly during the early nineteenth century, the number of poor was often so large in many districts that there was no way that the schools could be properly supported through the payment of rate-bills.

The development of philanthropic educational programs, such as that of the Free School Society of New York, represented an attempt to overcome some of the problems inherent in the funding system of the district schools. Serving only the poor, the basis of their support was limited. Widespread support for public schooling did not exist among the majority of the population. In general, given the choice of paying less in taxes or supporting the schools, most individuals seem to have chosen the easy way out.

The failure to support effectively the district schools by taxpayers reflects to a large extent what the main needs and concerns of people were during the period. In a primarily agricultural society, as in early nineteenth century America, where land was cheap and opportunities were numerous, the need for schooling was probably not perceived as a particularly important issue. Except for a limited number of professions, formal schooling did not in most instances contribute significantly to the average individual's success. On the frontier, where personal initiative, physical strength, and native shrewdness often counted for a great deal, schooling often counted for very little. In fact, formal education was frequently looked down upon as an aristocratic and unnecessary luxury.

In the South, public education received relatively little attention. Schooling continued well into the nineteenth century along much the same lines that it had followed during the Colonial era. Schooling was basically perceived as a luxury whose pursuit was a matter of individual discretion. When free public schooling was supported, it was typically as philanthropy. The free school law adopted in South Carolina in 1811, for example, was intended only for orphans and poor children. Similar laws passed in Virginia at about the same time also provided only for the education of the poor.

Exceptions can be found to the South's tendency to ignore education as an important issue. At the meeting at Rockfish Gap, Virginia, in the summer of 1818, Thomas Jefferson not only outlined the plans that eventually lead to the establishment of the University of Virginia, but also once again reiterated, as he had in 1779, the need for a state-supported system of primary education. Although figures like Calvin Wiley effectively lobbied in states such as North Carolina for the support of public education during the late 1830s and 1840s, the tendency in the South prior to the Civil War was to disregard free universal education as an important issue.

Although admirable in many respects, philanthropic and charitable programs of education in both the North and South were inadequate to meet the demands of the culture. Support for the development of the common schools began to come from many different groups. Often the reasons for these groups' interest in education were widely different. One of the earliest authors criticizing the charitable schools and urging the development of a broader-based system of public education was James G. Carter, whose *Essays upon Popular Education* were published in the mid-1820s. Carter called for a revival and improvement of public schools. He maintained that the poorer and ignorant members of the population did not voluntarily seek education. Yet unless properly educated, they posed a serious revolutionary threat to the integrity of the republic. The government, through the enforcement of education, had the obligation to eradicate ignorance for the government's own political good.

Beginning with figures such as Carter, there is an interesting and subtle shift in the attitude taken toward schooling, when compared with the educational theorists of the late eighteenth century such as Webster, Rush, and Jefferson. Throughout the works of these earlier writers, there is a consistent emphasis upon properly educating individuals so that they can assume the responsibilities of citizenship. With the growing waves of immigrants who entered the country in the 1830s and the 1840s, the schools were seen as having an increasingly important role in helping to bring about the process of assimilation and neutralizing the newcomers as a political threat. To be an American was to support and become part of Anglo institutions. As Calvin Stowe, a major figure in the Common School Movement, explained in 1836:

> It is altogether essential to our national strength and peace, if not even to our national existence, that the foreigners who settle on our soil, should cease to be Europeans and become Americans; and as our national language is English, and as our literature, our manners, and our institutions are of English origin, and the whole foundations of our society English, it is necessary that they become Anglo-American.

Biculturalism was seen as being un-American, and was felt to represent a potential threat to the political stability of the nation.

The primary impetus for the early support of the common schools has typically been seen as coming from a select group of liberal New England reformers. Yet interest in free public education was also an important issue for lower-middle- and working-class groups in the Northeast during the late 1820s and early 1830s. Interest in education on the part of these groups was socially and economically motivated. Factory-produced items were beginning to threaten the traditional markets of skilled craftspersons and small businesspersons. Education would provide the means by which working-class and lower-middle-class children could achieve economic and social equality.

The workingmen's parties clearly associated education with privilege. Charity schools were inherently discriminatory. As Stephen Simpson argued in *The Working Man's Manual...* (1831):

> ... the scanty pittance of education termed *charitable*, has never realized the *equal benefits of instruction*, to which the working people have been entitled as the producers of all the wealth of society. When it is solemnly inscribed upon our constitution, that education is an essential preliminary of government, its diffusive dispensation becomes a duty and a right of the first importance and magnitude: we are bound to consider it, not as an *accidental* but as an *integral* part of government. ...

The workingmen in their concern for education were reflecting views quite similar to those of the earlier republican educational theorists. Education was to act as an equalizer for the citizens of the republic. Ironically, in their criticism they often tended to repudiate many of the achievements of these same theorists. In Pennsylvania and Connecticut during the early 1830s, for example, the workingmen's groups mounted a major campaign against the granting of state funding to colleges and universities, since they tended to benefit the wealthy, rather than the general population.

The issues addressed by the workingmen's movement provide an interesting contrast to those issues addressed by leaders of the Common School Movement, such as Horace Mann, Henry Barnard, and others. The workingmen's movement called for a new type of educational program: one that, as Rush Welter has explained, "would abridge—not enhance—the authority of the established leaders of the society."

Traditional pre-Revisionist interpretations of the Common School Movement tend to present the programs of reformers such as Mann and Barnard as receiving widespread and immediate support from all members of the society. This was hardly the case. The movement itself was beset by fundamental contradictions. Following the older republican conception of education, the leaders of the Common School Movement saw education as serving Americans by helping them find their identities and realizing their full potential not only as individuals, but also as citizens. At the same time, the Common School Movement leaders felt it was their duty to sustain political stability by properly shaping the attitudes and values of the younger generation.

The goal of the Common School Movement—to provide for the personal development and education of the individual and at the same time to maintain political order and stability among the members of the society—often created serious contradictions and inconsistencies within the movement. Such inconsistencies were evident not only in the major programs that were put into effect by different state boards of education, but also in the personal philosophies of Horace Mann, Henry Barnard, and other members of the movement.

Undoubtedly, the leading figure in the Common School Movement was the Massachusetts educator Horace Mann (1796-1859). Originally trained as a lawyer, Mann supported major social and humanitarian causes such as the reform of debtor's laws, abolition, temperance, prison reform, and the improvement of the treatment and care of the mentally ill. By the middle of the 1830s, Mann had a reputation throughout Massachusetts as a gifted politician, one whose ability might eventually lead him to the governorship of the state, or to a seat in Congress.

It was therefore something of a surprise to Mann's friends when, in 1837, he accepted the post of Secretary of the Massachusetts State Board of Education. In May of 1837, Mann had been approached by Edmund Dwight, a prominent industrialist from Springfield, about accepting the position as head of the recently established State Board of Education. Dwight had persuaded Governor Edward Everett (who eventually became the president of Harvard University) that the secretary's position was too important to the State's future to be held by "just an educator." Instead, Dwight maintained that the position required someone of broader experience. Mann, whose previous work indicated a strong interest in social and humanitarian reform, was considered an ideal choice for the position.

When Mann took over as Secretary of the Board of Education in 1837, the situation in the Massachusetts schools was extremely discouraging. Although innovations, for instance, the "English Classical School," which was the forerunner of the modern high school, had been introduced in Boston as early as 1821, few tangible improvements had been made in methods of school administration or instruction since the time of the Revolution. The schools that were successful were usually private and did not meet the needs of the general population. According to educational reformer James G. Carter, only one third of Massachusetts school-age population attended school for some part of the year in 1837.

Part of the failure of the schools can be understood to be a result of older methods and approaches to education and schooling, which were no longer able to fulfill the complex and changing needs of the industrial and urban society that was beginning to emerge in Massachusetts, as well as in other parts of the country during this period. As the educational historian Michael Katz has argued, when Horace Mann was born in 1796, no one could have predicted that within his life-time the state's well-ordered Yankee farms would give way to burgeoning factories and mills. Old expectations and traditions were torn apart and new ideals and values were established in the radically changing society that was emerging during this period.

The new society that came into existence during Mann's lifetime forced education to assume an increased importance. Between 1820 and 1850, the per-centage of workers involved in agricultural occupations in Massachusetts fell from 58 percent to 15 percent. Traditional methods of learning no longer met the needs of many individuals—particularly those working in the newly industrialized sectors of the economy. The popular education proposed by the Common School Move-ment fulfilled the needs of many different individuals and interest groups within the culture. Utilitarian values were emphasized. It was widely assumed that educa-tion that promoted a disciplined working force would also bring about the growth of prosperity for both the individual and the society as a whole. As Mann explained in his *Fifth Report* (1842) as the Secretary of the Board of Education:

> ... Education is not only a moral renovator and a multiplier of intellectual power, but ... also the most prolific parent of material riches. ... It is not only the most honest and honorable, but the surest means of amassing prop-erty.

In his work with the Board of Education, Mann clearly saw the schools as an impor-tant vehicle for not only bringing about social reform, but also for maintaining the stability of the republic. Mann genuinely feared that the fabric that held American society together was in danger of being torn apart as a result of growing social pressures and conflicts. The burning of the Catholic Ursuline convent and school in Charlestown, across the river from Boston, by an antiforeign mob in 1834 was a "terrible outrage" for Mann. Not only was it a violation of the rights of the Catholic nuns who lived in the convent and ran the school, but also a threat to the general welfare of the nation.

Mann saw industrial expansion, which increased personal prosperity and wealth, as having the potential to provide a fuller and more complete life for all citizens. But education was the key to Mann's reform of society. As he explained:

> Education, then beyond all other devices of human origin, is the great equal-izer of the conditions of men—the balance wheel of the social machinery. ...

It gives each man the independence and the means by which he can resist the selfishness of other men. . . . The spread of education, by enlarging the cultivated class or caste, will open a wider area over which the social feelings will expand; and if this education should be universal and complete, it would do more than all things to obliterate factitious distinctions in society.

Mann was clearly espousing a conservative philosophy, one which suggests that public schooling would provide the talented and ambitious with the means to advance themselves socially and economically.

In certain respects, Mann's educational philosophy reflected the ideas of Thomas Jefferson. Like Jefferson, he promoted a meritocracy, which was supported by a system of free universal public schools. Unlike Jefferson, however, Mann was more interested in promoting the education of the general population than in isolating and educating a special elite group. Leadership would come from talented individuals within the general populace who were recognized by their peers as being particularly capable. Significantly, however, these leaders would not be separated by education from the people who elected them.

In this respect, Mann placed a tremendous amount of faith in the educational system's ability to provide the general population with a strong sense of morality and with the ability to critically judge the political and social needs of the nation. In this sense, the Common School Movement had as its purpose the training of an educated citizenry. For Mann, the Common Schools would create a uniform political consciousness—one in which the potential for political, religious, and social discord would be eliminated. Once the common schools were properly established, there would be no social issue or problem that could not eventually be solved by them through their educated citizenry.

Such an absolute faith in the schools as a tool of social reform was almost utopian in nature. As Mann argued:

In universal education, every "follower of God and friend of humankind" will find the only sure means of carrying forward that particular form to which he is devoted. In whatever department of philanthropy he may be engaged, he will find that department to be only a segment of the great circle of beneficence, of which *Universal Education* is centre and circumference; and that it is only when these segments are fitly joined together, that the wheel of Progress can move harmoniously and resistlessly onward.

The development of Mann's educational philosophy is most thoroughly chronicled in the twelve annual reports (1837-1848) that he submitted while he was the Secretary of the Massachusetts Board of Education. Remarkable for their insight and comprehensiveness, the *Reports* were widely circulated in both the United States and abroad. Taken as a collective whole, they represent perhaps the best source for understanding Mann's ideals and purpose as an educator.

Included in the twelve annual reports are discussions relating to almost every aspect of education and schooling. The development of better schoolhouses and responsible local boards of education is discussed at length in Mann's *First Report*

(1837). Objecting to the tendency of private schools to encourage their students to adopt a limited political perspective, and to "wield the sword of polemics with fatal dexterity," Mann strongly emphasized the need to encourage and promote the development of common schools in their place.

Mann's insights into the instructional needs of the child are remarkable for their time. In his *Second Report* (1838), he addressed himself to the needs of intellectual development on the part of the student. Discussing instruction in reading, spelling, and composition at length, Mann recognized that "Knowledge cannot be poured into a child's mind," but must be reached out and grasped by the children themselves. Rather than being a passive recipient in the process of learning, the child must be actively involved in the acquisition of knowledge. Mann placed a great deal of importance on the child's mastery of basic skills. Recognizing the importance of reading in his *Third Report* (1839). Mann advocated the establishment of a free circulating library in every school district throughout the state.

As Mann's work with the State Board of Education continued, his *Annual Reports* increasingly provided him the opportunity to address specific reform issues. The consolidation of small impractical school districts into larger ones was discussed in his *Fourth Report* (1840), along with his ideas on the basic qualifications for a teacher. In the 1840 *Report*, Mann emphasized the ability of teachers to teach subjects, rather than the curriculums outlined in manuals. He criticized the fact that the memorization of facts and data dominated most learning, rather than the understanding of principles. For Mann, the ability to communicate complex ideas, as well as to maintain order in the classroom was of critical importance in a teacher. As a skilled publicist, Mann used both the *Annual Reports* and *The Common School Journal*, which began publication in 1838, to promote the common schools. In his *Fifth Report* (1841), Mann included arguments, specifically directed toward the business community, which maintained that the schools would promote a suitable morality that would protect the rights of individuals with property.

Many different intellectual forces influenced Mann in his work. In 1837, when he was considering whether or not to accept the Secretariat of the Board, Mann had read the work of the Scottish phrenologist George Combe. Combe's most important work, *The Constitution of Man* (1828) attempted to combine the utilitarian aspects of traditional Scottish philosophy with the phrenological theories of F. J. Gall (1809). Phrenology represented a crude attempt, by today's standards, to develop a psychology of human behavior. According to Gall, the human mind was divided into more than thirty faculties, or propensities, that included characteristics such as "benevolence," "self-esteem," "inhibition," and so on. By observing the measurements and configurations of the skull, it was felt that the mental capacity and character of an individual could be determined.

Significantly, it was believed that the negative propensities of an individual could be discouraged and positive tendencies encouraged by means of proper training. Some of phrenology's most extreme practitioners argued that by massaging certain parts of the skull, positive or negative propensities or tendencies in an

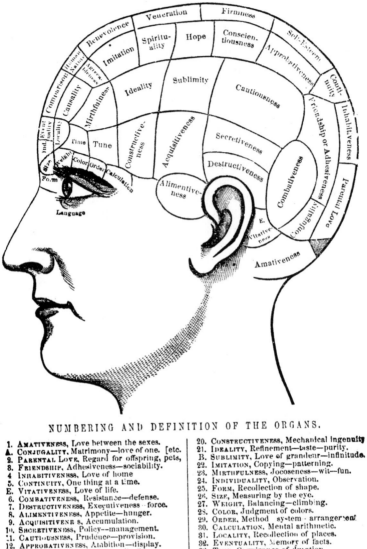

NUMBERING AND DEFINITION OF THE ORGANS.

1. AMATIVENESS, Love between the sexes.
A. CONJUGALITY, Matrimony—love of one. [etc.
2. PARENTAL LOVE, Regard for offspring, pets,
3. FRIENDSHIP, Adhesiveness—sociability.
4. INHABITIVENESS, Love of home
5. CONTINUITY, One thing at a time.
E. VITATIVENESS, Love of life.
6. COMBATIVENESS, Resistance—defense.
7. DESTRUCTIVENESS, Executiveness - force.
8. ALIMENTIVENESS, Appetite—hunger.
9. ACQUISITIVEN S, Accumulation.
10. SECRETIVENESS, Policy--management.
11. CAUTIOUSNESS, Prudence—provision.
12. APPROBATIVENESS, Ambition—display.
13. SELF-ESTEEM, Self-respect - di nity.
14. FIRMNESS, Decision—perseverance.
15. CONSCIENTIOUSNESS, Justice equity.
16. HOPE, Expectation - enterprise.
17. SPIRITUALITY, Intuition—faith—credulity.
18. VENERATION, Devotion—respect.
19 BENEVOLENCE, Kindness—goodness.

20. CONSTRUCTIVENESS, Mechanical ingenuity
21. IDEALITY, Refinement—taste—purity.
B. SUBLIMITY, Love of grandeur—infinitude.
22. IMITATION, Copying—patterning.
23. MIRTHFULNESS, Jocoseness—wit—fun.
24. INDIVIDUALITY, Observation.
25. FORM, Recollection of shape.
26. SIZE, Measuring by the eye.
27. WEIGHT, Balancing—climbing.
28. COLOR, Judgment of colors.
29. ORDER, Method system - arrangement
30. CALCULATION, Mental arithmetic.
31. LOCALITY, Recollection of places.
32. EVENTUALITY, Memory of facts.
33. TIME, Cognizance of duration.
34. TUNE, Sense of harmony and melody.
35. LANGUAGE, Expression of ideas.
36. CAUSALITY, Applying causes to effect. [tion
37. COMPARISON, Inductive reasoning—illustra
C. HUMAN NATURE, Perception of motives.
D. AGREEABLENESS, Pleasantness—suavity

FIGURE 4-2 Frontispiece to O. S. and L. N. Fowler, *New Illustrated Self-Instructor in Phrenology and Physiology* (New York: Fowler and Wells, 1859).

individual could be stimulated. Thus by massaging the top of the skull where "veneration" was supposed to be housed, this characteristic could be encouraged in the individual.

Mann readily adopted phrenology into his philosophy of education. Basically, phrenology provided Mann with a means by which to predict and shape human behavior. Although now discredited, phrenology did provide a primitive theory of personality and psychology around which educators such as Mann could develop specific educational programs. By encouraging the total balanced development of the individual, phrenology encouraged the introduction of subjects such as music, art, and physical education into the common schools.

John D. Davies in his work *Phrenology: Fad and Science, a Nineteenth Century Crusade* (1955), points out that Mann's *Sixth Report* was heavily dependent upon Combe's *The Constitution of Man* for many of its ideas. Mann's interest in phrenology was to follow him through the rest of his life. Having met Combe and attended his lectures in Boston in 1838, Mann traveled extensively with him throughout the United States during the Spring of 1840. In 1844, they again met and traveled together while Mann was on a six-month tour of European schools.

Mann's European tour provided the basis for his *Seventh Report* (1843). He was particularly impressed by the schools he observed in Prussia and discussed their programs at great length. To a large degree, Prussian schools were based on Pestalozzi's philosophy of gearing education to the developmental level of the children and their natural interests and, according to Mann, many positive features of their curriculum recommended them to the American educators. Of the thousands of students Mann claimed to have observed while in Prussia, he explains that never once did he see a "child in tears from having been punished, or from fear of being punished." Rather than harsh discipline Mann saw teachers deal gently with their students as individuals, while providing them with basic instruction. According to Mann, the relationship the teachers had with their pupils seemed

> ... to be one of duty first, and then affection, on the part of the teacher, ... The teacher's manner was better than parental, for it had a parent's tenderness and vigilance, without the foolish doatings or indulgences to which parental affection is prone.

Pestalozzi's ideal of the teacher being a guide and respected friend of the student was clearly at work.

Mann was by no means the only American educator to visit and write about the Prussian schools. Calvin Stowe, for example, had been sent by the Ohio state legislature in 1836 to study the schools in Prussia. A year later he published a report on his trip that was circulated by the legislature in every school district in Ohio. Stating that he was impressed by the "excellent order and rigid economy with which all the Prussian institutions are conducted," Stowe's report had a widespread impact beyond Ohio.

Mann's visit to Europe further impressed upon him the importance of the schools as a vehicle for social reform. Mann observed the great gulf that separated the wealthy from the working class in countries such as England. He considered it a terrible threat to society. By denying the working class access to free public schools, the English ruling class was threatening the country's political and social stability.

In his *Eighth Report* (1844), Mann discussed at some length the employment of women teachers and the need to develop effective teacher training institutes. Along with figures such as Charles Brooks, James G. Carter, Edmund Dwight, and Samuel R. Hall, Mann had advocated the establishment of special teacher training institutes as early as the late 1830s. In 1838, Dwight, a Boston businessman, contributed $10,000, to be matched, for the establishment of some sort of teacher training institute in Massachusetts. As head of the state board of education, Mann was left to develop the specific plans of the institution.

Attempts to establish teacher training programs date back to the beginning of the nineteenth century. Thomas B. Hall's private normal school, established in 1823, was unsuccessful. He later taught courses for would-be teachers at Phillips Academy at Andover, Massachusetts. A few academies, especially in New York State, offered teacher preparation courses, but this too was unsuccessful.

It was not until the very end of the 1830s that the first state-supported teacher training institute, or *normal school*, was established by Mann and his colleagues in Lexington, Massachusetts.

Opened on July 3, 1839, the normal school in Lexington was placed under the direction of Harvard graduate Cyrus Pierce. Only three students enrolled on the first day, although twelve eventually were enrolled for classes before the end of the first quarter. Several other normal schools were opened in rapid succession. In September of 1839, a school was begun at Barre, Massachusetts; another in Bridgewater, Massachusetts, the following year. The importance that Mann placed upon the normal schools is indicated in an address he made for the dedication of the normal school in Bridgewater, Massachusetts, in August of 1846. As he explained:

> I believe Normal Schools to be a new instrumentality in the advancement of the race. I believe that, without them, Free Schools themselves would be shorn of their strength and their healing power, and would at length become mere charity schools, and thus die out in fact and form.

Mann's desire that the normal schools would become strongly linked to the growth of the common schools was eventually borne out.

In the *Ninth Report* (1845), Mann emphasized the primacy of moral education over intellectual training. Basically Mann believed that the ideals of a republican democracy would never be fully realized until the common schools created "a more far-seeing intelligence and a purer morality than has ever yet existed among communities of men." (1849) Moral education for Mann provided a means of ensuring the promotion and development of the Republic:

> In order that men may be prepared for self-government, their apprenticeship must commence in childhood. The great moral attribute of self-government cannot be born and matured in a day: and if school children are not trained to it, we only prepare ourselves for disappointment, if we expect it from grown men.

Until his final annual report was submitted in 1848, Mann continued to use the reports to promote the idea of the common schools as providing the training necessary for the individual to become a useful citizen. While discussions of the state education code are included in the *Tenth Report* (1846), and the belief that education has the power to redeem the state is discussed in the *Eleventh Report* (1847), it is in the final *Twelfth Report* that Mann's ideas are best summarized.

Mann wrote the *Twelfth Report* after he had been elected to a seat in the U.S. House of Representatives in 1848, and had resigned as Secretary of the School Board. In the report he drew together the basic principles and ideas he had been promoting for the past twelve years as an advocate of the common schools. Mann once again emphasized that the destiny of the school is the same as that of society.

> . . . the true business of the schoolroom connects itself, and becomes identical, with the great interests of society. The former is the infant, immature state of those interests; the latter, their developed, adult state. As "the child is father to the man," so may the training of the schoolroom expand into the institutions and fortunes of the state.

The crusade Mann led for the establishment of common schools represented part of a more general educational movement that developed in the second half of the nineteenth century through which schooling came to play an increasingly important role in American culture. As an idealist, Mann had little notion of the extent to which his ideas on free universal schooling would be used to maintain the existing political and social order. Michael Katz has argued that the purpose of the public schools over the course of at least the last hundred years has been the inculcation of attitudes into children that reflect the dominant social and industrial values of the culture. In his reform of the common schools, Mann had no way of knowing the extent to which bureaucratic structures would come to dominate the operation and organization of the public schools in the years following his death.

Mann obviously contributed to the development of the bureaucratic system that would eventually come to so totally dominate American schools. His opposition to democratic localism on the part of individual school boards and his development of an increasingly centralized system of schools throughout Massachusetts are perfect examples of how his work tended to encourage the subsequent development of a bureaucracy. Yet in assessing Mann's work, one is left with something of a paradox. Assuming that the development of free public schools was an important ideal to be realized for the culture, one must ask how these schools could be developed without the implementation of a centralized administrative system and, along with it, rigid bureaucratic and often class-dominated structures.

Mann's work with the common schools was closely paralleled by that of Henry Barnard. Barnard was born in Hartford, Connecticut, in 1811. Like Mann, he was the product of a traditional Protestant upbringing. Educated in a local district school, Monson Academy in Massachusetts, and Hopkins Grammar School, Barnard entered Yale University when he was sixteen in 1826. Graduating in 1830, he taught for a single term at Wellsborough Academy in Pennsylvania. Teaching, however, did not agree with Barnard. In 1831 he returned to Hartford, where he became increasingly involved with Whig politics. Having spent a brief period of time observing the political scene in Washington, Barnard returned to Connecticut to study law at Yale. Passing the bar exam in 1834, he gravitated toward a political career.

Having traveled briefly in Europe, Barnard returned to the United States because of the death of his father. He was elected to the Connecticut legislature in 1837. Like Mann, Barnard was a Whig and supported a series of social and humanitarian causes similar to those supported by his Massachusetts counterpart. Included among the legislation that he sponsored in the legislature were programs to improve conditions for the blind, the deaf, and the mentally ill. Advocating the reorganization of the penal system in Connecticut, Barnard eventually became interested in the reform of the state's school system.

In 1838, Barnard introduced a bill in the legislature creating a Board of Commissioners to supervise the Common Schools. The board, under the supervision of a secretary, was to collect information on the schools and evaluate them with the purpose of improving their organization and the quality of education that they provided. Barnard's bill passed the legislature with little difficulty, and he accepted a position as one of the board's eight commissioners. Elected secretary of the board, Barnard intended to hold the position for a period of only six months. Persuaded to stay on for a four-year term, he became increasingly interested in using the schools as a means of reforming the culture. Barnard truly believed that with an educated populace most social problems would be eliminated. Vice and crime would be reduced, the quality of family life would be improved, justice and liberty would flourish.

Like Mann in Massachusetts, as secretary of the education board, Barnard assumed the role of an agent for promoting the common school cause. During the late 1830s and early 1840s, he traveled extensively throughout Connecticut, collecting school statistics, writing annual reports, and editing the *Connecticut Common School Journal*. It was in this capacity as a publicist and editor that Barnard undoubtedly made his most important contribution to the development of education in the United States during the middle and late nineteenth century.

Beginning with his editorship of the *Connecticut Common School Journal* and continuing to the end of his life, Barnard systematically wrote about, edited, and assembled an extraordinary collection of documents and critical essays relating to education in Europe and the United States. In doing so, Barnard continued the popular early nineteenth century tradition of disseminating educational ideas through the publication of popular journals and magazines. As early as 1811, for example, Albert Pickett published the first American educational magazine. Although Pickett's magazine ultimately proved to be a failure, the basic concept did not. Between 1811 and 1830, according to Sheldon Davis, a total of nine journals pertaining to the subject of education were published in the United States.

In 1855, Barnard began the publication of what was to be the greatest of the nineteenth century American educational journals, the *American Journal of Education*. Published in huge annual volumes until 1881, the journal was primarily underwritten by Barnard. The publication represented the most comprehensive journal that had been published up until that time dealing with the subject of education. In addition to republishing impotant documents related to the history of schooling (a complete copy of the *New England Primer* was reprinted in one of the early issues, for example), the journal included important biographies of educators, descriptions of educational innovations, essays on school architecture, descriptions of the education of the deaf and blind, as well as discussions of juvenile reformatories and the education of the poor.

Although the journal's cost was far beyond the means and interest of the average teacher, it was widely available in major libraries, school systems, colleges, and teacher training institutions. In addition, the journal was circulated internationally to such places as Chile, Argentina, Scotland, Belgium, Canada, Germany, France, Switzerland, and Italy. Surviving documents from the period seem to indicate that the impact of the journal as a vehicle for disseminating and promoting new educational ideas was enormous, although its influence is hard to assess accurately.

Barnard's efforts were by no means limited to the *American Journal of Education.* In 1838, for example, he had presented an address on the unfortunate condition of most schoolhouses in the United States. In 1842, his ideas were further developed and published in a manual or architectural pattern book entitled, *School Architecture, Or Contributions to the Improvement of School-Houses in the United States.*

Interest in the design of schoolhouses in the United States goes back to the beginning of the 1830s. In 1830, the American Institute of Instruction sponsored a competition on the construction of schoolhouses. Barnard credited his own interest in school architecture to Alonzo Potter and George B. Emerson's book *The School and the Schoolmaster.* Included in Barnard's *School Architecture* were not only designs discussed by Potter and Emerson in their work, but plans and elevations actually executed by Barnard himself for the Windsor and Washington district schoolhouses in Connecticut.

Barnard saw the well-designed school as not only a place where education could be properly conducted, but also as a model of good taste, worthy of imitation by the general population. As he explained in an article published in 1839 in volume two of the *Connecticut Common School Journal,* every village, town and school in Connecticut

> ... would have at least one edifice in good taste,—in a conspicuous and agreeable situation,—a correct model of architecture,—pleasing to the eye of every spectator, and agreeable to those for whom the school house is designed. ... How would such edifices adorn our streets, and arrest the eyes of the travellers along our roads, rivers; and sea coast! What an influence, also, would models of this kind soon exercise on the taste of our people, and their views of domestic architecture, and the arrangement of their own grounds!

Barnard felt that most schoolhouses were badly sited, situated in noisy places too often close to highways, unattractive, and built at the least possible cost.

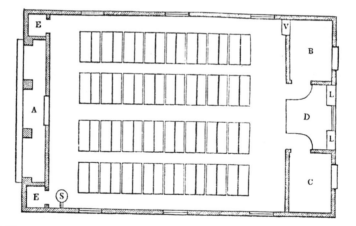

FIGURE 4-3 View and floor plan of a Greek Revival primary school included in Henry Barnard, *School Architecture* (New York: A. S. Barnes, 1848).

A careful examination of the designs included in Barnard's *School Architecture* is revealing. As in almost any type of architecture, there is inherent in the designs for schools a clear philosophy and set of social values. The consistent selection and use of classic revival style for many of the schoolhouses included in Barnard's book reflects not only the then current interest in classic Revival style for both domestic and public architecture, but also recalls in a physical form the rationalism of the Greeks. The schoolhouse becomes a "sacred space" or literally a temple of wisdom. Similarly, the emphasis upon Gothic styles of architecture for schoolhouses, which was popular as a style in both England and the United States, recalled not only the tradition of the medieval universities, but also the tradition of ecclesiastical architecture. As a result, the school as a "sacred" architectural space was once again emphasized.

Barnard included in *School Architecture* a great deal more than just floor plans and elevations for schoolhouses. Toward the conclusion of the book, he went into detailed discussions of different pedagogical systems, such as the monitorial system and the Facher system. In addition, he discussed the use of pedagogical devices ranging from movable blackboards to globes of the earth, desk designs, and even ventilation and heating systems.

In 1842, the same year that *School Architecture* was published, Barnard lost the secretaryship of the Connecticut Board of Education as a result of the Democrats coming to power. He immediately set out on a fifteen-month tour of the United States, collecting materials for a history of American education. While collecting his data, Barnard also lectured on the need for the establishment of Common Schools to various state and local groups. On completing the trip, Barnard assumed the post of Commissioner of Public Schools in Rhode Island, a position that he held until 1849.

Barnard subsequently served as the principal of the Connecticut State Normal School and State Superintendent of Common Schools, Chancellor of the University of Wisconsin and agent of the Wisconsin Normal School Regents. In 1867, Barnard was appointed as the first United States Commissioner of Education. With the change of political administrations in 1869, the Department of Education was made a bureau of the Department of the Interior. Barnard lost his job and returned to live in Connecticut, where he worked on his history of American education and the *American Journal of Education*, which he continued to publish until 1881.

Barnard's work as a proponent of the Common Schools was only exceeded by that of Horace Mann. His work as an educational administrator was largely a failure. As head of the University of Wisconsin, he never assumed a position of strong leadership, while his work as the United States Commissioner of Education was too short lived to bear any fruit. Instead, Barnard's most lasting contribution seems to have been derived from his work as an editor and writer—one who provided critical direction and purpose to the relatively new enterprise of public education in the United States.

ACADEMIES

The development of the common schools during the 1830s and 1840s was accompanied by a continued growth and development of the academies. Until roughly the centennial year of 1876, the academies enrolled more students than the high schools. Thousands of academies had been established. There were military academies, monitorial academies, manual labor academies, and preparatory academies. There were academies for boys, for boys and girls, and for girls. An academy for Indians operated for nearly twenty years, and after the Civil War there were a few academies for Blacks.

The first military academy in the United States was, of course, the army academy at West Point, patterned after military schools in France. Before Sylvanius B. Thayer replaced Alden Patridge as superintendent in 1812, West Point seems to have had a course of study like that of academies generally. Thayer laid the foundation of West Point's traditions of drill, polish, and discipline, Partridge established the American Literary, Scientific, and Military Academy at West Point, a private military school. He later aided in the establishment of other military academies.

The United States Naval Academy at Annapolis, Maryland, was established forty years later by Secretary of the Navy George Bancroft, by administrative sleight of hand, without Congressional approval. Until then, navy midshipmen had been expected to study at sea. For example, when the frigate *Potomac* sailed around the world (elapsed time 1002 days), in its crew were nineteen midshipmen and Schoolmaster Francis Warriner, who was outranked by them. Bancroft was sure this was an unsatisfactory arrangement.

FIGURE 4-4   New cadets arriving at West Point. From *St. Nicholas: An Illustrated Magazine for Young Folks,* Volume 14, 1887, p. 522.

In the twenty years after the Revolution, Boston produced a generation of American intellectuals. Conservative, Federalist, self-styled "natural aristocrats," they were dissatisfied with what they saw as vestigal grammar schools, rudimentary academies, and tradition-bound Harvard. Several young intellectuals were sent to Europe by Harvard President John T. Kirtland to complete their preparation for Harvard professorships. One was Edward Everett, who became a famed orator and politician. A second, George Ticknor, was an unsuccessful reformer at Harvard. Two others, Joseph Green Cogswell and George Bancroft, later established the Round Hill School, which was to be the prototype for preparatory boarding schools.

Cogswell visited von Fellenberg's school for young aristocrats twice in 1818. (That year Robert Owen of New Harmony sent his son, Robert Dale Owen, there.) At von Fellenberg's school for aristocrats the first concern also was for the development of the student's moral facilities. Students studied Latin, Greek, French, German, science, drawing, and music, and exercised by doing calesthenics. The school for young aristocrats was a boarding school also. About the same time Bancroft visited German secondary schools, *gymnasiums*, in which students studied and learned far more quickly and thoroughly what American students learned in the classical departments of academies and their first years of college.

Cogswell and Bancroft taught at Harvard upon their return, Cogswell as professor of science (and librarian), and Bancroft, after preaching a few months, as tutor (instructor) in Greek. The students saw Bancroft as a demanding tyrant in his classroom. After Harvard's "great rebellion" of 1822-23, forty-three of the seventy members of the senior class were expelled and President Kirtland was forced to retire. Cogswell and Bancroft resigned and founded Round Hill School, near Northampton, Massachusetts.

Like von Fellenberg's, Round Hill was a boarding school. Round Hill was concerned first with the development of "character." Cogswell and Bancroft undertook to provide a vigorous preparation for higher education, as the German gymnasiums did. Classes were small. Much of the teaching was tutorial, individual. Students began their studies there at the age of nine. When they had completed the Round Hill course of study, they were prepared to enter Harvard or Yale, sometimes even the junior or senior classes there. Round Hill was the prototype for Eastern preparatory schools, the schools which, at least by legend, have prepared the sons of the elite for Ivy League colleges. Bancroft left Round Hill in 1831, and in 1834, Cogswell closed the school.

Compared with the preparatory school, the range and variety of academies is difficult to overstate. Before the Civil War, Colonel Dick Johnson's Choctaw Academy had an Indian student body. On the eve of the twentieth century, Orange Park Normal and Industrial School for Negroes was closed by Florida Superintendent of Schools William F. Sheats because it had admitted seventeen white students. Frederick William Coleman's academy in Virginia was a small log cabin copy of the University of Virginia, complete with quadrangle. Mr. Coleman heard recitations when he was ready, early or late. Many of his scholars entered college. Fairfield Academy in upstate New York offered medical school courses. Gardiner

Lyceum in Maine was a school for "farmers, millwrights and other mechanics" from 1824 until 1831. Other smaller agricultural academies survived more briefly. To repeat, the academies were generally small. In New York State in 1850, even the best funded academies averaged only 4.4 teachers and 108 students. In North Carolina, then 272 academies had 403 teachers and 8,000 pupils, an average of 1.5 teachers and 29 pupils each.

After their first beginnings, academies for females multiplied rapidly. From first to last their aim was to educate girls and women so that they would be better wives and mothers and for the good of society generally. They did not educate women for professions or occupations, except for teaching. By 1839, nearly 500 former students at Zilpah Grant's Ipswich Female Academy alone had become teachers, and twenty more, teachers in female seminaries.

In 1876, there were still questions concerning appropriate studies for women, where they would go to college, and whether they should go to professional school. Underlying these, of course, were questions concerning suitable occupations for women, and most fundamentally, women's roles in society. These issues and questions arose outside the academies, which had made their contributions.

The supporters of the public schools portrayed the academies as unfortunate and inadequate, and their criticisms have outlasted the academies. However, if one starts with the proposition that secondary education should be privately supported,

FIGURE 4-5   The new school mistress. From *Harper's Weekly*, Vol. 17, p. 817.

as much of higher education still is, and if demand is so scattered that students must leave home, then perhaps they had their virtues. They were responsive to community and student needs, as part of the cost for their survival. They were small enough to avoid impersonality. Students and their parents had wide choices in courses of study and academys' religious stances. Tuition costs surely prevented some from attending an academy, but the first high schools were not for the poor—wages not earned were an important consideration too for those planning to go beyond common school. Most young men and women in the 1800s had no such plan or wish.

The virtual extinction of types of schools has been rare in our past; only the academy and the Latin grammar school have suffered that fate. A brief post mortem is appropriate. As a first approximation, tuition-supported academies were replaced by tax-supported high schools. During Horace Mann's superintendency the enrollments in Massachusetts schools rose much faster than total enrollments in Massachusetts academies. In 1839, in the town of Cambridge, 69 percent of the pupils attended common schools. Seven years later, 90 percent did. It seems likely that teachers who were well thought of preferred to teach in public schools, public or high, instead of in private schools or academies. In Buffalo, New York, the new school system recruited half its teachers from local nonpublic schools in the later 1830s. Some sixty academies in New York State were transformed into high schools, and a very few became colleges. Others closed when buildings burned or respected principals left education, as Bruce Catton's father did during World War I. A few closed later when their endowments were exhausted. A scattering of academies survive, in rural New England, or as preparatory schools, or schools closely related to churches. In the last twenty years, hundreds of new academies have been established, as refuges from school desegregation or from what has been seen as the mediocrity of the public schools and their "immorality." But they are a part of more recent history of education.

CONCLUSION

The first half of the nineteenth century saw the emergence of a distinct American identity and the development of a school system consistent with it. New attitudes toward childrearing reflected a specific set of values and beliefs concerning the child and the family that were unique to American culture. Democratic ideals combined with the demands of a rapidly expanding industrial system encouraged the "Common School Revival."

New and important educational ideas were promoted by leaders of the Common School Movement, such as Horace Mann, Henry Barnard, and Calvin Stowe. Older and more traditional approaches to schooling survived in the form of the academies. As had been the case with Republican educational theorists after the Revolution, the leaders of the Common School Movement saw education as a means of reforming American culture. In doing so, they failed to realize that they were promoting a philosophy that was specifically their own, rather than one that was universally held. Their faith in the efficiency of the schools and their ability to reform American culture had at times almost religious overtones. This belief in the school's ability to reform American culture has continued into our own era, and only in recent years has begun to be seriously questioned.

The significance of the Common School Movement ultimately lies in the patterns that it set for the subsequent development of education in the United States. The roles now defined for teachers and administrators within the school system, the relationship of the school to the family and to minority groups, systems of finance and administration clearly have their roots in the Common School Movement. As a result, the Common School Movement is of particular importance and interest to those concerned with understanding the history of American education.

CHAPTER FIVE
THE GROWTH OF THE COMMON SCHOOLS

The second half of the nineteenth century was the great period of expansion and growth for the common schools, and of the development of what David Tyack has called "the one best system." Common schools spread from New England and New York westward, and southward after the Civil War. They served (though that was not always an appropriate word) older students in high schools and vocational schools, and younger pupils in kindergartens. Partly because of compulsory attendance laws, a larger proportion of children attended schools.

As the common schools grew, there were strong arguments and seemingly good reasons for more centralized control, and also for more authority for state superintendents of schools, the establishment of the county superintendency, and the development of the city superintendency. With increasing enrollments, the division of the labor of teachers was more desirable. A need for coordination arose, and administrators, especially the city superintendents, acquired further duties and authority.

However, large segments of schooling remained outside the "one best system." Members of the Roman Catholic Church had preferred to build Catholic schools rather than send their children to Protestant-dominated public schools. Despite the efforts of radical Republicans and Blacks after the Civil War, only a much-modified form of schooling was available to Blacks. Girls and women were often consigned, at first, to different and inferior secondary schools, and were not admitted to colleges. American Indians also attended different and, in a sense, "colonial" schools. The common school as it was extended was not for everyone at every level.

EXPANSION

The concept of the common school spread in part because it was an institution whose time had come. Horace Mann, and also Henry Barnard and others, expressed what many people, particularly influential people, felt. Mann's and Barnard's reports and papers were read nationally, and approved and often acted upon. In other states there were also advocates of the common schools, who were respected and influential; Norman Angell of Michigan and John Swett of California were in their place and time ardent advocates. (A might-have-been of history opens an interesting speculation: If, for whatever reasons, Mann and Barnard had not been active in the Common School Movement, would it have been as strong and widespread? One of the authors thinks it might have been. That belief presupposes that public opinion or functional necessity, rather than inspired leadership, produced an institution. The question is illuminating because it shows alternative lines of historical explanation.) The common schools seem to have spread, too, because an extraordinarily large proportion of schoolmen and teachers had come from New England, presumably bringing with them devotion to the common schools. In large cities, particularly, some old residents felt threatened and were alarmed by the large numbers of people different from themselves. The common schools were established in some part to protect things as they had been, to protect against Irish and German immigrants in Buffalo, to protect against the Spanish-speaking residents of Los Angeles, and newly freed slaves in Charleston, South Carolina. In some cities, the men whom Bayrd Still called "civic boosters" established common school systems. In any event, the common school revival spread fast and far. In California, common schools appeared within a year after the gold rush of 1849. By then common schools had been established or reestablished in the Old Northwest, bounded by the Ohio and Mississippi Rivers, and in the states and populated territories west of there.

Organizationally, the "high school" was an extension of the common schools for older and more advanced pupils. If *high school* is understood as meaning a secondary school supported by taxes and controlled by public authorities, the line between academy and *high school* blurred because the later sharp distinction between "public" and "private" had not come into being. The source of the name *high school* was probably the Edinburgh High School, wich had been founded in 1566 and was controlled and funded by the city. John Griscom, the monitorial school enthusiast and professor of chemistry, had visited it and had published descriptions. Bostonians may have borrowed the term. The *English Classical School*, an alternative to Latin Grammar schools, was established in Boston in 1821 as a public secondary school. After 1824, it was called the *English High School.* It is thought of as the first high school in the United States.

The spread of high schools was slow at first, but by 1851, there were high schools in eighty American cities, and other high schools opened soon after. In some states new laws authorized the establishment of high schools. In other states courts held that common school laws had authorized the establishment of high schools. The most famous of these court cases was *Stuart et al. v. School District No. 1 of Kalamazoo*, which was decided in 1874.

There was as much variation in the curricula of early high schools as there was in the academies. Some subjects were extensions of those of the common schools: The English High School of Boston offered the common school subjects of reading, arithmetic, and geography, as well as more advanced courses. Others had curricula parallel to those of the academies. Some high schools offered the courses in Latin and Greek that had been taught in the Latin grammar schools and that were still needed for admission to colleges. Less often, high schools were seen as "people's colleges": A very few of them even awarded bachelor's degrees. Until nearly 1880, there were more academy than high school students. Enrollments in high schools increased after that, and academy enrollments declined.

The issue of the high school versus the academy was important in its consequences. However, most of the pupils, even at the end of the 1800s, had no plan or wish to continue their schooling. In 1880, only one adolescent in fifty was attending a high school, and fewer were attending an academy. Even in 1920, only one out of five adolescents would be attending high school. Nine out of ten of those who went to high schools in the 1880s did not graduate. Students dropped out for all the reasons still heard, and many high schools offered only one or two years of instruction. The importance of completing high school—graduating—was a later convention. High school students in Dedham, Massachusetts received a certificate for completing each year's work.

David Nassau has said that academies "were abandoned by parents unable to pay both tuition and taxes." It was more complicated than that, of course. Public high schools grew as cities grew, because in cities there were many potential pupils, and because real property—land and buildings—in the cities was valuable and profitable enough to bear taxes to support schools.

THE FORMING OF CITY SYSTEMS

From the first erratic beginnings of city school systems, in the 1830s, to their generally uniform organization, by about 1900, is a history that has gotten considerable attention, although it has not been fully explored. The general tendency, clearly, was toward regularization and regulation, toward more elaborate formal organization and bureaucratization. But there were many cases of delayed modernization, and even some cases of regression when the city superintendent was weak or unfortunate. In a few cities, superintendencies were even abolished for a time.

The history of Chicago's schools is in many ways illustrative. The first school there to receive public funds, in 1833, was that of Miss Eliza Chapell, who had moved her charity school from a lent storeroom to the Presbyterian church. Miss

Chappell's memoirs show that she was much more missionary than teacher, which should not be surprising.

After the time of Miss Chappell, who went on to better missionary fields, one first sees the enormous growth of enrollments in the Chicago schools. In 1837, the year of a particularly painful and costly panic, 325 children were enrolled. (The schools shut down because there were no tax revenues to support them.) Herrick, in her recent study of the Chicago schools, gives enrollment figures from time to time, which are shown in the accompanying table. The rate of increase in numbers of

TABLE 5-1   Chicago Pupils and Teachers, 1837-1970[a]

Year	Elementary enrollment[b]	High School enrollment[c]	Total Enrollment[d]	Number of Teachers[e]	Teacher: Pupil ratio
1837	325	—	325	4	1:81.2
1840	317	—	317	4	1:79.2
1850	1,919	—	1,919	21	1:91.4
1860	6,539	312	6,851	135	1:50.7
1870	27,342	602	38,939	537	1:72.5
1880	58,519	1,043	59,562	958	1:62.2
1890	131,341	2,825	135,541	2,711	1:50.0
1900	215,660	10,201	255,221	5,786	1:44.1
1910	257,620	17,781	300,472	6,357	1:47.3
1920	291,678	36,433	392,914	8,740	1:45.0
1930	326,000	103,851	440,161	13,479	1:32.7
1940	318,443	144,671	391,171	13,532	1:28.9
1950	293,142	96,786	389,928	13,423	1:29.6
1960	410,206	102,886	513,092	20,276	1:24.0
1970	433,319	142,843	576,153[f]	26,884	1:21.4

Notes:

[a]Data from Mary J. Herrick, *The Chicago Schools: A Social and Political History* (Beverly Hills: Sage, 1971), pp. 403, 406. Enrollment figures may be a third higher than average attendance in early years.

[b]Includes 7th and 8th graders in junior high school.

[c]Includes 9th graders in junior high school.

[d]Includes summer, evening, special students, 1890-1950. Normal school and college students not included.

[e]Includes special teachers, 1880, 1900, 1910, 1940, 1950, teachers not assigned to schools, 1970.

[f]Apparent discrepancy not explained.

pupils was far greater in Chicago, and in the other big cities, than any seen in our century. In the eight years ending in 1845, enrollments tripled. In the thirteen years ending in 1850, they increased nearly ten times. In the next ten years, they again more than tripled; and in the following ten years, nearly doubled again. By 1890, there were 135,431 pupils enrolled in Chicago schools. Because Chicago was one of the most prosperous and fastest growing cities of the time, its school enrollments were among the fastest growing. The sheer weight of numbers was one of the most important shapers of city schools in the later 1800s.

Miss Chappell's school and the other schools of that time were not publicly controlled, although they were partly supported by taxes. A new city charter put Chicago schools under the city's control in 1839, only two years after Horace Mann had become de facto superintendent of Massachusetts schools. The first Chicago superintendent of schools, John Dore, from Boston, was appointed in 1854. It was not unusual that he was a New Englander; most of the early superintendents were. The first big city superintendent, Oliver Steele, had been appointed in Buffalo seventeen years earlier. Dore was a *schoolman*, as they called themselves, who had previously taught, but he later became a Chicago businessman. Steele was a businessman, owner of a bookstore and bindery, before and after he was superintendent of schools, which seems to have been less common. But of Steele's seventeen successors in Buffalo before 1890, only four were schoolmen. Herrick gives no details as to why the Chicago schools were put under the control of the city government. The founders of the Buffalo school system were civic "boosters," who established the school system for the same reason they established police departments and fire departments, and built water systems: Those were good for the city and for business.

It is convenient to talk about public schools as isolated institutions, but it must be remembered that in the 1800s the schools were only part of a matrix of institutions intended to educate. In Chicago and elsewhere, many private schools continued after city public schools came into being. Herrick has not provided details about other educating institutions in Chicago. Those in Buffalo have been more thoroughly examined. In Buffalo, secondary studies could be undertaken at academies that thrived for a time even after a public high school was opened. There were private instructors in many subjects—one of the early Buffalo superintendents had been a private "writing," or penmanship, teacher. There were frequent lyceum sessions, and a privately supported school of art, and a large but privately supported library. There were, of course, newspapers. Parochial schools had appeared. The individual who wished to could, unless he was too poor, be educated in both practical and the finer things.

A Chicago Board of Education was appointed in 1857, replacing earlier "inspectors." In some places, including Buffalo, city governments continued to control the public schools directly. In others, such as Brooklyn and Pittsburgh, there was a school committee for each school. Their consolidation into one city-wide board of education, and its reduction in size, seemed at the time to be one of the greater advances of the late 1800s.

Dore was followed as superintendent by William Henry Wells of Connecticut. Wells had not attended college, but had been thought well enough of to be awarded an honorary master of arts degree by Dartmouth College. (Masters of Arts were generally honorary then, but were normally awarded to a college's own graduates.) Before coming to Chicago, he had written an innovative grammar book.

The first Chicago high school opened in 1856, at least fifteen years after it was first proposed. In 1856, most big cities already had high schools. There were 169 pupils in the high school its first year, admitted by competitive examination.

There were three programs. One was *Classical*, primarily the study of Latin and Greek, as preparation for college or, as some believed, to strengthen the mind. This was reminiscent of the Latin grammar schools. The second program was *English*. Greek and most of the Latin coursework was replaced by English literature and, by Herrick's count, sixteen other subjects. This was in the academy convention obviously.

NORMAL SCHOOLS AND
TEACHER PREPARATION

The third program in the high school was a two-year program, open to students at least sixteen years old, a *normal* program for would-be teachers. They studied history, "mental philosophy" (a kind of prescientific psychology), and "theory of teaching." Teacher training was one of Wells' greatest interests. He had been Samuel A. Hall's student in the normal department in 1834 at Phillips Academy at Andover, Massachusetts. There were scattered efforts to prepare teachers in other academies, sometimes with state funding, but the first state normal school, in Massachusetts, would not be established until 1839. A normal school in Albany,

FIGURE 5-1   Chicago high school building in 1857. From *The American Journal of Education,* Volume 3, 1858, p. 536.

New York, was established five years later. David P. Page was the first principal there; his book, *Theory and Practice of Teaching. . .* , moralizing, advocating, giving practical suggestions for classroom management, would still be seen as a classic fifty years later. But there were only nine state-supported normal schools when the Chicago program opened in 1856, and there were no more than a few normal programs in cities. Even Boston had not established a normal school until 1852. It was part of a girl's high school when the Chicago program opened.

A few years later Edward A. Sheldon saw an "object lesson" display in Toronto, a formalized English version of the Pestalozzian teaching method. Sheldon returned to Oswego, New York, with the display, recruited Hermann Krüsi, Jr., son of one of Pestalozzi's assistants, and the Oswego normal school, state supported after 1866, became famous and successful. Thereafter, normal schools, supported by states, cities, or occasionally counties, rapidly increased in number.

In 1883, Colonel Francis W. Parker became a principal of the Cook County Normal School near Chicago. During the Civil War, Parker, who had enlisted as a private, won his promotions by bravery. He had studied in Europe and had been the successful superintendent in Quincy, Massachusetts. The "Quincy System," which he established, called for learning and teaching directed by the interests of the pupils and the creativity of the teacher. As a supervisor in Boston, Parker was not successful; the system there seemed too rigid to change. Parker was a latter-day romantic who believed first of all in the natural gifts of the individual, particularly the child, but also the teacher. With this he coupled, rather oddly, faith in science. In principle, judging by the curricula he suggested, the child would learn by inventiveness, and would learn about the world by learning science. But Parker's greatest strength was his faith, which cannot be recaptured in a few lines.

Wells "graded" the Chicago elementary pupils, placing each of 14,000 of them in one of ten grades. Although grading had often been discussed earlier, John Philbrick is given credit for having first "graded" a grammar school, in Quincy, Massachusetts, in 1847. Perhaps the idea had been a kind of translation from the old Latin grammar schools, which had had "forms" since their beginnings in America. Perhaps the idea was borrowed: Mann had been impressed by grades in German schools. "Grading" was quickly and widely adopted. Most often, there were eight grades in a grammar school, but in the South there were seven, and many of the city schools added kindergartens. Usually a "grade" covered a year's work (and a year in the school life of the pupil, or more if the pupil "failed"). Many city grade schools had promotions twice a year, and a few even more often. Buffalo's schools had only three grades, or "departments," although nine years of instruction after kindergarten was offered—perhaps this was not grading at all. Chicago and a few other cities numbered grades starting with the highest; the student in first grade was in the graduating class. (West Point and Annapolis still use this sytem.)

A graded school had immediately obvious advantages. A class could be taught as a whole, and the old endless routine of one-by-one recitation would have been abandoned. A teacher in a graded school could specialize in teaching one grade, and would be more productive: Adam Smith's principle of division of labor had been applied. A third advantage was that discipline, especially in the earlier grades, would be easier to maintain.

The difficulties were less obvious. One of them was, and is, that the pupils could no longer advance at their own rate. Another probably more subtle disadvantage was, and is, that pupils met, studied, and played only with their agemates, and tended to lose contact with the worlds of those who were older or younger. The advantages were more obvious than the difficulties, and one might judge that they were greater if classes were huge, as they were during Wells's superintendency. In his last year as superintendent, there were 121 enrolled pupils for each teacher. Even taking into account the high absence rate (perhaps in the general neighborhood of 30 percent) a class of ninety is hard to visualize, but classes were that large. Also, teachers were unprepared by today's standards. As late as 1870, fewer than half the Chicago grade school teachers had completed either high school or normal school. In those schools at that time, however, perhaps the advantages were greater than the disadvantages.

Grading the schools also added an organizational difficulty. If graded schools were to be effective and satisfactory, content overlaps or omissions had to be avoided. That made necessary courses of study, which took much of the time of early superintendents. Wells wrote *A Graded Course of Instruction with Instructions to Teachers.* Much of it was taken up with essays, most of which were surprisingly humane and progressive. The book was far better known for its detailed course of study, an elaborate catalog of what was to be taught when. It was used in many school systems.

Wells resigned in 1865 because of poor eyesight and health. Chicago teachers loyal to him presented him with a $400 gold watch, a spectacular gift considering teachers' pay and the times. Wells stayed on in Chicago as a businessman and member of the Board of Education of Chicago and of the State of Illinois. He also helped establish the Chicago public libraries, the astronomical society, the Chicago Academy of Science, and the Chicago Historical Society. One infers that Chicago institutions for education also went much beyond the public schools.

AN ASIDE: MCGUFFEY'S AND OTHERS

The knowledge and values that schools tried to teach in this era are preserved like fossils in the schoolbooks of the time. The most famous of them was *McGuffey's,* eventually a set of six readers, starting with a primer and ending with a reader for what would now be a capable high school student. (*Webster's Blueback Speller,* survivor from early times, was probably next most famous.) *McGuffey's* is still well known because it was enormously popular. More than 100 million copies were sold. It is better known than competing readers, *Sanders* and *Appleton's,* for instance, not only because it outsold them, but because automobile manufacturer Henry Ford studied *McGuffey's.* He later purchased the log cabin in which the first compiler,

William Holmes McGuffey, had been born and had it restored at Greenfield Village outside Detroit. Ford also encouraged McGuffey societies. Nevertheless, there were better reasons for remembering *McGuffey's*.

The first of the *McGuffey's Eclectic Readers* appeared in 1836 and was compiled by William H. McGuffey, a former teacher, and president of a new college in Cincinnati, Ohio. His wife and younger brother aided in the compilations. Later there were revisions by the publisher's editors. Compared with the readers published after 1920, The *McGuffey's Readers* were over-moralizing, although they lacked much of the grim Calvinism of the various editions of the *New England Primer*. They have been accused of upholding conventional Victorian morality, which, in general, they did. *McGuffey's* were not openly abolitionist, for which they have been sharply criticized. Perhaps selling books in the South was too important to the publishers. (Another publisher printed practically identical books in the South during the Civil War.) However, it should be recalled that most northerners were not abolitionists before the Civil War, that Cincinnati was a border city, and that William Holmes McGuffey was a professor at the University of Virginia from 1845 until he retired in 1873. Conventional as *McGuffey's* was in other ways, it was first and last pacifistic, even in times of war.

Aside from values and issues, many of the *McGuffey's* selections were rememberable. Even Aesop's fable of the boy who cried "wolf" has remained in many minds. At worst, *McGuffey's* were stuffy. At best, they were much nearer to being literary than the primers that appeared after 1920. The 1857 edition of the fifth reader had two selections from William Shakespeare (edited and simplified) and selections from Joseph Addison and George Gordon (Lord Byron). One reader was criticized by some because English authors were favored. In the same reader there were also selections by Washington Irving, Nathaniel Hawthorne, William Cullen Byrant, and John Greenleaf Whittier. The readers were criticized by some because they favored American writers too much.

CHICAGO, 1864

Josiah L. Pickard was Chicago superintendent of schools for twelve years from 1864 until 1877. Pickard, a native of Massachusetts, had been Wisconsin state superintendent of schools before he had come to Chicago, and in 1871, he was the first president of the National Education Association (N.E.A.). Pickard was Chicago superintendent during the last year of the Civil War, when Whites' resentments of Blacks, an early sort of "backlash," had resulted in the segregation of pupils from 1863 until 1865. He was superintendent of the Chicago schools at the time of the Chicago fire in the fall of 1871. A third of Chicago's school buildings were burned then, and after the fire the high school was closed so that the building could be used for the courts.

As they did in every other big city, Irish and German immigrants had poured into Chicago. In Pickard's time they had acquired political power. As in New York

City, Catholic immigrants objected to the reading of the Bible in the schools, and Lutheran Germans joined with them in complaining. By forbidding the reading of the Bible, the Chicago Board of Education met that objection. Germans also succeeded in introducing German language in the schools, over the opposition of other ethnic groups. Discontinuing Bible readings was not common then, but many cities put German into the course of study. In a few places, such as Cincinnati, German became the language of instruction. The German version of *McGuffey's* primer is evidence of that.

In Chicago in the 1800s, the range of pupils attending the public schools increased enormously. At first the children of merchants and journeymen had attended private academies and schools, but they were increasingly drawn to the public schools—the establishment of the high school was probably related to that. Catholic parishes established schools, but many Catholic children attended public school. Many children, particularly the children of the poor, did not attend any school. In 1850, there were 13,500 school-aged children in Chicago, but only 1,919 enrolled in public schools. Herrick says enrollments in other schools were greater than in public schools, but perhaps half the children did not attend at all. Six years later Wells said that there were at least 3,000 children who had never been to school. A compulsory education law had been recommended as early as 1838, but it was 1883 before one was enacted in Illinois, thirty-one years after the first compulsory attendance law had been enacted in Massachusetts.

Like the earlier Massachusetts law, Illinois required all children between the ages of eight and fourteen to attend schools at least twelve weeks a year. The law was not fully enforced, and probably—in an age of child labor in sweatshops and before birth certificates—was not fully enforceable. There was not enough space in the schools for all the "truant" boys and girls. Nevertheless, in 1888 Chicago truant officers placed 9,799 children in public, parochial, or night schools. (In Chicago and in many other cities, night schools were at first for children who worked during the day.) The law was amended in 1889, to require eight consecutive and a total of sixteen weeks of school attendance each year.

In 1893, after several ineffective laws, the Illinois General Assembly passed an act forbidding the employment of children under the age of fourteen in workshops and factories. Compulsory education laws were generally ineffective unless there were also child labor laws. Although there were still children who worked in stores and still a diminishing number of truants, greater proportions of children attended school. As a result, the common schools in the cities, which most children would attend, required changed curricula, a subject we will return to.

Relatively little is known of Chicago teachers as individuals. Most of them were women. During the Civil War, women teachers outnumbered men teachers by sixteen to one, and by twenty-three to one in 1885. There were several causes for the employment of women and girls rather than men as teachers. Most obviously, women, who had fewer other career opportunities, could be employed for smaller salaries. In 1860, men beginning teaching in the elementary schools were paid $500 a year; women, $200. Twenty years later, when the starting pay for female high

FIGURE 5-2 The extraordinary popularity of McGuffey's work is indicated by the fact that special German editions like the one illustrated above from 1854 were published for German Americans.

school teachers was $850 a year, men were paid $2,000. It would not be difficult to cite a dozen or so speeches and papers arguing that women, because of their maternal—or perhaps submissive—nature, were best suited to be grade school teachers.

As Tyack has pointed out, the proportion of teachers who were women was greater where schools were graded; presumably it was easier for women to manage and teach a primary class, at least. However, there are still unexplained regional differences. Most teachers in Montana in 1880 were women, but most teachers in Indiana were men. It has been suggested that normal schools, because they cost time and therefore income, made teaching less attractive for men. The general matter should be further explored.

Most of the Chicago teachers were young. Some graduated from the normal program at eighteen, and those who graduated from high school were about that age. We would suppose that the other new teachers, appointed because of politicians' endorsements, were not much older. Not many of the woman teachers were married, although regulations against married teachers had not yet appeared. They were not married because, by the middle-class conventions of the time, many were too young to marry. Herrick remarks that the average teacher then had only seven years of experience. If she means that literally, Chicago teachers in the 1800s had more experience on the average than teachers in the 1960s, though probably less than now.

As far as we know, only three biographies of Chicago teachers have been printed. Eliza Chappell's biography suggests that she was a convert of the *New Reawakening*, passionately concerned with the redemption of souls, whether those of Indians or Whites. She was the first public school teacher in Chicago, as some calculated it. In Chicago she married a missionary and accompanied him in his missionary tasks. She survived long enough to spend her last winters in the warmth of Southern California and Florida. At the time of her death, on New Year's Day, 1888, nearly 130,000 pupils were enrolled in the Chicago public schools.

The second printed biography of a Chicago teacher is that of Chester C. Dodge, who was largely inconsequential. The third Chicago teacher who escaped anonymity was Ella Flagg (later Ella Flagg Young). Her family moved to Chicago from Buffalo when she was thirteen. In Chicago she had been a monitorial instructor in arithmetic, then had completed the two-year normal course. At eighteen she was assistant principal of the elementary school from which she had graduated, then was in charge of what would now be called "observation, participation, and student teaching" in the normal program. When it was eliminated, she transferred to high school teaching. One has the impression of Ella Flagg as a whirlwind of energy, a woman of great determination.

Pickard resigned in 1877 after a dispute with the board of education. By then the outlines of a city system had emerged. There were grade schools and high schools, and night schools for daytime workers. There was a normal school which, like those in most big cities, trained at least some new teachers in the system's ways. (Outside critics said city normal schools resulted in inbreeding, produced new teachers no different from the old by some kind of parthogenesis or cloning.) Within a relatively few years the city would have a vocational school: Pickard had already introduced manual training on a trial basis. As in many other cities, the first manual training school and kindergartens were privately supported. Kindergarten classes became part of the Chicago system in 1892.

Chicago school organization and staffing when Pickard left had assumed the form that would last without basic changes for a hundred years or more. The schools were under the direction of a central board of education, instead of local school committees or city government directly. The board of education (usually) delegated authority and responsibility to the superintendent, who was becoming increasingly powerful. There were assistant superintendents who were the beginning of a central office staff. In every school there was a principal in authority, and sometimes even an assistant principal.

Pickard became a professor at the University of Iowa, and then president there. He established some of the first university courses in education in the United

States, but only at the preparatory level. Later he wrote a book on the superintendency, one passage of which was a foretaste of what was to come. He saw the school as a factory, which was not new, but went on to describe the superintendent as a factory manager:

> In every branch of human labor the importance of supervision has grown with the specialization of labor. The more minute the division of labor, the greater the need of supervision. . . . [To each], what he has done is complete in itself. He has accepted his place in the plan about which he gives himself no anxiety. But his work is only a part, in the great plan. . . . He might acquire the knowledge, but at the expense of his efficiency in the special work he is to perform. Over him . . . stands one whose special work is to adjust the parts, make himself familiar with each, but freed from active work in any part. He is the overseer, the superintendent.

"MANUAL LABOR" SCHOOLS

In 1818, Joseph Green Cogswell, a New England intellectual, had visited a school, or rather a complex of schools at Hofwyl, near Berne, Switzerland. The founder and principal of the schools was Phillip Emmanuel von Fellenberg, Swiss aristocrat, onetime assistant to Pestalozzi. Von Fellenberg believed that, in the words of John

FIGURE 5-3   Fellenberg's Institute at Hofwyl. From a nineteenth-century illustration republished in Paul Monroe (editor), *A Cyclopedia of Education,* **Volume 2 (New York: Macmillan, 1911).**

Griscom, society was "divisible into three parts, the higher, the middling, and the poor." The higher were to be taught values; the lower, acceptance of their station in life. The Hofwyl schools were for the sons of the higher and the sons of the poor. They were boarding schools, intended, as we think of it now, both to educate and to socialize.

In von Fellenberg's school for the sons of the poor, pupils were taught piety and were to learn to be satisfied with their places in life. They were also taught elementary school subjects and, by working in shops and in the fields, vocational skills. That school was also an important model, a model for "manual labor" or "industrial" schools in the United States.

The apparent survival and application of von Fellenberg's model is informative. The concepts for it were imported to the United States by several returning visitors, including John Griscom, who also visited Hofwyl in 1818. "Manual labor" academies were briefly popular in the United States for several reasons: exercise was good for students, costs were lower, and pupils would learn skills or trades. There was even a Society for Promoting Labor in Literary Institutions. But manual labor schools fell from popularity quickly, and the Society died before it held its first meeting. Perhaps it was inappropriate to teach trades and farming in academies that many attended so that they would not be mechanics or farmers.

It has been argued that the Morrill Act land grant universities showed the influence of the manual labor movement, and that may be. We will discuss land grant colleges in a later chapter. In the meantime, the manual labor academies were copied in Hawaii. New England missionaries had arrived there in 1821. Their first concern was to bring Christianity to the Hawaiians, the old fashioned hellfire-and-brimstone Christianity which had regained favor in New England in the "New Re-awakening." From this followed the familiar imperatives: To be saved one must know the Bible; for that it was necessary to know how to read, at first in one's own language and then in English. Common schools of a simple sort were established early. After that, it was important to teach Hawaiians everyday working skills. Girls and women were taught to spin and weave and sew, because cotton grew on Hawaii and the other islands, and inferentially so that the unclad naked shame of Hawaiian bodies would be hidden. Hawaiian students learned to farm, and they learned to be printers and bookbinders so that Bible translations and homilies could be given to prospective converts. The manual labor schools were not intended to be like academies in the United States.

In 1831, The Rev. Richard Armstrong came to Hawaii to do missionary work. Like several other missionaries, he became a government official, the "minister of education" of Hawaii. His son, Samuel Chapman Armstrong, who had "come home" to New England to attend college, became the commanding officer of a black regiment in the Civil War. He founded Hampton Institute in Virginia in 1868. Established for newly freed Blacks, it operated on the lines of a manual labor school. That inspiration, he said in his autobiography, had come from the manual labor schools he had known in Hawaii. Manual labor schools, modeled directly after Hampton Institute and indirectly after the Hofwyl school, became one of the most popular, and, many thought, the most appropriate schools for free Blacks. The influence of Hofwyl might have stopped there, but as it happened, it did not.

By the beginning of the 1880s, a few years after the Indian victory at Little Big Horn, many concluded that it was cheaper (as well as more humane) to school Indians, or Native Americans, instead of shooting them. One possibility was to bring Indians, children or young adults, to school in the East. For a time Hampton Institute had an "Indian Department." Later, Indians attended Carlisle School in Pennsylvania, which followed Hampton Institute's—and von Fellenberg's—principles. We will return to the Carlisle School. Another obvious possibility was to build schools where the Indians were. In the Sioux reservation in what would become South Dakota, manual labor, or "work-and-study" schools were introduced. It was no accident, we are sure, that one of the first missionary teachers there in the 1880s, and the first superintendent of the reservation's schools, was Elaine Goodale, who had been a teacher at Hampton Institute. An "industrial room" was added to her schoolhouse immediately after she arrived. Manual labor schools were also established on the Navajo reservations in Southern Arizona and New Mexico. One of their promoters was a Navajo, J. C. Morgan, himself a graduate of Hampton Institute.

To trace the transit of the manual labor schools from Switzerland to the Navajo reservations, one starts by noting that the manual labor school, originated by von Fellenberg, became popular in the United States after John Griscom and others returned from visiting Hofwyl. We cannot show which missionaries, or missionary teachers, took the concept to Hawaii. Perhaps it was Richard Armstrong, who arrived in Hawaii the year the first manual labor school was opened there, was later an avid admirer of Horace Mann, and had a longtime interest in schools. We have General Armstrong's word that he brought the plan back from Hawaii. Richard Pratt, the founder of the Carlisle Indian school, was an admirer of Hampton Institute. Goodale, who set up manual labor schools for the Sioux, had taught enthusiastically at Hampton Institute, and Morgan had graduated from there. There are social reinventions, just as there are mechanical reinventions, but the record of the transmission of the manual labor school seems credible. Thriftiness aside, the manual labor school had benefits. Some benefits were to students. A sociologist might say that the manual labor schools were functional, in that they contributed to the preservation of society. Perhaps, taking the long view, von Fellenberg's school for the poor did indeed do as he intended, and teach them to accept their humble places in the world.

THE CATHOLICS AND EDUCATION

The rapid growth and expansion of the common schools was accompanied by the development of an alternative educational system for the Catholic population in the United States. Opposition to Catholicism had been strong during the early Colonial period. Although greater toleration of Catholicism had developed during the late eighteenth and early nineteenth centuries, anti-Catholic feelings were never completely eliminated. A latent fear of Catholicism persisted among Protestants during the early nineteenth century and became intensified as increasing pressure resulted from the waves of large numbers of Catholic immigrants who came to the United States during the first half of the nineteenth century. In many respects a new phenomenon developed: *Catholic* became synonymous with foreigner.

Opposition to Catholic immigration to the United States became strong during the 1830s. Many native-born Americans feared that the massive Catholic immigration to the United States would transfer Papal, or Romish, power to the North American continent. The Catholic church in the United States was in fact going through a period of extraordinary growth. In Ohio, for example, there was not a single Catholic church in 1816. By 1830, there were twenty-four priests, twenty-one churches, a newspaper, college, and seminary.

Other factors during the late 1820s and early 1830s contributed to the "Catholic problem." In 1827, the Papal Jubilee of Leo XII was celebrated, and led to an increased interest in Catholicism throughout the world. In the United States, Catholics attempted to win converts to their faith, which caused them to come increasingly to the attention of anti-Catholic groups within the country. Of even greater significance was the assembly by Bishop John England of Baltimore of the first Provincial Council of Catholicity, which met in Baltimore in October, 1829. Ostensibly, England's purpose in calling the Council was to calm the fears of many native Americans about foreign churchmen taking control of the Catholic church in the United States. It was intended to encourage the growth of a more American church with native, rather than foreign, leadership.

Rather than quieting nativistic fears, however, the Council had just the opposite effect. A total of thirty-eight decrees were issued by the Council. American Catholics were warned against corrupt translations of the Bible and were encouraged to build parochial schools for their children. The dangers inherent in a secular education were clearly outlined by the members of the Council. As they explained in their report:

> Listen not to those who would persuade you that religion can be separated from secular instruction. If your children, while they advance in human sciences, are not taught the science of the saints, their mind will be filled with every error, their hearts will be receptacles of every vice, and that very learning which they have acquired, in itself so good and so necessary, deprived of all that could shed on it the light of heaven, will be an additional means of destroying the happiness of the child, embittering still more the chalice of parental disappointment, and weakening the foundations of the social order.

Such statements, combined with the suggestions that non-Catholic children should be baptized if there was a possibility that they might eventually be raised as Catholics, tended to raise antagonism among non-Catholics.

During this early period, anti-Catholic sentiment was focused in New York, Philadelphia, Boston, and other urban centers. Organization of those opposed to the Catholics was relatively limited and ill defined. Beginning during the late 1820s, however, both in England and the United States an increasing number of tracts and articles were published that were critical of Catholicism. In New York on January 2, 1830, the first issue of the anti-Catholic newspaper *The Protestant* was published under the editorship of the Reverend George Bourne. Bourne saw himself as defending Protestantism against "Romish corruptions" and "monkish traditions." Although the newspaper initially met with opposition and underwent major editorial reorganization, its influence increased. Changing its name to *The Protestant Magazine* and becoming a monthly in 1833, it spawned other publications, such as *The Anti-Romanist*, which began publication as a weekly newspaper in 1834.

Anti-Catholic feelings were by no means limited to the press during the early 1830s. Under the leadership of Reverend W. C. Brownlee, the editor of *The Protestant*, and others, the New York Protestant Association was organized in 1832. The association was "to promote the principles of the Reformation by public discussions which shall illustrate the history and character of Popery." Meetings were open to the public and Catholics were in regular attendance, although the Bishop of New York eventually prohibited priests from attending the meetings and answering the charges of the Protestants. Violence often interfered with the sessions. In May of 1832, Catholics attending a meeting of the association became involved in a minor riot. At a meeting in 1835, where the subject "Is Popery Compatible with Civil Liberty?" was being discussed, a mob largely made up of Catholics broke into the hall where the meeting was being held, drove out the speakers, and destroyed the furniture.

Rioting and mob violence tended to create sympathy for the Protestant Association and focus attention on its cause. By the end of the decade published debates between the anti-Catholic and pro-Catholic groups were being regularly published in journals and newspapers. The outcome of these debates seems to have consistently been in the favor of the Catholics, and as a result a new type of strategy began to be employed by anti-Catholic groups. Beginning at this time a number of major anti-Catholic works were circulated and popularly received, including Anthony Gavin's *Master Key to Popery*: Scippio de Ricci's *Female Convents. Secrets of the Nunneries Disclosed*; Maria Monk's *Awful Disclosures of the Hotel Dieu Nunnery of Montreal*; and Richard Baxter's *Jesuit Juggling: Forty Popish Frauds Detected and Disclosed*. All of these works depicted Catholicism as a highly immoral religion in which priests kept convents in order to avoid their vows of celibacy. They told of secret passageways connecting the homes of priests with convents and of the bodies of babies found abandoned under convents.

The establishment and running of schools by the Catholics was seen by many anti-Catholics as a deliberate attempt by the Catholic leadership to indoctrinate children, especially Protestant children, into their system of values and beliefs. Opposition was early directed against the organization of Catholic schools. In some instances, this opposition took the form of mob violence. In August of 1834, for example, the school run by a community of Ursuline teaching nuns was burned by an angry mob in Charlestown, Massachusetts.

The burning of the Ursuline convent in Charlestown, brought national attention to the anti-Catholic movement. By 1836, the American Society to Promote the Principles of the Protestant Reformation had come into existence as an offshoot of the New York Protestant Association. It was the first national group of its type. The group had two purposes: the first to distribute anti-Catholic materials that would make clear the threat of popery, and the second to convert Catholics to Protestants. The group was extremely successful, sponsoring lecturers and organizing affiliate groups throughout the country.

If various Protestant groups feared the corruption of the Republic by the Catholics, the Catholics were likewise fearful of the corruption of their childrens' faith by Protestant educators and their schools. As the Common School Movement became an increasingly powerful force during the late 1830s and early 1840s, many Catholics saw it as posing a threat to the religious values that they held to be important. Religious materials were being consistently introduced into the curricula of the common schools. Above all, Catholics complained about the use of Protestant hymns, prayers, and, in particular, the King James version of the Bible as a regular part of the instruction. Even the reading of the Bible without interpretation was anti-Catholic.

The inclusion of "Christian" material in the curricula of the common schools had been suggested by nearly all of the early leaders of the Common School Movement, including Horace Mann. Mann argued that a common core of Christianity

FIGURE 5-4   "The American River Ganges" by Thomas Nast, *Harper's Weekly,* **Vol. 15,** September 30, 1871, p. 916.

THE AMERICAN RIVER GANGES.

could and should be taught in the common schools. Specific sectarian creeds and beliefs were to be transmitted through the home. Through appeals to the traditional Protestant doctrine that the Bible was the principal source of knowledge about Christianity, the Bible continued to be a major source of religious instruction in the common schools.

Mann's philosophy, while excluding the specific doctrines of any Protestant sect from the schools, did not exclude what may be termed a more general or universal Protestant outlook. It was this general Protestant philosophy, evident in the common schools, that many Catholics strongly opposed. They believed that their faith was the true faith. The recognition of other religious beliefs on an equal footing with Catholicism was a denial of the basic truths believed to be inherent in Catholicism.

It was in New York that the Catholic schools developed their strongest following. Although there were five Catholic schools in New York City when the first Plenary Council met in Baltimore in 1829, the schools were hardly able to meet the needs of the Catholic population of the city, which numbered approximately 35,000. Under the leadership of Catholic bishop John DuBois, attempts were made to cooperate with the Public School Society in order to provide Catholic children with schooling. Despite numerous attempts at compromise, the leaders of the Public School Society could not comprehend why Catholics, in particular the poor Irish, were unwilling to send their children to the Society's schools.

With the death of Bishop DuBois in 1838, John Hughes, DuBois's assistant, was ordained the bishop of New York. Hughes was forty-one when he became bishop and was highly energetic in defending the Catholic cause. Of poor Irish origins, Hughes established himself as a militant defender of Catholic interests.

When Hughes assumed the position of bishop in 1839, there were a total of about 60,000 Catholics living in New York City. Approximately 3,000 children attended the Catholic schools. Arguing that the entire population of Catholic children should be provided the opportunity to receive a Catholic education, Hughes sailed to Europe in the fall of 1839 to seek funds for a new college and seminary (later to become Fordham University) and to bring back priests and teachers who could work in the Catholic schools.

While Hughes was visiting Europe, the Governor of New York, William H. Seward, took a remarkable stand in his second annual report to the legislature. Seward had been informed that very few Irish Catholic children were attending the public schools. As a result, he called for a system of schools to be established at public expense that would be acceptable to the Catholics from a religious point of view. According to Seward, the Catholics had special educational needs. Calling for the establishment of schools in which teachers spoke the same language and were of the same religious faith as those whom they taught, Seward advocated a remarkably sensitive (for a Whig politician) and radical solution to the Catholic school problem.

The Catholic leadership, under the direction of Dr. John Power, who acted in Hughes's absence while he was in Europe, interpreted Seward's report as an invitation to apply for state funds to support their schools. Traveling to Albany and consulting with various legislators who were close to Seward, Power was encouraged to submit a request for a public subsidy for the Catholic schools in New York City.

The Catholics submitted a request to the New York Common Council legislature for financial support on the basis of need. The public opposition was overwhelming. Members of the Public School Society quickly objected to the petition. Arguing that the Common School Fund was a civil fund intended to benefit all members of the community, the Public School Society asserted that the Catholics' schools served a limited and narrowly defined segment of the population. The Public School Society further argued, with some justification, that if public funds were given to the Catholics, then other sects would have an equal right to request support. Considering the limited resources available, the funds would be so seriously limited if the Catholic request received support that sectarian education would displace public or general education in New York City.

After reviewing their request for a month, the Common Council rejected the Catholics' petition for funding. Hughes returned to the United States from Europe shortly afterward and launched into a major campaign to receive financial support for the Catholic schools. Compromises, including the revision of textbooks that were offensive to Catholics, with the Catholics were attempted by the Public School Society. What the Public School Society failed to understand was that the Catholics were opposed not only to the schools and curricula of the Public School Society, but to the basic idea of common schooling as well. The Catholic outlook concerning the common schools and public education was clearly outlined in the Pastoral Letter of 1840 for the Provincial Council of Baltimore:

> . . . it is not through any reluctance on our part, to contribute whatever little we can to the prosperity of what are called the common institutions of the country, that we are always better pleased to have a separate system of education for the children of our communion, but because we have found by a painful experience, that in any common effort it was always expected our distinctive principles of religious belief and practice should be yielded to the demands of those who thought proper to charge us with error: . . .

Catholics' complaints were clearly justified. Readers, as the New York Common Council School Committee admitted, included passages offensive to the Catholics. The King James version of the Bible was used to the exclusion of any other translation. More important, the Catholics objected to non-Catholics interpreting scripture to their children.

In late September of 1840, Hughes supervised the drafting of a new petition to the Common Council requesting funding for the Catholic schools. Significantly, the new request was not based on need, as the earlier request had been, but as a matter of conscience. It was argued that public school education was a threat to the morality of Catholic youth. Under the supervision of the Board of Aldermen, a debate was held, on October 29 and 30, to allow both the Catholics and the Protestants to present their respective points of view.

Hughes led the debate for the Catholics. Arguing that the Public School Society monopolized public education funds, he maintained that individuals who held different attitudes and beliefs concerning the education of their children were no less deserving of public support. Representing the position of the Public School Society was Theodore Sedwick. According to Sedwick, the Public School Society was not involved in any type of dogmatic Protestant instruction of the type that the Catholics were talking about, but instead a generalized moral education. He argued that sectarian views were not a part of the schools and should not be as long as they were supported by public funds.

Attempts were made by the committee of aldermen to reconcile the differences between the Public School Society and the Catholics. Compromises were proposed. Catholics offered to place their schools under the supervision of the Society. The Public School Society agreed to submit its textbooks to Catholics for review. Neither proposal was accepted by the other group.

After inspecting the schools of both groups and debating the issue for more than two months, the committee advised the Board of Aldermen, on January 11, 1841, to reject the Catholics' petition, which it did by a vote of fifteen to one. Having suffered defeat at the hands of the New York City Aldermen, the Catholics took their case to the legislature in Albany.

Governor Seward, in his annual message in January 1841, again reconfirmed his support for the Catholics' receiving a share of the school fund. After prolonged discussion and debate, the legislature passed the MacLay Bill on April 9, 1842, which created a system of public common schools in New York City. Under the bill, no school teaching any religious doctrine was to receive financial support. This included the schools of the Public School Society. The bill also provided for Board of Education members to be elected by wards. The power of the Public School Society had been broken and, in its place, a more democratic ward system of representation established.

If the MacLay bill represented a defeat for the Public School Society, it was by no means a victory for Catholics. The MacLay bill had the effect of establishing a system of public schools in New York that were supposedly totally free of sectarian influences and that were ultimately under the control of a board of trustees drawn from the various wards of the city. The legislation also placed the schools under the supervision of the state superintendent of education. In July, following the passage of the bill, William J. Stone, a prominent nativist, was appointed to the superintendency. Despite the stipulation in the MacLay bill that sectarian influences be excluded from the schools, Stone allowed the use of the King James version of the Bible in the schools during his term of office. Following various protests, Catholics received some relief by bringing pressure to bear through their elected trustees.

The Catholic school controversy had three major effects that are of particular importance for the subsequent history of American education and culture. The first was to exacerbate during the period the feelings that were held by the nativists against the Catholics. The second was to undermine the domination of the New York City schools by the Public School Society and to substitute in their place a system of public common schools administered by ward-elected commissioners or trustees. And finally, it encouraged Catholics to establish an extensive system of parochial schools that would operate on a parallel basis with the public, or common, schools.

CONCLUSION

The second half of the nineteenth century saw the steady growth and expansion of the common school movement. Extending their influence beyond the elementary level, the common schools expanded to include secondary education by the beginning of the Civil War. By the end of the nineteenth century, the growth of public high schools had become so successful that they totally superseded the tradition of the academies.

Accompanying the growth of the city schools was an increasing tendency toward regulation and regularization. Administrative systems expanded along with increased enrollments. Regularization was also evident in curriculum and textbooks, with works by authors such as McGuffey reaching a national audience.

In the school systems that developed during the second half of the nineteenth century are rooted many of the bureaucratic and social traditions that have been responsible for shaping education in our own era. They were also responsible for encouraging alternative models of education such as the Catholic schools—alternatives that remained powerful forces into our own era. Yet the structure and intention of the schools was by no means set in stone. As will be seen in future chapters, many directions and many alternatives developed in the American educational system that were responsible for the definition of schools that exist in our own era.

CHAPTER SIX
COLONIALISM AND
SCHOOLING

The growth and development of the Common School Movement expanded the educational opportunities of many Americans. Yet the schools also severely limited equal access to and equal opportunities for many. We believe that for women. Blacks, and Native Americans, schools often served as a deterrent rather than as an aid in achieving equality.

For the purpose of discussing these groups, we believe that the concept of "colonial" schooling may be helpful. Our model is drawn from the work of comparative educationist Gail P. Kelly, who has constructed an "ideal type" of colonial schooling. Kelly describes the similarities of schools established in the 1800s by several European imperial states and imposed on their subjects in Asia and Africa. With the schools a set of values and norms were imposed. The imposed schools sometimes paralleled "homeland" schools, at least superficially, but transfer from colonial to homeland schools was impossible or difficult. Colonial schools did not afford entry into higher-status occupations. Therefore, they perpetuated inequality, sometimes in spite of the best intentions of their founders. Much of the school experience of women, Blacks, and Native Americans during the 1800s fits Kelly's model. It is our belief that schools have contributed to injustice and the perpetuation of inequality throughout much of our history.

WOMEN

Although Puritan women were taught to read so that they could know the Scriptures, they were considered to be easily corrupted. The account in Genesis of Eve's tempting Adam with an apple and leading him into original sin was a constant reminder of what was believed to be women's natural inferiority to men. Women were encouraged then to pursue domestic, rather than intellectual, ideals. Pressure for them not to engage in intellectual pursuits seems to have been fairly constant, even though, as has always been true in history, there were exceptions to the rule. Anne Bradstreet wrote

> I am obnoxious to each carping tongue
> Who says my hand better a needle fits
> A poet's pen all scorn I should thus wrong,
> For such despite they cast on female wits:
> If what I do prove well, it won't advance,
> They'll say its stol'n, or else it was by chance.

At another time Bradstreet felt compelled to justify her poetry, written only after she had cared for her husband and her children.

Interest in women's rights and education increased during the later 1700s as a result of Enlightenment debates on the rationality of women and their educability. Jean Jacques Rousseau in *Sophia*, his companion work to *Emile*, outlined in detail the possibilities and limitations of education for women. American thinkers contributed to the debate. In his "Reflections on Courtship and Marriage" (1746) Franklin argued that women should concentrate their educational development on fully developing their potentialities as wives. Benjamin Rush in his essay, "Thoughts upon Female Education" (1787), maintained that the education of the American woman should be quite different from that of an Englishwoman. Rush said the American should have a good knowledge of English, that she should learn to write clearly and to keep accounts. An acquaintance with geography and history would also be helpful. She should be instructed in music and dancing, as well as in the basics of the Christian faith.

In Europe much more radical theories concerning women were emerging. Among the most interesting of these theories were Mary Wollstonecraft Godwin's. She was born in Ireland in 1759 and was self-educated. A radical thinker for her time, she consistently protested against the low status of and limited opportunities for women. She did not hesitate to break accepted norms. In France, at the age of thirty-three, she lived with an American, Gilbert Impay, and gave birth to a daughter. Later, as wife of English philosopher William Godwin, she died giving birth to their daughter, Mary. (Mary would later write the novel *Frankenstein* and marry the great English poet Percy Bysshe Shelley.)

Wollstonecraft's first published work, in 1787, was titled *Thoughts on the Education of Daughters*. In many respects it was typical of the pedagogical and childrearing manuals written during her era. The primary purpose of girls' education was to prepare them for their roles as wives and mothers. In 1790, she wrote her first political work, *A Vindication of the Rights of Men*, a rebuttal to Edmund Burke's criticism of the French Revolution. Wollstonecraft wrote then in the belief that in France a new and just system of government was being created. When Talleyrand proposed a system of national education that excluded women, she realized that the rights of men proclaimed by the French Revolution would apply only to men. Shortly afterward she published *A Vindication of the Rights of Women*, which was to be the most important statement in the 1700s concerning the rights of women.

Sexual tyranny was no different from political tyranny, she wrote. While admitting that most activities of women were domestic, she argued that women must be their husbands' intellectual companions and that they should be capable of supporting themselves if necessary. To do so, education was imperative. Wollstonecraft called for a system of nationally supported elementary day schools for all children. Equal schooling would be provided for boys and girls, and there would be equal expectations for men and women. What Wollstonecraft desired was ultimately a society in which the qualities of individuals, rather than their sex, would determine what they would do and how they were to be treated. When she wrote, Mary Wollstonecraft's ideas were a radical departure from the accepted wisdom.

However, in the United States then, even liberal thinkers advocated schooling for girls so that they would be good daughters and become good wives and mothers. This was the stated purpose of Miss Pierce's Litchfield Academy, as the commencement speaker there expressed them (see page 139). Noah Webster, far better known for his "Blue Back Speller," wrote in 1804 about his ideal young woman, calling her "Sophia." Webster described a virtuous woman who had learned to obey and serve in her parents' home and did the same in her husband's household. As Webster explained:

> Without much knowledge of the world, she is attentive, obliging, and graceful in all she does. A good disposition does more for her than much art does for others. She possesses a degree of politeness which, void of ceremony, precedes from a desire to please, and which consequently never fails to please.

Virtue was Sophia's greatest strength. Such virtue was "the glory of the female sex."

Virtue and morality were seen as being an essential quality for the American woman after the Revolution. In the childrearing literature of the time, as well as in much of the educational writing, women were seen as being the guardians of the republic. A woman's personal needs were meaningless, except as they affected her as wife or, especially, as mother. Women were placed in the ironic dilemma of being exalted because of important spiritual and domestic qualities and, at the same time, being made most abject. The form of schooling was roughly parallel to Kelly's colonial schools. The values to be imposed upon girls and women were those of men. Aside from teaching, schooling admitted them to no vocation, except those of daughter, wife, mother.

Miss Pierce's Female Academy was exceptional, since most of the first academies for girls and women were, like other academies, short-lived, transitory, and operated by men. One of the more influential of these men was The Reverend Joseph Emerson, whose academies for girls and women were at Byfield and later at Saugus, Massachusetts. One of Emerson's students was Zilpah Grant, who became the principal of female academies at Londonderry, New Hampshire, and then at Ipswich, Massachusetts from 1828 until 1837. Students at Ipswich Female Academy became in turn principals of other academies for girls.

Two women, Mary Lyon and Emma Willard, are remembered as the founders of the first women's colleges, begun as Troy (New York) Seminary in 1821, and Mt. Holyoke (Massachusetts) Female Seminary in 1836. Willard had been born in 1787, and had taught at several schools before she opened her own school for girls in 1814. Believing, as Wollstonecraft did, that women were entitled to the same educational opportunities as men, she acted upon her beliefs by teaching her students philosophy, mathematics, and other subjects normally only taught to men. In 1819, she proposed that the New York State Legislature sponsor the establishment of a female seminary, which would be a model for similar schools throughout the country.

FIGURE 6-1   Mount Holyoke Female Seminary. From Edward Hitchcock, *The Power of Christian Benevolence Illustrated in the Life and Labors of Mary Lyon* (Northampton, Massachusetts: Hopkins, Bridgman and Company, 1852), pp. 288-289.

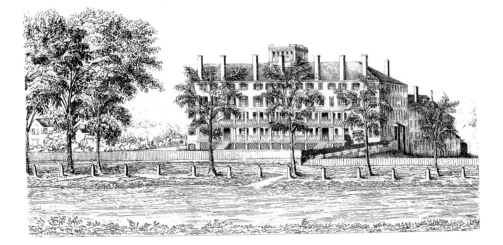

In her proposal, Willard presented four areas of instruction: religious and moral training, literary training, domestic training, and ornamental instruction. The proposed curriculum and stated purposes of the seminary recall Miss Pierce's Litchfield Female Academy. The primary purpose of educating women was to be a means of preparing them for family duties.

Religious and moral training for Willard meant instruction in Christianity. In her rationale for the literary training of young women, she argued that they should be familiar with the operations of the mind. As she explained:

> The chief use to which the philosophy of mind can be applied, is to regulate education by its rules. The ductile mind of the child is instructed to the mother; and she ought to have every possible assistance, in acquiring a knowledge of this noble material, on which it is her business to operate, that she may best understand how to mold it to its most excellent form.

Domestic training was intended to provide young women with the skills necessary "to make either good wives, good mothers, or good mistresses of families." Drawing, painting, elegant penmanship, music and "the grace of motion" would provide ornamental skills. One is struck by the apparent contradiction between intent and means. The proposal did not receive support in the New York legislature.

However, upon the invitation of the city of Troy, Willard established a female seminary there. Its curriculum included history, geography, chemistry, and mathematics. Many students were trained as teachers. "If the women were properly fitted by instruction, they would be likely to teach children better than the other sex; they could afford to do it cheaper. . .' she wrote.

Lyon had attended Byfield Academy and then taught with Zilpah Grant at Ipswich Female Academy. (Grant was in ill health; otherwise she might have been the college founder.) Lyon's intent was to set up a college-level school that would attract the daughters of the well-to-do but also young women of moderate financial means.

Lyon strongly emphasized religion as a part of the school's training. Domestic skills were not formally taught, but the students were expected to perform domestic activities as part of their normal activities. Lyon's curriculum was patterned after Amherst College's. A sophisticated curriculum it included subjects such as mathematics and chemistry. Students were to attend the school for three years. The school had laboratory facilities and a library.

Despite the efforts of Willard and Lyon, the general acceptance of higher, and even secondary, education for women was gradual during the nineteenth century. Women were simply not seen by many as needing schooling. In a satirical article in the Springfield, Massachusetts *Republican and Journal*, March 14, 1835, the establishment of a proposed college for women in Lexington, Kentucky, was discussed. The author suggested that the college seriously consider awarding the degrees of M.P.M. (Mistress of Pudding Making), M.D.N. (Mistress of the Darning Needle), and so on.

By the first half of the 1800s, schooling for women had become more freely available and was more extended. However, values and norms—and roles—were still imposed. Just before 1850, English author Harriet Martineau had written that in the United States there were only seven kinds of jobs for women: to teach, to do needlework, to keep boarders, to set type, to bind books, to work in a cotton mill, or to be a servant. That does not suggest that women's schooling had prepared them for more prestigious occupations. In the mid-1800s, schooling for women was still, as in Kelly's model, colonial.

After the Civil War there was increased support for the establishment of institutions of higher education for women. Women's colleges appeared more rapidly. Vassar had been established in 1861, Wellesley was established in 1870, and Bryn Mawr in 1885.

As early as 1837, women had been admitted to Oberlin College. Yet, as historian Jill Conway and others have pointed out, women were not treated as men were. Oberlin's male students worked on the school's farm to pay for their education. Women performed domestic duties, such as cooking and waiting on tables. Work roles were defined by sex and recreated norms and values then prevalent in the larger culture. But by 1900, approximately 80 percent of the professional schools, universities, and colleges admitted women. Schools of law and of medicine enrolled female students.

In 1869, in his inaugural address as president of Harvard, Charles W. Eliot said that although Harvard had excluded women for practical reasons, it was his belief that

> The world knows next to nothing about the natural capacities of the female sex. Only after generations of civil freedom and social equality will it be possible to obtain the data necessary for an adequate discussion of woman's natural tendencies, tastes, and capabilities.

Although somewhat less so, schooling for women tended to be colonialist even in 1900. There were still inequities, especially in professional and graduate education. However, secondary courses were the same for young men as for young women. Vocational education had appeared for both of them at the high school level. In 1900, there were colleges for women, although there were more colleges for men. Many colleges were coeducational, but men there outnumbered women.

Mary Calkins, the first woman to complete doctoral requirements in the Department of Philosophy at Harvard, was never awarded her Ph.D. because she was a woman. As a guess, only one student in twenty-five in schools of law, medicine, or dentistry was a woman.

However, like nearly all else, colonialism in education is a matter of degree. The degree of colonialism was not of much interest to women who were discriminated against then. But, that there was a change, a lessening, is informative.

BLACKS

Slavery during the South during the early 1800s became a carefully regulated institution. Slave codes prohibited slaves from holding property, from leaving their master's land without specific permission, from carrying firearms, and from striking a white man even in self-defense. Laws throughout the South prohibited slaves' learning to read and write. A law, for example, was passed in Mississippi in 1832, making illegal the assembly of "slaves, free Negroes, or mulattoes" for the purpose of teaching them reading or writing. In Louisiana in 1830, a law was passed that stated:

> ... all persons who shall teach, or permit or cause to be taught, any slave in this State, to read or write, shall, upon conviction thereof, ... be imprisoned not more [sic] than one month nor more than twelve months.

Legislation from this period clearly showed the conviction that educating slaves had the "tendency to excite dissatisfaction in their minds, and to produce insurrection and rebellion." The North Carolina General Assembly passed a law that provided for fines of from $100 to $200 upon any white person selling a book to or teaching a slave to read. A free Black teaching a slave to read could receive a minimum of twenty lashes with the whip. A slave found guilty of teaching another slave to read or write was to be sentenced to thirty-nine lashes. As the law implied, there were some free Blacks and a few slaves who had learned to read.

Many justifications were provided for not educating slaves. Most important, an eduated slave population would be much more likely to rebel than one that was kept ignorant. Insurrections were a real problem and a dread. In 1800, "Colonel" Gabriel Prosser organized a thousand slaves in revolt outside of Richmond, Virginia. In 1822, a free Black, Denmark Vesey, attempted to organize a major revolt in Charleston, South Carolina. A rebellion in 1831, under the leadership of slave preacher Nat Turner, caused the death of sixty white men, women, and children in southeastern Virginia.

Slave tradition, custom, and oral learning formed a subculture that could not be eradicated. The rhythms of African music would echo in spirituals and reecho in jazz. The syntax of African languages was transliterated, to contribute to "Black English." On the isolated Sea Islands of Georgia, Gulla, an African language, was preserved and perhaps survives still. Although some families were broken up when a member was "sold down the river" (to the Louisiana sugar cane plantations), there were many stable, and extended, slave families.

Although slavery was abolished in the northern states in the late 1700s and early 1800s, Blacks were neither welcomed, treated as equals, nor encouraged to become educated in the North. Even after the common school movement was embraced there in the 1840s, Blacks were discriminated against in schooling. In

New York City the "African School" was resumed, and "African schools" or segregated schools predominated there despite the efforts of some Blacks and their white supporters to achieve integrated education. In Chicago, elementary schools would never be legally segregated; in Massachusetts, segregated schools were banned in 1852, but those were exceptions. Free Blacks in the North established several literary societies. Their purpose was to provide libraries and reading rooms for Blacks and to encourage the literary endeavors of their members and to sponsor speeches and debates. These groups seem to have been patterned largely after the lyceums and were undoubtedly established because Blacks could not become members of white literary societies and lyceums.

Abolitionists, as might have been expected, gave important support and encouragement to the schooling of Blacks: The association of black schooling with abolitionists provided many people with an easy excuse not to support the educational cause of northern Blacks. Leon Litwak, in *North of Slavery: The Negro and Free States, 1790-1860*, describes the interesting example of Prudence Crandall's school for black girls.

Crandall was a young Quaker teacher who became an abolitionist. In 1831, she established a successful girls' boarding school in Canterbury, Connecticut. In the school's second year Crandall admitted a black student. Immediate protests were made by many of the white parents who were sending their children to her school. Support for the school by the community ended. Crandall contacted leading abolitionists, including William Lloyd Garrison, about the possibility of opening the school for black women and girls only. With the support of nearly all the major black leaders in the North, Crandall opened an academy for black women and girls in 1833.

The citizens of Canterbury violently opposed the school, arguing that it would lower the value of property in the town, and that Blacks living in the town would claim to be the equals of black students, and so equal to the local white citizenry. The school was seen as an abolitionist plot to foist "upon the community a new species of gentility, in the shape of sable belles."

Offers to purchase Crandall's home and school were made by local townspeople. Crandall refused their offers and persisted. In April 1833, when the school opened, Crandall and her students were consistently harassed. Manure was thrown down the school's well, stores refused to sell to Crandall, the local physician refused to treat ill students, and local officials threatened to enact vagrancy laws against them. The town appealed to the Connecticut legislature to take action against the school. It responded by passing a law prohibiting the establishment of any school or literary institution for the education of Blacks who did not live in the state. Crandall refused to close the school and was arrested. She was brought to trial, but the jury was unable to reach a verdict. A second trial found Crandall guity, but the case was overturned in appellate court, for technical reasons. Attacks against the school continued, and there was an attempt to burn it. Finally, in September, 1834, Crandall closed her school and moved to Illinois.

Four years later, in 1838, the state repealed the law. Yet the climate in which it was passed was not much changed. Although Blacks in the North felt less opposition to their schooling during the years just before the Civil War, theirs was consistently inferior schooling. Segregated schools predominated.

Blacks were denied access to most colleges and universities during the first half of the nineteenth century. By midcentury, liberalized admission policies more often allowed the admission of qualified black students. By the beginning of the Civil War, Amherst, Dartmouth, Oberlin, Union, Princeton, and other colleges had accepted black students, but very few Blacks attended colleges. Most Blacks were not qualified for admission. Black leaders complained that without equality of elementary and secondary schooling, there would be little access to higher education.

The Civil War profoundly redefined the condition of the American Black. In September 1862, President Lincoln issued the Emancipation Proclamation, which declared that slaves in the Confederacy were to be permanently free. The ratification of the Thirteenth Amendment, on December 18, 1865, freed all slaves.

As Union troops fought their way into the South, it became necessary to resettle Blacks displaced by the war. General Sherman and other northerners called for philanthropic support for resettlement and for schooling. Responses to their appeals came quickly, from philanthropic freedmen associations. Money, food, clothing, teachers, and ministers were sent to the South to aid the refugees.

Schooling, although not the first concern of freedmen programs, soon became important. At the instigation of General Edward L. Pierce and the philanthropic New England Freedman's Bureau, the Port Royal experiment was begun in March 1862. Thirty-five New Englanders were sent to teach Blacks living on the Sea Islands off the coast of Georgia. Union forces had captured the islands; the plight of Blacks there was desperate. An additional forty-one New England teachers followed that year. Some teachers left in disgust; one stayed on for decades.

Hundreds of other teachers supported by philanthropic societies went to the South to teach the freed slaves. The federal Freedman's Bureau, established in 1865, supported schools and also hospitals. Freed slaves, and Blacks from the North also, taught Blacks—by 1869, 600,000 of them. Booker T. Washington's boyhood schooling demonstrates the variety of sources of support (and its slenderness) for the schooling of Blacks. The school he attended, in Malden, West Virginia, began in the home of a black preacher. His teacher was a black Union veteran from Ohio. The school was supported by the Freedman's Bureau ($200 for a new schoolhouse), by local taxes ($40 a month for four months each year), and by tuition paid by black parents. Three years later, after graduating from Hampton Institute, Washington taught in the same one-room, one-teacher school, where there were as many as ninety daytime pupils, and ninety more at night. He found time somehow to establish a library and debate society.

Black institutions of higher education were established. By 1865, Fisk University at Nashville, Tennessee; Talladega College in Talladega, Alabama; and what would become Atlanta University had been begun. At first they offered secondary school education. Only Howard University, founded in Washington, D.C., in 1866, offered essentially collegiate courses.

With the support of the American Missionary Association, Hampton Normal and Agricultural Institute of Virginia was established in 1869. The driving force at Hampton was General Samuel Chapman Armstrong. The son of a missionary to Hawaii, Armstrong had been the commander of a black regiment during the Civil War, and then became an agent of the Freedman's Bureau. He decided to establish a school for Blacks patterned on the Hilo, Hawaii, Boarding and Manual Labor School. Its emphasis upon the development of basic occupational skills combined with a work-study program was particularly attractive to Armstrong. He felt that it was well suited to the needs of recently liberated Blacks (as perhaps it had been for von Fellenberg's peasant pupils forty years before).

With the help of the American Missionary Association, Armstrong purchased a 159-acre plantation as the site for the school, at the mouth of the James River. It opened with two teachers and fifteen students. Hampton was to train students to be of service, to themselves and to the white community. With strong support from prominent men, including former teacher and brigadeer general and future President James A. Garfield, and Mark Hopkins, president of Williams College, the school was rapidly expanded. Armstrong's purpose was clear in 1868:

> ... [T]o train selected Negro youth who should go out and teach and lead their people, first by example of getting land and homes; to give them not a dollar that they could earn for themselves; to teach respect for labor; to replace stupid drudgery with skilled hands; and to these ends, to build up an industrial system, for the sake not only of self-support and intelligent labor, but also for the sake of character. And it seemed equally clear that the people of the country would support a wise work of the freedmen.

FIGURE 6-2   Hampton Normal and Agricultural Institute shortly after its founding. From Mary F. Armstrong and Helen W. Ludlow, *Hampton and its Students* (New York: G. P. Putnam, 1875), frontispiece.

An 1873-74 Hampton Institute catalog outlined a three-year teacher training course of study based on English grammar and composition, mathematics, history, and natural science. In agriculture such subjects as crop and livestock management and crop rotation were studied. The commercial course emphasized bookkeeping skills. The mechanical course provided instruction on household industries, sewing, printing, and mechanical drawing and penmanship.

Armstrong's ideal for his students was perhaps most thoroughly personified by Hampton's most famous student, Booker T. Washington. Washington, as he described it in his autobiography *Up From Slavery*, walked part of the 500 miles from his home in Malden, West Virginia, to attend Hampton. He arrived at the school after three weeks' journey, with only 50 cents in his pocket. He applied to Miss Mary F. Mackie, the head teacher, for admission. After Washington waited several hours, Miss Mackie directed him to clean a recitation room. Washington wrote that "the sweeping of that room was my college examination." Feeling that his future depended upon the impression he made on Hampton's head teacher, Washington swept the floor three times and dusted the room four times. Mackie accepted Washington, who quickly became a model student. After graduating, three years' teaching, and a year at Wayland Academy in Washington, D.C., he returned to Hampton as its first black instructor.

Washington's private papers show that he was a politic and sometimes dissimulating man. Publicly, Wasington saw the black man's place as being in the agrarian South. Education for the Black had as one of its primary aims "the fitting of him to live friendly and peaceably with his white neighbors both socially and politically." From the beginning of his career, Washington tended to accommodate and conform. Many critics have commented that rather than shaping the beliefs of his era, his public behavior was shaped by the values and attitudes of the culture then. (Or perhaps he had learned too much and too well at Hampton.) In 1881, at the suggestion of Armstrong, Washington was appointed the head of Tuskegee Institute, an industrial school for Blacks in the heart of rural Alabama. Washington modeled Tuskegee largely after Hampton Institute. The school was constantly short of funds in its early years, but Washington was an inspired fund raiser. By the beginning of the 1890s, Washington had fully formulated his philosophy of the institute and the means by which racial equality would be achieved:

> The Tuskegee idea is that correct education begins at the bottom, and expands naturally as the necessities of the people expand. As the race grows in knowledge, experience, culture, taste, and wealth, its wants are bound to become more and more diverse; and to satisfy these wants there will be gradually developed within our ranks—as already has been true of the whites—a constantly increasing variety of professional and business men and women.

Washington said that the Blacks in America would be accepted by Whites in time as a result of having demonstrated their merit and worth.

In that scheme of things, equality and respect had to be earned. He said that agitation by the black population for social equality was "the extremist folly." In

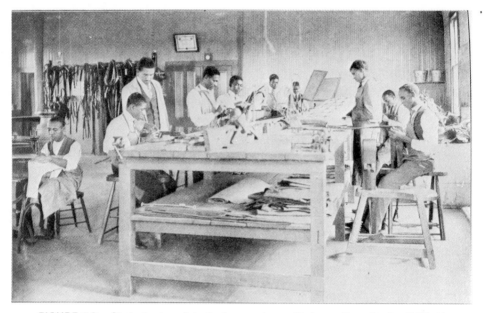

FIGURE 6-3   Students at work in the harness shop at Tuskegee. From Booker T. Washington (editor), *Tuskegee and Its People: Their Ideals and Achievements* (New York: D. Appleton and Company, 1906), pp. 270-271.

his address before the Cotton States Exposition in Atlanta in 1895, he renounced the idea of demanding social equality for Blacks. Arguing that the future of black people and white people in America were inevitably linked, Washington maintained that in the case of the Blacks

> In all things that are purely social we can be as separate as the fingers, yet one as the hand in all things essential to human progress.

The segregationist governor of Georgia congratulated him after the speech. Known as the Atlanta Compromise, Washington's speech was extraordinarily well received by the general public. Black protests about its denial of racial equality were largely ignored. A position was formally established by Washington, having consequences that would be felt well into the twentieth century.

Washington's Atlanta Exposition speech also established him as the principal spokesman for the American black community. He predicted that the Black in America would eventually come to be accepted for his or her own worth. Washington publicly ignored, however, the pervasive racism during the second half of the nineteenth century. Educational opportunities for Blacks, which briefly flourished after the Civil War, became increasingly limited and circumscribed.

Overt racism was evident in many forms. The organization of the "Ku Klux Klan," the "Knights of the White Camellia," and "White Empires," were obvious demonstrations of the hostility and prejudice of the white South. "Black Codes," or "Jim Crow Laws," after the Civil War, severely limited the rights of Blacks throughout the South. The Civil Rights Act in 1866, and the Fourteenth Amendment two years later, were unsuccessful attempts to provide Blacks with significant protection of their rights.

When Union troops left the South at the end of Reconstruction in 1877, Blacks' rights were eroded. Support for white supremacy came from many sources. In the Civil Rights Cases of 1883, the Supreme Court took the position that the Fourteenth Amendment prohibited states from discriminating against individuals on the basis of color, but that the provisions of the amendment did not prohibit racial discrimination by private citizens. Thus, the owners of restaurants, hotels, trains, and theaters could legally practice segregation. In the 1896 *Plessy v. Ferguson* case, the Court supported state legislation that separated Blacks and Whites. The Court's decision was that separate accommodations on railroads and other public transportation did not deprive Blacks of their rights as long as the segregated accommodations were equal. This same principle was upheld with the schools in 1899, with the Court case of *Cummings v. Richmond County Board of Education*, which held that separate schools for Blacks and Whites were acceptable if the facilities in each school were equal.

Critics representing the black cause voiced eloquent protests, but remained largely unheard. For example, in 1880, Frederick Douglass, the great abolitionist and black orator, maintained in a speech in Elmira, New York, that the rights of citizens guaranteed under the Fourteenth Amendment and the right to vote guaranteed under the Fifteenth Amendment had become a mockery. A "master class" had emerged as triumphant and the Blacks were in little better condition than they had been before the war.

Among the most powerful black critics, particularly in matters related to education, was William E. Burghardt DuBois. DuBois had been born in Great Barrington, Massachusetts, in 1868. Educated at Fiske University, Harvard, and the University of Berlin, DuBois was the first Black in America to be awarded a Ph.D. In his book *The Souls of Black Folks* (1903), Dubois directly challenged Booker T. Washington's version of the Black's role in American culture. DuBois opposed educational programs for Blacks that primarily emphasized the development of manual skills and acceptance of an inferior status. He argued for the education of the most "talented tenth" of the black population, preparing them for positions of leadership and authority in not only the black community, but also in society as a whole.

DuBois's arguments received relatively little support. They were clearly too divergent from the times to receive widespread acceptance. There is a certain irony in the fact that some of his proposals that were revolutionary at the turn of the century provided an important philosophical foundation for the Civil Rights Movement of the 1960s.

The system of education developed for Blacks during the eighteenth and nineteenth centuries clearly reflected the racism and bias of the larger culture and society. Black education fits well into the colonial model outlined by Kelly. Education was significantly different for Blacks than for whites. It was overall at a lower level; facilities were usually inferior to those of the white schools. Vocational rather than intellectual training was emphasized in the black schools. Black students were rarely able to transfer from their own schools into those of the mainstream white society. While higher education was available in black colleges and universities, it was generally inferior when compared with white institutions of higher education. It imposed Whites' values and customs. Finally, education did not provide general opportunities for advancement. As in Kelly's model, the schools were largely a dead end in terms of advancing the economic, social, and political needs of the black population in the United States.

It is our conviction that as long as a segregated system of schools for Blacks existed, opportunities for both education and equality could only be inferior to that of the majority culture. In essence, a colonial system was clearly functioning, effectively limiting the possibilities of education and advancement for Blacks in America.

NATIVE AMERICANS: INDIANS

Similar discriminations and limitations were placed upon the Native American, or Indian, populations. The history of Indian education in the United States can only be understood in the larger context of the European settlement of North America. Colonial settlers, whether French, English, or Spanish, viewed the "Indians" of the regions they were settling as a single people. The distinct character of individual cultures, their individual linguistic identities (there are at least 200 distinct Indian languages of at least six unrelated basic linguistic roots), were largely ignored.

Schooling for Indians was intended from the first to Christianize and "civilize" them. Some teaching missionaries realized that, in some senses, religion was dependent upon a way of life, so that it too must be changed. It is also true that missionaries had the cheering, and as yet unexamined, belief that their own way of life was best. Further, schooling served (even if that was not intended) to teach and maintain subservience of the Indians. Understandably, Indians often rejected missionary schooling. It is said that in 1744, the Iroquois were invited to send their sons to Williams and Mary; they declined.

> We know that you highly esteem the kind of learning taught in those Colleges. . . . We are convinc'd, therefore, that you mean to do us Good. . . . But . . . our ideas of this kind of Education happen to be not the same with yours. . . . Several of our young People were . . . brought up at the Colleges of the Northern Provinces; . . . they were bad Runners, ignorant of every means of living in the Woods, knew neither how to Build a Cabin, take a Deer, or kill an Enemy, spoke our language imperfectly, were therefore good

for nothing. . . . [I]f the gentlemen of Virginia will send us a Dozen of their Sons, we will instruct them in all we know, and make Men of them.

This became one of Franklin's favorite tales, a parable about appropriate and useful education. The Virginians declined the Iroquois offer, of course.

The incident was at least partly fictional, but it does emphasize one of the most important issues arising from attempting to educate Native Americans, or Indians. In general, attempts to "civilize" and Christianize Indians were a failure.

Between 1778 and 1871, a total of 389 treaties were made with tribal groups. They put under federal control 1 billion acres of land, four-tenths of the area of the United States. "Reservations" retained 155 million acres for the Indians, one seventh as much, and that was later halved. In addition, the federal government promised to provide medical, educational, and technical services.

Government funds were made available for Indian schools for the first time in 1819, when the Office of Indian Affairs was established. At the request of President James Monroe, Indians would be introduced to "the habits and arts of civilization." Money for the support of schools was turned over to various Protestant missionary programs who were responsible for establishing and running the schools.

The Reverend Cyrus Kingsbury, superintendent of schools in the Choctaw mission, which was run by the American Board of Commissioners for Foreign Missions (a sub-group of the Congregationalist church), reported in 1822 to the Secretary of War John C. Calhoun that the school which he was responsible for running for Indian boys was based on the monitorial method of instruction. In addition to being employed in various agricultural endeavors, some of the boys at the school were being taught to be blacksmiths. Women attending the female school were being taught domestic skills. An attempt was made to have the school, as much as possible, be self-supporting.

Support for the "civilization" policy of the Indians was widespread by the middle of the 1820s. In 1824, the Committee on Indian Affairs of the House of Representatives reported that eighteen new Indian schools had been established under federal sponsorship since 1819. The outlook provided was extremely optimistic. As the committee reported:

> It requires but little research to convince every candid mind that the prospect of civilizing our Indians was never so promising as at this time. . . . The instruction and civilization of a few enterprising youths will have an immense influence on the tribes to which they belong.

According to the committee, the educational program which it supported would grow in "geometrical proportion" as educated Indians convinced their fellow citizens of the virtues of the white man's culture.

Such an interpretation was overly optimistic. Attempts at providing education for various Indian groups proved to be largely a failure prior to the Civil War. Tribal resistance made the work of missionary educators extremely difficult. Few of those promoting Indian schooling were aware that most Indians saw themselves as surrendering their culture and traditions by accepting the white man's education. Katherine Iverson, in "Civilization and Assimilation in the Colonized Schooling of Native Americans," has argued that

> As "wards" of the federal government, Indians have found the land which was finally left as reservations to be held "in trust" by the United States. The economic as well as political decisions of tribal councils are subject to the approval of United States Bureau of Indian Affairs officials. Often "tribal" businesses are initiated and administered by federal bureaucrats. The federal government is responsible for the education of most Indian children, either through funding or direct school administration. Indeed it is surprising that more scholarly work has not employed what Cherokee anthropologist Robert K. Thomas calls the BIA agents' presence on Indian reservations, "a classic model of colonialism."

Evidence of educational colonalism is found in the establishment of boarding school programs by Captain Richard Henry Pratt and General Samuel Chapman Armstrong in the decades following the Civil War.

Richard Henry Pratt first became involved in Indian education in 1875, when as a young army lieutenant he had placed under his supervision at Fort Marion, St. Augustine, Florida, a group of seventy-two Kiowas, Cheyennes, and Comanches. They had been captured during the Red River War and sent to Florida in order to remove them as far as possible from their tribes and the setting of their uprising. While they were under Pratt's supervision, he was convinced that they could benefit from regular instruction.

Pratt's clear intention was to demonstrate that Indians could be civilized. Henry Benjamin Whipple (1822-1901), a champion of Indian rights, visited Pratt and his captives at Fort Marion in April of 1876. Recounting a visit of his to the school, Whipple wrote that Indian students were

> ... beginning to read and write. They have learned the Lord's prayer. They sing very sweetly several Christian hymns. I was never more touched than when I entered this school. Here were men who had committed murder upon helpless women and children sitting like docile children at the feet of women learning to read. Their faces have changed. They have all lost that look of savage hate, and the light of a new life is dawning on their hearts.

Pratt was convinced that the Indians could abandon their primitive ways and adopt white civilization and culture. His philosophy was neatly summarized in a speech before a Baptist convention in 1883. Where Indians were concerned, he explained that he was a Baptist and believed in immersing the Indians in white civilization and holding them there until they were thoroughly soaked.

Pratt's experiment in Florida received much attention. Although many political leaders were at first skeptical of his accomplishments, his experiment was conducted when attention was increasingly turning away from conquering the Indian population in the West to integrating them into American culture.

In 1878, the government ordered the Indians under Pratt's charge returned to the West. Most of them requested permission to stay in the East and continue their education at eastern schools. Permission was eventually granted by the Bureau of Indian Affairs, provided that they could find private support for their education. Private subscriptions from wealthy winter residents of St. Augustine eventually made it possible for Pratt to send seventeen students to Hampton Institute to continue their studies. General Samuel Chapman Armstrong, who had begun Hampton shortly after the Civil War, saw the opportunity to work with the Indians in much the same light as Pratt.

With the help of Pratt, Armstrong began the training of his Indian charges. Before the first year was over, he received permission from Carl Schurz, the Secretary of the Interior, to recruit an additional fifty students at government expense. Pratt was sent West, where he found forty Sioux boys and nine Sioux girls to attend Hampton.

A year later Pratt obtained permission and support to open an Indian school in the deserted army barracks at Carlisle, Pennsylvania. Pratt opened the Carlisle Indian Barracks school in October of 1879, with eight-two Sioux students. At first the Sioux leader, Chief Spotted Tail, was strongly opposed to sending Sioux children to the school, but eventually his objections were overcome. More children than could be accommodated applied to the school.

Before the end of the first year, forty-seven Pawnees, Kiowas, and Cheyennes were also enrolled in the school. Over the course of the next two decades, the school rapidly expanded. By 1900, more than 1,200 students from seventy-nine different tribes were attending the school. Support for Carlisle and Indian education was extremely widespread. In spite of whites' belief that the Indians were an inferior race with only limited potential, the programs at Hampton and Carlisle clearly demonstrated that the Indian people had the ability and intelligence to become members of the mainstream American culture.

Significantly, the curriculum at Carlisle emphasized industrial and manual training. In this way, the school was following the same approach taken in the education of the Blacks at Hampton. Indian youths were almost totally excluded from higher education and professional training. Although at first the Hampton and Carlisle experiments seemed successful, it is extremely doubtful that they were effective on a long-term basis. Part of the problem lay in the fact that once the students completed their training, they were returned to the reservations, where there was little opportunity for them to exercise their new skills. Many of them entered a limbo in which they were accepted neither in the Indian world, because of their training, nor in the white world, because of their race. Many cast off the veneer of civilization imposed on them by their school experience and assumed their prior Indian identities. In a well-known and extreme case, the Sioux youth, Plenty Horses, murdered Lt. Edward W. Casey during the Ghost Dance troubles at Pine

FIGURE 6-4   A group of young Indians before and after their education at Carlisle. From "Indian Education at Hampton and Carlisle," *Harper's New Monthly Magazine,* Vol. 62, April 1881, pp. 660-661.

Ridge in 1891. At his trial, Plenty Horses explained that he had committed the murder to wipe away the stain put upon him by his experience and to win a respected place among his people.

It is clear that by 1900, federal educational programs for the Indians were having relatively little positive impact. For example, among the Navajos, in 1901, there were between 4,000 and 5,000 children of school age, but only 300 of them attended schools. Limited reforms were attempted in the early decades of the twentieth century, but educational opportunities opened to the general population were shared by only a very limited number of Indians and with a very limited degree of success.

CONCLUSION

Despite its democratic principles of government, the history of the American people reflects a tradition of discrimination. The experience of various religious, ethnic, and minority groups, as well as women, has been critically shaped by this discrimination. The public schools, and the educational system in general, have played an important role in promoting the oppression of these groups.

The educational experience of women, Blacks, and Native Americans to a large extent followed models of colonialism. The education provided all three groups was imposed upon them and tended to reinforce stereotyping. Little control of their own education was given to any of these groups. Subject matter and information was imposed from without. Racial and sexual discrimination, inequalities of income, and the inequality of education between socioeconomic groups ultimately reflect the fundamental values and beliefs of the dominant or colonizing culture.

Yet, if the educational system often perpetuated oppression, it also—if imperfectly—provided individuals with limited opportunities to advance themselves within the culture. The development of education for women during the nineteenth century is a clear-cut case of how education was used as a means of redefining the status of an individual group. As will be shown in subsequent chapters, schools do have the capacity to advance the causes of various minorities. The extent to which they can do so, however, is ultimately dependent upon forces at work beyond the educational system and within the larger culture.

CHAPTER SEVEN
SCHOOLING AND
INDUSTRIALISM

The year 1876 marked an important psychological turning point for the American people. During its first century, the United States had emerged as a major social, political, and economic power. Western expansion had opened new lands and provided new opportunities. Three foreign wars and a Civil War tested the strength and will of the American people. The population had grown tenfold, swollen by waves of European immigrants. The Centennial provided an opportunity to pause and reflect on what had happened over the course of the preceding century and to consider the possibilities for the future.

The Americans did not celebrate their Centennial alone. Numerous foreigners came to the United States in 1876. Most came to participate in the Centennial Exhibition held in Fairmount Park in Philadelphia. Visitors often found the exhibits of machines and manufactured goods at the Fair the most tangible evidence of the accomplishments and power of the new nation. The unofficial symbol and technological wonder of the Centennial Exhibition—the 700-ton Corliss steam engine—pointed to this newly found power as perhaps no other single display could. For the visitors to the Centennial Exhibition, the message was clear—new types of industry and technology would dominate American culture during its second century.

If foreign visitors came to the United States to celebrate its accomplishments, they rarely left without commenting about the Americans and their culture. Among the most perceptive of these visitors, particularly concerning matters related to education, was the French educator, M. Ferdinand Buisson.

Buisson came to the United States in 1876, as the French Commissioner of Education, to the Philadelphia Centennial Exhibition. Although mainly concerned with preparing exhibits for the Fair, Buisson met numerous American educators, and also visited schools throughout the country. His reactions to these experiences were recorded in the report that he and his staff submitted on their return to France.

Buisson explained that schooling in the United States had become an essential part of the system of state and local government. As he perceived the situation, the Americans saw education as being far too important an issue to leave in private hands. They had united their national destiny with their system of public schools. As the early Republican educational theorists had hoped, the schools served the function of educating the nation's children to be patriots.

Buisson also recognized that the public schools were to be the primary means by which immigrant children were drawn away from their traditional cultures and Americanized. In his comments, Buisson was clearly critical of the idea of biculturalism. His praise of the American school system focused on its ability to take its recently arrived immigrants and to assimilate them quickly into the mainstream of the culture.

Yet, political and cultural socialization were not the only distinguishing features that Buisson recognized as part of the American public school system. Economic growth and development were also clearly linked to the American educational system:

> If the political future of the United States depends on the efficiency of her schools, her commercial future is no less directly interested. The conditions of labor in the New World are such that success depends, as it were, on a certain degree of education. . . . education has a double value: it has besides its real value a kind of surplus value, resulting from its practical and commercial usefulness. . . . The wealth of the United States is incalculable precisely because intellectual wealth counts for an enormous proportion. We sometimes think that the eagerness of the Americans to support and improve schools is a kind of national pride, vanity or show. Not at all. It is a calculation, and a sound one; enormous advances are made, but it is known that they will be returned a hundredfold.

Buisson's comments are confirmed by the educational trends evident in American schools during the second half of the nineteenth century. Beginning approximately at the time of the Civil War, American education became increasingly focused on issues related to industrial and technical training. In the case of higher education, this interest can be seen in the passage of the Land Grant College Act on July 2, 1862.

INDUSTRY AND EDUCATION

The Land Grant College Act, or Morrill Act, granted federal funding for the support of colleges and universities whose primary purpose was to teach engineering and agriculture. Under the grant, payments for the sale of federally owned lands were turned over to the different states in order to set up agricultural and engineering colleges. Each state received 30,000 acres of land for each of its senators and congressmen. Money from these sales was to be invested at a rate of no less than 5 percent a year, thus providing a perpetual endowment for the schools. A total of 17,430,000 acres of land was eventually turned over to the states. California, Ohio, Arkansas, and West Virginia used the money to establish state universities with agricultural and engineering programs. In Connecticut, the money received from the Land Grant College Act was used to endow the Sheffield Scientific School at Yale. In New York, special funds were provided to Cornell for the establishment of its agricultural and engineering programs. The same type of program was set up in Indiana at Purdue University.

The establishment of the land grant colleges clearly represented a major redirection in American higher education during the second half of the nineteenth century. But the program was not without controversy. Questions arose as to the relationship these new technically oriented universities would hold with the nation's older and more traditional private colleges and universities. The land grant schools were also reflections of an increasing process of modernization and industrialization sweeping across American culture. Higher education was seen in a new light. In 1872, the dean of the college of agriculture at the University of Missouri was maintaining that the purpose of the college was to "teach the science of high production" and to make farming competitive in attracting the nation's most talented youth.

The establishment of the land grant colleges reflects an increasing tendency toward the "industrialization" of American education. This was also evident at the elementary and high school levels, for example, programs in art education were first established in American schools in Massachusetts during the late 1860s. The motivation for the establishment of these courses was not to improve the aesthetic sensibilities of the children attending the schools, but instead was to train skilled draftsmen for industry.

As the Unitarian minister Edward Everett Hale maintained, the need to establish art programs as part of the Massachusetts public school system was because of their contribution to the development of the Massachusetts industrial system. As he explained:

> It will be impossible for Massachusetts to maintain any eminence in the higher manufactures if the great body of workmen of other countries are the superiors to our own in the arts of design, in the drafting of machinery, and in the habits of observation which spring from such accomplishments.

American interest in vocational training can be traced back to the early Colonial period. Besides traditional apprenticeship methods of instruction, proposals can be found as early as the end of the seventeenth century supporting the establishment of schools that would instruct children in basic trades.

Thomas Budd, for example, in his work *Good Order Established in Pennsylvania and New Jersey* (1685), argued that schools should be established throughout the cities and towns of Pennsylvania and New Jersey that would not only teach Latin and English, but also provide instruction in trades such as the making of mathematical instruments, woodworking, clock making, weaving, and shoemaking. In his *Proposals Relating to the Education of Youth in Pennsylvania* (1749), Benjamin Franklin repeated many of Budd's arguments.

Yet, the origins of what can accurately be called modern industrial education in the United States did not occur until the first decade of the nineteenth century. During the 1820s, vocational instruction was included as an important part of the educational programs of reform schools such as Boston's House of Reformation, and Philadelphia's and New York's Houses of Refuge. Training in these programs was not systematic, however, and was simply an attempt to have the children attending the reform schools contribute to their own support, as well as to teach morality and sound work habits.

The first major attempt to develop a systematic industrial education program in the United States was in conjunction with the school established during the 1820s by Robert Owen at New Harmony, Indiana. Owen, whose work at New Harmony was discussed in Chapter 3, placed particular emphasis upon manual and vocational training. Taxidermy, printing, engraving, drawing, carpentry, wheelwrighting, woodturning, blacksmithing, cabinet making, hatmaking, shoemaking, agriculture, washing, cooking, sewing, housekeeping, and dressmaking were among the subjects taught. Although Owen's utopian and educational experiment at New Harmony was ultimately a failure. it was an important early attempt to systematically introduce manual and industrial training into an educational program.

During the first half of the nineteenth century, a number of orphan asylums in the United States also included programs in vocational training. Among the best known was the program at Girard College in Philadelphia. Programs emphasizing several types of craft training were developed within a few years after the opening of the college in 1848. By 1864, provisions were made for the orphans at the college to learn trades as sophisticated as typesetting, printing, bookbinding, woodturning, photography, and even telegraphy.

Important programs in manual and industrial training were introduced by individuals such as General Samuel Chapman Armstrong at Hampton Institute in Virginia during the late 1860s, but it was not until the late 1870s that widespread interest in industrial education began to develop throughout the United States. Much of the foundation for this interest was the result of a modest exhibit of Russian drawings, tools, and models used for teaching manual and industrial arts that were on display at the 1876 Philadelphia Centennial Exposition.

The Russian materials were sent to the Exposition by the Moscow Imperial Technical School and were based on the work of its director, Victor Della Vos. Begun in 1830, the school was reorganized in 1868 under imperial sponsorship. Primarily for training draftsmen, industrial foremen, and chemists, as well as civil and mechanical engineers, the school provided not only theoretical training in various specialized fields, but also practical courses in subjects such as wood turning, carpentry, metal turning, fitting, and forging.

Under the supervision of Della Vos, the school's new system of manual and industrial training was developed during the late 1860s. It deemphasized apprenticeship training and focused instead on the principles of design inherent in the manual arts. Rather than following the traditional apprenticeship method in which a student learned a trade or craft by copying the work of a master craftsman, students under the Della Vos system learned the basic principles of design and fabrication that were the basis of the manual or mechanical arts. Della Vos's purpose was to teach students to become skilled in each craft area as quickly as possible and to learn the proper use of tools in each of the manual arts.

As part of his system of instruction, the following procedures were laid out: 1—each mechanical art or trade, such as metal forging, wood joinery, or carpentry, was assigned a separate instruction shop; 2—each shop had as many working places and separate sets of tools as students; 3—exercises done by the students were arranged in a hierarchy of difficulty; 4—all work was done from drawings rather than models; 5—drawings used by students in the beginning classes were prepared by students in the advanced classes; 6—students could not advance to a new project unless they had completed what they were working on and it had been approved by the instructor; 7—the grading of projects became stricter as the student advanced in the program; and 8—each instructor teaching a specialized trade, such as carpentry or forging, had to be an expert in his area. Training at the Imperial Technical School included both the secondary level and the collegiate level and took three years to complete for each level.

When Della Vos's method was put on display at the Centennial Exposition in 1876, the possibilities of using it in an American context were immediately recognized. For example, John D. Runkle (1822-1902), the president of the Massachusetts Institute of Technology, recalled how

> At Philadelphia, in 1876, almost the first thing I saw was a small case containing three series of models, one of chipping and filing, one of forging, and one of machine tool work. I saw at once that they were not parts of machines, but simply graded models for teaching manipulations in those arts. In an instant, the problem I had been seeking to solve was clear to my mind; a plain distinction between a mechanic art and its application in some special trade became apparent.

Runkle's interest in the Russian exhibit was a result of his experience with the problem of providing shop training for engineering students. On his return from the Centennial Exposition, Runkle recommended the establishment of a program in shop training based upon the Della Vos method.

On August 17, 1876, the trustees of the Institute approved not only a set of shops for the students in engineering, but also a School of Mechanic Arts at the secondary level for those interested in receiving general industrial training.

FIGURE 7-1 The exhibit of the Moscow Imperial Technical School at the 1876 Philadelphia Centennial Exhibition. The materials described by Runkle were included in the display cases in the lower left-hand corner of the photograph. Courtesy of the Free Library of Philadelphia.

Runkle was soon promoting Della Vos's method in reports to the Massachusetts Board of Education and the National Education Association. According to Runkle, students from M.I.T. trained under the method were clearly superior in shop skills to students trained under the more traditional apprenticeship system. Claims were made that if the Della Vos method came into wide use in the schools, it would be possible to double national production and to increase the wages of laborers by 300 percent. Through the introduction of Della Vos's system, workers would be elevated not only in terms of their skills, but in their social status as well. Conflicts between labor and management would be eliminated. Unionism, which was just beginning to emerge as a force at this time, would cease as a result of not having a cause or reason to exist.

Runkle's suggestion of establishing mechanic arts schools as part of the public school system quickly came to the attention of Calvin Woodward. Woodward was a professor of mathematics and applied mechanics and dean of the Polytechnic

(Engineering) faculty at Washington University, Saint Louis. An experienced secondary and collegiate teacher, Woodward, like Runkle, faced the problem of providing engineering students with training in shop skills. Having established shop training as part of the university program as early as 1872, Woodward began to argue the need for industrial training, not only as part of the program of specialized polytechnical schools, but also in the public schools in general.

In 1877, Woodward acquired the use of an old dormitory in Saint Louis known as the "Philbert Mansion" to set up a more extensive workshop for his students. Charles F. White, who had attended the Worcester Free Institute and the Stevens Institute of Technology, became the shop superintendent. Under White's direction, graded exercises in the use of machine tools were introduced as part of the program. White had seen the Della Vos method at the Centennial Exposition and had developed his own exercises based on it. In the "Philbert Mansion" were a blacksmith shop, a machine shop equipped with vises and lathes, and a woodworking shop.

In May of 1878, in an address before the Saint Louis Social Science Association, Woodward called for the establishment of a secondary school emphasizing both intellectual and manual training. With the help of Samuel Cupples, a Saint Louis businessman and philanthropist, Woodward began to assemble the support necessary for a new secondary school. After lengthy discussion, it was agreed that the Manual Training School be established as a permanent part of Washington University's Polytechnic School. Instruction in the new school would include mathematics, drawing, the English branches of the high school curriculum, and training in the use of tools.

A new building was completed for the school in the summer of 1880. Opening for classes the following September, the school was to provide students with a liberal education that emphasized the development of mechanical arts and skills rather than a specific vocational training. The school's program took three years to complete. By electing to take a foreign language as part of their coursework, students were able to complete three years of college preparation at the school. Most students, however, were expected to enter the work force once they had completed their course of study at the school.

The Manual Training School was an immediate success. Enrollment increased from fifty students in September of 1880 to 176 students when the first class graduated in June of 1883. While interest quickly developed throughout the nation in the school and its programs, there emerged at the same time a strong anti-manual-training sentiment among many educators. According to Lawrence Cremin, the debate that developed during the 1880s over the acceptance or rejection of manual training in the schools was the most vigorous pedagogical battle of the decade.

As one would expect, Woodward led the pro-manual-training forces. Support came from many sources. Graduates of the program vigorously promoted the establishment of new manual training schools throughout the country. On February 4, 1884, the second manual training school in the United States was opened in Chicago. Known as the Chicago Manual Training School, the school was privately

FIGURE 7-2   The wood-working shop of the Manual Training Institute, Washington University. From C. M. Woodward, *The Manual Training School* (Boston: D.C. Heath & Co., 1887), p. 26.

supported. On March 3, 1884, the first publicly supported manual training high school was opened in Baltimore. The programs of both of these schools were closely modeled after those of Woodward's schools in Saint Louis. Before the end of the decade, manual training schools could also be found in cities such as Philadelphia, Toledo, Cincinnati, New Orleans, Brooklyn, and Cambridge, Massachusetts.

Woodward clearly believed that manual training could provide students with a balanced general education. Writing in 1887, he argued that manual training programs would not only encourage students to stay in school longer, but also provide them with a superior intellectual background. Besides material success, the education provided by the manual training schools would help the worker deal with the demands of an increasingly complex technological society:

> The new education will give more complete development, versatility, and adaptability to circumstance. No liberally trained workman can be a slave to method, or depend upon the demand for a particular article or kind of labor. It is only the uneducated, unintelligent mechanic who suffers from the invention of a new tool.

Significantly, opposition to Woodward's ideas came not only from traditional educators, but from an important segment of the labor movement as well. A survey undertaken in New York in 1886 showed that the state's labor organizations favored trade schools and manual training by a margin of only two to one. Manual training further weakened traditional apprenticeship programs. Although cooperative efforts were gradually worked out between the various labor organizations and many of the early manual training programs, opposition came from powerful union leaders such as Samuel Gompers, who argued that the workmen produced by the manual training schools not only did botched work, but that they undercut the wages of skilled union workers as well.

Organized labor's opposition to manual training focused primarily on its introduction at the elementary level. Arguing that children were inadequately trained in various crafts, critics felt that emphasis on manual training, denied the worker's children the opportunity to study more traditional subjects. D. J. O'Donoghue, writing in the *American Federationist* in 1895, for example, argued that

> . . . even now too many children are obliged to leave school and fight for a livelihood long before they are grounded in even a fair elementary education, and yet we are told, and many of us are gullible enough to believe, that the time which is now devoted to imparting such an education in our public schools could, with advantage, be reduced so that our children may receive a technical education—and their minds directed away from higher pursuit! . . . A little careful attention on the part of the careful workingman will readily demonstrate that the first aim of the average advocate of manual training in the public schools is that of *utility*, rather than physical or intellectual improvement.

Schoolmen presented similar arguments. Among the most important of these critics was William Torrey Harris. Harris was the superintendent of the Saint Louis public schools from 1868 to 1880. Among the most distinguished American educators of the second half of the nineteenth century, Harris later headed the Concord School of Philosophy and served as United States Commissioner of Education from 1889 until 1906. His work combined both the practical and the theoretical. Under his supervision, the Saint Louis schools became known throughout the nation as a center for innovation in education. As the leading Hegelian philosopher in the United States, Harris spearheaded what became known as the "Saint Louis Movement," or "American Hegelian Movement," in philosophy. Harris was editor of the *Journal of Speculative Philosophy*, the first modern scholarly philosophy journal published in America. Besides providing a forum for the dissemination of German philosophical ideas, Harris's journal had the distinction of publishing the first articles of a young Vermont high school teacher named John Dewey.

Harris, like Horace Mann, believed that universal public elementary education would provide the children of the working class the tools by which to participate in the more general culture. He defined these tools as being grammar, literature and art, mathematics, geography, and history. Through their use, these "five windows of the soul" would allow the child the means by which to master both the mysteries of nature and of the human mind.

When the manual training movement became popular during the early 1880s, Harris opposed the movement because it emphasized the physical development of individuals instead of their spiritual development. Harris felt that manual training did nothing to develop the higher faculties of the individual. Training in manual arts, such as woodworking or forging, provided children with only a limited knowledge of themselves and nature.

Described by the historian Merle Curti as a "conservator," Harris supported a capitalist economic system. He felt that socialism discouraged the initiative of the individual, an initiative that was critical to the creative growth and development of the culture. As a follower of the German philosopher Hegel, Harris saw the process of history as being an ever more powerful movement of the individual toward personal freedom and away from domination by the group. For Harris, manual training did not contribute to the development of the individual's spirit. Hence, Harris rejected the ideas outlined by Karl Marx in *Das Kapital (Capital)*, and argued that in making his profits, the businessman or industrialist was in fact benefiting the entire society by developing more effective means of production and distribution, as well as by providing jobs for workers.

Despite arguments such as Harris's, support for the manual training movement increased during the last decades of the nineteenth century. Educators throughout the country argued that manual training would provide modern factory workers an effective means by which their children could receive the technical training necessary for them to be able to succeed in work.

Through the introduction of manual training in the schools, a partial solution was provided to the problems imposed by industrialization in the United States. The increasing use of mass production techniques meant that the worker did an increasingly narrow range of work. Under the older craftsman and artisan system, a clock, for instance, was made from beginning to end by a single highly trained individual. Using mass production techniques, factories in places such as Massachusetts would employ dozens of workers doing different tasks to make a single clock. Although efficiency was gained, the new methods left the worker with little sense of accomplishment at having produced a complete item or an actual understanding of the work process.

The tradition of the craftsperson and skilled worker was giving way to a new ideal of efficiency. Unlike traditional craftsmen, the new industrial workers in most instances had neither the means nor the skills to provide their children with the training necessary to effectively enter the work force. As a result, it became necessary for the school to assume many of the functions of the more traditional education. According to many educators of the period, children would once again have reinforced in them the traditional values of industriousness, thrift, and pride in work through the virtues inherent in manual training.

Marvin Lazerson has maintained that the manual training movement was perceived as a means of reconstituting American society. It was also seen as a vehicle for social reform. By providing practical education and training that would be of value in the everyday world of work, it was felt that manual training would help reduce truancy among the children of industrial workers.

Although compulsory education laws had been established in Massachusetts as early as 1852, such legislation had met with only limited success. Under the 1852 law, children under fifteen could only be employed if they had received three months of schooling in the year prior to their employment. Attempts to make the law apply to children working on farms and in stores, as well as to factory workers, failed. Similar types of legislation were passed, prior to the Civil War, in northern states such as Rhode Island, Connecticut, Vermont, New Hampshire, Maine, and Pennsylvania.

Factory owners and the parents of working children often found ways to get around the laws requiring compulsory school attendance. Careful birth and school attendance records were deliberately not kept by many factory owners so that they could not be held responsible for violations of the compulsory schooling laws. Children were often moved from one factory to another every nine months in order to avoid the requirement of being in school at least three months each year. Parents often cooperated in having their children work in the factories rather than attend the schools.

Although greed, and possibly fear, often motivated the parents of child laborers to cooperate with factory owners in ignoring the laws, economic survival must also have been a factor for many parents in sending their children to work. A working child could contribute an additional quarter or third to the income of a family, which in a period of extremely low wages could provide the additional means necessary for a family to survive.

Lucy Larcom (1824-1893), a onetime child worker, recalled in her autobiography, *A New England Girlhood* (Boston, 1889) just how important her working in a factory was for her family.

> When I took my next three months at the grammar school, everything there was changed, and I too was changed. . . It was a great delight for me to study, and at the end of three months the master told me that I was prepared for high school.
> But alas! I could not go. The little money I could earn—one dollar a week, besides the price of my board—was needed in the family, and I must return to the mill. It was a severe disappointment to me, though I did not say so at home. . . .

Stephen A. Knight, another child worker, recalled working in a cotton mill during the mid-1830s for approximately fourteen hours per day, with a half hour out for breakfast and lunch. Knight was paid 42 cents per week, or 7 cents a day—an hourly rate of one-half cent!

As mentioned earlier, vocational training was an important part of the educational programs of orphan asylums during the first half of the nineteenth century. By the 1850s, it was widely maintained that industrial training would not only provide an effective means of reforming juvenile delinquents, but would also act as a means of training the children of the lower classes to be industrious and virtuous.

The success of city and state reform schools by the late 1860s is indicated by their proliferation throughout the country. In their 1867 survey, *Report on the Prisons and Reformatories of the United States and Canada*, Enoch C. Wines and Theodore W. Dwight noted the existence of seven state reform schools outside of New York State, as well as municipally sponsored reform schools in cities such as Providence, Cincinnati, Louisville, Baltimore, Saint Louis, and Chicago.

As an attempt to prevent children from becoming delinquents, the New York Children's Aid Society (1853), the Boston Children's Aid Society (1864), and other groups were organized. The work of these groups was part of the earliest attempts in the United States to respond to the problems of children living in an urban environment. Earlier groups, such as the New York Association for Improving the Condition of the Poor (A.I.C.P.) established in 1843, had attempted to address the miserable living conditions that had begun to develop in New York and other major cities by the end of the Jacksonian era. Arguing that individuals raised in the squalid moral and social conditions of the slums would be insensitive to Christian morality, the A.I.C.P. attacked the overcrowded conditions of the slums, the lack of adequate sanitary facilities, poor ventilation in buildings, and the general conditions that they felt produced disease, intemperance, and a lack of morals among the urban poor.

The A.I.C.P. assumed throughout its early years that an enlightened capitalist system could provide good housing for the working class and still make a substantial profit on their investment. Promoting the development of housing with superior structural and sanitary features, the A.I.C.P. built its first model tenement in 1854. Located in the general neighborhood of Elizabeth and Mott Streets, near what today is Chinatown in New York City, the building included nearly 100 units with rents from $5.50 to $8.50 per month. The project proved to be a financial failure and was sold by the A.I.C.P. in 1867. Degenerating into one of the worst tenements in the city, the building was actually condemned by a committee of the A.I.C.P. during the 1880s.

Underlying much of the early work of the A.I.C.P. was the assumption that enlightened real estate investors would provide good living conditions in the tenements they built, while still making a reasonable profit on their investment. For too often, however, investors sought the maximum profit possible from the buildings they owned. Tenements were built as cheaply as possible, while forcing together as many people as possible in the smallest amount of space.

If attempts to improve the physical conditions of the urban poor met with little success during this early period, greater success was achieved with the various child welfare agencies such as the New York Children's Aid Society. Founded by Charles Loring Brace in 1853, the society had as its purpose meeting the needs of the destitute children of New York. Brace, a minister, set up Sunday meetings, established industrial schools, opened lodging houses for newsboys, and established reading rooms for poor children. Acutely aware of the physical and personal needs of poor urban children, Brace and the Children's Aid Society were also intent on providing them with religious and moral training. In doing so, Brace felt that the integrity of the American political system would be maintained. Referring to the boys and girls served by the Children's Aid Society, Brace argued in his work, *The Dangerous Classes of New York* (1880) that they would

> ... soon form the great lower class of our city. They will influence elections; they may shape the policy of the city; they will, assuredly, if unreclaimed, poison society all around them. They will help to form the great multitude of robbers, thieves, vagrants, and prostitutes who are now such a burden upon the law-respecting community.

Other sources from the period confirm that the children of the poor were perceived as being potentially dangerous to the future political stability of the nation. Wines and Dwight in their 1867 report on prisons and reformatories strongly recommended that compulsory education laws be established in every state in order to insure that all children learn proper moral habits and industriousness.

Calling for the establishment of public nurseries and industrial schools, Wines and Dwight clearly saw such institutions as providing substitutes for the family.

FIGURE 7-3   The night school of the Children's Aid Society. From *Harper's New Monthly Magazine*, Vol. 47, August 1873, p. 327.

Arguing that the discipline of the industrial schools should be of the family character, they explained that the arrangements of the schools should be such that they would

> ... cultivate industrious habits, and prepare their inmates for the stations they are afterwards to fill.

Practical labor promoting moral development was advocated as fundamental to the purposes of industrial schools. Skills for the workshop or farm or home, suitable kinds of recreation, and particularly appropriate schooling would reform poor urban children and provide them with the kinds of character and skills necessary to become members of the larger American culture.

The early initiators of child welfare reform programs, such as the Children's Aid Society, obviously did much to meet the immediate needs of poor children. They also consciously tried to impress upon their charges a specific set of moral values and limited economic expectations. We agree with Samuel Bowles and Herbert Gintis, who argue in *Schooling in Capitalist America* that most educational reformers during the later nineteenth century did not question capitalists' ownership and control of production. The purpose of educators was to help "preserve and extend the capitalist order." Schools were intended to inculcate students with values supporting the existing social system. If they were successful—the point is moot without good evidence—the schools contributed to the strength of the existing order and also encouraged its further expansion and growth.

Nearly a century ago the French sociologist Emile Durkheim pointed out that almost all educational systems tend to perpetuate the existing values and traditions of the cultures of which they are parts. In fact, Durkheim argued that it would be foolish to imagine that an educational system could exist for very long if it did not serve to maintain the status quo. Conservatism, rather than change, is encouraged by most educational systems, a conservatism that preserves existing power structures and sources of influence and privilege within the society. The extent to which this is true can be and has been debated at great length. Simple answers are not evident. In any case, Durkheimian and anti-Durkheimian arguments both rest on the assumption that educational systems have been or are successful in transmitting to pupils values or traditions. There is no hard, clear demonstration, historical or sociological, that this is true.

If the present social order is accepted by the educator, he or she may still favor mobility of the individual within that system, and most educators have at least paid lip service to that. In carefully examining the past of American schools, it is clear that schooling has, even at the same time and place, held some back and given others the means to advance socially and economically. Nevertheless, school systems, like other organizations, usually function to preserve themselves and their existing practices. Even so, some significant number of people have been able to use schools to meet their needs and approach their personal goals.

During the first half of the nineteenth century, institutions other than schools began to play increasingly important roles in the education of many Americans. As early as 1826, Josiah Holbrook (1788-1854), a graduate of Yale, had organized the first lyceum in Massachusetts. Loosely organized, the purpose of the lyceum was to sponsor lecturers, to encourage the public discussion of ideas, and to provide reading material for the general public. According to Holbrook in his *Proposal for a Constitution for the American Lyceum* (1828), the object of the lyceum was the promotion of "useful knowledge" among its members and the advancement of popular education by encouraging improvements in the common schools. Because the services of the leading speakers of the period were enlisted, interest in the lyceum movement spread rapidly. By 1830, approximately 3,000 communities in the United States had such organizations, providing a major source of adult education.

The lyceum movement, as shown by its widespread popularity, was an important vehicle of popular education. Closely paralleling the movement was the rapid proliferation and development of libraries. Although individuals including Benjamin Franklin had supported the development of free libraries in America as early as the middle of the eighteenth century, it was not until the beginning of the nineteenth century that libraries began to be available to the public on a widespread basis.

As early as 1820, the Boston Apprentice's Library was formed. In 1829, a similar library was set up in New York City. Mercantile libraries were organized in business districts in various east coast and midwestern cities. In 1849, New Hampshire passed the first law establishing libraries on a statewide basis. Yet, despite the steady growth of interest in libraries, it was not until the last quarter of the nineteenth century that successful attempts were undertaken to organize the library movement on a national basis.

Although a convention of leading American librarians was called as early as 1853 in order to set up a national library organization, it was not until 1876 that this goal was finally accomplished. Under the direction of Melvil Dewey, the librarian at Amherst College and the creator of the Dewey Decimal System, a meeting of librarians was held in October of 1876 as part of the Centennial Exposition in Philadelphia. Ninety men and thirteen women attended the meeting. By the meeting's end, the American Library Association had been organized with Justin Winsor, a Boston librarian, its head.

At the American Library Association meeting, the U.S. Bureau of Education presented a massive two-volume report on the *Public Libraries of the United States.* The most detailed and comprehensive document produced until then addressing library organization and history, the report also included the first comprehensive explanation of Dewey's system of decimal classification for libraries. The report clearly reflected the new direction libraries were beginning to take in the second half of the nineteenth century. According to the report, the twenty-nine public libraries in the thirteen original colonies had approximately 45,000 volumes in

1776. A hundred years later, there were 3,682 libraries in the United States, with a total of 12,276,964 volumes and 1.5 million pamphlets. The sheer volume of material and information that had become available made it imperative that new systems of classifying and disseminating it become available.

The literature from this period clearly indicates that the librarian was seen as being a special type of "public educator." Casting aside to some extent the traditional model of the scholar-librarian, librarians were recognized as being popular educators. As explained in the Education Bureau's report:

> ... the librarian has silently, almost unconsciously, gained ascendency over the habits of thoughts and literary tastes of a multitude of readers, who find in the public library their only means of intellectual improvement. That educators should be able to know the direction and gauge the extent and results of this potential influence, and that librarians should not only understand their primary duties as purveyors of literary supplies to people, but also realize their high privileges and responsibilities as teachers, are matters of great import to the interest of public education.

Traditional interpretations have presented the growth and expansion of libraries after 1876 as being part of an idealistic, liberal humanitarian movement that functioned as a counterpart to the common school movement. Under what has been described by the historian Dee Garrison, in her work *Apostles of Culture*, as the "progressive interpretation," the public library has been looked upon as part of the general movement toward social reform and moral improvement coming out of the late nineteenth century.

Garrison has argued that the traditional interpretation of American library history has been too simplistic. According to her, the traditional approach places too much emphasis on the support for library development that came from the working classes. It does not take into sufficient consideration the extent to which the public libraries were seen by the middle and upper classes that sponsored them as a means of "arresting lower-class alienation from traditional culture." While altruism and humanistic ideals were undoubtedly key factors in the development of libraries in the United States during the second half of the nineteenth century, leaders in the development of their institutions tended to support moral and economic values that were consistent with their middle- and upper-class backgrounds.

Yet, despite the fact that most library leaders of the period had highly conservative points of view, significant advances were made over the course of the late nineteenth century to counter the paternalistic nature of most American librarians and their programs. Unlike the schools, which had much tighter control over their charges and the materials studied, librarians had relatively little control over what their patrons read. Although librarians made consistent attempts to discourage the reading of popular novels (in most cases, romances), little could be done to effectively shape the tastes and interests of most readers. Fiction collections were tolerated in many libraries only as a means of attracting readers into libraries. As the 1876 Bureau of Education report maintained:

> The old recipe for cooking hare, which begins with "first catch your hare" may well be applied to the process of elevating the tastes of the uncultivated masses. Let the library, then, contain just enough of the mere confectionary of literature to secure the interest in it of readers of the lowest—not depraved—tastes; but let this be so dealt out as may best make it serve its main purpose of a stepping stone to something better. . . .

In the 1890s, innovations such as the "two-book" system, in which fiction readers were required to check out a nonfiction book for every volume of fiction that they took from the library, became popular among librarians.

These attempts by many librarians to impose what they considered suitable reading material were largely unsuccessful. A significant minority of librarians opposed placing restrictions on the selection and use of reading materials by their patrons; popular tastes could not be curbed. Strict censorship was impossible. The library by its nature encouraged the free flow of information, providing educational opportunities to a significant portion of the population. In doing so, the library movement, whether consciously or in spite of the intention and purpose of many of its founders, contributed significantly to the development of a free society.

THE DEVELOPMENT OF KINDERGARTENS

The contradictory tendencies of both formal and informal institutions of education to impose upper-middle-class values, as well as to provide limited opportunities for economic and social advancement, is particularly evident in the early kindergarten movement. The kindergarten movement was first transplanted from Germany to

FIGURE 7-4   The New York Public Library by E. J. Meeker. From *The Outlook,* Vol. 83, May 19, 1906, p. 199.

the United States during the years immediately preceding the Civil War. Privately sponsored, and led by educators with strongly humanitarian concerns during its early years, the kindergartens were eventually absorbed into the public school system, where their original intention and purpose was radically redefined as part of the American cultural experience.

Although the kindergarten was originated in Germany during the 1830s and 1840s, it was in the United States that it achieved its greatest success. Conceived by the German educator, Frederich Froebel (1782-1852), as preschool instruction for children between the ages of three and seven, the kindergarten curriculum emphasized not only the physical and intellectual development of children, but also their moral development.

Froebel began his first kindergarten in Blankenburg, Germany, in 1837. Its roots, however, go back not only to the earlier part of Froebel's life, but also to the educational philosophies of Jean Jacques Rousseau and Heinrich Pestalozzi. Froebel's own childhood seems to have been relatively unhappy and may explain part of his concern with early childhood education. Entering the University of Jena in 1799, Froebel concentrated his work for the next three years mainly in the areas of mathematics, physics, and architecture. Evidently strongly influenced during this early period by the philosophical ideas of the German philosophers Johann Fichte and Friederich von Schelling, Froebel developed a philosophy in which he maintained that all life was based on an eternal law of unity. According to Froebel's scheme, God was the ultimate or "Divine Unity." All things having evolved from this divine unity, for Froebel it was the purpose of education to teach children to observe and understand the divine characteristics of all things in the world around them.

Froebel proposed a philosophy in which the spirit of God was infused in all things. This being the case, it followed that all things were interconnected. Each man, although an individual, was part of a larger whole. Following such a philosophy, it is not surprising that Froebel was an ardent German nationalist. He enlisted in the infantry to defend the German fatherland against Napoleon; Froebel's pursuit of unity realized itself not only as part of his educational philosophy, but of his political consciousness as well.

Froebel's philosophical ideas were merged with a great deal of practical experience as a teacher. Having decided upon a career as an educator shortly after having completed his work at the university, Froebel became involved in a number of different educational enterprises. In 1808, he went to Yverdun, Switzerland where he worked and studied with Heinrich Pestalozzi.

In 1810, he left Yverdun to continue his studies at the University of Göttingen. After serving in the army from 1813 to 1817, Froebel became the principal of a school in Kielhau, Germany. It was at Kielhau that Froebel wrote the most complete exposition of his philosophy, *The Spirit of Man* (1826).

Froebel's liberal political point of view eventually led him into difficulty with the Prussian government, which investigated his school for socialist influences. The school was forced to close. From 1831 to 1837, Froebel tried to set up a number of schools in Switzerland, but met with strong opposition from local authorities because of his religious point of view and the fact that he was a foreigner.

Returning to Germany in 1837, Froebel set up the school in Blankenburg that was eventually to become known as the kindergarten (child's garden). Lacking adequate financial support, the school was finally forced to close in 1844. Attempting to promote the idea of the kindergarten, Froebel traveled throughout Germany during the next five years. In 1849, he set up a kindergarten in Libenstein, Germany, where he met the Baroness Bertha Von Marenholtz-Bülow. Quickly convinced of the value of Froebel's work, the Baroness began to work intensively with him in the promotion of his ideas. Helping Froebel to establish a teacher training school, the Baroness attempted to enlist the support of leading educators for Froebel's work and in turn the support of the government. Despite the support of the Baroness and prominent educators throughout Germany, the Prussian government not only did not lend its support to the establishment of kindergartens, but also actually forbid them in August of 1851!

The rejection of the kindergarten in Germany was largely a result of its association with a radical political ideology in the minds of political leaders. Yet except in the broadest philosophical context, Froebel's ideas as an educator were apolitical. Froebel seriously considered leaving Germany and emigrating to the United States. Froebel died, however, in June of 1852, and the promotion of the kindergarten was left to his followers.

Froebel's ideas concerning the education of young children were a radical departure from the traditional approaches. Abandoning the idea of John Locke that a child is a tabula rasa, or blank slate, upon whom ideas are impressed, Froebel argued that the child was a self-generating force. Education, rather than impressing ideas upon the child, had as its purpose helping children realize their natural potential. Through the process of education, children would have their inner potentials revealed to them.

Froebel included a wide range of activities in his curriculum for the kindergarten. Gardening, circle games, and group singing taught children how to work and play with one another and be part of a group. Of greatest importance to Froebel's pedagogical scheme was his set of "Gifts" and "Occupations." These involved a series of twenty teaching devices and tasks that would provide the child with an increasingly sophisticated understanding of the world in which they lived.

Froebel's system of Gifts and Occupations had as its purpose helping children to understand not only the spiritual relationship and unity supposedly inherent in all things, but also to provide them with the tools necessary to master and shape the world in which they lived. To what extent the Gifts succeeded in this purpose is, of course, impossible to know. It is interesting to note that the American architect Frank Lloyd Wright felt that the Froebelian materials had a major impact upon his growth and development as a designer. Recalling his using the kindergarten materials as a child during the 1870s, Wright commented that

A small interior world of color and form now came within grasp of small fingers. Color and pattern, in the flat, in the round. Shapes that lay hidden behind the appearances all about. . . . Here was something for invention to seize, and use to create.

According to Wright, the virtue of the Froebelian materials

. . . lay in the awakening of the child-mind to rhythmic structure in Nature— giving the child a sense of innate cause-and-effect otherwise far beyond child comprehension. I soon became susceptible to constructive pattern *evolving in everything* I saw. I learned to "see" this way and when I did, I did not care to draw casual incidentals of Nature. I wanted to design.

At least for Wright, the Froebelian materials had helped him to not only master methods and materials, but also to understand the rhythmic unity that drew the world together.

In the United States limited discussions and experiments in kindergarten education were underway by the middle of the 1850s. Henry Barnard had published an article in the *American Journal of Education* describing the kindergarten display held in conjunction with the London educational exhibit of 1854. In 1856, Margarethe Schurz, wife of a German political exile and former student of Froebel's, established a German-speaking kindergarten in Watertown, Wisconsin.

In 1859, Schurz visited Boston, where she met Elizabeth Peabody. Peabody was one of the famous Peabody sisters of Salem. Her sister Sophia was the wife of novelist Nathaniel Hawthorne and her other sister, Mary, the wife of Horace Mann. Among her intellectual associates and friends were the leading figures of the New England intelligentsia, such as Ralph Waldo Emerson and the Unitarian leader, Dr. William Ellery Channing. Widely experienced as an educator, Peabody had been involved in a number of major educational and literary experiments associated with the Transcendentalist movement in philosophy. During the 1830s, Peabody had taught in Bronson Alcott's Temple School, which had attempted to help children develop the ability to express themselves with the ultimate purpose of leading them to a greater spiritual development. Peabody had also been involved in the founding of the utopian Brook Farm experiment and the great Transcendentalist literary magazine, the *Dial.*

Peabody's involvement with the Transcendentalist movement laid an important foundation for her acceptance of kindergarten ideals and practices. The Transcendentalists argued that the essence of human nature was spiritual and ideally in tune with God's universal spirit. Contradicting traditional religious views, the Transcendentalists believed that God was an "oversoul." Ideally, the human spirit would transcend the physical and material aspects of existence and become one with God's divine spirit.

Having been introduced to the concept of the kindergarten by Schurz, Peabody began to read and study Froebel's works. In 1860, she opened the first English-speaking kindergarten in the United States at 15 Pickney Street, Boston. Assisted by her recently widowed sister, Mary Mann, Peabody actively promoted the ideals of kindergarten instruction. In 1863, she published with her sister Mary the *Kindergarten Guide*. Unsure of her knowledge and mastery of the kindergarten system, Peabody went to Europe in 1867-68 to study more thoroughly Froebelian theory. On her return to the United States, she gave up teaching and focused her energies on the promotion of the kindergarten. Repudiating her earlier work, Peabody advanced her ideas through public lectures, private correspondence, and the publication of a new journal, the *Kindergarten Messenger*.

Peabody's efforts on behalf of the kindergarten met with a remarkable degree of success. As the result of a speech she gave in Springfield, Massachusetts, Peabody managed to engage the interest of game manufacturer Milton Bradley in the idea of the kindergarten. In 1869, Bradley published Edward Weibe's *Paradise of Childhood*, which was the first American study of the Froebelian system. At the same time, Bradley began to manufacture kindergarten materials. Peabody also, after several unsuccessful attempts, convinced the Boston school system to open an experimental kindergarten as part of the public school system. Unfortunately, the kindergarten proved a failure and was finally forced to close in 1869.

Success in introducing the kindergarten into the public school system came about partly as a result of Peabody's efforts with the Saint Louis superintendent of schools, William Torrey Harris. Having met Harris on one of his frequent trips back East, Peabody sent a long series of letters to him in 1870 and 1871, urging him to set up kindergartens as part of the public school system in Saint Louis. Harris initially showed little interest in Peabody's proposal to establish kindergartens as part of the school system, although as early as 1871, he did mention in his annual superintendent's report the possibility of adapting various kindergarten methods to instruction in the primary grades. The major impetus for the establishment of kindergartens in Saint Louis, however, came from a young socialite, Susan Blow.

Blow was the daughter of a wealthy Saint Louis businessman, Henry Blow. An outspoken abolitionist prior to the Civil War, Henry Blow also had a distinguished public career serving not only as a state senator and congressman, but also as the American minister to Venezuela and Brazil. In 1871, Blow took his family on a trip to Europe. It was while they visited Germany that his daughter Susan first saw a kindergarten class. After taking extensive notes on what she had seen, Blow returned to the United States and began to inquire into the possibilities of establishing a kindergarten in Saint Louis.

Initially, Blow's father wanted to finance a private kindergarten run under Susan's direction. Susan evidently declined his offer and talked with superintendent Harris about setting up a kindergarten as part of the public school system. Harris agreed to operate a kindergarten on a trial basis and promised that he would assign a teacher from one of the primary schools to work with Blow, as well as provide the classroom space needed to set up the school.

Before Blow actually began the experiment, she went to New York City, where she studied for a year under the direction of Maria Boelte, a German who had studied kindergarten methods under the direction of Froebel's widow. Blow had tremendous hopes for the success of the kindgergarten in Saint Louis. Writing to Harris from New York in the spring of 1873, she explained that

> . . . we shall see the day when this mustard seed will have grown into a mighty tree [sic], and I am more than ever anxious to see the system introduced into our Public Schools.

Blow's kindergarten began regular classes in August of 1873, at the Des Peres School in Saint Louis. It is commonly recognized as the first successful public kindergarten program in the United States. Mary A. Timberlake was assigned to Blow as her assistant. Blow provided her own services on a voluntary basis.

The kindergarten quickly proved to be an enormous success. By 1879, there was a total of 53 classes and 131 paid teachers working in the kindergartens. Also working in the kindergartens were many unpaid assistants, most of whom were receiving training in order to become kindergarten teachers.

Numerous arguments were put forward opposing the establishment of the kindergartens. It was argued that setting up kindergartens would be extremely expensive, that they would spoil the children attending them, and that it would be almost impossible to find or train teachers who could effectively handle the demands imposed by the kindergarten curriculum.

FIGURE 7-5   The interior of the Des Peres Kindergarten. Courtesy of the Audio-Visual Department of the St. Louis Public Schools.

Blow and others who shared her view argued for the establishment of the kindergartens primarily on the basis of the opportunities for happiness and personal growth that the kindergartens would provide the individual child. Harris and the Saint Louis School Board took a more pragmatic approach in their reasons for supporting the kindergarten. For example, Thomas Richeson, the president of the board, explained in the superintendent's report for 1875 that

> It is in its industrial aspect chiefly that our recent experiments in Kinder-garten education promises the most satisfactory results. At a tender age, when the child is plastic in his nature, and easily moulded in any direction, he commences a training adapted to give him great skill in the use of his hands and eyes. . . . The influence of the Kindergarten will be felt on all subsequent education. The early impulse given to mechanical skill and to taste, in regard to form an design, in the Kindergarten, reinforced by a thorough course of instruction in industrial drawing in the primary and grammar schools, is suffi-cient to work a revolution in the manufactures of the country, and cause our goods to obtain the preference in foreign as well as domestic markets.

While Harris recognized the fact that children would be better able to become use-ful workers in the industrial system as a result of the habits and skills they obtained through their kindergarten training, he was more concerned with the fact that the kindergarten would provide children in the manufacturing districts of the city with an additional year of schooling. In his report for 1872-73, Harris argued that the kindergarten would remove children in poorer neighborhoods from the corruption of the streets. According to Harris:

> We do not look so much to gain in intellectual possessions as to the training of the will into correct habits, during the years previous to the seventh. . . . Such careful training in habits of regularity, punctuality, industry, cleanliness, self-control, and politeness, as are given in the ordinary primary school, and still more efficiently in the well-conducted kindergarten, are of priceless benefit to the community. They lessen the number of rough, ungovernable youths whose excesses are the menace of the peace of society.

Harris's comments reflect the increasingly important role the kindergartens were perceived as having in the reform of urban society during the final decades of the nineteenth century.

The kindergartens were seen as providing the poor child the opportunity to rise above the poverty and neglect that was supposedly so much a part of their lives. By providing the children with kindergarten instruction for three hours a day, and having teachers work with the parents of these children, sweeping reforms and improvements were believed to be possible. Children, still flexible, could be shaped in ways that would allow them to overcome the debilitating environments in which they lived. The negative influence of the home and the neighborhood would give way to the supposedly superior influence of the schools and its teachers. By culti-vating the spiritual and moral aspects of the child, as well as providing them with practical training, it was believed that the fragmentation and alienation caused by urbanization and industrialization could effectively be overcome. In doing so, the needs of the society as a whole would be met.

Paralleling the growth of the public kindergartens were charity kindergartens such as those sponsored by Mrs. Quincy Adams Shaw in Boston's North End, Jamaica Plain and Brookline, beginning in the early 1870s. As part of the North End charity kindergarten, teachers spent half their days away from the classroom visiting parents and enrolling children in school. In this context, the teachers in many of the early charity kindergartens were fulfilling the roles of social workers.

As late as 1903, the kindergarten was seen as being an important vehicle for the Americanization of immigrant children. In an address included in the National Education Association Proceedings, Richard Gilder commented:

> You cannot catch your citizen too early in order to make him a good citizen. The kindergarten age marks our opportunity to catch the little Russian, the little Italian, the little German, Pole, Syrian, and the rest and begin to make good American citizens of them.

As the kindergarten movement received greater support from the public schools, it moved away from working with parents and became more and more integrated into the general school sytem. By the end of the 1890s, the kindergarten had become a major force in American education. In 1873, according to the United States Bureau of Education, there were a total of twelve kindergartens in the United States, with seventy-two teachers and 1,252 students. By 1898, this number had increased to 4,363 kindergartens with 8,937 teachers and 189,604 students.

The rapid growth of kindergartens in the late nineteenth century was accompanied by important efforts to go beyond the work of Froebel. Anna E. Bryan, for example, argued in a major address to the National Education Association in the early 1890s that the use of Froebel's Gifts and Occupations discouraged spontaneity and creativity on the part of the child. A few years later, G. Stanley Hall rejected much of Froebel's work because it was not derived from systematically observing young children, while John Dewey argued against Froebel's concept that the child's mind contained certain specific universal principles.

Hall and Dewey, with kindergarten leaders such as Anna E. Bryan and Patty Smith Hill, laid the foundations for what would become the Progressive kindergarten movement. Rejecting what they saw as an overly romantic approach to culture by the traditional Froebelians, the progressives felt that the primary purpose of the kindergarten should be to help the individual child learn to cope with the demands of an increasingly complex culture and environment. Unlike the traditional Froebelians who saw morality as being fixed and defined within each individual, the progressive kindergarten supporters saw it as defined by the social environment in which the child lived. Essential to their philosophy was the realization that the children they were teaching were members of a larger and more complex society in which they would have to live and function as adults.

CONCLUSION

By the late 1860s, American culture was being reshaped by rapid industrialization and urbanization. Education, in turn, was affected. The demands of industry for workers with specific skills led the schools to develop programs in industrial arts. As the cities grew, and with them the problems resulting from rapid expansion and overcrowding, the school came to be looked at increasingly as a source of stability and direction for the culture.

The development of the land grant colleges, the manual training schools, free libraries and even the kindergarten were responses to the new social and political order. A new society was coming into being—one radically different from the agrarian society of America during the late eighteenth and early nineteenth centuries. With the creation of this new society there developed in turn a radically different educational system, shaped by the new industrial and urban culture.

PART THREE
FROM FARM TO CITY

At the beginning of these times, in the Centennial Year of 1876, there were elderly men and women who as children had been among the witnesses of General Lafayette's last year-long triumphal tour of the United States in 1825 and 1826. Now, in the 1980s, men and women only a few years into retirement have at least fragmentary memories of headlines and military music and the olive drab uniforms of the first World War. As adolescents, some men and women now in retirement may have tasted illegal home-brewed beer or even homemade "bathtub" gin. As young adults, they were without jobs, or at least many of their friends were. Marriages were postponed, mortgages foreclosed, and for ten years and more, prosperity and jobs for everyone seemed no more than a memory and faint hope that was in some ways misleading.

Because of the way they directly or indirectly affected schooling and education, or because they were affected by education, parts of national political history, that of the Progressive period near 1900, and of the New Deal in the 1930s, are parts of the most important context for education and schooling. The first World War was a dividing time in American politics and thought. The shape not only of schools, but also of society and culture, was modified by the growth of knowledge, professionally applied and pure; most of that knowledge was spread by the schools, and much of it was generated there. Industrial production increased enormously as steam power nearly replaced water power in manufacturing, and then was in turn replaced by electricity. New manufactured products, from phonograph records to diesel locomotives, poured into markets in the United States and abroad.

New products and growing production, at least until 1929, created a demand for labor that was an important cause of the greatest flood of immigrants. The new immigrants were no longer distant cousins of the "old" Americans, but came from outlandish places along the Mediterranean Sea, the Balkans, and from elsewhere in Eastern Europe. Industrialization, improving transportation and distribution, completely changed the American ways of life in the cities and also on farms. The economy grew, although some benefited much more than others. Prosperity ended in 1929 with the Depression, the longest and most severe American economic crisis ever.

POLITICAL REFORMERS, AND OTHERS

Perhaps the Civil War for a time exhausted American energy and enthusiasm for reforms. In any event, although there were some small reform parties and reform causes (for instance, in free coinage of silver), the next important reform era did not come for thirty years or more. It was already slowing, then it was brought to an end by the United States' entry into the first World War. The war was followed by another ten years of conservatism, as if American zeal had again been used up in the war's effort and frenzy. The second reform period of the 1900s was the *New Deal*, the response of President Franklin D. Roosevelt and government to the calamity of the Depression.

President Theodore Roosevelt (a distant cousin of Franklin) was inaugurated in Buffalo, New York, on September 14, 1901, after President McKinley died a lingering death from a gun wound by a perhaps deranged self-styled radical. Roosevelt, not yet forty-three when he became president, is as representative as any man of the Progressive era. The time for reform had come: It seemed to many that there was one law for the poor, another for the rich—and no law at all for big business. Theodore Roosevelt became the most popular president since Andrew Jackson and the most powerful since Abraham Lincoln. Roosevelt was a whirlwind of energy. He was rancher, author, explorer, soldier, and Nobel Prize winner, as well as president. He was the enemy of corruption and of "the wealthy criminal class." He was an early conservationist, foe of harmful business monopolies, believer in just and popular rule.

Now the times had come for change, and the Progressives undertook them. Writers, intellectuals, journalists, and politicians took part. The future was to be taken in hand and planned so that a better future might be brought into being. There were to be changes in government: secret ballots; "women's suffrage," the right of women (but not Blacks) to vote; an expanded civil service; responsible and honest city, state, and national government. Wretched, unhealthy slum housing was to be improved; the prisons, reformed. Child labor in factories was to be ended;

drinking, prohibited; and trusts and monopolies harmful to the public good were to be controlled and, if necessary, dismembered. Outrageous freight rates would be corrected by government control. The impulses for school reform were part of the same Progressive movement, and they too would be called "Progressive." The Progressive era in politics ended in 1917 when the United States entered the war against Germany and Austria.

THE FIRST WORLD WAR, AND OTHERS

The United States' participation in World War I disrupted and reshaped America's society and economy. The United States entered the war, which was already two and a half years old, in April of 1917 for a variety of reasons, most of them debatable, but many of them honorable. There was some resistance to going to war, most of it also honorable. The war required huge amounts of food, supplies, and weapons for our allies, as well as for our own troops. Factories were converted, and a million women employed in war-related jobs. The demand for industrial labor attracted to northern cities a half million Blacks from the South.

The Navy saw action at once, in antisubmarine patrols and escorting ship convoys. Later the Navy laid the mine fields in the North Sea, which prevented German submarines from entering the North Atlantic. On July 4, 1917, the first American soldiers were greeted in Paris, but even at the end of that year there were only 200,000 soldiers and marines in France, most of whom had not been in combat. But in the summer of 1918, when Russia had withdrawn from the war, a quarter million Americans defended the line against German attacks at Château-Thierry. In September more than 1 million U.S. "doughboys" were in the Battle of the Meuse, and one tenth of them were wounded or killed. The Armistice took effect on November 11, 1918. By then, more than 5 million men had served in the armed forces. It was the greatest military effort since the Civil War.

There were other military actions, more or less minor, before and after the first World War. The summer of the Philadelphia Centennial Exposition was the summer of the Battle of Little Big Horn, Sitting Bull's triumph and General George A. Custer's defeat and death. Some of Custer's cavalrymen were killed by Sioux tomahawks. Only forty-two years later, soldiers in France were killed by poison gas. (One of the least pleasant contributions of technology has been to make even ways of killing more efficient and less personal.) The Spanish-American War, in 1898-99, was fought in the Caribbean and in the Philippine Islands. "A splendid little war," Theodore Roosevelt called it. For two years afterward, United States troops pursued and supressed Philippine nationalists. In 1916, General John J. Pershing pursued Francisco "Pancho" Villa into the mountains of Mexico. After World War I, in 1919, United States and Japanese troops occupied the port of Vladivostok in Asiatic Russia. Marines were stationed in Santo Domingo into the 1930s.

KNOWLEDGE, POWER, AND PRODUCTION

From colleges and new American universities, from abroad, and from American workshops, there was a continuing accumulation of knowledge and theories, of knowing why and of knowing how. A segment of that knowledge had direct effects upon thoughts and beliefs: The "higher criticism" of the Bible suggested that it had been written by many men at many times, that it was not in any literal sense the "Word of God." Geologists, particularly George Lyell, and evolutionists, above all Charles Darwin, drew theories from assembled facts. They argued that the creation of the earth had been by natural processes over an enormously long period rather than by "cataclysm," and that "the origin of the species" was a natural process and not the direct act of God. This was painful for some, especially for church members who were "fundamentalists," who held that the Bible was truly the "Word of God."

Knowledge also affected the professions. For the first time in a hundred years, one historian of medicine has concluded, it was beneficial to one's health to be under the care of a physician. The role of bacteria in infection and disease was better understood. Sanitized operating rooms and anesthetics made operations that had been all but impossible feasible and often successful. It was known that purification of water would reduce typhoid fever outbreaks and that the extermination of mosquitoes would prevent the spread of malaria.

Knowledge came also from the machine shop, the foundry, the factory. Given the concept that experiments, sometimes even cut-and-try experiments, could add knowledge about how to accomplish given objectives, knowledge of that kind had been accumulated for a full century and more. Frederick Taylor's improvement of metal-cutting methods, which is to be described in Chapter 9, is one of the more successful examples. A more famous illustration, although in some ways misleading, is Thomas Edison's testing of thousands of materials as filaments in incandescent lights. Edison was a great exponent of trial-and-error experimentation. In public he scoffed at pure, theoretical scientists, but in private he employed them.

From the expanding knowledge of theoretical physics and by use of mathematics, as well as from accumulated experience, engineers acquired stores of expert knowledge. In the older fields, engineering knowledge surpassed that of the traditional master craftsmen. In new fields, electricity for example, there were no old master craftsmen, and electricity belonged to the scientists and engineers. Successful engineers, as well as inventors, were esteemed men, even popular heroes. John A. and Washington A. Roebling, father and son, were famed for building the Brooklyn Bridge. James B. Eads, bridge builder (across the Mississippi at Saint Louis), was also famed as boat builder and hydraulic engineer. John Stevens and Colonel George W. Goethals were well known for supervising the building of the Panama Canal.

Edison, born in Ohio in 1847, said he had attended school only three months. He was a newsboy, a candy hawker on the trains, and then a telegrapher. His inventions included not only the incandescent electric light, but also the stock ticker, the mimeograph, the phonograph, and motion pictures. In the summer of 1876, Edison opened his laboratory in Menlo Park, New Jersey, intending to produce many minor inventions and one or two major inventions each year. Edison not only received a thousand patents in his lifetime, but also, in a sense, reinvented inventing—inventing for the marketplace.

It was a relatively short step from Menlo Park to General Electric's laboratory in Schenectady, New York. It was organized by Willis R. Riley, graduate of Massachusetts Institute of Technology, and holder of a doctorate from the German University of Leipzig.

The G.E. laboratory produced in due time tungsten lamp filaments, cathode and radio tubes, and even an atomic theory. As Daniel Boorstin has pointed out, the research and development ("R&D") laboratory has become an essential part of industry, a massive undertaking in its own right. It is seen by many as the appropriate organization for research and development in education.

America had acquired technology that expanded and grew almost day by day. Faith in technology was not new, but vastly increased. America had accumulated knowledge of how things function, and was acquiring research and development laboratories, and also new universities in which laboratories and professors would become acknowledged leaders in expanding "pure" scientific knowledge.

One of the most important and general fields of technology was the generation and use of electrical power in factory production. By 1870, steam power had become more used than waterpower in factories: The Corliss engine at Philadelphia had been a symbol of that, as well as of other changes. By the early 1900s, steam was being replaced by electric power, which was more readily distributed from a central generating plant, and more readily controlled. Water power could be used to generate electricity; enthusiasts planned to divert all the flow of Niagara Falls into power plants. For other uses, water wheels, windmills, and even treadmills served special purposes, or survived as quaint relics.

With more available power, its more effective use, a thousand other cumulative technological developments, and year-by-year increases in efficiency, the volume of factory output increased year by year—in the 1920s, faster than markets, contributing to the coming of the Depression. Larger investments in larger factories allowed the use of more expensive and more specialized machines. At best, the factories were impressive collections of machines unfamiliar to outsiders; of punch presses and drop forges, of turret lathes, of shears and brakes, and of a thousand others, linked by belts, wires, and conveyers. At worst, the factories were dehumanizing, dangerous sweatshops. The factory laborer had replaced the craftsman. Big factories and plants hired hundreds and thousands of workers, most of whom worked too-long hours in dangerous, disagreeable places: in the stench of Chicago meat packing houses, at moving conveyers where carcasses were methodically dismembered; in the gigantic auto plants of Detroit; in the searing heat of Pittsburgh steel mills; in the sweatshops of New York City's garment district; and in the hot, humid, dusty cotton mills. In the South, whole families worked in such environments. Work was dangerous. About 15,000 workers were killed annually in factory accidents, and in the 1920s, more than ten times as many were injured. Few factory workers belonged to unions. Most earned less than $10 a week when they worked. Layoffs and unemployment were commonplace.

LIFE IN CITIES AND FACTORIES

The requirements for mass production were for capital, management, materials, and labor. Capital, in very large sums for the time, came from investors, from bank loans, and from earnings. Materials came, usually, from American farms and ranches, mines, and forests. A new specialization, management, was appearing. It will be discussed in Chapter 9, since it was also applied to the schools. The additional labor that industrialization required was comprised of journeymen whose skills were no longer needed; of farm laborers, who were also being supplanted by mechanization; and of Blacks and Whites who came from the largely unindustrialized and still poor South. Millions of the new factory workers and their families were immigrants from the Mediterranean's shores and from Eastern Europe. The demands of mass production shaped the workers' hours on the job, and determined exertions and repetitiveness of work. After hours, and for mothers and children, new communities set ways of immigrant life, in some ways new and in other ways old.

As factories expanded, jobs were divided, subdivided, and divided again, in accordance with the principles of division of labor that Adam Smith had employed. A hundred years before, for example, a family of craftsmen on eastern Long Island had made furniture and clocks—some of those items are now in museums—by hand from their own or inherited patterns, from boards and brass to finished piece. In the 1920s, workers on the Ford Model "A" assembly line at the River Rouge plant in Detroit tightened only one nut on each car. If he was fortunate, the craftsperson became a supervisor or foreman. More often he, like others, took a job requiring much less skill. He became a factory hand. Many journeymen were displaced that way and became factory workers, often dissatisfied and resentful.

The mechanization of farms and farming had started before the Civil War. Reapers, mowers, threshing machines, cream separators, and dozens of other machines reduced the need for farm labor, though they increased the need for farming capital. Farmhands and farm sons came to the city to work in mills and factories, especially after the costs of farmland and equipment had risen. Rural Wyoming County in western New York State, as an example, had a decreased population in every census year from 1850 until 1960. Its inhabitants were moving away, many of them to the cities.

Especially during the 1914-1918 wartime labor shortages, southern Blacks were recruited to work in war and other industries. Some were recruited as strike breakers, but most simply to provide labor. Others, naturally, heard of work for relatively good pay and so came North. Southern and border cities had already had comparatively large black populations. During the war more than half a million

Blacks moved to northern cities, and the flow resumed during the Depression. Southern whites, especially poor mountain people from Appalachia, also came North for factory jobs.

Many, probably most, of the new factory workers were immigrants. Between 1890 and 1914, more than 15 million immigrants came to the United States, and by 1920, more than half of all those living in big cities were immigrants or the sons or daughters of immigrants. The new immigrants—by 1907, four fifths of them— came from southern or eastern Europe, although many others came from Asia, the Caribbean, Mexico, and other places. In every big city outside the South, there were immigrant ethnic communities.

There was too much variation for any ethnic community to be "typical." "Buffalo Polonia," the "Polish Village" of Buffalo, New York, can serve as an example. "Polonia" (the living place but also the spirit of the Poles) was near its zenith in 1914, when the first World War cut off immigration. Polonia was then more than forty years old. It had grown east of the city's center, because there was no nearer place and no housing cast off by others. The population of Polonia was difficult to estimate, but the first Catholic parish, St. Stanislaus, had once had more than 30,000 Polish communicants, most of the population of Polonia. By 1914, there were four other Polish Catholic parishes.

Immigrants had come to Buffalo Polonia because Buffalo was prosperous, because there were friends and relatives there, because there were jobs, because "w ameryce kazdy ma dobrze" (in America everyone has it good). At least one non-Polish agent advertised for and recruited Poles from the homeland. Many of the immigrants were from Poznania in Prussian Poland and spoke German and had friends or acquaintances who were German. ("Kaisertown," a German community, was adjacent to Polonia on the south, and there was another German community to the northwest.) Although Poles said they came to Buffalo "za chlebem," "for bread," that was a figure of speech. Poles came to Buffalo Polonia to earn money, but they did not come moneyless. Many of them had worked in factories in Germany, although others had come from the countryside in search of success. "Success" was owning "grunt," ground and house, and security. Poles of Buffalo worked, some remembered, to buy a cramped one-story wood house. Some families lived in small additions at the rear and rented the best rooms for mortgage payments. As money was saved and families grew, there were additions to the houses and additions to additions, until some houses stretched nearly to the back of deep lots. When money could be spent for it, houses were furnished in bright, exuberant, rather old-fashioned ways, with the feel of the late Victorian era. A lot even only twenty feet wide, and a one-story wooden house and its furnishings, were proof of prosperity.

Success in Polonia's way of thinking came from hard physical work, from sweat. It did not come from schooling, unless for the priesthood. Most Polish children in Buffalo did not even hope to enter other professions. Far more often boys hoped to be craftsmen. There were a few Polish physicians and lawyers, but many Polish boys and men attended vocational schools days or at night. If it would lead to a trade and so to high wages, schooling attracted Buffalo Poles, but school was not to stand in the way of jobs and wages. Only one Polish child in five, we estimate, completed elementary school. (But only one Buffalo child in four completed elementary school then.)

Many of those living in Buffalo Polonia not only spoke German, but had experienced life in bicultural cities. Polonia was, in the words of a man still living, expected "to last a thousand years." (Although it seems unlikely that it will, there is still a Buffalo Polonia in the 1980s.) It was, and is, above all a community, a place where personal and institutional connections link people together. In the immigration, many men had been joined by their wives and children. By 1914, there were third-generation Polonians and there were extended families: aunts, uncles, in-laws, and cousins sometimes living in the same house, more often on the same block, and usually in the same parish. Beyond the families there was the Catholic Church. The "mother parish" church, St. Stanislaus, was more imposing and more impressive than the Roman Catholic cathedral. St. Stanislaus's pastor was one of the most prominent men in Polonia, and in Buffalo. It was said that there had been hopes that St. Stanislaus would become the cathedral of a Polish diocese, hopes which were in vain. The church's teachings, celebrations, and feasts united Polonia, and the church was the symbol of hope for the Polish nation that had lived under German, Austrian, and Russian rule for a hundred years. There were many church organizations—of choirs, altar boys, and ushers—and an insurance society. Children, especially before their first communion at about age eleven, attended parish schools. Women belonged to the Women's Circle, mothers' clubs, rosary societies, and, of course, there were Polish nuns who lived in parish convents and taught in parish schools. Beyond the church, there were the Polish Falcons, a young men's gymnastic and patriotic society. "Dom Polski," the Polish home, housed a score of organizations. The Polish Union, Polonia's own insurance company, provided a library and meeting rooms. The Chopin Society sang traditional Polish songs. There were shops and stores, some of them owned by Polish-speaking Jews (but to be Polish was to be Catholic). There was at least one Polish newspaper and sometimes two. At the market there were sweet Polish holiday breads; strong spiced kielbasa sausages; live ducks for czarnina, duckblood soup; and fresh vegetables and fruit in season. At Christmas and Eastertime the market itself was a festival, with warmth and numberless greetings. One could live and die in Polonia rarely hearing even a word of English. One could even be buried by a Polish undertaker. Life and death occurred among relatives, friends, acquaintances, supporting if binding. When one family of White Russians, another ethnic minority, found its name difficult for others, it is said that their surname was changed to one familiar and easily spelled and pronounced, "Sobieski," the name of one of Poland's first great heroes.

There were incursions, of course. Policemen were not Polish, and occasionally Poles were arrested for drunkenness or minor crimes, although Polonia was generally law abiding. Some Polish children attended public schools, especially after primary grades and religious instruction in parish schools taught by the nuns. There were almost no Polish teachers in the public schools. At least one Polish boy's first independent excursions out of Polonia were on a bicycle, an American-made bicycle, and at least one rich Pole owned American-made Packards. The onetime bicyclist remembers a Polonia Christmas when he was given maple sugar candy, an American candy if ever one was.

Above all, there was the job. Most jobs were outside Polonia, in factories, machine shops, grain mills, at the blast furnaces. The work was hard and dirty: the first was not bad, the second a minor annoyance. German might do at first, but a factory worker needed to know English. Women worked in factories too, or as housemaids outside Polonia, and so also needed to know English. As strong as the community was, it could not be completely insulated from the rest of America.

There were other Polonias—in Chicago, Detroit, Pittsburgh, Scranton, and elsewhere. Of one national origin or another, there were ethnic communities in all nonsouthern cities: Chinese in San Francisco, Polish Jewish in Manhattan, Greek in the old New England seaports, and French-Canadian in New England mill towns, Lithuanian in Chicago, Mexican in Los Angeles. There were "Dago Hills" or "Little Italies" in nearly every big city. There were communities of ethnic farmers, too. Swedes, Norwegians, and Germans who had arrived earlier had settled in a band of border states from Michigan through the Dakotas, and although most Italians settled in big cities, there were, and are, Italian-American vegetable- and fruit-growing communities.

Restrictionists saw several disadvantages to unlimited immigration. Other Californians' prejudices against those of Oriental origin led to the Chinese Exclusion Act as early as 1882, and to excluding the Japanese by the "Gentlemen's Agreement" of 1907. Some conservatives believed in the "natural superiority" of fair Nordics, and others in traditional ways of life. Labor leaders believed that immigrants who worked for low wages kept all wages lower. World War I almost stopped immigration, which was restricted by quota laws in 1921 and 1924, when all immigration of Asians and Africans was forbidden. During the worst years of the Depression, a greater number of recent immigrants returned to their homeland than arrived here.

Working conditions for immigrant and other workers were generally poor. Factory jobs usually were low-paying, dangerous drudgery. Maxine Seller quotes a description, from 1907, of children who did piecework sewing at home: "...pallid boy or spindling girl ... backs bent under a heavy load of garments ... the little worker sits close to the inadequate window ... a child may add to the family purse from 50 cents to $1.50 a week. ..."

Perhaps the Ford River Rouge plant at Detroit was at another extreme. It had been built so that the flow of materials from iron ore to finished Model "A" and of 60,000 workers could be fully coordinated. Defenders of Henry Ford called the management "friendly autocracy." Pay was high, at least compared with that of other factory work. In 1925 the average automobile worker had earned $1,627. (Henry Ford's personal income in the 1920s averaged $4.5 million a year, roughly 2,700 times as much.) A nourishing meal on the job cost 15¢, buildings were freshly painted, clean, and well ventilated, and Ford Motor Company had a good job safety record. But there was no union. There were assembly line "speed-ups," and supervisors spoke of "driving" men, using the same word and ideas that cotton plantation owners had applied to their slaves a hundred years before.

Ford Motor Company and a few other corporations grew to giants while most others disappeared. From the beginning until now, there have been more than a thousand American manufacturers of automobiles, alphabetically from Abbott (1916-18) to Zimmerman (1908-16). Most were forced out of business. Some became parts of the biggest motor companies; General Motors was made up of fifteen such companies, Chrysler of twenty-two. As early as the spring of 1934, the Big Three—General Motors, Ford, and Chrysler—sold 91 percent of all new automobiles. Automobile manufacture is a late but informative example of the consolidation of corporations that took place in many industries beginning even before the Progressive era. Personal wealth was also being concentrated. As never before, a few Americans were becoming rich while many grew poorer.

Although there were pauses during panics and lulls, the economy was turning from farming to manufacturing and becoming one of the largest in the world. Of course this was not helpful to the farmer selling wheat at a loss or to the laid-off and moneyless factory hand. But the poor were nearly invisible. Public attention was on other things, on new cars, on new houses in new suburbs, on common stocks, on movies, on jazz, on flappers.

WAYS OF LIFE

Looking back at the 1920s, one can see most of the shape of life in the United States today. It took shape then from changes of that day. It came, by paradox, from near-constants: the Protestant Work Ethnic, "boosterism" and enthusiasm for improvement, and our practicality.

In the 1920s, businessmen commuted from suburbs by car. New houses at the edge of the city had not only running water, but also bathtubs and toilets, and electric lights. There were telephones and central heating, and by the mid-1920s, there were already millions of radios. For workers and their families there were older and smaller houses nearer the old center of the city and nearer the factories. The city poor lived in slum tenements, but apartment houses had already appeared before 1876. The Dakota, still standing in New York City; overlooking Central Park and inspired by a German castle, had been built in 1880, and in the late 1920s, more apartment units than one-family houses were built. Macy's department store in New York City, Wanamaker's in Philadelphia, and Marshall Field in Chicago were famous. They displayed merchandise that all could see and many could buy, one low price, satisfaction or your money back, even on time payments. Before 1900, stores sold ready-made clothing for women and children as well as for men. Wonderfully elaborate furniture was factory made—elaboration by machine was cheap, no matter how vulgar. Groceries might come from the A&P or another chain store, maybe even from a "self-service" food store. There was Shredded Wheat and other prepackaged foods. For farm families there were Sears, Roebuck and Montgomery Ward, and other catalog mail order companies. When they could afford them, farm families more and more bought clothes, furniture, and even food like that of city families. Telephones, radios, and rural free delivery of mail made farms less isolated, and old farming communities were wasting away.

By 1876, "Victorian" houses, huge ornamented turreted boxes, had ornateness too. About 1920, the "bungalow," smaller, heavily trimmed, story-and-a-half boxes came into fashion. There were "Spanish mission" bungalows of imitation adobe, and carpenters built Dutch colonial and New England colonial reproductions (more or less).

At home the phonograph replaced the reed organ or piano. Reproduced music—Enrico Caruso, John Philip Sousa, Rudy Vallee, according to taste—replaced music made for the occasion. For other amusement there was baseball, which produced as its greatest hero, Babe Ruth. The Yale football stadium, completed in 1914, had 80,000 seats. Boxing was still of questionable morality, but 118,736 rainwet spectators saw Gene Tunney win the world championship in 1926. There were still touring theater and vaudeville companies. In the 1920s, they competed against feature-length motion pictures, with sound starting in 1927.

And then—

CHAPTER EIGHT
PROGRESSIVE REFORM

INTRODUCTION

Progressive reforms, beginning in the late 1800s, were intended to improve government, to aid the exploited and defenseless, and to increase efficiency. The development of one of the streams of Progressivism, of which Progressive education was a part, is discussed here. Progressivism grew from new intellectual activity, the growth of social conscience, and changes in culture.

The 1890s were an important turning point for America. According to the Census of 1890, the West had been populated; the useful free land was gone. The frontier was officially closed two years later. In 1893, a young professor of history at the University of Wisconsin, Frederick Jackson Turner, addressed the American Historical Association. In a paper entitled "The Significance of the Frontier in American History," Turner argued that the American character had been shaped not so much by the East Coast or European cultural traditions as by the vast opportunities provided by the virgin land of the frontier. The frontier had critically molded and shaped the American people. By having provided an almost limitless expense of land for settlement and exploitation, the frontier had stimulated democratic values, individualism, and even a sense of national identity.

Beginning in the 1890s, a new conception of American culture emerged. The frontier and its possibilities, which had for so long dominated the minds of the

American people, had suddenly given way to the city. An agricultural society was acquiring an increasingly urban orientation.

The changes that were taking place in American culture were most evident in the cities. It was here that rural Americans and the newly arrived immigrants most often came in search of new opportunities. In 1860, approximately one sixth of the people lived in towns with a population of 8,000 or more. By 1900, this figure had increased to one third. Cities and towns were growing larger. Chicago, which had a population of 100,000 in 1860, had more than a million inhabitants by 1900. New immigrants from Europe contributed much to this growth. Between 1860 and 1900, a total of 14 million immigrants came to the United States. During this same period, the population more than doubled, increasing from approximately 31 million to 76 million people.

If America's physical frontiers were closing during the 1890s, the country's intellectual frontiers were expanding as they had never done before. As Lawrence Cremin has pointed out, the 1890s were a brilliant period for American scholarship. Largely under the influence of Darwinian theory, nearly every field of knowledge made important advances. Psychology, social theory, philosophy, physics, chemistry and biology were each profoundly reformulated. So too were the theoretical foundations of education. In 1890, William James published his *Principles of Psychology*. Other works, such as Francis W. Parker's *Talks on Pedagogics* (1894), Edward L. Thorndike's *Animal Intelligence* (1898), James's *Talks to Teachers on Psychology* (1899) and John Dewey's *The School and Society* (1899) were to radically reshape the meaning and purpose of American education during the early decades of the twentieth century.

The development of an increasingly progressive urban and intellectual consciousness in the United States during the 1890s is recognized by most historians as being part of a larger reform movement. Reformers sought to reshape the city through the improvement of the physical environment and the establishment of a sense of community. With agencies such as the settlement house and the popular press, the schools were to play a crucial role in the development of this sense of community.

BUSINESSMEN, SOCIAL DARWINISM, AND URBAN REFORM

The growth of business and industry during the second half of the nineteenth century led to the emergence of a new economic elite. By 1892 there were more than 4,000 millionaires living in the United States. Many had acquired their wealth and prestige with the help of family connections and inheritances. Others were "self-made" men, typified by John D. Rockefeller and Andrew Carnegie. Rockefeller began his career working as a clerk in a Cleveland commission house. As a child, Carnegie had been a worker, a bobbin-boy in a Pittsburgh cotton mill.

The Carnegies and Rockefellers achieved their wealth by largely disregarding the welfare of the public. Likened to the "robber barons" of the Middle Ages, the new economic and business leaders in the United States often rationalized their wealth as being simply the result of hard work, thrift, and "good living." Many believed they had achieved what they had because they deserved to. John D. Rockefeller argued that his wealth had been given to him by God. The implication underlying this point of view was that somehow those who had achieved less were less deserving.

Historian Richard Hofstadter has suggested that the business leadership of the late nineteenth century had adopted a philosophy of social Darwinism to justify the social inequities in America, but the extent to which American business leaders were aware of either Spencer's or Darwin's ideas is doubtful. Irwin G. Wylley in *The Self Made Man in America* (1954) maintained that businessmen in the Gilded Age evolved their belief in the philosophy of the self-made man from a deeply rooted Christian morality, and from faith in reason that had its origins in the eighteenth-century European Enlightenment, rather than from a knowledge of evolutionary theory.

If the concept of social Darwinism was largely unknown to the businessmen and financial leaders of the late nineteenth century, the application of Spencerian and Darwinian concepts to social theory and reform was a subject of increasing interest to American intellectuals. Two leaders who held largely opposing views were Lester F. Ward and William Graham Sumner. Sumner, a professor at Yale in political and social science from 1872 to 1910, argued that true scientific progress could take place only if nature was allowed to take its natural course in the evolutionary process. Defending the notion of social Darwinism, Sumner argued that those who held positions of influence and power did so because they were most suited to do so, as demonstrated by their survival in the system. Sumner opposed government reform because it upset the natural evolutionary process. State-supported education he saw as a vehicle for improving society, but only useful to the extent to which it encouraged political order.

The work of Lester Frank Ward was in contrast to the ideas of Sumner. In *Dynamic Sociology* (1883), Ward drew upon Darwinian theory to develop a theory of culture. Unlike Sumner, however, he argued that when applied to a modern society, different forces altered the evolutionary process. Base desires and needs could be overcome through the active use of intelligence. The intellect was able to overcome man's natural desires, and methods could be developed by men to improve their evolutionary future. Ward emphasized the importance of "intellect" and "culture" in human evolution. Calling for increased government regulation and reform, he emphasized that if natural forces were left to themselves, they would tend to be destructive and counterproductive for the culture.

Ward's ideas, along with those of other social theorists of the period, generated increased interest in reform during the late nineteenth century. A new America was emerging, and with it a new set of social problems. Rapid industrialization and urbanization, combined with successive waves of immigration, were reshaping New York, Philadelphia, Boston, Buffalo, Saint Louis, Chicago, Cincinnati, and other great cities. Increasing efforts were made in the late 1880s and early 1890s to combat crowded tenements, exploitative labor practices, unemployment, and dangerous working conditions. At the same time, important efforts were made to provide the city poor with a sense of community.

The problems of poverty that were the focus of the reform movement during the late 1890s were not new problems. What was new was an articulate and well-educated middle-class urban leadership that emerged during the late 1880s and early 1890s and addressed the problems of the poor. Philanthropic, perhaps at their worst paternalistic, the "progressives" were concerned with promoting "social justice and governmental reform."

In its broadest sense, the Progressive movement of the late nineteenth century was an awakening of social consciousness and an awareness of the need for education in its broadest sense. As Lawrence Cremin explained in *The Transformation of the Schools*:

> To look back to the nineties is to sense an awakening of social conscience, a growing belief that this incredible suffering was neither the fault nor the inevitable lot of the sufferers, that it could certainly be alleviated, and that the road to alleviation was neither charity nor revolution, but in the last analysis education.

Reform was pursued in many ways and received the support of many groups. Ministers, priests, and rabbis were among the leaders of the progressives, as were newspaper reporters, politicians, and businesspeople. The strength and zeal of the reformers was often impressive. The Salvation Army could claim 20,000 privates and 3,000 officers in its ranks by 1900. Intellectuals such as Jane Addams and John Dewey were among the reformers, as were politicians such as Theodore Roosevelt.

The reform movement had many sources, but probably the social settlement movement was most important and best typified its spirit. The social settlement movement began in England in the early 1880s, and had as its origins ideas of Christian Socialists Frederick Denison Maurice and Charles Kingsley. Strongly influenced by Hegel and Carlyle, the Christian Socialists believed in the unity of mankind and abhorred the artificial divisions created between men by social class and wealth.

Kingsley promoted his ideas in essays, articles, and books, while Maurice brought them to the attention of the public through his establishment of the Working Men's College in London in 1854. According to Maurice, such institutions as the Working Men's College would eventually eliminate, through equal education, distinctions in English society based upon class and social status. Maurice received the support of art critic, writer, and social reformer John Ruskin. Together with Kingsley, Maurice and Ruskin were to inspire the principal leader of the English settlement house movement, Samuel A. Barnett.

Barnett was a Church of England minister who for some years had worked in a parish in one of London's worst slums. Interested in helping the working people in his parish and taking advantage of the energy and enthusiasm of university students with whom he had contact, Barnett organized the first university settlement in 1884. It was named Toynbee Hall after Arnold Toynbee, a young English reformer who had died while working to improve the lives of the poor. Rather than contributing to the poor as an act of charity, Barnett had young university-educated men live and work in the worst neighborhoods in London and share their lives with the poor. In doing so, they would make their settlement house a center for culture and education, and bring with it a new sense of community.

Toynbee Hall was an important early experiment in social work and served as an inspiration for similar programs in the United States. Stanton Coit, a graduate of Amherst and a Ph.D. from the University of Berlin, spent three months at Toynbee Hall in 1886 and brought the settlement idea back to the United States. Strongly influenced by Felix Adler and the ideas of the Ethical Cultural Movement, Coit established a settlement house on Forsyth Street in New York's Lower East Side.

The key to Coit's program was a system of neighborhood guilds, each guild containing 100 families who would work together in improving their neighborhoods and their lives. Coit believed that his neighborhood system would bring about a civic Renaissance in America, but he moved to England in 1887, and his plan for revitalization of American civic life collapsed. His place was quickly taken by a number of other individuals. Four Smith College graduates, led by Jane Robbins and Jean Fine, were responsible for setting up New York's College Settlement in late 1889. In Chicago, at the same time, Jane Addams and Ellen Gates Starr began what was to become the most famous of the American settlements, Hull House.

Addams saw herself and her coworkers as going into the immigrant slums and taking over where the city officials had failed. Through the settlement house, a sense of order and community would be established. Programs organized by the settlement houses would be based on the needs of the local community. If the filthy tenements were infested with lice, then Addams and her coworkers would show the immigrants how to exterminate them. If gangs of "street arabs" and urchins were a threat, then the settlement house would organize the children into clubs, provide opportunities for them to take part in organized sports, and instruct them in arts and crafts. If immigrant mothers had to work, then the settlement house would provide day-care nurseries and kindergartens for their children. Immigrants were taught to read and speak English. Social clubs were organized. Music lessons were provided, and choral groups regularly presented concerts.

Addams had as her purpose the regeneration of urban society. Her program was educational in the broadest sense. Hull House was to represent a center for practical education and culture. Lectures were a regular part of the activities at Hull House; John Dewey and Frank Lloyd Wright were among the most prominent speakers there. Reproductions of well-known works of art covered the walls of Hull House, and numerous art exhibits were held. The success of the lecture series and art exhibits as educational endeavors is somewhat doubtful. Hull House was probably most successful in the practical areas with direct impact on the lives of the immigrants.

Addams accepted the fact that industrialism and the factory had become a permanent part of American culture and society. She felt that it was crucial that the immigrant industrial workers understand and appreciate the important part they played in the industrial system. Innovative approaches to education were undertaken. With the help of Ellen Gates Starr, Addams set up the Hull House Labor Museum in 1900, through which she and Starr hoped to make people more aware of the importance of labor and of the role of the practical crafts and arts immigrants had brought with them.

The programs developed at Hull House were an important alternative to the public schools' relatively restricted and narrow version of education. Increasingly, those involved in the settlement house movement began to set in motion reforms within the schools. For example, Lillian Wald of New York City's Henry Street

FIGURE 8-1   A back-alley in the Hull House neighborhood of Chicago. From Jane Addams, *Twenty Years at Hull House* (New York: Macmillan, 1910), p. 95.

Settlement persuaded the New York City Health Department to hire school physicians for the first time. Her colleague Elizabeth Farrell was responsible for starting, under the sponsorship of the board of education, the first classes for handicapped children. Individuals other than the settlement house leaders turned to the question of education and urban reform. Among the most interesting of these was Jacob Riis.

Riis came to the United States from Denmark in 1870. After a difficult period of adjustment and settlement, in 1877 Riis became a reporter for the *New York Tribune*. His firsthand experience as an immigrant suited him ideally to report the problems and lives of the immigrants increasingly filling New York City below Fourteenth Street in the Bowery. He worked for more than ten years as a police reporter for the *Tribune*, then went to work for the *Evening Star*.

Riis's work as a reformer was at the time of massive immigration into the United States. Between 1890 and 1900, approximately 2.8 million immigrants came from Italy, Germany, Russia, England, Austro-Hungaria, Norway, and Sweden. They crowded into cities such as New York, where populations were already swelling because of an increasing shift of American rural population to urban centers.

In 1890, Riis permanently established his reputation as an urban reformer with the publication of his book *How the Other Half Lives*. Based on his own first-hand experiences in the slum and tenement districts of New York, it brought attention to the immigrants' unhealthy living conditions and poor wages, and the destruction of the integrity of the individual. He was particularly concerned for children, and felt that with their purity of spirit they did not deserve the tragic fate that most would meet in the slums. Riis was essentially an environmentalist. He argued that the corrupt environment of the cities threatened the institutions of democracy, that corrupt politics sprang from and were encouraged by unstable homes, poor schools, and an unhealthy physical environment. "A man cannot live like a pig and vote like a man," Riis wrote.

Education and improvement of the physical environment were the keys in Riis's belief in city reform. Riis, like Jane Addams, hoped that through proper education, the importance of the home and the school would be reestablished in the lives of the immigrant poor. He felt that the New York schools, overcrowded, poorly designed, and extremely limited in curriculum, inadequately met the needs of poor children.

Riis strongly favored the establishment of industrial schools. "The industrial school plants itself squarely in the gap between the tenement and the public school," he wrote. These schools would provide the link between the immigrant culture and the larger American culture. Like Horace Mann fifty years earlier, he felt that the schools should provide immigrant children with educations adequate to vote and to become good citizens.

Many of Riis's articles and books were illustrated, and he used a projector when he lectured. The illustrations were based on his research photographs. Consistently used to document educational conditions, Riis's pictures of childhood in New York are among the most valuable resources on urban life and education in the period.

An excellent example of Riis's educational photographs is his "A Class in the Condemned Essex Street School." The inadequate facilities were clearly illustrated. On overcrowded, poorly lit, and badly heated classrooms such as this, Riis commented:

> . . . In New York we put boys in foul, dark class-rooms, where they grow crooked for want of proper desks; we bid them play in gloomy caverns which the sun never enters, forgetting that boys must have a chance to play properly, or they will play hooky; we turn them away by the thousands from even such delights as these, and in the same breath illogically threaten them with jail if they do not come. . . .

Riis also focused attention on the need to establish playgrounds for children living in the poorer neighborhoods. Although by 1887, legislation had been passed in New York City calling for the establishment of small parks with playground equipment for children, none had been built by 1894. Then Riis began to lobby

FIGURE 8-2   The Essex Street Market School; photograph by Jacob Riis. Courtesy of the Library of Congress.

strongly for them. In *The Century* magazine, for example, he proposed that sufficient land be condemned around every school in the city to build a playground, a "people's park" in which children could play during their recesses and where mothers living in the neighborhood could take their babies during the day.

The city government was unwilling to spend the money necessary to tear down the tenements surrounding schools, and roof-garden playgrounds were proposed as alternatives to playgrounds at the street level. The plentiful supply of light and air, while not improving classrooms, would provide some relief from the dark and cramped conditions in which many children were forced to learn. Riis argued that there were dangers of fires, and that by placing playgrounds on the roofs of schools, it would become much more difficult to have the entire community take advantage of them.

Playgrounds, whether on the roof or at street level, would induce tenement and immigrant children to attend school more regularly. With the choice of staying at home in their dark airless tenements, or coming to school where they could enjoy a playground full of air and light, Riis believed that the children would choose the latter. As he explained, "Instead of being repelled, children would be attracted to a school that was identified with their playground. Truancy would cease." Ideally, children would come to identify with the school. An identity and sense of self, rather than being shaped in the alleys and back streets of the tenement district, would be formed in the fresh air and wholesome environment of the playground.

Riis wished to make the schools community centers that would provide a wholesome alternative to the squalor and destructive environment of the tenements and streets.

> . . . [T]he churches, clubs, schools, educational and helpful agencies . . . make a front of 756 running feet on the street, while the saloons, put side by side, stretch themselves over nearly a mile; so that ideals of citizenship are minting themselves on the minds of the people at the rate of seven saloon thoughts to one educational thought.

Riis's encouragement of the establishment of parks and improvement of physical conditions of the schools and tenements in New York City were his principal contributions as an urban reformer. He knew, however, that, by itself, physical reform of the urban environment would not be enough. While establishing better schools, recreation centers, and parks was critically important, the immigrant children and their parents must be properly educated if the conditions of the city, and life within it, were to be improved. Thus, Riis's reform attempts can best be understood as combining reform of the physical environment with the general moral and intellectual education of the individual.

Riis drew ideas from the Children's Aid Society, the Fresh Air Fund, and other groups. Rooftop playgrounds and evening programs in the schools had been successful in England for some time. Sol Cohen has argued in *Progressives and Urban Reform* that Riis's ideas were not original and that Riis was "a great propagandist, rather than a great innovator." Even if propagandistic in intent and purpose, Riis's photographs nonetheless tell clearly an invaluable story of the overcrowding, cramped, sordid conditions in the New York City schools—and reform, like all else, requires a variety of talents.

CRITICS OF THE SYSTEM

Although the reform movement of the 1890s focused initially on the physical conditions of the city, it expanded to address other social issues. In the case of the schools, increasing criticisms were made of their organization and curriculum. The most powerful of the school critics was Joseph Mayer Rice.

Rice was a young New York City pediatrician, who had studied education and psychology in Germany between 1888 and 1890. Back in the United States, Rice published a series of articles on education. The editor of *The Forum*, Walter Hines Page, was impressed, no doubt, by the prospect of the articles. And then, too, Rice's brother was *The Forum's* owner.

Under the sponsorship of *The Forum*, Rice toured the country examining every possible aspect of the public schools. He observed classrooms; talked to children, teachers, and parents; and interviewed school board members and administrators. His findings were published as a series of articles in *The Forum*.

Between January and June of 1892, Rice visited thirty-six cities and interviewed more than 1,200 teachers. The first article in the series appeared the following October. They continued to be published until June of 1893. They raised extraordinary controversy among educators and the general public. Rice reported that in city after city, political corruption, apathy, and incompetence were responsible for creating inadequate and badly run schools. In New York City, for example, a principal whom Rice had interviewed totally disregarded the idea that the children for whom she was responsible as a supervisor might have any knowledge or experience of their own. Rote memorization and parroted answer were the principal's ideal for a properly schooled child. As Rice explained:

> The principal's ideal lies in giving each child the ability to answer without hesitation, upon leaving her school, every one of the questions formulated by her. In order to reach the desired end, the school has been converted into the most dehumanizing institution that I have ever laid eyes upon, each child being treated as if he possessed a memory and the faculty of speech, but no individuality, no sensibilities, no soul.

Rice wrote that the principal and her program received high praise from the local superintendent. The school was based on the maxim of "save the minutes." Rather than thinking, children were commanded to simply absorb and memorize whatever was presented to them. When Rice asked the principal why the children were not allowed to move their heads or arms and legs when they were having their lessons, she responded saying, "Why should they look behind when the teacher is in front of them"? Rice's contempt for her approach was complete.

Rice's picture of the schools was in general a discouraging one. A teacher in Chicago was quoted as haranguing her students with the command: "Don't stop to think, tell me what you know." Bright spots did emerge at a few points. In La Porte, Indiana, Rice saw important progress in classes in art. (A Froebelian, W. N. Hailman, was superintendent there.) Francis W. Parker's Cook County Normal School was providing outstanding models of teaching and instruction.

Rice called for basic and sweeping reforms. He maintained that if the schools were to improve, they must be totally divorced from local politics. School boards could have one and only one purpose in mind—providing the children under their charge the best education possible. In addition, proper supervision of teachers must be introduced into the schools. Incompetence would be checked and eliminated from the classroom as the result of proper examination and supervision on the part of the school's administration.

Rice was advocating in his proposals a system of accountability for the schools. His primary emphasis was on how the schools were administered and the quality of their curriculum. Other critics and reformers addressed similar issues. At the meeting of the National Education Association in Saratoga Springs in 1892, a group that eventually came to be known as the Committee of Ten or Secondary School Studies, was organized by the N.E.A.'s National Council of Education. The committee, which was headed by Charles W. Eliot, the president of Harvard University, was established in order to try to determine a standard set of entrance requirements for those applying to college.

Until this time, most colleges required applicants to have completed a Classical course of study at the secondary level. This normally included four years of Latin and two or three years of Greek. Students who had followed the English course of study were usually not admitted to universities or colleges. Under the leadership of the Committee of Ten, an attempt was made to broaden the criteria under which people would be admitted to college and university study.

Meeting over a period of a year and a half, the Committee of Ten completed its report in December of 1893. A total of 30,000 copies were sent throughout the country by the United States Bureau of Education. Against Eliot's desires, the report outlined four courses of study for the high school: Classical, Latin-Scientific, Modern Language, and English. In the Classical course, greater emphasis was placed on the inclusion of subjects such as English, history, and science. In general, the report argued that the primary purpose of the secondary schools was to prepare students for life, rather than just for college. At the same time, the report maintained that those individuals who had successfully completed the high school curriculum should be able to continue on to college without difficulty. From a practical point of view, the report of the Committee of Ten had the effect of making higher education more accessible to a larger number of people.

While the Committee of Ten was preparing its report, a second N.E.A. committee was appointed in February of 1893 to address the question of elementary education. Known as the Committee of Fifteen, this group was specifically charged to examine the training of teachers, the reorganization and combining of school subjects, and the organization of the schools. Under the direction of William H. Maxwell, the superintendent of schools for Brooklyn, the Committee appointed three subcommittees including one on "Correlation," reorganizing and combining school subjects.

The subcommittee on correlation was chaired by United States Commissioner of Education, William Torrey Harris, who wrote its report. The subcommittee report strongly upheld the value of the traditional divisions of subjects in elementary schools.

At issue in the debates of the subcommittee on correlation was not only the course of study, but also the question of what the philosophical bases of education should be. By the end of the 1880s, a number of new educational theories had begun to emerge in the United States. Among these was Herbartianism. Based on the ideas of the German philosopher Johann Friederich Herbart and his followers, the Herbartian movement in the United States was led by Frank and Charles McMurry of the Illinois State Normal University, and Charles DeGarmo of Swarthmore College.

Herbartianism is difficult to define precisely. There was much disagreement, even among those who considered themselves leaders of the movement. Basically, the Herbartians rejected the traditional idea of mental "faculties." They saw little value in mental discipline, as reflected in exercises involving memorization and recitation. Instead they placed greater emphasis on the subject matter being taught.

Such an approach was in considerable conflict with views held by Harris. In February of 1895, the Committee of Fifteen finally presented its report. In presenting the report of his subcommittee, Harris strongly opposed the Herbartians and their philosophy. While a number of issues were discussed, the most important was Harris's conviction that the Herbartian theory denied the concept of free will.

The arguments made for and against Herbartianism in the 1890s are tedious and obscure. What is perhaps most important is that an important choice was being made between philosophies. A new educational leadership was emerging. Whether or not they realized it, the curriculum reforms these new leaders were supporting implied more than a shift of philosophy. They were supporters of a new psychology. Harris's idealism was being replaced with materialism. New and different answers were being developed about how the human mind related to matter.

PSYCHOLOGY AND THE NEW PEDAGOGY

Herbartianism was by no means the only new educational philosophy to emerge from the 1890s. Of far greater importance, for example, was the *Child Study Movement*. Dating back to the 1880s, the Child Study Movement was devoted to attempting the study and understanding of the child's behavior and development through systematic observation. The leader of the movement in the United States was the psychologist, G. Stanley Hall.

Hall, the son of an old but impoverished Massachusetts farm family, was born in 1844 in rural hilly western Massachusetts. Exempted from the Civil War draft, he graduated from Williams College, studied theology for a year, and then studied in Germany for three years. After teaching at Antioch College in Ohio, he became William James's student at Harvard and completed his doctorate in psychology, the first in the United States. In 1882, at age thirty-eight, he was named a member of the faculty at newly established Johns Hopkins University in Baltimore, and his career had begun.

Hall was one of the founders of psychology in the United States; perhaps only William James was more important. He was *the* founder of child psychology. An admiring biographer called him the "playboy of Western scholarship." His enthusiasms, "crazes" as he called them, led him into a variety of fields: theology and philosophy initially, then psychology, pedagogy (the science of teaching), child study, history, sex education, adolescence, and Freudian psychology all caught his interest. Unlike many researchers in education who would follow, Hall seems to have begun with an interest in "why," research to satisfy a need for knowledge. His interest in "how" was usually secondary. He was another of those individuals with inexhaustible energy. He was scholar, lecturer, journal founder, and editor, and after 1889, president of Clark University. He wrote hundreds of articles, supervised dozens of doctoral dissertations, and wrote half a dozen books. He was a founder and first president of the American Psychological Association. In the 1960s, he was described as having had values ". . . ominously parallel to twentieth century totalitarianism." It is true that he was nostalgic and felt that earlier times had been better times. With other prosperous citizens of his age he shared a longing for public order, and was a staunch antifeminist. Staunch antifeminism was not rare then, but Hall gave it an aura, and so aided its perpetuation.

Hall's first paper on the contents of children's minds—what preschoolers did and did not know—was published in 1883, and marks the beginning of *Child Study* (or, in a Latin form, *paidology*). Hall returned to child study in the 1890s, when due to his influence several child study associations were established. The Department of Child Study of the N.E.A. was established in 1893. There were thousands of published papers on Child Study, and tens of thousands of unpublished case studies. By 1896, aspects of childhood that had been studied included physical measurements, death rates, stammering, hearing losses, memory, games, children in primitive cultures, secret languages, imitation, home environment, and punishment. The Child Study Movement had a common subject—the child. It had no common approach, no linking theory. For instance, a theoretical connection between children's heights and stammering is unimaginable. Child Study was outlived by Hall, who lived and wrote until 1924. Child Study was an idea whose day would never come.

In the late 1800s, psychology was emerging as a special discipline or branch of learning. It was founded upon a philosophical base and upon research by early German physiological neurologists. Psychological theories that now seem crude were developed. Hall's approach to psychology came from his longtime conviction, acquired at Williams, that human behavior should be interpreted in the light of Charles Darwin's evolutionary theory. That theory explained the improvement by adoption of each species, including mankind, Homo sapiens. It had been argued that the individual's growth followed the evolution of his species. "Phylogeny recapitulates ontogeny," in learned language. The growth of the body and intellect retraced that of the race. (A game of cowboys and Indians was the reliving of a barbaric "epoch.") This general theory, however dubious it seems nearly a century later, was the theoretical, or paradigmatic, basis for Hall's psychology of children and education. It would be disproved and discarded within a few years, but that is often the fate of theories.

From Hall's theory it followed that evolution, which was indeed right, should not be contradicted by education. Schooling should be adjusted to the age and "culture epoch" of the child. The Herbartians and the Child Study Movement were eventually linked through the cultural epoch theory and the concept of recapitulation. Other theorists picked up these ideas, the most interesting and important of whom was John Dewey. Dewey, although a member of the Executive Committee of the National Herbart Society and a supporter and critic of the Child Study Movement, cannot be accurately portrayed as a member of either group. Instead, he was an original thinker and force of his own—perhaps the most important in the history of American education.

Dewey was born in 1859 in Burlington, Vermont. After attending traditional district schools in the area, Dewey went to the high school in Burlington and then entered the University of Vermont when he was sixteen. Evidently his early experience in school had little impact on him. In recalling the experiences of his childhood some years later, Dewey remembered that the most important part of his early education was obtained outside of the schoolroom in the Burlington community and the nearby countryside.

While at the University of Vermont, Dewey developed what was to be a lifelong interest in philosophy. Upon completing his degree in 1879, he went to Oil City, Pennsylvania, where he taught high school for two years. Free to spend much of his time reading, Dewey began to pursue systematically the study of philosophy. Returning to Burlington, he taught briefly in a nearby village school. While in Burlington Dewey was tutored in philosophy by H.A.P. Torrey. It was then that he submitted, and William Torrey Harris accepted, several articles for the *Journal of Speculative Philosophy.*

While Dewey's interest in philosophy began to expand, an imaginative experiment in higher education was being undertaken in Baltimore, Maryland. A local businessman, Johns Hopkins, had endowed what became a research university based upon German models. Dewey read the university's inaugural address by evolutionist Julian Huxley. Highly impressed, Dewey decided to apply to study philosphy at the new university. Failing to receive a fellowship (the great sociologist Thorstein Veblin, a fellow student of Dewey's, was also refused support), Dewey borrowed $500 and entered the university in the fall of 1882, as a student of G. Stanley Hall.

(Their relationship seems to have been a cool one.) Dewey received a fellowship the following year and completed his doctorate in 1884.

Johns Hopkins was a remarkable place to be in the early 1880s. It was expected that both advanced students and professors would be involved in original research. Dewey's early coursework was in history and political theory with Herbert B. Adams. During his second year he took courses in history and political science (Woodrow Wilson was a fellow student), animal physiology, elocution, and philosophy and logic. While at Hopkins, he studied under such major figures as G. Stanley Hall, Charles S. Pierce, and George Sylvester Morris.

Morris undoubtedly had the greatest impact on shaping Dewey's career. Under his supervision Dewey began to study the work of the German philosopher Hegel. More important, after Dewey finished his thesis, *The Psychology of Kant*, in 1884, he went as an instructor with Morris to the University of Michigan where Morris had been made chairman of the department of philosophy. Dewey was to remain (except for a year teaching at the University of Minnesota) at Michigan for ten years. It was while teaching at Michigan that his interests in primary and secondary education began to develop. Beginning in 1871, the University began to admit the graduates of any secondary school whose program had been approved by the university. Faculty committees were sent by the university to determine the quality of various schools' programs. Dewey often served on these committees. He also became active in the Michigan Schoolmasters Club, serving as its vice-president in 1887 and 1888.

During this period, Dewey frequently spoke to teachers' groups and published a number of articles addressing general educational questions. While working with the schools in Michigan, Dewey became convinced that the quality of secondary schooling was ultimately dependent upon the type of instruction students had received in the earlier grades. While at Michigan, he became convinced that the schools were failing because of lack of coordination between programs, poorly conceived curricula, and limited understanding of methods of teaching.

In 1894, Dewey accepted an offer from the University of Chicago to head the combined departments of philosophy, psychology, and pedagogy. Included among his responsibilities at Chicago was the organization and administration of an experimental school for the university. Eventually known as the Laboratory School, Dewey saw the school as an ideal setting for experimental work in education. As he wrote in an early report:

> The conception underlying the school is that of a laboratory. It bears the same relation to work in pedagogy that a laboratory bears to biology, physics, or chemistry. Like any such laboratory, it has two main purposes: (1) to exhibit, test, verify and criticize theoretical statements and principles; (2) to add to the sum of facts and principles in its special line.

Dewey was not interested in creating a practice school for training teachers, but in creating a laboratory where pedagogical ideas could be practically tested.

Implicit in Dewey's work at the Laboratory School was the desire to establish a "science of education." Much of his work in education was based on the work of earlier educational theorists, including Johann Pestalozzi, Frederich Froebel, and Johann Herbart. Like them, he believed that children learned best by doing things for themselves and learning directly from the environment in which they lived.

Dewey argued in *The School and Society* (1899) that what the best and wisest parents wanted for their children, the community must want for its children as well. Only by helping each child to become all that he or she was capable of becoming could the community achieve its maximum potential. Dewey maintained that changes in the culture and society were necessitating the development of new curricula and methods that were responsive to the needs of the new society. He objected to traditional rote learning from textbooks and instead advocated a type of instruction that focused on the interests and activities of the child.

Dewey believed that children were active and inquiring beings with impulses, concerns, and desires of their own. Breaking with earlier traditions, he argued that the teacher's duty was not just to impart knowledge. Instead,

> His problem is that of inducing a vital, personal experiencing. Hence, what concerns him, as teacher, is the ways in which that subject may become part of experience; what there is in the child's present that is usable with reference to it; how such elements are to be used; how his own knowledge of the subject matter may assist in interpreting the child's needs and doings, and determine the medium in which the child should be placed in order that his growth may be properly directed. He is concerned, not with the subject-matter as such, but with the subject matter as a related factor in a total and growing experience.

For Dewey, the world of the child was a world of individuals with personal interests, rather than a realm of facts and laws. The ideal school and teacher respected these interests on the part of the student. At the same time the teacher attempted to shape the direction of the students' interests so that they conformed with social needs and requirements.

Dewey attempted to make the school into a cooperative community. He did this by making occupations such as cooking, weaving, carpentry, sewing, and metalwork the basis for much of the experience of the child. Dewey felt that by integrating traditional subjects, it would be possible to develop not only children's intellectual abilities, but their imaginative, emotional, creative, and social capacities as well. Textbooks were rarely used at the Laboratory School. Instead students were encouraged to search for information themselves, as well as to draw upon the skills and knowledge of highly trained and competent teachers.

Learning at the Laboratory School was seen as a synthetic process. In the textile room, for example, the children were able to learn about different textiles by processing and weaving them themselves. Looms, dying vats, and spinning wheels were included in the textile room. Samples of different types of fabrics were available for the students to study along with exhibits on their history and use. As Dewey explained: "You can concentrate the history of all mankind into the evolution of flax, cotton and wool fibers into clothing." Reading, writing, arithmetic, and spelling were related to the activities undertaken by the students in the textile room. Traditionally different subject matters were correlated and a unified curriculum was achieved.

The textile curriculum was one small example of the curriculum developed by Dewey and his colleagues at the Laboratory School. Essentially what Dewey attempted to do was to integrate the activities of the school with real life experiences. "Learning by doing" became the motto for the school. Instead of being a place to learn lessons, the school became a process of directed learning.

Dewey's emphasis upon learning by doing was picked up in many interesting ways by educators throughout the country. Increasingly, the community was seen

FIGURE 8-3   The Textile Laboratory of the University of Chicago Laboratory School, c. 1896. Courtesy of the Department of Education, University of Chicago.

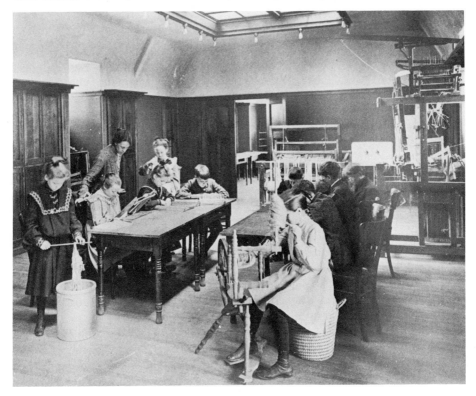

as having the potential to educate the child. In 1899, for example, the Brooklyn Institute of Arts and Science began the first children's museum in the United States. Known as the Brooklyn Children's Museum, the purpose of the museum was explained in an early brochure:

> ... to build up gradually for the children of Brooklyn and the surrounding neighborhood a collection that will delight and instruct the children who visit it; to bring together collections in every branch of natural history that is calculated to interest children, and to stimulate their powers of observation and reflection; and to illustrate by collections of pictures, cartoons, charts, models and maps, each of the important branches of knowledge which are taught in the elementary schools.

Children would visit the museum on a voluntary basis, attracted as a result of their natural interest and curiosity to its programs and activities. The museum would allow children living in the tenements and brownstones of Brooklyn to escape the urban environment in which they lived by taking advantage of a cheerful and exciting museum in a park-like setting.

As in the case of Dewey's curriculum, the Brooklyn Children's Museum hoped to bring children of all ages, whether or not they were attending school, into direct contact with the subjects and objects that

> ... appeal to the interest of their daily life, in their school work, in their reading, in their games and rambles in the fields, and in the industries which are carried on about them.

Dewey had included an instructional museum as part of his plan for an ideal school described in *The School and Society*. While the Brooklyn Children's Museum represented one type of approach to hands-on education similar to that of Dewey's, a second interesting alternative was developed by the Saint Louis Board of Education in 1905.

As a result of the 1904 Louisiana Purchase Exposition in Saint Louis, interest had developed among teachers and school administrators in providng more hands-on learning experiences for children in the public schools. After the exposition was closed, the assistant superintendent of schools, Carl Rathmann, persuaded the school board to set aside funds for the establishment of an educational museum. A museum was started the following year, using exhibits left over from the World's Fair, as well as specially purchased collections of lantern slides, botanical collections, and stuffed animals.

The motto of the museum was "Bring the world to the child" and represented a continuation of the spirit of the Louisiana Purchase Exposition, which through its exhibits had brought the world to Saint Louis. Instead of having children visit the museum, collections of objects and slides were sent out to the public schools throughout the school system. Instead of just studying maps and materials in textbooks in geography class, students were given the opportunity to actually handle the raw materials and industrial products of a country. Under the guidance of their teacher, the students would be introduced to the climates, products, and occupations of different people from around the world. Stereoscope views, lantern slides and photographs would provide students a clearer sense of the people they were studying, their ways of life, and the society in which they lived.

Parallels to the Dewey curriculum at the Laboratory School were to be found throughout the curriculum of the Educational Museum. Carl Rathmann, for example, explained in his first report concerning the Museum that

> By means of the cotton exhibit, we take the children to the cotton fields, where they study the plant, the method of preparing the soil, the harvesting; to the cotton gin, where the seed is separated from the lint; to the markets to see the bailing and the shipping; to the large cotton factories where the lint is spun and woven into fabrics; and to the refineries to learn how cotton seed oil, oil cake, cottonlene, and soap are made.

Lantern slides and photographs were used to develop comparisons between how cotton was processed in primitive cultures and how it was done in modern factories.

The development of "teaching" museums such as the Brooklyn Children's Museum and the Saint Louis Educational Museum are just a few examples of the influence of Dewey's work at the Laboratory School. By 1900, the school had come to the attention of educators throughout the country. Although Dewey left Chicago in 1905 to assume a position in the philosophy department of Columbia University, his influence in education continued to spread. The influence of Dewey

FIGURE 8-4   Deliveries being made for the Educational Museum of the St. Louis Public Schools, c. 1905. Courtesy of the Audio-Visual Department of the St. Louis Public Schools.

on various schools and curricula, and his role in the development of "progressive education" will be discussed in subsequent chapters.

YOUTH

Throughout his writings in the late 1890s, Dewey indicated that he saw American culture undergoing profound change. An urban industrial consciousness was increasingly dominating American culture. New values were emerging along with important changes in the social and economic system. Perhaps nowhere were these changes more evident than with the youth population.

During the late nineteenth century the role of youth in the economic and social system underwent a major alteration. Throughout the nineteenth century, youthful workers represented a critically important part of the labor force in the United States. By the turn of the century, however, younger workers were becoming less important in the economic system. Technological improvements in farming meant that fewer youths were needed to work in the agricultural sector of the economy. Rural populations were moving to the cities. Increased industrial efficiency eliminated many jobs that had traditionally been assigned to younger workers. Older established workers opposed young workers since they undercut wages and threatened job security. Opportunities to enter the job market were more limited. Protective legislation in the field of child labor, while preventing children from being abused, also made it increasingly difficult for youths to enter the job market.

During the first half of the twentieth century, with the exception of the periods of the two world wars, the number of youths engaged in work steadily decreased. Statistics cited by the contemporary educational historian, Joel Spring, indicate that while the male labor force between the ages of fourteen and nineteen increased from 50 percent to 62 percent between 1890 and 1900, the employment figures for this same youth group decreased to 51.5 percent by 1920, and to 44 percent by 1940.

As the need for youth labor decreased during the twentieth century, there developed a corresponding growth in interest in the problems of youth. As early as 1904, for example, the psychologist G. Stanley Hall published his pioneer two-volume study, *Adolescence*. Hall's definition of adolescence as a functional stage in human development was based as much on a social perception as on the recognition of a stage of physiological development. Unlike earlier times, when children with the onset of puberty were largely expected to enter into the responsibilities of adulthood, an intermediate period of transition, adolescence, was increasingly recognized as existing between the end of childhood and the acceptance of full adult responsibilities. The vicissitudes of this period of development for the youth were clearly defined by theorists such as Hall:

> The functions of every sense undergo reconstruction, . . . The voice changes, vascular instability, blushing, and flushing are increased. Sex asserts its mastery

in field after field, and works its havoc in the form of secret vice, debauch, disease, and enfeebled heredity, cadences the soul to both its normal and abnormal rhythms, and sends many thousand youth a year to quacks, because neither parents, teachers, or physicians know how to deal with its problems.

The energy of youths during this period of their development was seen as having enormous potential. Hall, as well as individuals such as the pioneer social worker Jane Addams, argued that the energies of the youth population should be used for the betterment of the culture.

The development of an increasingly sophisticated technological culture beginning in the early decades of the twentieth century had the effect of making the services of the youth population more nearly superfluous. As the work of youth was needed less and less, enrollment in school began to increase dramatically. In 1900, according to Spring, 78.7 percent of the population between the ages of five and seventeen attended school. By 1926, this figure had jumped to 90.4 percent. Similar increases had taken place during this period in the number of youths attending college.

With the decline of the need for youths in the labor force during the early twentieth century, there was a corresponding increase in compulsory schooling. Although local compulsory education laws were passed during the early colonial period, their implementation on a statewide basis did not begin until the middle of the nineteenth century when Masschusetts in 1852 passed the first statewide law requiring children to attend school. Yet, despite such laws, attendance in school throughout the nineteenth century was largely voluntary. Relatively little concern was given to teenagers who dropped out of school to find employment. Loopholes in the various attendance laws were easily found so long as there was a demand for the services of young workers.

The enforcement of compulsory education laws seems to have increased as adolescent workers were increasingly superfluous. Selwyn K. Troen has pointed out that in the 1870s, one third of the employees in Macy's department store in New York City were cash girls, while the same proportion worked as cash boys in Marshall Field in Chicago during the 1880s. In 1902, Macy's, and then Marshall Field, introduced a pneumatic tube system that eliminated the need for young messengers to carry money back and forth between the store's sales counters and the bookkeeping department. This relatively simple innovation, combined with the invention of devices such as the cash register in 1878, and their widespread adoption and use by the turn of the century almost completely eliminated the need for cash boys and cash girls. Technology was similarly affecting other areas of employment. Improvements in communications systems, such as the invention of the telephone, quickly eliminated the need for messenger boys to carry information between different offices in downtown business districts. As a result, another important source of youth employment was also eliminated.

Interestingly, as youth labor became less and less needed, increasing efforts were made to regulate and limit it. Reformers increasingly saw child laborers as being exploited by the capitalist system. In addition, psychologists, such as G. Stanley Hall, began to warn that interference with the child's natural development would not only be destructive to the development of the individual, but to the normal evolution and development of society as well.

The new psychology of Hall and the child study movement, as well as the educational ideas of Dewey and his followers, stressed the physiological and psychological importance of play. "When children are robbed of playtime, they too often reassert their right to it in manhood, as vagabonds, criminals, and prostitutes." Such views not only encouraged the establishment of public playgrounds, but also led an increasing number of individuals to criticize child labor.

By 1904, the National Child Labor Committee had been organized. Headed by Felix Adler of the Ethical Culture School in New York, the committee had a board that included Florence Kelley, Jane Addams, Lillian Wald, Edgar G. Murphy, Edward T. Devine, Robert D. DeForest, and Homer Folks. The N.C.L.C. had as its purpose the investigation of working conditions, the establishment of more stringent legislation, and the enforcement of existing laws. Promoting its course through a wide range of activities, the N.C.L.C. made extensive use of photographs to document the working conditions of children in America.

Numerous books and articles were published at this time describing the conditions of child labor in America. Full-length works included Ernest Poole's *The Street: Its Child Workers*; Robert Hunter's *Poverty*; and John Spargo's *The Bitter Cry of the Children*. Articles condemning child labor began to appear regularly in periodicals such as *The Survey, The Outlook, McClure's, The Independent*, and even *The Saturday Evening Post* and *Cosmopolitan*. Among the most interesting of these articles were the photo stories of Lewis Hine.

Hine was born in Oshkosh, Wisconsin, in 1874. He went to New York in 1901 to teach at the Ethical Culture School. Hine resigned from teaching in 1908 to work full time as a documentary photographer. As the staff photographer for *The Survey*, Hine also undertook work for the N.C.L.C. Traveling thousands of miles over the course of the next seven years, Hine took photographs of children working in canneries, coal mines, sweatshops, tenements, and cotton fields and cranberry bogs. Following the reform tradition of Riis, Hine produced some of the great documentary and reform photographs of his era.

Although primarily a photographer, Hine often wrote about the materials he photographed. In an article published in *The Survey* in 1913 entitled "Baltimore to Biloxi and Back," Hine described the conditions of children working in oyster and shrimp canneries. Children seven and eight years of age were forced out of bed at three o'clock in the morning to work shelling shrimps. Hine explained how

When they are picking shrimps, their fingers and even their shoes are attacked by a corrosive substance in the shrimp that is strong enough to eat the cans into which they are put. The day's work on shrimp is much shorter than on oysters as fingers on the worker give out in spite of the fact that they are compelled to harden them in an alum solution at the end of the day. Moreover, the shrimp are packed in ice, and a few hours handling of these icy things is dangerous for any child.

Hine was also upset because their work in the factories kept them from attending school. For pay of 25 or 50 cents a day they not only endangered their health, but were also deprived of any formal education. In those few instances where Hine did observe children going to school, he found that they attended only a few hours a day, often having worked since the early morning.

Hine fought to expose children working illegally in factories. His camera took him anywhere children were at work. Unlike Riis's, Hine's concern for reform went beyond the city. His photographs of "breaker boys" in coal mines in Pennsylvania,

FIGURE 8-5 Cover photograph by Lewis Hine for the September 23, 1911 issue of *The Survey* magazine.

child cotton spinners working in rural factories in North Carolina, and child agricultural workers engaged in almost every task imaginable provide us with remarkable documentary sources for the history of child labor.

The work of Hine and groups such as the N.C.L.C. was eventually responsible for bringing about the passage of important state and federal legislation limiting child labor. When the N.C.L.C. was originally organized in 1904, there was virtually no legislation existing in any of the states concerning child labor. By 1914, thirty-five states a fourteen-year-age minimum, and an eight-hour-day maximum for workers under sixteen. Thirty-four states prohibited children from working at night, while thirty-six states had appointed factory inspectors to enforce child labor regulations.

By 1916, the federal Keating-Owen Act was passed. Providing for the protection of child laborers on a national level, the passage of the law was the triumph of the Progressive reformers, such as Hine, who were concerned with child labor reform. Failing to address the needs of domestic and agricultural workers, the law was eventually repealed in 1920. Its effects on reducing child labor and the child labor reform movement in general, however, are clearly evident in statistics from the period. In 1900, the census listed 790,623 children working who were between the ages of ten and thirteen, and 959,555 working who were between fourteen and fifteen years of age. By 1920, these figures were reduced to 378,063 children working between the ages of ten and thirteen, and 682,795 children working between fourteen and fifteen years of age.

CONCLUSION

This strain of the Progressive reform movement in education was an important attempt to deal with the problems created by an increasingly complex urban industrial society. Jane Addams, Jacob Riis, John Dewey, and other reformers had as their purpose the improvement of the environment in which people lived and were educated. Realizing that traditional models of education and reform were inadequate to meet the demands of the new society and culture emerging by the end of the nineteenth century, they provided important alternatives.

In retrospect, many of the innovations undertaken by these reformers seem naive and overly optimistic. Yet despite this, these reformers did help to create a better life for many people, and laid the foundations for much of our modern education system.

CHAPTER NINE
EFFICIENCY AND
MANAGEMENT

There were two streams of reform in the Progressive era, between roughly 1896 and 1920. One stream of reform, which we have already discussed, included within it thought that led to the establishment of settlement houses and of visiting teachers, and ideas such as Dewey's.

There was another stream of reform that was in many ways more influential than the first. It led first to the reform of city government. The continued and rapid growth of cities made them more and more subject to control by political bosses. Trickery, bribery, and graft enabled the city bosses, or at least the most greedy of them, to divert city funds into their own pockets. The phenomenon of city bosses was not new in 1896, but to reformers and respective reformers they seemed to have become too numerous, too audacious, and much too voracious.

Reformers sharing the same general convictions also found reason for concern in the growth and increasing power of big business. Even before the Civil War the railroads had been big business by most standards. Before 1900, many other big businesses had appeared. Oil refining was dominated by Standard Oil. The production of chemicals and explosives was dominated by Du Pont. Many other industries were controlled by oligopolies, combinations of a few firms. For some reformers, bigness was badness. For other reformers, of whom the most prominent by far was Theodore Roosevelt, bigness was acceptable, although badness demanded strong responsive action by the government.

One variety of school reform reflected this second philosophy. Progressive reform led, even in the 1890s, to efforts to centralize control of the city schools. At least some reformers in the city schools would discover "efficiency" as industry knew it. At about the same time, "scientific management" was introduced in the schools. These innovations had other effects, but they created a demand for exact measurement of what pupils had been taught. Reformers urged centralization of control and administration in the schools, efficiency and scientific management, and the management of what had been taught.

Historians in the last twenty years have subjected these Progressive reformers of education to the strongest of criticisms. Some of these criticisms we accept and will express. We think other criticisms have been based upon unexamined assumptions or, to put it bluntly, gut feelings. We agree more than disagree with criticisms and critics of this stream of reform in the Progressive era. But, even though it complicates matters, we are persuaded that there are human explanations for these turns of events. We are also persuaded that although by our standards the outcomes were more unfortunate than fortunate, there were also positive and useful contributions from this strain of reform.

SCHOOL REFORM AND SCHOOL CONTROL

The most powerful men, and women, in the progressive reform movements were members of the middle class and the well-off, members of the "elite." This was true not only of the city reformers, but also of the school reformers. Public statements supporting school reform were often made by the prominent and the successful. University presidents Eliot of Harvard, White of Cornell, and Harper of Chicago were staunch supporters of school reform. They were joined, of course, by school superintendents, for instance Blewett of Saint Louis and Maxwell of New York City. Supporters of centralization of school control in New York City were, as David Hammack has shown, business and professional men, advocates of efficiency in city government generally, and also old-fashioned Protestant moral reactionaries. The supporters of school reform in Philadelphia were prominent businessmen and lawyers.

One of the first aims of the reformers was to reduce the size of school boards, on the grounds that smaller boards and appropriate board members would enable school boards to function in ways similar to business boards of directors. School boards were reduced in size in many cities. The Saint Louis School Board was reduced from twenty-eight members to twenty-two, and then to twelve. The Philadelphia School Board was reduced from forty-two to twenty-one, and the New York City School Board from forty-six to seven, although that process took nearly twenty years.

As the size of school boards was reduced, the proportion of middle- and upper-class members in Saint Louis increased from 17 percent in 1896 to 86 percent in 1903. The Saint Louis School Board was made up then of three lawyers,

FIGURE 9-1   The St. Louis School Board, c. 1875. Courtesy of the Audio-Visual Department of the St. Louis Public Schools.

four businessmen, two engineers, a physician, a newspaper manager, and an educator. It is incontestable that most board members, at least since Scott Nearing's investigation of 1916, have been members of the middle class.

If it has generally been in the interest of the middle class to prevent school change in order to prevent social change, then the middle-class makeup of school boards has been a preventative of change. However, one might ask whether middle-class parents have indeed preferred the status quo in schooling. One might also ask if school board members have in general voted on the basis of their social class membership, a question which, as Charters pointed out some years ago, has not been answered. It could be argued that the decisions to be made by school boards were and are essentially moral decisions. If so, then a school board, like a jury, should represent as fully as possible the community from which it comes. However, if school board decisions have technical elements in them, then knowledge as well as wisdom may be valuable. We are disinclined to offer personal judgment in the matter.

The school reformers, like the city reformers, felt that politics should be kept out of education. Lord Bryce, who had said that the quality of American life was pleasant, found little to admire in American political parties and party politicians: "We place at the head of the list of evils under which our municipal administration labors, the fact that so large a number of important offices have come to be filled by men possessing little, if any, fitness. . . ." Schisel notes that political scientists have found that nonpartisan elections favor, once again, members of the middle class. That aside, it is also argued that keeping politics out of school board elections and appointments has made the schools less responsive to local neighborhood influence. It must be granted that schools have been wonderously immune to such influences, but we have not seen persuasive evidence that party-affiliated board members have been effective in presenting local preferences in schooling.

Nearly all school superintendents avoided party politics. The party person who was a superintendent, as John Hancock of Ohio was, and who served as superintendent whenever a solid Republican was called for, was part of a small minority indeed. If *politics* is defined more broadly, then of course the control and financing of the schools is of necessity political—but that objection comes from a difference in definitions.

Inside and outside schools, in municipal government the reformers argued that more decisions should be made by experts, as decisions in private businesses were made by experts. The most powerful of the school experts was, of course, the school superintendent, who in addition to being an executive was ideally an expert in all things educational. Decision making in and about schools was more and more the responsibility of the superintendent, as at least two surveys made at the time show.

The Progressive reformers of schools argued that decision making should be centralized in the office of the superintendent, and then went on to advocate the development of city school district organizations very much like those of business organizations. Such school organizations were developed. However, the possible future disadvantages of such organizational patterns were not considered at the time. Large organizations may, or may not, function well when they are established. However, the same organizations become nearly impossible to change if they become obsolete or otherwise inappropriate. This, we have found in the last twenty years, is particularly true of public organizations, the staffs of which are protected by civil service regulations. To centralize and organize school decision making was to generate an organization that would be the greatest of bulwarks against subsequent change in schooling. The Progressive reformers did not foresee that difficulty, and perhaps could not have foreseen it, and that circumstance is partly extenuating.

Partly because they were outcomes of a kind of Progressive reform of schools, and partly because they accompanied it, "efficiency," the ready-made bromide, and scientific management and measurement in the schools should be discussed and considered in the wider context of Progressive reform.

EFFICIENCY IN THE SCHOOLS

Definite qualitative and quantitative standards must be determined for the product. ... Where the material acted upon by the labor processes passes through a number of progressive stages from the new material to the ultimate product, definite quantitative and qualitative standards must be determined for the product at each of these stages. ... The worker must be kept up to standard qualifications for this kind of work during his entire service.

Pupils were the "materials" and the "product."
Teaching was the "labor." Teachers were the "workers."

The author was Dr. Franklin P. Bobbitt, instructor in education at the University of Chicago. These passages were first published in 1913, when efficiency in the schools was a popular issue.

"Efficiency" in the schools was borrowed from efficiency in factories. Although there had much earlier been suggestions of its coming, schoolmen were converted to efficiency starting about 1910 because they had been subject to stinging criticisms, and because "efficiency" was the most popular of remedies for evils, real or imagined.

Because of its origins, school efficiency and its popularity are more understandable with the history of industrial efficiency as background. For a similar reason, we have followed the history of industrial and business management. Even in factories, efficiency was useful, if it was useful, as a management tool. Efficiency required a different form of management, "scientific management." School administrators and others including Bobbitt saw school efficiency as a tool, a tool for the scientific management of the schools. If we are to tell the history of one, we must tell the history of both.

In a sense, scientific management of the schools rested upon a kind of school efficiency, but school efficiency rested upon educational measurement. After all, the meeting of "quantitative" standards could only be verified or demonstrated by measurement. There were unremitting efforts to measure school learning and so to measure school or teacher effectiveness.

Efficiency and *efficient* have had several meanings, as Samuel Haber has pointed out. First, in an everyday sense in the 1800s, to be efficient was to be fit or powerful. Second, to scientists and engineers, *efficiency* meant and still means a machine's ratio of output to input. An automobile engine, for example, may be 25 percent efficient. Third, business "efficiency" has meant the ratio of dollar output to dollar input. In all these senses, "efficiency" was something to try to gain or to increase, something good and valuable. "School efficiency" was an attempt to be efficient by all three of these definitions. It also meant *efficiency* with a fourth definition, of "social harmony and the leadership of the competent."

The first meaning of *efficiency* is not particularly important to us here. *Efficiency* by the second definition, the engineer's, is important. *Efficiency* does in this sense determine an automobile's rate of fuel consumption. However, when used in this sense, the measurement of efficiency requires that input and output be measured in comparable units. This is a requirement that is nearly impossible to meet in schools, as is obvious after a moment's reflection. There is a similar difficulty with *business efficiency*. Even if school input is seen (inhumane as that is) as money alone, it is, again, nearly impossible to measure output only in money terms. *Efficiency* by the last definition, leadership by the (self-proclaimed) "competent," may have been most damaging, both by efforts to attain efficiency and by the exercise of efficiency after some slight approximation of it was attained.

School efficiency was most popular during the early 1900s. It became popular for a variety of reasons. It was a response to, and perhaps a defense against, reformers. Attacked by Progressive reformers, particularly by the "muckrakers" who were the advocacy journalists of their day, city school superintendents felt threatened and "vulnerable." They needed, for their own defense, to find ways of showing their usefulness and competence. For superintendents, efficiency seemed a way to ward off a terrible threat, the threat of being fired. For them, there was another advantage to efficiency, because administrators who were seen as efficient had additional justification for increasing their control and power. Perhaps, more benignly, school administrators came to favor efficient methods because businessmen and engineers favored efficient methods, and businessmen and engineers had come to be the most admired and respected men in American society. Some professors of education also became ardent supporters of efficiency. Their zeal seems to have been often excessive, and it is difficult to believe that none of them was opportunistic.

School efficiency and the beliefs and values that supported it came from many sources. Efficiency was in accord with the tradition-honored values of thrift and economy and the husbanding of worldly goods. There is a sense in which efficiency was a part of a longtime drive to rationalize, to make more logical.

There were also sources in the schools' past of support for efficiency. As we have said, the monitorial schools at the beginning of the 1800s had incorporated concepts of schooling as manufacturing and of the school as a factory. It had not been accidental, as John Griscom wrote in 1823, that ". . . the establishment and progress of the Lancastrian or monitorial Schools, have been contemporaneous with the improvements of the Steam Engine, and with the wonderful applications of that new power to the wants of mankind." Nor do we think it coincidental that S. Chester Parker, dean of education at the University of Chicago when school efficiency came into fashion, was nearly the first writer in a half century to praise the orderliness and systematic arrangements of the monitorial schools.

It has been said that Benjamin Franklin was the first efficiency expert. That has a grain of truth in it. Franklin was surely a practical man interested in practical solutions to practical problems. Although American practicality did not originate with Franklin, it has been one of Americans' first interests, the interest which made Americans tinkerers and master mechanics, inventors, and engineers.

The most noteworthy thing about American machines a hundred years ago was that they worked well. In 1876, English visitors to the Philadelphia Centennial Exposition noted that the hidden nonoperating parts of American machines were roughly made, although the operating parts were made with great care and precision. That was good enough. "Good enough" became an important consideration for American industry. (We most often complain because "good enough" is not good enough.) "Good enough" became a commonplace idea. It was not surprising that an analog, a like concept, was applied to schooling at about the time of the efficiency movement. In schooling the near-equivalent of "good enough" was "minimum essentials," minimum essentials that each pupil was to master in order to be a satisfactory citizen and worker. "Minimum essentials" received much consideration during the time of the school efficiency movement.

To repeat, school efficiency was largely an adaptation of industrial factory efficiency. The synthesis that produced industrial efficiency was primarily the contribution of Frederick W. Taylor. Taylor was the son of an old and well-to-do Philadelphia Quaker family. Born in 1856, Taylor is described by one of his biographers, Sudhir Kakar, as having a personality—formed by his first experiences—that was neurotically compulsive; as ritualistic and combative, profane but prudish. Kakar does not err on the side of generosity.

Although not generally considered a likable man, it can be argued that Taylor had a streak of genius. He attended an academy in Germantown, by then a prosperous part of Philadelphia, and in Germany when his family made a prolonged visit there. Back in the United States, he was sent to Phillips Exeter, to prepare to enter Harvard. Taylor was admitted to Harvard but did not attend because, he said, studies had weakened his eyes. One of Taylor's biographers has concluded that Taylor's eyestrain had psychological origins. But on the other hand, young Philadelphia gentlemen had often started their careers with an apprenticeship, as Taylor did in 1874.

As an apprentice, incidentally, Taylor was an attendant at his firm's display at the Philadelphia Centennial Exposition. In 1878, at age twenty-two, he was employed by Midvale Steel Company, which produced heavy parts for railroads and for the Navy. At Midvale he began the first of his tens of thousands of experiments on machining steel.

Taylor's objective was to cut away metal on a lathe, as quickly and inexpensively as possible. The problem was a complicated one, in which there were a dozen variables: depth of the cut, shape of the cutting edge, cooling, and so on. Taylor's work was a model of excellence in applied science. Among other things, he determined that around cutting edge was quicker than a diamond-shaped one. Later he invented "high speed" chromium-tungsten alloy steel, which is still in use for cutting edges.

Taylor was also interested in increasing the output of the worker. The first step was to replace traditional skills with technology, a process already many years old. Taylor's metal-cutting experts made part of machinists' traditional knowledge obsolete and useless, and made the lathe hand a worker semiskilled at best. Worker output could also be increased by division of work, or division of labor. That had served as one of the key concepts in Adam Smith's *Wealth of Nations* in 1776, although that idea was then already old, too. In 1835 Charles Babbage, an Englishman, had calculated that while one worker could make twenty pins in a day, ten workers could together make nearly 9,000 pins a day.

Like Adam Smith, Taylor saw the worker as being motivated by money or lack of it. This would have been unfortunate if it had been true, and it is demonstrably untrue. However, it was possible to think of a worker in terms of money. As another efficiency expert wrote in 1913:

> On a punch press costing $3,000, the yearly cost . . . would be $450. The operator of this machine would probably be paid $3 a day, a total of about $900 a year. The only apparent difference is that the machine is paid for in

advance, while the labor is paid for in weekly, bimonthly, or monthly installments.

Taylor had not voiced that thought, but the thought did lead to the efficiency
expert's conception of the worker, worker as machine, money-driven rather than
power-belt-driven. Like any other machine, the worker could be adjusted and read-
justed. The other variables would be the worker's speed, strength, and endurance.

The most famous man-as-machine description was written by Taylor. The
worker was called "Schmidt." The task, at Republic Steel, was loading ninety-
pound iron pigs into railroad box cars. First there was a step-by-step analysis of
activity and time required, from "(a) picking up the pig from the ground or pile"
to "(e) walking back empty to get a load." Schmidt was selected from among the
Republic Steel laborers. He was an "energetic little Pennsylvania Dutchman" who
was known for "placing a very high value on a dollar." Like the other laborers, he
had been loading into box cars twelve and a half tons of pig iron a day. For a 60-
cent raise, to $1.85 a day, he was to move forty-seven tons of pig iron a day.

> ". . . you will do exactly as this man tells you tomorrow, from morning till
> night. . . . When he tells you to pick up a pig and walk, you pick it up and
> you walk, and when he tells you to sit down and rest, you sit down. You do
> that right straight through the day. And what's more, no back talk. Do you
> understand that? When this man [Taylor's assistant] tells you to walk, you
> walk; when he tells you to sit down, you sit down, and you don't talk back
> at him. . . ."
>
> Schmidt started to work, and all day long. . . . He worked when he was
> told to work, rested when he was told to rest, and at half past five that
> afternoon had his forty-seven and a half tons loaded on the car. . . .

Schmidt's work output increased by 280 percent, his pay by 60 percent. Taylor
argued that increased overhead costs were part of the price of efficiency. Republic
Steel had employed Taylor in order to increase profits, of course. There were many
other applications of efficiency, and time-and-motion study, in factories whose
products ranged from bicycles to field artillery.

In 1910, northeastern railroads applied to the Interstate Commerce Commission for a freight rate increase to cover the additional costs of wage increases. One
of the attorneys arguing against the rate increase was Progressive liberal Louis
Brandeis. Brandeis argued that the railroads' inefficiency cost $1 million a day. He
called ten witnesses who testified on the application of efficiency and scientific
management in industry.

The Interstate Commerce Commission hearings gained public attention, and
"efficiency" was the hope of the hour. "Efficiency" was advocated for every part
of life, even for churches and homes, and of course for schools. One author,
Fletcher Durell, undertook building a formal philosophy with efficiency as its base.

"Efficiency" was exported to France to aid in winning World War I. In Russia Lenin wrote a pamphlet in its praise.

"School efficiency" was the subject of many speeches and innumerable articles. Bobbitt's full-blown book-length presentation, from which the quotations at the beginning of this chapter are taken, appeared in 1913. The next year one of the few superintendents with public doubts said that "so many efficiency engineers [were] running hand carts through the schoolhouses in most large cities that grade teachers can hardly turn around without butting into two or three of them." In 1915, a National Society for the Study of Education yearbook on the measurement of teacher efficiency was published, and in 1916, efficiency and testing were important topics in the most important textbook on school administration.

Franklin Bobbit's book that appeared in 1913 was a yearbook of the National Society for the Study of Education, then the most prominent of scholarly education societies. The book was an exposition of Taylor's principles of efficiency and management, and of their application to schools. This would be valuable to teachers, Bobbitt said, because they would know exactly what was required of them. It would be valuable to supervisors, who could simply compare the achievements of a class with standards for its grade. The superintendent could "instantly locate the strong, the mediocre, and the weak teachers." He could assess differences in teaching methods and textbooks.

FIGURE 9-2   **Plan of educational organization for a large city school system. Adapted from Ellwood P. Cubberley,** *Public School Administration* **(Boston: Houghton Mifflin, 1916), pp. 172-173.**

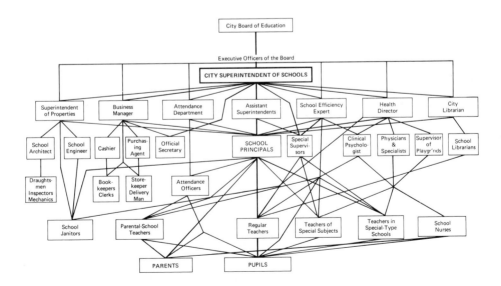

A simple calculation of efficiency in schools was in terms of dollar cost. (This was like the business input-output dollar efficiency, only by mistaken analogy. No dollar measure of output was available or even sought.) The most prominent expositor of dollar efficiency was Frank Spaulding, who had earned a Ph.D. in Germany, and having been superintendent of schools in Passaic, New Jersey, was superintendent of schools in Newton, Massachusetts. As early as 1909, he had said that "The demand for efficiency . . . is urgent and universal."

Spaulding's definition of *efficiency* was nearest to that of the businessperson. It was true, he said then, that school outputs were unmeasured and ultimately unmeasurable. Measurements of instructional cost were to the informed eye measurements of inputs. Spaulding demonstrated his methods. First, he had discovered that per pupil instructional costs in a small school in Newton were greater than in a large school there. On the other hand, the large school had cost more, per pupil, to build. These findings do not seem to be surprising or even particularly informative.

As a second example, he discussed the costs of high school instruction on a per pupil per recitation basis. He found that

> . . . 5.9 pupil-recitations in Greek are of the same value as 23.8 recitations in French; that 12 pupil-recitations in science are equivalent in value to 19.2 pupil-recitations in English; and that it takes 41.7 pupil-recitations in vocal music to equal the value of 13.9 pupil-recitations in art. . . .

Presumably the audience found this at least somewhat impressive, even though hard to follow. The conclusion was school efficiency reduced to dollar cost, pure and unmitigated.

> . . . I know nothing about the absolute value of a recitation in Greek as compared with a recitation in French or English. I am convinced, however, by very concrete and quite logical considerations, that when the obligations of the present year expire, we ought to purchase no more Greek instruction at the rate of 5.9 pupil-recitations per dollar. The price must go down, or we will invest in something else.

This was, of course, *efficiency* redefined as *economy*, and *economy* defined as *cheap*. There seemed to be no other consideration.

SCIENTIFIC MANAGEMENT IN THE SCHOOLS

Management, as we will use the term here, means oversight of an enterprise and organization, public or private. It means choosing goals and strategies and, on that basis, distributing resources. Organizationally, management divides labor, logically defines jobs, and distributes monetary and other rewards. Hastened by its inheritance from Taylor, management has been in part a systematic process of transferring skill from workers to management.

Patterns of school management have been derived largely from, and much modified by, patterns of management of private enterprises. This took place more than at any other time when schools adopted Taylor's "scientific management." "Scientific management" itself is more readily understandable against the background of the practice and theory of private enterprise management.

The simplest form of management is direct personal management by the owner. As an example of owner management, John W. Cannon was both captain—management—and owner of the record-making Mississippi River steamboat *Robert E. Lee* (New Orleans to Saint Louis, three days, three hours, forty-four minutes). In some industries there was little advantage in consolidation, or in elaborating management.

However, as industrial enterprises became ever larger and more complex, there was pressing need for coordination. At that point it was necessary to develop more detailed arrangements for management. The first of the elaborated management systems in the United States were the railroads' systems. Investments in railroads were huge for the time, far greater than in any other enterprise. By 1850, there were already two railroads capitalized at over $10 million. In 1860, there were ten such railroads, and five capitalized at nearly twice that. Not only were they huge enterprises, but they were geographically dispersed—by 1855, there were at least thirteen railroads that each had more than 200 miles of track in use. It was necessary to coordinate operations. A locomotive derailed and damaged in Buffalo would affect the delivery of passengers and freight in New York City. The operation of a railroad increasingly called for technical expertise in operations, in maintenance of track and rolling stock, and also in accounting and other areas. Organized and centralized management was advantageous, and the appearance of the telegraph made it feasible.

In 1847, Benjamin H. Latrobe, chief engineer of the Baltimore and Ohio Rail-Road, put into operation a new management system. (Engineers would be important in these matters.) Financial accounting, receipts and disbursements, were to be the responsibility of a comptroller. There were separate departments for track maintenance, for rolling stock, and for transportation operations. The heads of the departments were to be responsible to the chief engineer or general superintendent, who with the comptroller reported to the Baltimore and Ohio's president and board of directors. Engineer David C. McCallum refined the management system for the Erie Railroad in 1855. He said then that the management of the Erie Railroad system called for, first, an appropriate division of responsibilities, and with it, appropriate division of authority. It followed that there must be ways of verifying that responsibilities had been met, and that therefore all "derelictions of duty" were to be reported at once (via telegraph most often) for quick correction. Concerning operations, daily or even hourly reports were required.

What McCallum formulated was the line of command portion of management organization. Additional staff positions for expert advisers would be added as the need and knowledge arose. (Although the language and spirit of this kind of organization and management have a military air, they did not arise in the military services, but in private enterprise. They were largely copied by the Army and later by the Navy.)

To management, Taylor made two important contributions. First, he offered a related set of ideas, a synthesis, and a refinement of the management techniques by then available. Second, perhaps without intent, he was instrumental in the popularization of a management plan, as well as his plan for worker efficiency. Taylor started with time-and-motion study, or the immediate development of efficiency. The next step, Taylor wrote, was the development of standards for tools and work. Then, there was the task, to be worked out by a planning department, and with it bonus plans for payment for work. The "planning department" would develop the knowledge that would replace that of the journeyman, the skilled craftsman. A part of planning was to be the careful recording of production costs. Finally, Taylor's plan called for "functional foremen" whose primary responsibility was to teach workers how to perform tasks; this part of Taylor's scientific management was least often used.

As we have said, school administrators had appeared long before Taylor's scientific management and efficiency became popular. The drift of school administration toward business methods had started with the Interstate Commerce Commission hearings. W. E. Chancellor, who had written books on school administration in 1904 and 1908, had more often than not portrayed the city superintendent as a business manager. Early in 1910, Frank Spaulding was arguing not only that the school administration, as it then existed, was "grossly inefficient," but also that the training of the administrator should be based on "sound and simple business principles."

At the first meeting of the Department of Superintendence of the N.E.A. after the Interstate Commerce Commission hearings, Spaulding was invited to deliver a major address. His topic was "Improving School Systems through Scientific Management." Spaulding's version of "scientific management" bore little resemblance to Taylor's. Spaulding reported on the procedures that he had used with great success in Newton. He had eliminated small classes and reduced the number of classes offered, so that fewer teachers were needed. Spaulding used several graphs and charts that provided at least the pretext of science, although he had applied not much more than rudimentary cost accounting. His conception of what the school administrator should be was obvious.

An alternative form of efficiency would have been based on Bobbitt and at least indirectly upon Taylor. However, superintendents adopted Spaulding's formulas, and so could reduce schooling to dollars and meet the economy-minded critics on their own ground. Spaulding gave to the work of the administrator the appearance of scientific respectability. He contributed to the improvement of the status of administrators and also provided them with a professional reason for great emphasis upon the dollar aspects of education. If there were doubts of the effectiveness of Spaulding's approach, they might have been dispelled by witnessing Spaulding's career. For ten years he had kept his job at Newton, the "burial ground of superintendents," at one of the highest Massachusetts superintendents' salaries. In 1914, he would be appointed superintendent at Minneapolis at $8,000 a year, and three years later he would move to Cleveland at an annual salary of $12,000.

It was Spaulding's ideas, not Bobbitt's, that were accepted by most of those who wrote on educational administration after 1913. Spaulding's principles were easy to apply, economy was achieved, and the schools appeared to be run efficiently. Bobbitt's system would have required elaborate and expensive research and planning divisions, for which even the largest school systems had neither money nor talent. That aside, the public seemed to be primarily concerned with cost. Although there was not much objection to Bobbitt by administrators, and although he was praised, Bobbitt's description of children as "raw material" and of teachers as "workers" seems to have been too extreme.

The most widely used and most influential administration textbook of the time was Ellwood P. Cubberley's *Public School Administration* (1916). Cubberley incorporated into his text concepts from Chancellor, Spaulding, and Bobbit. The textbook pictured the superintendent as nearly superhuman. His was the office "up to which and down from which authority, direction, and inspiration flow." As Cubberley saw him, the superintendent was to be familiar with Bobbitt's efficiency and Spaulding's cost accounting, but was to be neither time-and-motion expert nor cost accountant. The superintendent was to be an executive in every way, much like the successful business executive, the captain of industry. Cubberley's definition of the role of the administrator left the teacher without authority outside the classroom. The teacher might advise, but was not to make important "administrative" decisions.

FIGURE 9-3   The development of the Efficiency movement depended heavily on the results of quantitative research.   Elaborate methods of recording the progress of students, such as this Courtis scorecard in arithmetic, came into widespread use as part of the movement.   From Ellwood P. Cubberley, *Public School Administration* (Boston: Houghton Mifflin, 1916), p. 334.

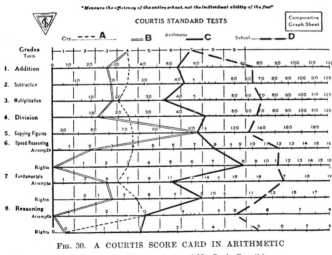

Fig. 30.   A COURTIS SCORE CARD IN ARITHMETIC

(Reproduced by permission of Mr. S. A. Courtis)

In the figure above curves A and B are of two individuals in the same class. From an Indiana school. Note that A is practically normal except in the last test (shown by the fact that the curve is almost a straight line and lies almost wholly within the boundaries of the fourth grade), while B is below grade in every test but one and is particularly weak on reasoning.

Curves C and D are two measurements of the same child, one in September and the other in June. From a Michigan school. Note the correction of many defects and the balance of the final scores.

MEASUREMENT IN THE SCHOOLS

Returning to Schmidt's and to Taylor's efficiency, it is obvious that efficiency depended upon measurement. In the case of Schmidt, the necessary measurements were time (spent by Schmidt) and the weight of pig iron he moved. Time and weight together, as tons per day, were the measure of Schmidt's productivity. If the efficiency and productivity of schools were to be calculated, it would be necessary to have ways of measuring. Therefore, the popularity of school efficiency increased interest in productivity measures.

There were other sources of interest in measurement. At the beginning of the 1900s, Americans were increasingly impressed with the importance of pure science. Until then the sciences and scientists had been relatively unimportant in the development of new technologies and industries. The development of electric and chemical industries, however, depended heavily upon the pure sciences. Thomas Edison, the practical inventor, sold his electrical business, which became General Electric. General Electric relied upon Charles Proteus Steinmetz for technical advice. Steinmetz was a German-trained physicist, whose approach was mathematical and quantitative. It was clear that there were new areas for technology that demanded science and demanded measurement.

Although pure science had gotten some attention in American colleges since the 1820s, it seemed more important by 1900. Kelves points out that in that year there were 200 physicists in the United States. One of the most prominent of them was Henry A. Rowland, professor at Johns Hopkins University whose vastly improved diffraction grating had made it possible to measure light spectra much more accurately. Another prominent physicist was Albert A. Michelson, born in Poland, brought up in Murphy's Camp, California, and graduate of Annapolis Naval Academy. Michelson studied in Germany and began there an investigation of "luminiferous ether." This in turn required the most precise possible measurement of light. (Einstein's special theory of relativity rested upon Michelson's results.) For his measurement Michelson was awarded a Nobel Prize in physics in 1907, the first to an American. Science would be important in America, and measurement would be a necessary part of science.

The secret of factory mass production then was, as we have said, the standardization of products and their parts. This also required measurement of lengths and weights. The European standards would no longer do, it was said, and most of the states had no standards at all. To provide these measurement standards, the National Bureau of Weights and Standards was established in 1902. Fair standard weights and measures for the consumer was one of the goals of some Progressive reformers. *Cosmopolitan*, one of the popular magazines, carried a muckraker article on short weights. Measurement would not only aid in production. It would aid and protect the consumer, too.

Under the circumstances, interest in educational measurement increased. It had begun earlier, of course, with the work of Joseph Mayer Rice, who in the fall of 1894 turned from his exposes of the school to measurement. Rice's first question was about the relationship between the length of spelling lessons and the pupil's ability to spell. Spelling lessons' lengths were measured in minutes per day; ability to spell was to be measured by spelling tests. Since it was impractical for Rice to teach spelling, he relied upon teachers for information on the customary length of spelling lessons. (Technically this was what is called a *quasi-experimental research design*, which is still in use.) The spelling tests, fifty words long, were administered by Rice personally to, eventually, 14,000 pupils. Rice himself scored and corrected their papers. Rice concluded that there was no relationship between the length of spelling lessons and pupils' ability to spell. One might have inferred, therefore, that spelling lessons should be short. (It now seems that Rice's tests were too easy.) Rice's results, presented in 1896, did not please the superintendents. Perhaps they still resented his earlier muckraking, and the days of measuring educational products had not yet come.

In 1909, the year before the Interstate Commerce Commission rate hearings that publicized efficiency, Leonard P. Ayres, in *Laggards in Our Schools*, compared fifty-eight cities, by the ages of pupils and the grades they were in. This had been done earlier by New York City superintendent William H. Maxwell and by Robert L. Thorndike at Teachers College, Columbia University. A city school system, he argued, was most efficient if none of its pupils were "retarded," or too old for the grade they were in. Since 75 percent of the pupils in Memphis black schools were "retarded," those were the least efficient of schools. There are obvious limits to the conclusions that might be reached this way. Ayres had mentioned none of them.

More direct measures, achievement tests, had already begun to appear. Several were developed by Edward L. Thorndike and his doctoral students at Teachers College, Columbia University. The first achievement tests, carefully validated, pre-tested, and standardized, were C. W. Stone's arithmetic tests, which appeared in 1908. Thorndike's handwriting scale appeared the next year. Developing it was more complicated; there are objectively correct answers in arithmetic, but handwriting is good if it is judged to be good. S. A. Courtis's arithmetic tests, with grade level norms, also appeared in 1909. In 1912, there was a measure of composition achievement; and in 1913, B. R. Buckingham's spelling test. In 1918, Walter S. Monroe listed 109 achievement tests. After that there were too many to list, or even to count. The interpretations of test scores rested on at least elementary statistics, which were made (relatively) accessible by Robert L. Thorndike in 1904 in *An Introduction to the Theory of Mental and Social Measurements*. The inter-relations between measures were, as it developed, complex, and the interrelation-ship was never one to one. Thorndike provided information on correlations, calculations, that is, of the degree of interrelatedness. That was necessary, of course, because one set of scores by itself was uninformative.

Achievement tests, checklists, and other measurements were used in every imaginable way. Teacher outputs were measured. Two or more methods of teaching were compared. Schoolhouses were rated on long or short forms. The heights of boys and girls were measured annually and carefully tabulated.

A popular use of achievement measures was in school surveys. The *school surveys*—the term was borrowed from the municipal reformers' *social surveys*—appeared about 1910. One bibliography lists six surveys in 1910 and 1911, seventeen in 1912 and 1913, twenty-one in 1914 and 1915, and twenty-three in 1915 and 1916. Surely there were many more. The most massive survey was that of the New York City schools, conducted by Paul H. Hanus of Harvard. That survey was in progress for three years and was reported in three volumes. It was the first survey to include achievement test results. Surveyers usually found that the schools were in most ways efficient, and provided evidence of the superintendent's competence and the system's merit. The schools of Boise, Idaho, were surveyed in 1910, 1913, and 1915 for reasons otherwise obscure, except that Boise School Superintendent Charles S. Meek was a survey enthusiast. School surveys would continue to be popular through the 1920s, and there are still occasional school surveys, though now for different purposes. In 1925, Jesse B. Sears in his book *The School Survey* explained the popularity of school surveys because of their resemblance to industrial efficiency studies, "... it was not strange that the public should take readily to the survey idea. People were already familiar with the work of the efficiency engineer and the accounting expert in business and industry...."

As an isolated force, out of context, measurements are nearly meaningless, and our criticism of them in isolation would be as meaningless. Undeniably, the surveys were misused in the name of efficiency, and their results were employed to

FIGURE 9-4   "What Is A School Survey And Why?" cartoon
published in *The Richmond News-Leader,* reprinted in *The Survey,*
Vol. XXXI, March 14, 1914, p. 747.

gratify and defend superintents. Perhaps one of the shortcomings of the measurement movement was that some of its participants had concluded that a science of education, and from it basic truths, would come from the refinement of measurement without other consideration. That, as we think everyone should now know, is false.

CONCLUSION

Of course there were dissents to the centralization of school control, to efficiency in the schools, to scientific management, and to measurement. Although the dissents were generally inconspicuous and generally ineffectual, teachers did object. They were joined in their dissent by a few professors of education, and even by a superintendent or two. As early as 1893, on the eve of the Progressive era, a pamphlet had appeared, "Mechanism in Education, Sacrifice of Education and Health to Mechanical Examinations," by one Louis Freeman. Identifiable teachers protested verbally, in the N.E.A. Department of Classroom Teachers. In 1916, its president, Sara Helena Fahey, attacked school efficiency.

> Then there is the constant effort to standardize the human relations of child and teacher. The unobtrusive sterling qualities, which so often characterize the faithful overworked teacher, are not the first things in sight during a survey. There is often a startling contrast between paper efficiency and field efficiency.

Teachers also expressed themselves in other ways. First, they unionized. Second, as World War I created boom times and a labor shortage, teachers quit. They became clerks, telephone operators, and typists in the war industries. In part this was self-protection against inflation, but it was also in part protest.

Several university professors also dissented. In 1914, A. W. Rankin of the University of Minnesota told the N.E.A.'s Department of Classroom Teachers that "the superintendent learns to copy the manner of the factory head toward the operatives. He is an autocrat, an overlord, a taskmaster to the teachers. He reigns as a monarch...." The next year W. A. Bagley of Teachers College, Columbia University also addressed the Department of Classroom Teachers. ". . . Getting the next generation ready for its serious responsibilities is being accomplished more and more on the factory plan," he said, and he disapproved. His comments are eye-catching because Bagley had been a few years before an efficiency enthusiast. In 1913, John Dewey, in the American Federation of Teachers' *American Teacher*, was arguing that teaching should be, if it was to be anything, an intellectual activity. Teaching as an intellectual activity was, clearly antithetical to factorylike efficiency. Even New York City Superintendent William H. Maxwell protested. The findings of the New York City survey were objectionable. Frank McMurray, one of the surveyers had, Maxwell said, concluded far too much from far too little.

He had, that is, gone too far beyond his data. Maxwell's complaints, as the others' had, seemed to so almost unnoticed.

We have misgivings about the school reformers who have been the subjects of this chapter, and we have expressed most of them. Only two after thoughts may be worth expressing here. First, although elaborated administrative organizations may have been promising, or even useful, when they were built, they were built more strongly than the builders could have known, and more lastingly than they could have intended. While the same organizations have, we concede, sometimes instituted change, they have at other times been impervious to it. Second, if one is discomfited at the thought or experience of depersonalized education, one is discomfited at overcentralization, overregulation, and mechanization and routinization. However, we must add that there were other efforts and accomplishments of the Progressive administrators that we admire. We will discuss them in the next chapter.

CHAPTER TEN
SCIENTIFIC PEDAGOGY: TEACHERS AND CURRICULUM

The 1910s were times of development and expansion of the one best system; the 1920s, times of its perfection; and the 1930s and early 1940s, times of its maintenance. The system's principles of organization and administration were adopted by or forced upon city schools, small town schools, and rural schools. Enrollments in schools generally increased, as pupils stayed on longer. City enrollments increased more rapidly as the urbanization of the United States continued. Especially after 1920, in the new suburbs made accessible by automobiles, one-room country schools developed within a few years into complete school systems.

As many have pointed out, the importance of schools and schooling was increasing more rapidly than before. The world had become more complicated; growing up on a farm did not automatically provide a knowledge of soil pH, especially if a youth's father was uninformed about it. There was no way of learning at home how to operate a punch press, the simplest and most vicious factory machine. Mastering the punch press, even without losing fingers and hands, did not teach one how to be a machinist. In 1918, Mississippi passed a compulsory school attendance law, and compulsory attendance became, at least in principle, universal. That required the attendance of some children who otherwise would not have been pupils. But increasing numbers of students stayed beyond fourteen or other minimum age set by law. The day of the high school had come, and high school enrollments increased most of all. College and university enrollments were also increasing, although most of the students who did complete high school did not enroll in colleges, public or private. Libraries multiplied, newspaper circulations increased, and motion pictures and radios appeared. Nevertheless, schools became more important.

The "science of education," aided by and aiding the one best system, continued to develop. Educational psychology provided a new, impressive, and convenient way of thinking about learning. "Mental" aptitude tests were developed to measure ability to learn, and achievement tests to measure what had been learned. Much of curriculum revision was a practical and empirical undertaking, concerned with practical, utilitarian efforts to prepare students for jobs.

Even history of education was of value for showing how much had been achieved and how successful the system had become. In fact, the most widely used textbook of history of education in the United States had been written by Ellwood P. Cubberley, who was also a leading authority on Progressive administration in public schools.

The science of education, like most human enterprises, has experienced success and failures. Judged by the highest hopes of those who encouraged it, its successes in those times were few, its failures many. Compared with other sciences, engineering and medicine most obviously, little was gained. Not surprisingly, precise measurement was a first goal. There were real successes, and new techniques did yield measures usable for some purposes. But a science is more than measurement. Because of a common intellectual history and the obvious connection, research in education followed many conventions of emerging psychology. Again there were advantages, but there were also drawbacks. Far too often it proved to be impossible to generalize from experimental findings, and for much research there was no obvious application. Other outcomes were trivial, and research too often yielded only frustration.

There was still great variation in schools, although it was decreasing because of the progressive administrators' emphasis upon uniformity. There were differences between schools for Whites and schools for others, and differences between city schools and country schools. There were rural one-room schools not much different from those fifty years before. There were city school systems with tens or even hundreds of thousands of pupils. Chicago, not the biggest system, had 226,000 pupils by 1910. City schools had better-paid teachers and far wider curricular offerings. It can be argued that small country schools were more responsive and less impersonal. Judged by most other standards, wealthier communities had better schools. There was a decreasing number of private schools, and an increasing number of parochial ones.

With a few exceptions, biographies of individual teachers no longer appeared, but there is partial compensation for the historian in "scientific" numerical and sociological studies. There were important exceptions to the generalizations, but the first survey of teachers in 1910 showed that most teachers—a huge majority of them women—were the daughters of native white small businessmen and farmers. That continued to be true, although less so as time passed. State and city normal schools prepared larger numbers of better-trained teachers, and an increasing minority of new teachers had studied in colleges and universities. Teachers were young, far younger than pictured by the myth of the faded "schoolmarm." Depending on the source, their lives were ordinary, or satisfying, or teaching was imprisoning and teachers were victims of politics. There is support for each of these views.

Much school teaching and learning was surely in the old convention—a schoolbook assignment, study or homework, and then, if you remembered enough of what it said, recitation, questions answered from memory. One plausible way to improvement was the straightforward application of plant efficiency methods. *Activity analysis* was widely praised, but not often carried out. In the early 1930s, however, there was an attempt to apply it to teacher training. (Teacher preparation seems particularly susceptible to some kinds of fashions and styles in education.) Another plausible approach was the *project method*, proposed and popularized by William H. Kilpatrick. The essence of the project method was a ". . . wholehearted purposeful act carried on amid social surroundings." The wholehearted purpose was that of the pupil, and the project was practice in "living well."

THE GARY PLAN:
THE CHILD AND EFFICIENCY

In 1906, United States Steel Company built a huge complex of blast furnaces and steel mills on the empty, sandy, southern shore of Lake Michigan. It built a city there, Gary, Indiana, named after Elbert H. Gary, U. S. Steel founder. William A. Wirt was employed as school superintendent to build a new system of schools for the new city. It was a rare opportunity and Wirt made the most of it. An admiring former student of Dewey, he installed workshops adjacent to classrooms to strengthen connections between school and work. The community became the schools' laboratory. The schools were to become the hearts of the community.

Wirt was also a rockribbed Republican conservative capitalist, and intended to make the Gary schools efficient, systematic, and economical. He developed the *Gary Plan*, with classes exchanging places at appropriate times in gymnasiums, auditoriums, shops, and classrooms. Better utilization of school buildings and more careful organization was to keep costs low and promote efficiency.

The Gary Plan was admired by all progressives, by Dewey himself for its curriculum and ways of teaching and learning, and by administrators for its low cost and businesslike management. There were faulty details, but they would be remedied. Randolph Bourne, darling of politically progressive intellectuals, wrote a series of approving articles for *New Republic*. Those who objected to the Gary Plan did so for the same reasons that others supported it. Abraham Flexner, official of the Carnegie and Rockefeller foundations, growing more conservative as he grew older, objected to the curriculum because conventional subjects were not well taught, having been sacrificed for immediate and real experiences. Much later

Callahan would criticize the Gary Plan because of Wirt's intent of efficiency. At least in appearance, the Gary schools were progressive in the two most important educationally progressive senses.

New York City rejected the Gary Plan when it was tangled in a political campaign there and because of the opposition of New York City school bureaucrats. Opponents even rioted before attempts to introduce it were abandoned in 1917. An evaluation of the Gary schools made with newly developed achievement tests raised doubts and opposition. Labor leaders in some cities objected to the Gary "platoon system" as cheapening schooling, and to anything connected with U. S. Steel or named for Elbert Gary. By the middle of the 1920s, the Gary Plan's unique popularity had passed.

No other plans or school systems got the support of Dewey's followers and also of efficiency enthusiasts. As an exception the Gary Plan may prove a rule. That Gary's popularity was isolated and unique seems to us to be evidence of the divergence of the views of educational progressives. Like political Progressivism, educational Progressivism had its origins in the reformers' beliefs in the 1890s. Progressive educators generally shared as a general aim the improvement of schooling and the improvement of society. In anything more specific than that educational progressives did not agree among themselves, although the extent of their disagreement would not be clear until later. A new curriculum, businesslike management, and perhaps the science of education were Progressive, depending upon the view of the educator. That *Educational Progressivism* was a single unified movement was far more apparent than real.

Since the 1960s, historians of education have argued that progressives in education were more interested in preserving than in changing, that they oriented toward the conservative, that their hoped-for reforms would have resulted in a more conservative or more nearly static society, and that they intended to preserve capitalism. These arguments have been useful in dispelling the too-cheerful view that all that the progressives did was right, and that schools and schooling in their time were in every way and at all times a blessing. They were not always a blessing or were they ever a blessing for every pupil, nor did every progressive have a clear vision of a transformed society.

Beyond that, the danger of overgeneralization seems to us great. It comes, as Kaestle has pointed out, from failing to distinguish the intent and effect of progressives. More than that it comes from not specifying which progressive, and with what intent and with what effect. The distinctions should be kept in mind.

THE SCIENCE OF EDUCATION, CONTINUED

Some deny that there is a science of education or that there can be one. However, argument as to the existence or possibility of a science of education in general is nearly meaningless, since there is no generally acceptable meaning of *science*. At one extreme, *science* is anything systematically arranged; by that definition it could

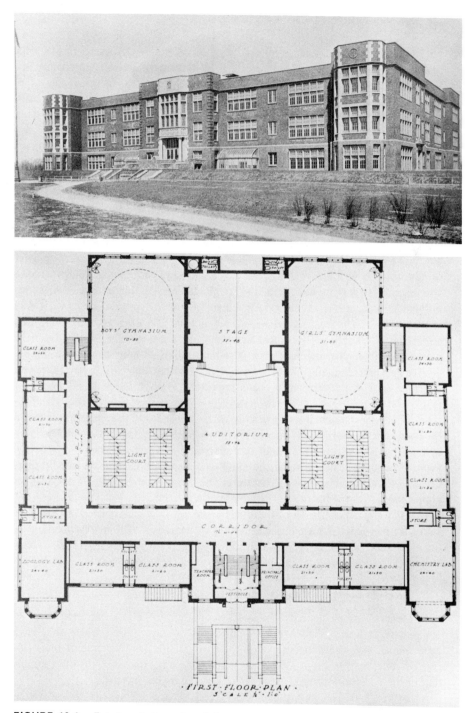

FIGURE 10-1 Exterior photograph and floor plan for the Froebel School, Gary, Indiana. From *Modern School Houses* (New York: The American Architect, 1915), Plates 117 and 119.

be said that there is a science of philately, that is, stamp collecting. In one sense philosophy, as the careful ordering and examining of human experience is a "science." At the other extreme, a "science" is made up of a set of "laws" or theories that allow precise prediction and control. Physics comes closest to being such a science. The "science of education" has been thought of in all these terms, and probably others. Among its supporters, it has probably most often been thought of as becoming a science in somewhat the same sense that engineering is a science. One of those who believed most strongly in such a science of education was Charles H. Judd of the University of Chicago. Education, he said in 1918, was becoming a science because, in the first place, it was studied by the scientific method (although he did not define *"scientific method"*). The sources of the science would be history of theory and practice, psychology and educational psychology, statistics, experiment, and the study of "retardation" and of administrative problems. It is a far more comprehensive formulation than that of the science of education as no more than a science of administration and management. Judd's visualization strikes us now as oddly composed, but his was a science in which influential men strongly believed. Whether "scientific" or not, or in what way scientific, the *science of education* and research in education have had important effects upon schooling. Even those who feel that a science of education has been premature, or empty pretense, or a false hope, and that educational research has been a misguided failure and a pure liability, cannot deny its importance. Our strongest conviction is that it has been important, is important, and will be important.

Educational researchers have not, with rare and odd exceptions, worked in isolation. They have most often been university professors, less often college professors, or occasionally public school or foundation officials. The origin or employment of many educational researchers and scholars in the early 1900s was Teachers College, Columbia University. Therefore, the history of Teachers College is an important part of the history of the science of education.

Like any other branch of inquiry, the science of education had its founders who set precedents and established patterns or paradigms. The most important of these founders in the order in which they appeared were G. Stanley Hall, Joseph Mayer Rice, and Edward L. Thorndike.

Teachers College, Columbia University

Research of most kinds is shaped, naturally, by the interests and talents of researchers. It is also shaped and supported by the institutions where they have been trained and where they carry on their work. This has been true of the scientists of education. In the earlier years of the science of education, the most important of these institutions was Teachers College, Columbia University.

Before 1900, increasing numbers of colleges and universities were offering graduate or undergraduate courses in education, or *pedagogy* (the science of teaching). The beginnings are difficult to specify, because of the existence of honorary faculty appointments and precollege-level and not-for-credit courses. However, Josiah L. Pickard, who left the superintendency of the Chicago schools in 1877 to become president of the University of Iowa, started education courses there. William H. Payne, appointed to the University of Michigan in 1979, had been the first identifiable full-time university professor of education. G. Stanley Hall had been named professor of psychology and pedagogy at Johns Hopkins University in 1884.

Institutions and professorships suggest the underlying development. Education—teaching and administration—was at least potentially-professional, based upon science and knowledge. That conviction led to the establishment of schools or departments of education intended primarily to offer graduate study and to support research. Clark University did so after G. Stanley Hall became its first president in 1888. There were other attempts, some short-lived and others only indifferently successful. A few developed substantial strengths. The outstanding success was that of Teachers College.

The earliest inspiration for Teachers College came from longtime Columbia president F. A. P. Barnard, a Unionist who had escaped from the South early in the Civil War and had stayed on as Columbia's president. More immediately, Teachers College was the creation of Nicholas Murray Butler, member of the department of

FIGURE 10-2   Teachers College, Columbia University, c. 1900. Courtesy of Special Collections, Teachers College, Columbia University.

philosophy of Columbia University, who had been encouraged by Barnard, and of Grace Hoadley Dodge, progressive-minded heiress. Teachers College was established in 1889, and became a part of Columbia University in 1893. In 1897, James Earl Russell, who had earned a Ph.D. at Liepzig in Germany (and had become acquainted with Joseph Mayer Rice) became its president. Russell had a miraculous ability to identify the most promising young scholar and to lead him to prominence. He recruited Edward L. Thorndike, who would become the most prominent educational psychologist and researcher of his time; Paul Monroe, an industrious and methodical man who would establish the field of history of education; Frank McMurray, who developed a new curriculum based on the new psychology, and who would be joined by his brother Charles A. McMurray, survivor of an unsuccessful attempt to establish a "School of Pedagogy" at the University of Buffalo; and Susan Blow and Patty Hill Smith, kindergarten reformers. George S. Counts, a new kind of sociologist of education and educational comparativist, and William H. Kilpatrick, inventor of the "project method" and disciple of John Dewey, would join the Teachers College faculty later. Dewey himself, who had had unpleasant misunderstandings with President William Rainey Harper of the University of Chicago, became a member of the philosophy department of Columbia University in 1905. Although he was not a member of the Teachers College faculty, he would serve as guide and inspirer. Russell recruited a number of subject matter specialists whose names are now less familiar, but who were outstandingly competent in their time. Outstanding graduates, such as George D. Strayer in educational administration, were kept on as faculty members.

Russell had, Cremin has said, four goals for Teachers College: It would provide liberal arts education, academic scholarship, professional knowledge, and technical skill. Russell's success in recruiting and his broad formulation of purpose and aim were sources of Teachers College's marvelous growth and success. By 1917 it had 2,500 students. There were other successful schools and departments of education at Stanford University, University of Chicago, and other universities, but Teachers College, Columbia University was by far the most prominent and successful of them all.

The rise of Teachers College is important not because of its fame or its material success. As measured by endowment, Teachers College has not been wealthy, and it is neither financially supported nor controlled by Columbia University. It is important because it was a "visible," formal college, the home of communities of scholars who continued and extended thought about schooling, and so modified practice. It was important also for the researchers and scholars it trained. It has by now awarded thousands of doctorates in education. In the ten years ending in 1927, Teachers College awarded a third of all doctoral degrees awarded in education in the United States. Teachers College is no longer more important than all other schools of education combined, but in the 1980s, Teachers College is still a prominent school of education, perhaps the most prominent.

Founders

Hall's research in psychology, pedagogy, and child study was in part a result of his lifelong unending curiosity. Many of his continuing inquiries were into the "whys" of child behavior and child learning. By intent his research was reality based, empirical. It was, at the beginning at least, partly anchored in the theories of genetic psychology, to which Hall was then committed. Part of Hall's legacy was a line of educational research devoted to learning "why," to discovering underlying variables.

Cremin has dated the beginnings of educational Progressivism as being in 1892, when Joseph Mayer Rice's scathingly critical descriptions of schools appeared in the journal *Forum*. However, Rice's "Futility of the Spelling Grind" also appeared in *Forum* in 1897, only five years later. It presented results of his research on the time spent studying spelling and spelling achievement. Similar studies followed.

Nontheoretical and utterly practical, presenting as results columns of numbers, Rice's research was solely concerned with "how." We can guess why his approach changed, since Rice, a near recluse, was always silent about himself, and because his papers were burned immediately after his death. Rice, too, set precedents for educational research. Unlike Hall, he proceeded without theory to find immediate practical solutions for practical problems. What was to be answered was how long to make spelling lessons. "How" was at the core of both the question and the research. Unlike Hall, Rice was a quantifier: he used, relied upon, and published numbers. He also used an experimental design or, to be more exact, a quasi-experimental design. He did not attempt to manipulate the lengths of spelling lessons, but instead located classes that had been given spelling lessons of varying lengths, and tested them afterward. This "after-only" design has been standard in education since. It has serious flaws, but is the simplest research design and sometimes the only feasible one. We would guess that Rice borrowed the design from medical research. He had been trained as a physician and the after-only design had been used in medical research by French physician Claude Bernard, fifty years earlier. But to repeat, Rice set precedents in education of quantified results and of addressing the question of "how."

Rice's precedent was followed by Leonard Ayres, who published *Laggards in Our Schools* in 1909. To measure school "efficiency," Ayres tabulated the number of pupils who were "retarded," older than expected for their grade in school, and calculated the proportion of retarded pupils in sixty-three school systems. This, too, was an after-only quasi-experimental design, and the question to be answered was "how"—how efficient the school systems were. This was the link to efficiency studies and the administrative progressives. "How" questions have predominated in educational research since.

Hall's and Rice's research had not been undertaken at Teachers College. In fact, Hall's study of "the contents of children's minds" had taken place some years before Teacher College's founding. Edward L. Thorndike, the third important figure at the beginning of educational research, spent nearly all his career there.

Thorndike has been the subject of a thorough biographical study, but Thorndike's personality remains an enigma. Some of his onetime colleagues remember him as completely matter-of-fact, and as cold and distant. Believing intelligence was in some large part inherited, he was accused of being politically and socially conservative. However, he demanded and got a retraction of that accusation. His last books were studies, in some ways stiff and mechanical, of the "quality of life," concerned with satisfaction and enjoyment for members of society at large, surely a liberal and progressive interest.

When asked to account for his success, Thorndike once said it was because he had strong eyes and good health. A more matter-of-fact and less informative answer is unimaginable. Certainly he was energetic and untiring. He published numerous books and articles. Thorndike unquestioningly accepted the existence and usefulness of a science of pedagogy, or education. As a researcher, he often had great insight in forming questions and hypotheses. At the beginning of his career he was an originator of experimental work in animal psychology. Into education he introduced descriptive and inferential statistics, and in many new applications of statistics. He and his students developed academic achievement tests. As a psychologist, he contributed an important learning theory that had value and influence. His work contributed to the psychological "behaviorism" that John B. Watson formulated and popularized. The most important of those who influenced him can be identified: His interest in psychology was kindled by William James; Thorndike, as well as G. Stanley Hall, had studied with James at Harvard. His interest in quantification was aroused by Franz Boas, pioneer anthropologist. J. McKeen Cattell, who was also at Columbia—until he was fired for "treason" and other indiscretions during World War I—emphasized the importance of individual differences. But none of this explains Thorndike's successes. He was indeed "seminal," as Cremin has said, and a father figure for future researchers, his apparently humdrum personal life notwithstanding.

The Measurement Movement

Counting and measurement, quantification, seemed to attract educators almost as a candle attracts moths. Ever since the time of Henry Barnard they had gathered columns and pages of numbers, and had compulsively counted almost everything. Rice had measured so that the achievement of classes of pupils could be compared. Ayers had calculated proportions and ratios so that school systems could be compared. Educators had been enormously impressed by Frederick Taylor's methods, which of course rested on timing and measuring.

There were precedents, European and American, for psychologists' quantification. A. Quitelet, a Belgian astronomer and public health official, had, by 1850, gathered physical, anthropometric data on the dimensions of men. In England

Francis Galton, who was interested in all things but most interested in heredity and eugenics tentatively undertook measurements of mental ability. J. McKeen Cattell had been administering "mental tests"—he coined the term—to University of Pennsylvania undergraduates in 1900.

In 1904, Thorndike published *Theory of Mental and Social Measurements*, the first and most important of elementary statistics textbooks. It dealt with descriptive statistics: units, scales, frequency distributions and their description, probability, measures and differences in measures, reliability, and correlations. This was the basis of descriptive statistics. Aside from perhaps some computational procedures, Thorndike's book was not original in content and he did not claim that it was. It did make widely available the statistical methods used to construct tests and interpret results. Other statistics textbooks followed, and Thorndike's remained in print for more than twenty years.

The most important other contribution, both in measurement and in content, was by French psychologist Alfred Binet and his colleague Théodore Simon. Binet had studied thought and reasoning for nearly twenty years, and for nearly ten years had attempted to measure it. The diagnosis of retardation, or feeblemindedness, was a first use, but the measurement of the "mental ages" of all children proved to be feasible. Simon and Binet published their first intelligence test in 1905, and an elaborated one in 1908. It was translated and first used in 1909 by Henry H. Goddard at the Vineland (New Jersey) Training School for retarded children. The intelligence test was important for what it measured, even though what that is remains perplexing. It was also important because it was constructed as a scale, as a set of subtests, fifty-six in 1908, for measuring mental ages of children from the age of three upward to thirteen. One subtest, for example, was "catch" sentences for eleven-year-olds:

> There was found in the park today the body of an unfortunate young girl, frightfully mutilated, and chopped into 18 pieces. It is thought that she committed suicide.

About half of the eleven-year-olds tested could see the absurdity of this and four other similar sentences. (This item was quickly replaced with a less bloodcurdling one.)

Thorndike and his students quickly applied the principle of scaling to achievement tests, as did some other researchers. The first normed and scaled achievement, in arithmetic, was C. W. Stone's, published in 1908. Many tests were constructed, and many applications were found for them. Walter S. Monroe said, in 1922, that there were by then seventeen arithmetic achievement tests, and nearly a hundred more for other academic subjects. The number of psychological tests increased in roughly the same proportion. Again and again, Thorndike argued that whatever existed, existed in some quantity, and that, therefore, it was measurable.

The measurement movement did not end in the 1920s, of course, and there are still numerous educational measurement experts gainfully employed. However, the gains and limits of the measurement movement in the 1900s, 1910s, and 1920s, can be considered. As a first generalization, the measurement movement was largely unsuccessful, if success is defined as advancing the science of education, or knowledge of education, or, more widely, as the improvement of schooling. There were exceptions, but in general, measurements did not fulfill the hopes and expectations of the times.

It was unsuccessful because it generated data and statistical results—numbers—not much related to each other or to any other perceptible thing. Again the exceptions: first, intelligence tests, which in spite of whatever flaws, did have correlates—substantial correlates; and perhaps second, research at the University of Chicago by Charles H. Judd and others on reading, in which the readers' eye movements were photographed and measured. But those were the exceptions: At the very beginning of the measurement movement, Clark Wissler found that there was no connection of consequence between, for instance, class standing and reaction time, and that almost all of his dozen or so mental measurements were for any practical purpose uninterrelated. Many findings carefully arrived at were trivial. As an analogy, with careful sampling and use of rudimentary statistics it would be possible to calculate the number of pebbles on Salmon Beach. But that would not matter much, either.

Early mental and educational tests left something to be desired in both reliability and validity, as tests still do. But that seems to have been a minor, though general, difficulty. What the measurements did not provide was information bearing on or coming from crucial, often theoretical, issues. Even Frederick Taylor's practical-to-a-fault experiments on metal cutting had been based upon considerable knowledge of the nature of metals, from engineering, physics, and chemistry. Albert A. Michelson's measurement of the speed of light, which had made him the first American to win a Nobel Prize, had been important not because of the ingenuity of his apparatus, but because it disproved a theory of "ether." Michelson's experiment was of lasting importance because it cleared the way for Albert Einstein's new theories. It is informative, no matter how unjust, to compare Ayers's study of "retardation" with Michelson's measurement.

Maybe it is putting it most simply to say that in the most important way the measurement movement was a failure in the same way that the child study movement had been. Each had yielded masses of data, but neither became a successful science. Each lacked the theoretical or conceptual framework that is necessary for a science to be successful by any intellectual, or most practical, standards.

Psychology and Educational Psychology

Educational psychology, as a branch of the discipline of psychology and as a part of a prospective or existant science of education, developed in the Progressive era, and in the decades that followed became firmly established. We must note that educational psychology lacks clear boundaries. There is a wide area that psychology in general and educational psychology have as joint territory, and another grey area that is jointly held by educational measurement experts and educational psychologists. We cannot trace here all, or even the most important, developments in the field of educational psychology and its jointly held territories. We will follow some developments in the measurement of intelligence, and the development of Thorndike's psychology, which would become for most purposes, though not all, the psychology upon which school administration was based.

The measurement of intelligence was a matter of fascination, as it still is. Knowing the "mental age" of a pupil was important for the assessment of instruction, for guidance, and eventually for personnel selection. (At first, there was an annoying and obvious flaw: Older children were, or at least acted, more intelligent than younger ones. That was resolved by using a method suggested by German psychologist William Stern. The child's mental age, as determined by an intelligence test, was to be divided by his or her real, or chronological, age. The ratio of the two, multiplied by 100 for convenience, was the child's *intelligence quotient*, or *IQ*, an informed calculation as to how intelligent the child was for his or her age.)

After granting the importance of IQ tests and agreeing that IQ tests did and still do predict pupils' success in school, there were and still are doubts about what was measured—what was learned or what was inherited. Doubts persist, too, as to its measurement of intelligence or measurement of training of some kind, or of the two in some combination. As one example, subtest number 18 of the 1908 version of the Simon-Binet test was "execution of a triple order," for the six-year-old:

"Here is a key; please put it on that chair. Then please close the door. Then . . . please bring me that box. Do you understand? First put the key on the chair, then close the door, then bring the box. Now, go ahead."

Of course some amount of thought—to use that soon-to-be outdated word—by the child was called for. But one would have suspected that obedience was called for too. That might have been reasonable, since the Simon-Binet test had been intended to identify the children who would not be successful in classrooms. As another example, subtest number 23, for seven-year-olds, required that the child copy, legibly in ink, "See little Paul." Later research showed that there was no important correlation, or relationship, generally between handwriting and "intelligence." At best, the item was influenced by the training of the child.

Soon after the Simon-Binet test was published, it was shown that children from wealthier, higher socioeconomic status homes performed better on it. This immediately raised doubts. IQ tests were not intended to measure socioeconomic status, after all. Another question that was perplexing then to the thoughtful—and which is perplexing still—is whether IQ tests measured some general ability called "intelligence" or some combination of abilities. That discussion was for a long time hot and has not yet ended. These perplexities puzzle the writers and, we hope, will puzzle the reader. However, they did not for a moment stand in the way of IQ enthusiasts.

One of the most prominent of these was Louis B. Terman at Stanford University, who was devoting his life, or at least most of his professional career, to the measurement of intelligence and to determining the consequences of high IQs. In 1916, he published the Stanford-Binet Intelligence Test, which was the most widely used American version of the individually administered intelligence tests and which in revision is still commonly used.

In 1917, 1918, and 1919, 1,726,966 soldiers, sailors, and marines underwent 1,793,313 mental tests. (There were retests and cross-validations. The precise numbers are in the 880-page official history.) It was testified that mental, or psychological, tests, identifying misfits at one extreme and potential officers at the other, made military personnel assignments more efficient and effective, and so helped win the war. Certainly they popularized mental, or psychological, testing.

Whatever else, the psychologists were prompt. On the day the United States declared war, April 7, 1917, American Psychological Association President Robert M. Yerkes wrote that

> In the present perilous situation it is obviously desirable that the psychologists of this country act unitedly in the interests of defense. [But psychologist Hugo Münsterberg, driven to a frenzy by American hostility to Germany, had committed suicide.] Our knowledge and our methods are of importance to the military service, and it is our duty to cooperate . . . toward the increased efficiency of our Army and Navy. . . .

Seven weeks later a committee of psychologists met at Vineland, New Jersey, and in ten days designed what would be known as "Army Alpha," a personnel classification test. It was followed later by "Beta," for men who did not read English. The tests were the first widely used group tests and were administered to up to 500 men at a time.

Alpha and Beta were quickly—hastily?—assembled from available tests, among them A. S. Otis's intelligence test. There were strong correlates, and Army Alpha and Beta did measure something. However, weighing, scoring, and subtests were changed until it is difficult to say what they did measure. They yielded results that would be debated for twenty years; Whites scored higher than Blacks, northerners higher than southerners, sailors higher than soldiers, and so on. Army Alpha and Army Beta convinced the public that useful group, paper-and-pencil tests could be constructed, even in spite of mare's-nests of army red tape and bureaucratic confusion. (There was a delay because army officers had mistaken *psychologists*, experts in mental measurements, for *psychiatrists*, treating the mentally ill.) The official history shows great industry and considerable ingenuity by the army psychologists. The popular acceptance of mental testing had been attained.

Thorndike directed the statistical analysis of the results of the preliminary form of Army Alpha, but is far better remembered for other and more important contributions. His key theoretical contribution had come from the study of animal psychology. (Some of Thorndike's early research had been with chickens, cats, and dogs.) If it was assumed, as Thorndike did, that animal and human learning were alike in kind if different in degree, then conclusions from animal psychology could be applied to humans. In 1898, Thorndike had published *Animal Intelligence*, which led to his "Law of Effect." Often modified, it said first that all behavior was "stamped in" when it was rewarded, and that behavior that was punished was stamped out. The relationship between stimulus and response became stronger if there was a reward, weaker if there was a punishment. Behavior was to be explained as a linking of stimulus and response.

As Cremin and others have pointed out, accepting Thorndike's concept of learning made "mind" unnecessary, and useful only as meaning total response. Since behavior was the outcome only of reinforced "original tendencies," mankind was not innately evil, as Calvinists had long since maintained. It was not innately good, as Jean Jacques Rosseau had maintained. It merely *was*.

Thorndike's psychological theory became by far the most important one in education. It was a psychology of learning, and therefore suitable. In contrast, German Gestalt psychology, which appeared a few years later, was a psychology of experience or patterns of experience, and Freud's psychology was personality psychology. Each had its supporters, but Thorndike's learning psychology was far more popular. More concretely, Thorndike's work was an influence on John B. Watson, who argued in 1919, in *Psychology from the Standpoint of a Behaviorist*, that only behavior—only stimulus and response—need be studied. Watson's work in turn influenced B. F. Skinner, whose "operant conditioning" would become important in late twentieth century education.

The purposes for which measurements and educational psychology were used were as one might have predicted. Titles of two National Society for the Study of Education yearbooks indicate them well enough. In 1916, a yearbook was titled *Standards and Tests for the Measurement of the Efficiency of Schools and School Systems*; and a 1922 yearbook, *The Measurement of Educational Products*. To utilize measurement for efficiency, at least seventeen city system bureaus of research had been established as early as 1916. There were a number of state bureaus of research, and university bureaus: The University of Illinois Bureau of Educational Research listed with pride seventy-nine of its publications between 1918 and 1927. (At least a few had residual value fifty years later. Educational research was not always uninformative.) A few private philanthropical foundations also conducted research, and supported financially some further research. Achievement measures, in particular, were used in dozens and hundreds of school surveys.

Walter S. Monroe listed, in 1928, what he saw as the most important areas of research then: reading, by Judd and his colleagues; school finance, under the direction of George D. Strayer of Teachers College; a recently completed study by Thorndike on the measurement of intelligence; a "genetic study of genius" at Stanford University, directed by Lewis B. Terman, in which the lives and fortunes of 650 extremely high IQ students would be followed for thirty years; and a study of nature versus nurture, sponsored by the National Society for the Study of

Education, also directed by Terman. There were also school surveys and research in the teaching of school subjects. These undertakings do not strike us as having had substantial positive long-range effects.

Researchers encountered serious difficulties. Experiments when repeated gave differing results. Findings sometimes seemed trivial: that George Washington had an estimated IQ of 135, or that it was more efficient to teach children the use of the period first, then the use of the comma. (But even a fragment of good research may seem ridiculous when out of context, standing alone.) Some research must have been utterly frustrating.

Given the conventions of experimental designs, research was perhaps more successful in demolishing, rather than rebuilding. There was, for instance, the hundred-year-old belief of pre-empirical psychologists in "faculties," of specific capacities of the mind. Faculties had been incorporated in phrenology by F. J. Gall. A later American phrenologist had in a self-improvement manual listed twenty-six faculties: "philoprogenitiveness," "vitativeness," "conscientiousness," and so on. Each faculty could be enlarged by training and exercise. But Thorndike and experimental psychologist R. S. Woodworth published in 1901 the quantitative results of a series of experiments which showed that faculties were not increased by use. One experiment, as an example, showed that learning to estimate the area of a triangle did not increase skill in estimating the area of a circle. As they put it, "Improvement in any single mental function [faculty] rarely brings about equal improvement in any other function, no matter how similar." There was no such thing as a "faculty," that was to say. The Report of the Committee of Ten and all emphasis upon "intellectual training" was based on a false premise.

However, the psychologists and other scientists of education had enormously underestimated the difficulties, the complications, the number of possible and plausible dead ends, the variety and vagary of human behavior. Few of them considered the possibility that measurements and psychology might be misused. It was not realized that putting the science of education at the service of efficiency might be costly if efficiency lost its lure—as it did. But there would be another day.

TEACHERS

If teachers had more often spoken for themselves during the period between the first and second World Wars, it would be far easier to say what it was like then to be a teacher. Generally, teachers did not leave records of themselves; they seldom wrote at all of their teaching. Rarely, teachers' letters and papers are preserved in some collection, as are those of Oliver Cromwell Applegate of Ashland, Oregon. Even more rarely a teacher, such as Beatrice Stephens Nathan, has left behind memoirs or reminiscences. Careful interviewing of now elderly survivors would be illuminating, but the results of such interviews have not yet been published. Far more often than not, we must rely upon surveys and sociological studies, sometimes written with much precision, but usually with limited intent.

The first of the almost over-plentiful statistical studies was Lotus D. Coffman's dissertation, *The Social Composition of the Teaching Population.* Coffman, who was then beginning a distinguished career, gathered data, in the fall of 1910, on 5,215 teachers. His sample was only more-or-less representative. There seem to have been no big city teachers in it, and men were overrepresented by 20 percent. However, Coffman's tabulations do roughly describe all white teachers whom pupils had encountered that September.* The median—that is, midway, approximately typical—white teacher was about age 25; almost 10 percent of Coffman's respondents were still in their teens. This median teacher had only four years of schooling beyond elementary school, little by present standards, but substantially more than the average woman then. Only one teacher in ten had four years of college or the equivalent. She was in her fourth year of teaching. Her median yearly salary was just under $500. No black teachers were included; they certainly earned much less and were not as well prepared as white teachers by their schooling.

Although Coffman's data do not clearly show it, many teachers began and ended their teaching in the same school at the same grade. For teachers there were two patterns of upward occupational mobility. One was geographic, from country school to small town school to small city school, and occasionally to a big city school. The other was from lower grades to higher grades, and perhaps to high school, where salary and prestige were greater. A few teachers followed both pathways. About one teacher in ten was a beginner. Apparently nearly one teacher in ten quit each year, a low proportion compared with, say, 1965, a high one compared with 1982.

Only 1 percent of Coffman's teachers had been born outside the United States, and only 12 percent had foreign-born parents. (Even this proportion of teachers of foreign extraction troubled Coffman.) None of the teachers had been born in Italy or Greece, origins of masses of new immigrants. Most teachers had been raised on farms, in relatively large families with relatively low incomes. Women teachers outnumbered men by three to one in Coffman's sample, by four to one in another study that year.

In September 1915, Beatrice Stevens, a twenty-year-old normal school graduate, began her teaching career in a one-room school in the mountains of California. She boarded with a rancher's family, and from there rode horseback or walked to the school. There were nine pupils: the youngest, age six; the oldest, seventeen years old. Progressive administration had already begun to impose uniformity. Pupils were assigned to grades, and there was a standard course of study and a countrywide examination for graduation. Stevens's yearly salary was $600.

After two years in her one-room school, she taught in a two-room school in a small town in the San Joaquin Valley. There were thirty-five pupils in her class, in grades five through eight. She remembered a Model-T truck that was used as a school bus, and living in a ramshackle, noisy hotel, and taking her class to swim in

---

*This was not representative of those who taught. Those with short careers were systematically underrepresented.

an irrigation ditch. The next year she taught in a larger school near her family's home, then was one of the first teachers in one of the new junior high schools that were coming into fashion. There she learned how children might be classified and tracked and stigmatized by IQ tests. . . .

Nearly forty years after Coffman, Frances R. Donovan's *The Schoolma'am* appeared. Donovan's description was in many ways like Coffman's. From the Census of 1930, she found that more than 3½ percent of the teachers had been foreign born, but Donovan was sure they had "American ideals—firmly planted in their hearts." In 1930, only one teacher in five was married. Most married women teachers were teaching in country schools, where monthly salaries averaged $22. There were 46,000 black women teaching then, the invisible women of their time. Except for those in New York City and a very few elsewhere, black teachers taught only black pupils. Only one teacher in five was 40 years old or over; only one in fourteen, over 50.

More new teachers had attended colleges and universities, and the era of the normal school was passing. Among new high school teachers, four out of five were college graduates, and a few city school systems—12 percent of them—required a master's degree for new high school teachers. Salaries had increased. In Chicago a high school teacher could earn as much as $4,800 a year, when a new eight-cylinder Buick cost perhaps $800. But the average yearly salary for a teacher was only $1,325 a year, and the average teacher earned less than the average carpenter, less in fact than almost anyone except farmhands, clerks, and factory workers. Teachers' salaries were no longer so low, but certainly were not high.

In smaller towns especially, there was religious bigotry, and Roman Catholics, Unitarians, Christian Scientists, and even Episcopalians were sometimes discriminated against. "There are communities today," Donovan wrote, "that prefer Methodist chemistry, and Spanish taught in a Baptist accent." But in the 1930s, in one Buffalo school, there were lessons about Hanukkah as well as about Christmas. Teachers in the big city school systems were different—possibly they long had been. The diversity of city dwellers resulted in diversity of teachers from and in the cities. George Counts wrote that in Chicago ". . . teachers vary almost as widely as the population itself in their cultural origins, their religious affiliations, their political beliefs, their economic prejudices, their social philosophies. . . ." Teachers were daughters (occasionally sons) of professionals and businesspeople or, increasingly often, of blue collar workers. In the 1930s especially, men and women who in better times would have become college instructors or professors became high school teachers. The pay was not nearly as bad. Washington's high school teachers were leading black intellectuals. Black teachers in Washington, and in other border and southern cities, taught in "Division II," black schools. In most northern cities there were few black teachers. In Buffalo, into the 1930s, they could have been counted on the fingers of one hand.

Williard Waller's *Sociology of Teaching* (1932) is still important as sociology. It is also a picture, a grim picture, of the life of a teacher in a small town in the 1920s. What a teacher did and was, Waller said, depended upon the public image, the stereotype, of "teacher." Long ago teacher stereotype had contributed to the forming of the common schools; by the early twentieth century, the school largely perpetuated the stereotype of the teacher. Her, or his, role was narrowly defined by the expectations of others. In the school the most important "others" were students. The teacher was always "at war" with students, Waller wrote, because the values of the school that she was to uphold were not those of the students. If the school was to function, the teacher was necessarily a despot, perhaps polite and kind and cheerful, but a despot nevertheless. The successful teacher maintained a distance from students, was isolated from them.

Outside the school, the teacher was a "stranger" in both the usual and a sociological sense. She came from elsewhere. The stereotypes that separated her from her students also separated her from the rest of the community. What was innocent amusement for others was forbidden to teachers. Custom determined where she could room. It was demanded that she attend church or even that she teach Sunday school. The teacher stereotype discouraged suitors. Women teachers were not to use rouge or lipstick, men teachers not permitted to even hear dirty jokes. Narrow roles and binding expectations made the teacher a prisoner and, at the same time, kept her an outsider. Teachers were forced to rely on other teachers for companionship.

Waller's sociological informants, teachers who were his students, did not teach in big cities, where presumably impersonality reduced constraint. Still, sociology aside (if that is possible), Waller captured a side of life of the teacher that had its share of reality.

The Case of Chicago

School and Society in Chicago appeared in 1928. Its author was George S. Counts, who was committed to social and political reform; the year before he had published research on school board members, showing that they were—as they still are—largely from the middle class, and that presumably the middle class was the chief beneficiary of the schools. In Chicago, Counts argued, politics could not be kept out of education. The Chicago School Board was not representative either, not representative of all social classes and not representative of all interest groups.

Chicago was a battlefield, a battlefield of political bosses, ethnic voting blocs, progressive "professional" school administrators, and even philosophic progressives, and some battles were fought over schools. That was true of many cities, perhaps of all cities. But in Chicago the battles were rowdier. Chicago was different in another important way. In Chicago, teachers—organized teachers—were important and powerful combatants.

"Machine politics" was not new in the 1920s. Municipal graft and municipal corruption had been one of the first targets of the political progressive more than twenty years before. It was not confined to Chicago. Other cities had famous or infamous bosses: Tweed in New York, Pendergast in Kansas City, Crump in Memphis, and the list could go on. The generally reigning boss in Chicago was

William Hale "Big Al" Thompson, who once promised that when he was mayor he would "punch the snoot" of the King of England. (That helped bring out the Irish vote.) Thompson was elected mayor in 1915, and left office in 1923, after a grand jury indicted his friends. He was elected again in 1927, with the support of Hearst newspapers and the alleged support of bootlegging gangster Al Capone.

Chicago, the fastest-growing American city—3 million inhabitants in its first hundred years—had large ethnic communities: German, Polish, Czech, Italian, Greek, and others. Ethnic voting blocs could control the outcomes of elections. (As a side effect, this resulted in the appointment of black teachers in Chicago's schools.)

Earlier there had been philosophical progressives in Chicago. John Dewey had been professor of pedagogy and psychology at the University of Chicago. Before him, Colonel Francis W. Parker had been a normal school principal near, and then in, Chicago from 1875 until 1899. Dewey's student, Ella Flagg Young, had been Chicago superintendent of schools from 1909 until 1915. Administrative progressivism was already being advocated in Chicago before 1900, first by University of Chicago President William Rainey Harper. He recommended centralization of authority, a "professional" superintendent, and reducing the size of the school board (which would make it more than ever middle class). Progressive administrator William McAndrew was appointed superintendent in 1924, by a reform, politically progressive-minded, mayor. McAndrew had written that

> ... [T]he fixing of responsibility, groups of workers responsible to the designated heads, an orderly graduation of duties and appropriate powers, must be maintained, or chaos, confusion, and waste ensue. These books [standard works on school management] chart the school system to show the regulation of authority.

Apparently on another occasion, he wrote

> Every organization which is planned to secure results devotes its energies not only to plans for maintaining and increasing efficiency, but to continuous follow-up of such plans to see that the efficency comes to pass.

This naturally displeased teachers, but McAndrew also displeased school board members named by Thompson, who had again been elected mayor. McAndrew was suspended, charged with "insubordination" and being a "stool pigeon of the King of England."

Three women played important parts in the governance of the Chicago schools: Ella Flagg Young, Catherine Goggin, and Margaret Haley. Catherine Goggin and Margaret Haley were the leaders of the Chicago Teachers Federation (C.T.F.), which had been founded in 1897. Its members were women elementary teachers in the Chicago schools, and within a year or two after its founding it had more members than the N.E.A. The C.F.T. was active on behalf of teachers and schools more generally, and in other public issues. Goggin (who was killed in a traffic accident in

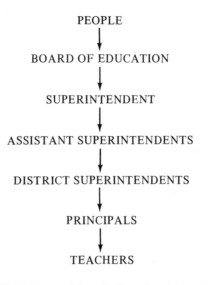

PEOPLE

↓

BOARD OF EDUCATION

↓

SUPERINTENDENT

↓

ASSISTANT SUPERINTENDENTS

↓

DISTRICT SUPERINTENDENTS

↓

PRINCIPALS

↓

TEACHERS

FIGURE 10-A William McAndrew explains the line of authority in Chicago schools. From George S. Counts, *School and Society in Chicago,* **1928.**

1916) and Haley believed that teachers' natural interests were the same as those of workers, that teachers were white-bloused blue collar workers. The C.T.F. at Goggin's and Haley's urging, became an American Federation of Labor (A.F.T.) affiliate. The affiliation was later discontinued to comply with a school board resolution, but the C.T.F.'s interests continued to be those of the unions. The C.T.F., for instance, strongly supported child labor laws, as did the unions.

Haley and the C.T.F. were, naturally, interested in the financial support of the Chicago schools. The C.T.F. discovered that Chicago's public utility companies—electric, gas, telephone, and public transportation—were not paying taxes upon the value of their franchises, although Illinois law made them taxable. C.T.F.'s attorneys argued a series of suits and appeals until taxes were paid. C.T.F. also discovered that several of Chicago's largest industrial firms, among them Pullman and Swift, were not paying taxes based upon their assets, although Illinois laws made them subject to it. Again, suits followed. The Chicago Board of Education still owned scraps of the land set aside for schools by the Ordinance of 1785. It was leased by contracts that called for rental payments equal to 6 percent of its value. The *Chicago Tribune* building, on one of the most valuable sites in the city, did not pay increased rents, under the terms of a contract change in 1895. Again suits were filed, but the C.T.F. was unsuccessful. Its hope, in suits against utilities, corporations, and leasers of school land, was to increase the revenues of the board of education, which it did.

Haley and the C.T.F. had expected the board's increased revenues to be used to increase salaries, which were low in the 1900s, and sometimes paid belatedly. Instead, the board used its new revenue for building and repairing schools. There were finally raises, but not until 1920. Another of C.T.F.'sconcerns was pensions for teachers. A teacher pension law was passed in 1895, five years after Chicago had started a pension system for its policemen. But contributions, as little as $6 a year, were too small to pay the scheduled pensions of $600 a year. A dozen years after the pension system was adopted, the C.T.F. succeeded in having it changed; payments by teachers were larger and were accompanied by payments by the board of education, and pensions were reduced. Later the C.T.F. became the trustee of the pension fund. Haley and the C.T.F. urged and finally secured a teacher tenure law, and arbitrary and political firings of teachers were prevented.

The C.T.F. also resisted the establishment of junior high schools, as did labor unions. It appeared to them, as it did to other unions in other cities, that junior high schools might be used to divert working class pupils from high schools and into vocational schools; the term *industrial education*, long out of use, reappeared. Perhaps it was natural to doubt what sounded like and looked like von Fellenberg's school for peanuts. The C.T.F. also opposed the classification of pupils on the basis of IQ scores, and the discontinuance of the teachers' councils, which had provided upward communication to accompany McAndrew's downward orders.

Counts's most important point in *School and Society in Chicago* was that the schools were enmeshed in society, politics, and the economy. They were not pristine, isolated institutions above politics and wordly concerns. With that there could be no disagreeing. From Counts's book it is entirely clear that teachers' lives were not always bucolic, that they were not always even mildly pleased with their pay and the wisdom of their superiors, and that they were sometimes little more than captives of the schools.

CURRICULUM BUILDING:
KNOWLEDGE AND THE CHILD

Before the end of the 1920s, curriculum research, design, and construction had become a recognized enterprise. In many ways it was the central and crucial issue in education. There was nothing more important in schools, after all, than what was to be learned. The implications were great, if not immediately clear.

Knowledge—what was to be learned—was most conventionally and simply subject matter, the substance and content of conventional school courses. In another view it was the accumulated knowledge within the culture. That knowledge was, in the wider view, artificially and harmfully compartmentalized by academic disciplines and conventional school subjects. From still another perspective, valuable knowledge was know-how, the knowledge needed for jobs and for lives. Valuable knowledge was practical knowledge. Knowledge that could not be used was not knowledge worth having. We will return to one assumption about the structure of knowledge.

Curriculum construction also depended upon assumptions, far more often than not implicit, about the nature of the child. Some aspects of the child's nature and learning were essentially psychological. Clearly, the child was not a bundle of "faculties," as the phrenologists had believed a century before, or as philosophical psychologists had more recently believed. Thorndike and other experimental psychologists had disposed of that. Dewey had argued that one critical consideration was the "interests" of the child, since activities that interested the child would be rewarding and therefore would hasten learning. That point could be argued, or ignored.

The child was seen as learner but also, necessarily, as a member of society, or perhaps as a potential member of it. A member of society might not be much other than a faithful and productive worker and law-abiding citizen. Or social roles might be seen as wider, as that of fully participating members. This was linked to further assumptions about whether or not society was essentially fixed and static, evolving if at all only by natural law, or whether, as many progressives saw it, society was to be reformed, "restructured," by its members so that it would be more democratic, less oppressive, more just.

The acceptance or rejection of assumptions was implicit far more often than explicit. Dewey had provided an admirable, but largely abstract, position; but even if it was accepted, the applications of it were difficult. Understandably, there were numerous approaches to the construction of curriculum.

Activity Analysis

As part of the science of education, *activity analysis* for curriculum building implied the precedence of social needs over psychological needs, of a society largely unchanging, and of the pupil as future worker and perhaps as a future "good citizen." Activity analysis was from all appearances a descendant of Taylor's job analysis in the shop. Curriculum analysis in this vein was a part of the science of education and the curriculum builder was the "great engineer." One of its chief advocates and practitioners was Franklin Bobbitt, not surprisingly. His *How to Make a Curriculum* (1924), and W. W. Charters's *Curriculum Construction*, published the year before, were the standard expositions.

Put most simply, activity analysis started by exhaustively describing a task, from opinion, observation, or record. If performance of the task was to be learned, its components were to be learned. To design a spelling curriculum, Leonard P. Ayers tabulated 23,629 words in business and personal letters and identified the 542 most commonly used ones. There were variations. Bobbitt and his associates tabulated 11,000 topics in *Readers Guide*. In a study that he directed, the 1,243 traits of good citizenship were tabulated.

Activity analysis as a basis for curriculum design was applied in nearly every field. Often it was applied to vocational training. That was nearest to its industrial origins, social considerations were less immediate, and it was not unreasonable to take for granted the interest of the student. We are particularly interested in the *Commonwealth Teacher-Training Study* because recent studies have been remarkably similar to it. We see it as resting on an assumption that is categorically wrong.

We also see "teacher-training" as entirely different from, say, training steno-graphers. The reader should keep that latter bias in mind.

The *Commonwealth* investigators, W. W. Charters, Douglas Waples, and their assistants, tabulated traits, or abilities, of good teachers, employing another minor variation. There were eighty-three major traits, alphabetically arranged from "accuracy" to "wittiness." This seems to us no more than a compilation of plati-tudes, and was not much more than preliminary. The larger and more serious part of the study was activity analysis. To list what teachers did, Charters and Waples sent 22,000 questionnaires to teachers in summer schools, who returned 6,000 of them. Previous studies were combed, then more teachers were queried. In all, there were 235,340 "activity statements." Duplicates were discarded, the near-complete-ness of the list was verified, and the items were classified. The result was a 168-page compilation of precisely 1,001 activities. This was to serve to evaluate education textbooks and courses in student teaching, methods, and theory, or teacher train-ing programs as a whole. Revisions and improvements in training could then be made, and new units and courses could be designed.

The minute division of activity and learning was primarily from shop effi-ciency studies, but the concept was, not even in the early 1900s, new in curriculum building. As we have said, the approach had been anticipated by Joseph Lancaster and other monitorial school enthusiasts, who used the analogy of school as factory. Surprisingly, almost no one then mentioned the parallels and possible precedents. Activity analysis in the schools was largely a reinvention or reapplication.

There is now substantial interest in "competence-based education," and especially in "competence-based teacher education." The similarity of the Florida Catalog of Teaching Competencies, computer-generated in 1976, and the *Common-wealth* list is remarkable. The Florida list is more extensive, with competencies enumerated. By the late 1970s, there was a rather extensive literature on compe-tence-based teacher education. As far as we know, the *Commonwealth Study* has never been cited in it. The general approach had again been reinvented. In this case, history does seem to demonstrate that nothing is learned from history.

Activity analysis as a basis for curriculum design was largely abandoned in the 1930s, for several reasons. First, it was, as Cremin said, enormously laborious and tedious to compile lengthy near-complete lists. Until the computer was available, it was too time-consuming.

Second, activity analysis did not seem to lead to important conclusions. In 1930, Abraham Flexner, in his *Universities, American, British, German,* singled out the *Commonwealth Study* to illustrate that research in education was more and more "technical, trivial, and sometimes absurd," and wrote that the *Common-wealth Study* was "... based, apparently, upon the assumption that American teachers have neither native sense nor ordinary good breeding ...." We would certainly agree that activity and competence analysis is often an elaboration of the obvious.

A third and more serious shortcoming was that in the name of objectivity, activity analysis was concerned with what *was* to the exclusion of what *should* have been. Boyd H. Bode criticized it in those terms in the later 1920s. Bobbitt seemed to feel that sole concern with what *was* was a strength. Of his compilations from *Readers Guide* he said: "They do not show, nor do they attempt to show, what educators . . . think the world should be concerned with. They show what it is concerned with." Bode's criticism deserves thought; Bobbitt seems condemned by his own words. If present practice is not satisfactory, it should not be perpetuated by schooling. Ayers's notiion that the spelling of the most common words should be learned first is reasonable enough, but professional education and spelling lessons are, or at least should be, different.

We add one further objection: We believe that fruitful knowledge, and therefore fruitful learning—professional or otherwise—is a knowledge of interrelationships. There is indeed more to playing a sonata than depressing piano keys three thousand times, and a cathedral is more than a high pile of rocks. As one further analogy, it is misleading to say that a container has in it an inflammable metal and a greenish gas if in fact the container has in it metal and gas in combination as sodium chloride, commonly known as salt, and is in fact a salt shaker. Knowledge is by nature molecular, with bits of information in combination, rather than atomic with bits of information isolated. Activity analysis was as near to atomic as its practitioners could make it.

Project Method

The *project method* was one of many other approaches to curriculum. Butts and Cremin mentioned the *unit method*, the Dalton and Winnetka plans, the *contract plan, activity plan,* and others. Some of these seem more or less workable still, but the *project method* was more straightforward and we think most influential.

The *project method's* originator was William Heard Kilpatrick, progressive by nature, onetime student of Dewey, later Dewey's colleague at Columbia University, and Dewey's popularizer. Kilpatrick was voluble, but a man who is an enigma. If anyone was, he was a Progressive by nature, and had had Progressive leanings even before he had become familiar with Dewey and his work. He began his career as a public school teacher and administrator. He was also a careful critical scholar; it was Kilpatrick who clarified the career of Adam Roelantson and the beginnings of schooling in New Amsterdam, and who did a critical study of Maria Montessori's method, and of the principles of Froebel. Kilpatrick was not only a philosophical progressive, but Dewey's chief evangelist. Kilpatrick's skill as a lecturer deserves to be legendary. It is said that each member of his classes, which sometimes had enrollments of hundreds, felt personally addressed and personally involved. To popularize, it was necessary to simplify. The most important simplification was the *project method*, which Kilpatrick formally introduced in a journal article in 1918. A book, *Foundations of Method*, followed in 1925.

Kilpatrick posited that what the child did and found rewarding would determine what was learned. What the child found rewarding was a "wholehearted purposeful act." Thorndike's psychology showed, he said, that without wholehearted purposefulness an act would not produce learning that was substantial and unified. With this there was another premise—that learning should be ethical and moral. Since ethics and morals had their origins in society, the child was to learn in society. "Education is life," he said, and the "rugged individualist" was not from Kilpatrick's point of view an admirable individual.

The spirit of the project method could permeate school programs in which there were only residual formal lessons and subjects. In the 1930s, Julia Weber Gordon spent four years teaching in a one-room school in rural New Jersey. Her account, *Country School Diary*, describes teaching in the spirit of the project method. There were projects as such: a presentation of "Pinocchio," a train ride, gardens, a school newspaper. Learning came from each of them: how to make a puppet, how a steam engine worked, the value of fertilizer, writing and calculating how long it had taken to produce a school newspaper.

Gordon's concern for the interests and needs of the pupils appeared again and again. She wrote of "capitalizing on their interest," on "meeting the needs of the

FIGURE 10-3   Outline of the Project Method in use for a curriculum on boats at the Lincoln School, Teachers College, Columbia University. Reprinted in Harold A. Rugg and Ann Shumaker, *The Child-Centered School* (New York: World Book, 1928), pp. 100-101.

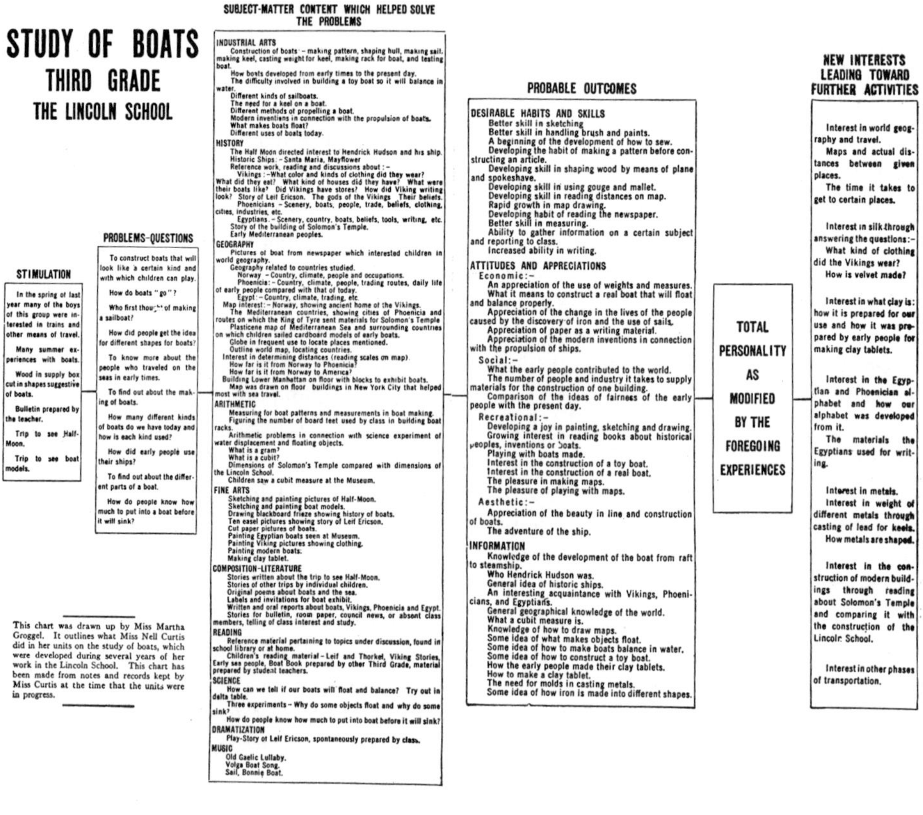

children," of "learning purposefully," of "meaningful geography." She was almost as much concerned with the social relationships of pupils. She wrote about a pupil's "being accepted by the group," and "group spirit and cooperation," and worried about a boy "folks don't like to have around."

Country School Diary says much less about more formal learning: a sixth grader, Warren, explained about rainbows; older pupils wondered how cities became so large, and consulted their geography books; a group discussed the impact of the mechanical cotton picker, although in 1939, in New Jersey, the matter must have been problematical. We are left with doubts. Nevertheless, Julia Gordon's school must have been a pleasant place, at least compared with the school one of us was attending then.

Cremin pointed out the difference between Dewey's intent and Kilpatrick's project method. Dewey had said that the interest of the child should be engaged, but Dewey had insisted that society's accumulated knowledge was of equal importance. Kilpatrick emphasized the interest of the child. Society's knowledge was less important, and was sometimes nearly ignored. Kilpatrick's project method pushed helter-skelter toward child centeredness. For romantics with bottomless faith in the innate virtue and goodness of the child, this has been an attractive formulation, even though only a distant approximation of Dewey's intent. For many of the tens of thousands who heard Kilpatrick speak of it, the project method had enormous merit. One of them may have been Julia Weber Gordon.

THE TURNING POINT TO COME

It would seem to many that the end of the world had come when the stock market collapsed, the Depression set in, and the New Deal took form. In some ways they were right. At least a different world and new public concerns would change both schooling and theories of schooling.

One unpredictable survival was that of the Gary Plan, part of which, as it has probably occurred to the reader, is still standard and conventional practice in high schools and junior high schools. In 1917, after failing to introduce the Gary System in New York City, Wirt returned to Gary. He continued to speak and to write, but the Gary, Indiana schools took more of his time, and general enthusiasm for the Gary Plan slackened. Renewed interest in it and its wide adoption in the next decade or so was more the result of the efforts of Alice Barrows than those of Wirt.

Barrows, a graduate of Vassar and member of the eastern establishment, had first visited the Gary schools in 1914. She wrote that her first day there was "one of the most astonishing and exhilarating experiences of my life." Barrows was a convert. When Wirt became educational consultant to the mayor of New York for the introduction of the Gary Plan in the city's schools, Barrows became his secretary and the Gary Plan's publicist and propagandist. Her friend Randolph Bourne praised her "generalship" and "supernatural energy," and Ray Mohl's study of a few years ago seems to bear out Bourne's opinion. When the attempt to introduce the Plan in New York City failed, Barrows became a staff member of the United States Bureau of Education. She would remain there until her retirement in 1942, and her efforts on behalf of the *platoon school* would be unceasing. (*Gary Plan* had become a controversial term, so the name was changed.) Barrows conducted surveys of more than a dozen city school systems, and the report of every survey advocated the platoon school. She organized conferences on the platoon school and spoke in its support, fifty times in twenty-four days during one survey. She wrote articles for the Bureau of Education's magazine, *School Life.* She taught summer school courses on the platoon school. She was founder and executive secretary of the National Association for the Study of Platoon, or Work-Study-Play Organization, and edited its journal.

Before the end of the 1920s, there were platoon schools, even at the elementary level, in 200 cities. Barrows's campaign for the U. S. Bureau of Education had been most successful. The platoon school thrived during the New Deal in the 1930s. The way in which Barrows brought about change from the inside should be a classic case in the study of innovation.

And yet there is room for doubt. After visiting Cleveland platoon schools, Barrows had written that "I liked the spirit of the children and teachers. . . . It was free and natural. . . . I felt that these children were learning how to think, that the school was a community in which they were engaged in worthwhile activities that had meaning to them. . . ." That might be difficult to observe in most high schools in the 1980s, although students and classes would still exchange places on a carefully planned schedule. Perhaps Barrows's humaneness and idealism had in the end served Wirt's efficiency.

The Depression was to show that business management was far less than a cure-all, and that it could be catastrophic. When business enterprise managers were to seem incompetent, verging on bankruptcy, and were unpopular, school administrators would portray themselves in different lights. After a thirty-year lapse, some administrators in the late 1970s and the 1980s would be proudly businesslike, but that would only be much later.

Research in education would continue after 1929. Thorndike would conduct research at Teachers College even after his retirement in 1942.

Other established researchers would continue their work. Nonetheless, research would lag. In the 1930s, philosophic progressives would argue that research of what *was* could not show what *should be*, which was of far greater importance. During the 1930s and 1940s, other efforts would have priority.

During the Depression of the 1930s, the spirit of the project method, its concentration on the interests and needs of the child, would gain support. There would be dark days for child-centered schooling, but not until the 1950s, when the Depression was long past. In the late 1960s, a generation later, child-centered schools would again be prominent. Educators then would discuss *Summerhill* and free schools.

CONCLUSION

The diverse educational thought and practice from the early 1900s until the Depression cannot be concisely summarized. Reforms and innovations were based upon reformers' social insights, upon the prestige of businessmen and managers, and upon science as some envisioned it. In the 1920s all these were extended, in complex and diverse patterns.

PART FOUR
FROM DEPRESSION UNTIL NOW

DEPRESSION

Almost no one was prepared, but looking back, one sees that there might have been warnings. High inventory levels, installment plan debts being the greatest ever, stock market speculation and margin buying, and fallen crop prices had gone nearly unnoticed. Looking back, one can view the Depression of 1929 as having begun with "Black Thursday," October 20, when the stock market broke and stock prices collapsed. In three weeks, stocks lost $30 billion in value. A conservative newspaper said that week "witnessed the greatest stock-market catastrophe of the ages." There were fables of suicidal brokers and speculators leaping from office windows to their deaths on Wall Street. Those fables were fortunately untrue, but the number of suicides at Niagara Falls more than doubled. In spite of minor rallies and pauses, stock market prices fell for two more years. By 1932, RCA stock had fallen from 101 to 2½, General Motors from 396¼ to 34. Farm prices had been falling since 1920, wheat from $1.98 to 38 cents a bushel, and cotton from 16 cents to 6 cents a pound.

As many as 30 percent of all workers and half of all factory workers were jobless. More than 40 percent of all New England textile workers were out of work. In East Saint Louis, Illinois, the unemployment rate was 60 percent. However, President Hoover insisted that relief, unemployment, and welfare payments were not the responsibility of the federal government. "The strength of our economy," Hoover maintained, was "unimpaired." The reputation of President Herbert Hoover, "the Great Engineer," has not recovered. The businessmen and engineers who had been respected and admired since at least 1910, had had reputations so badly soiled that they would not regain the confidence of the public for fifteen years or more. In the seventy years before 1930, there had been only two Democratic Presidents; Democratic Presidents would be elected in seven of the next nine elections.

The lowest, hardest time of the Depression may have been on the eve of Franklin Roosevelt's inauguration in 1933. Banks, suffering from after-effects of the stock market crash, had lost the confidence of their depositors, who in throngs demanded the return of deposits. Roosevelt was sworn into office on Saturday, March 4, 1933, and the next day declared a "bank holiday" to close banks officially to halt the public panic. At his inauguration Rooselvelt said that ". . . This great nation will endure as it has endured, will revive and will prosper. . . . [T]he only thing we have to fear is fear itself—nameless, unreasoning, unjustified terror which paralyzes needed efforts to convert retreat into advance."

New legislation and new programs began at once. New agencies, nearly three dozen of them, were created. Federal funds were appropriated for public welfare. The N.R.A., National Recovery Act, was intended to reduce competition and restore profits. Its symbol, the blue eagle, was everywhere for a year or two. Several agencies were established to provide jobs. Two and a half million workers became members of the Civilian Conservation Corps—the C.C.C.—and reforested, built fire trails, planted wind breaks, and dammed off gullies to stop erosion. C.W.A., W.P.A., and P.W.A. built the Holland Tunnel, Boulder Dam, and numberless courthouses, hospitals, schools, and levees. The N.Y.A.—National Youth Administration—arranged and financed part-time work for high school and college students. The A.A.A. supported farm prices. F.H.A. encouraged building and modernizing homes. (Critics complained of "alphabet soup.")

After hesitation, Roosevelt supported the labor unions, which had been declining in membership since 1920. One of the N.R.A.'s controversial sections was 7a, which said that "employees shall have the right to organize and bargain collectively . . . and shall be free from the interference, restraint, or coercion of employers. . . ."

In 1936, Roosevelt was reelected by majorities in every state but Vermont and Maine, but the New Deal faced opposition and had difficulties. President Roosevelt was the most widely hated man in America. The "nine old men" of the Supreme Court declared the N.R.A. and the A.A.A. unconstitutional, and it was only after Roosevelt threatened to name six additional Supreme Court judges that the Court showed signs of relenting. The distribution of welfare and work funds was never satisfactorily organized. Roosevelt's attempt to balance the budget was followed by another stock market slump. Unemployment continued. In the summer of 1939, the month before the beginning of the Second World War in Europe, 9.5 million workers were unemployed. Final relief from the Great Depression came only from an unwelcome event, the outbreak of war in Europe, when foreign orders for war-related supplies reenergized the United States' economy. However, this is not to say that the New Deal made no contribution. It established, lastingly, that the government of the United States was responsible for the well-being of its citizens, a principle that has since seemed so obvious that its recent source can be overlooked.

THE SECOND WORLD WAR

The first battle in what would become the Second World War was between the Japanese the Chinese at the Marco Polo Bridge near Peking in 1937. In Europe the war began with the German invasion of Poland on September 1, 1939; England and France went to war against Germany two days later. Although there were "America Firsters" and other noninterventionists in the United States, most people, including President Roosevelt, had come to feel that the United States would, and even should, go to war. Nevertheless, the surprise Japanese attack on the naval base of Pearl Harbor in Hawaii on the morning of Sunday, December 7, 1941, was enormously shocking. Those who cannot say now where and how they first heard of the attack are too young to remember, or were not living in the United States at the time. Roosevelt called it the "day that shall live in infamy," and the United States declared war against Japan. Three days later Germany and Italy declared war against the United States.

There was immediate certainty that life would be different: That proved to be true. For three and a half years, until the final victories in the spring and summer of 1945, the needs and demands of the war came first. Government control was wider than ever before. Industrial production was controlled by a priority system, and price ceilings were set by the O.P.A., Office of Price Management. The public's knowledge of the war largely depended upon the Office of War Information. Americans were taught to hate and exhorted to kill "bullet-headed Nazis" and "yellow squint-eyed Japs."

Although the war in Europe had brought foreign orders for war material and supplies and American rearmament had begun before Pearl Harbor, needs for equipment, supplies, and weapons, both for the United States and its allies, vastly increased: In an important way this war was won in the factories and shipyards of the United States. Manchester's statistics on wartime production are for once more eloquent than words. As examples: airplanes, 300,000; tanks, 100,000; large guns, 400,000; cargo ships, 5,500; small arms ammunition, 44 billion rounds. There were of course hundreds of other war products.

War manufactures demanded more workers. Nearly a million housewives took jobs. More than a million people moved from farm to factory, from country to city, from the South to the North and West.

The cost of living did not increase, at least after mid-1943, but better jobs and more overtime increased wages by 70 percent. One minor fictitious figure of wartime was "Rosie the Riveter," filling a job that until then had been for men only.

War and rumors of war seemed to overshadow all else. There were strange and inconvenient shortages, from military needs or production dislocations. Matches were scarce, but there were fewer cigarettes to light. Because the Japanese had overrun the rubber plantations, there was a shortage of tires. To reduce their use, there was gasoline rationing.

The war shaped even popular music: "Praise the Lord and Pass the Ammunition," a ballad (of sorts) about a fighting navy chaplain; "Don't Sit Under the Apple Tree," a departing soldier's admonition to his girl; "Roll Out the Barrel," borrowed from the Australians; even "Lili Marlene," translated German nostalgia; and Bing Crosby's lachrymose, homesick "I'm Dreaming of a White Christmas."

Science and scientists, as well as production workers, became part of the war effort, under the direction of Vannevar Bush and James B. Conant. Physicists and chemists had contributed in some ways to the winning of the first World War. Their contributions had been useful then, but not critical. But between the wars there were revolutionary theoretical developments, particularly in physics. As we have said, university faculties in science had grown in number, and in expertness.

The Second World War has been called, for rather good reason, the "War of the Physicists." The contributions of scientists were crucial and decisive. The successful defense of England against German bombing raids had depended upon early English radar. German submarine "wolf packs" were driven from the North Atlantic by U. S. Navy airplanes and ships equipped with improved American radar that located submarines and automatically directed gunfire. Germans developed the V-1 "buzz bomb" (remote ancestor of the cruise missile) and V-2 "flying stovepipe" (direct ancestor of all ICBMs), too late to change the war's outcome, but these were inklings of what was to come.

The crowning and most terrifying achievement was the American atomic bomb. Albert Einstein had shown in 1915 that, in principle, matter could be converted into energy: $E = mc^2$. In the 1920s, scientists produced far-reaching new theories about the structure of the atom. In 1939, German physicists demonstrated that some atoms of uranium could be split, releasing energy. Albert Einstein and other refugee physicists warned Roosevelt that Germany could develop an atom bomb. An American atom bomb was an imperative, they said. Its development began in the summer of 1941, after solutions were found for what would be difficulties in production. The first atomic reactor was built under the direction of Enrico Fermi under a football grandstand at the University of Chicago. It first began operating—"went critical"—December 2, 1943. The development of the first atom bomb, under the cover name of "Manhattan Project," was fully underway. There were many technical problems. How could U-238—the isotope of uranium, which was fissionable, or could be split—be separated from the U-235 that made up 99.3 percent of the uranium that was produced? What were the physical properties of plutonium, which did not occur at all in nature? They were determined from milligrams, specks, of plutonium made in the cyclotron at Washington University in Saint Louis. After Pearl Harbor, rifle-carrying soldiers were on guard there, though neither they nor many others knew what they were guarding. Oak Ridge, Tennessee, produced enriched uranium, and Hanford, Washington, plutonium.

By early summer of 1943, there were three atomic bombs. (No more could be produced in less than a year.) The first, code named "Trinity," was not really a bomb, but a test model to be fired statically from atop a tower. The uranium bomb, "Little Boy," was long and slender, like a streamlined ship's torpedo. "Fat Man" struck one observer as graceful, but a prototype in the Sandia museum today seems gross, obese, even obscene, and of course deadly. "Trinity" was fired before sunrise on the morning of July 16, 1945 at Alamogordo, New Mexico. The tower that supported it was vaporized; the desert sand beneath it melted into glass. The world saw its first artificial mushroom-shaped cloud. The Atomic Age had come.

It was clear at the end of the war that defense would continue to rest upon research, that the armed forces must depend upon scientists for new weapons, and also that the armed forces or other federal agencies must provide funding if scientific research was to continue. In the transformed world that appeared after the war, profits and prosperity would also depend upon scientific research. But that, of course, is hindsight.

After the news of Pearl Harbor there were floods of volunteers for the army, navy, and air corps. Even women were allowed to enlist as noncombatants. During the war draft calls grew until nearly 15 million American men had entered the armed forces. Most often there was for the inductee, the "GI," a basic or boot camp, then more often than not a specialized training school, maybe on a college campus where there was available space because college students too had gone to war. Having been assigned to a unit, the serviceman went to sea, or overseas to any of four or five continents. For some reservists, for instance college-trained R.O.T.C. officers, combat came much more quickly. Some were killed within a month in the first battle on Bataan.

The unsung heroes were the "GIs," particularly the "dog faces," the infantrymen. They wallowed in mud from Guadalcanal to the Rhine River, suffering everything from malaria to frostbite, and always from enemy action. They were often ignored by war correspondents. Only Ernie Pyle—killed on Ie Jima—and cartoonist Bill Maudlin seemed to seek them out. Nearly 400,000 Americans were killed in the war, three times as many as in World War I. But American losses were only one fifth of those of Germany, and only one thirtieth of those of Russia. Six million Jews were put to death by Nazi executioners at Dachau, Bergen, Auschwitz, and other concentration camps of the holocaust. That had long been rumored; the reality was almost too ghastly to believe.

President Roosevelt died on April 12, 1945, at Warm Springs, Georgia, of a cerebral hemorrhage. Adolph Hitler killed himself in a bomb shelter under Berlin at the end of April, two days after his ally, Benito Mussolini, had been killed by Italian partisans two days before the German surrender. On September 2, the official Japanese surrender took place aboard the battleship *Missouri* in Tokyo Bay. Six years and a day after the invasion of Poland, the Second World War had ended.

PEACE AND PROSPERITY, USUALLY

Almost a million of the new veterans were discharged within a month. That did not seem fast enough, or soon enough. Draft quotas were reduced, then drafting was ended. Lydon B. Johnson returned from the navy to his seat in Congress. Richard M. Nixon, also a naval officer, was elected to Congress, as was John F. Kennedy, who had been discharged earlier. The "G.I. Bill" provided for veterans mustering out and unemployment pay, and payments for schooling. More than a million veterans went to college. College administrators had had misgivings at first, and educational benefits had been seen by some as a kind of welfare. In spite of over-crowded dormitories, rickety housing, and too-large classes, the veterans were better students than most.

Although some had not realized it, the American economy had been trans-formed, and with it society. Wartime had raised wages, and at the same time high taxes had reduced the incomes of the richest: There had been a major redistribution of incomes. Improved wages and wartime savings made possible more and larger purchases. There were accumulated demands from wartime and even from the Depression. Birth rates climbed, creating further demand.

The years after the war are remembered by historians of foreign relations as the time of the *Cold War* against Russia and communism. A satirist might call them the age of the Edsel, an overlarge, overweight automobile calculated—miscalcu-lated—by Ford Motor Company to appeal to the rising organization man. Many remember the years after the war as the good years.

The returned veterans wanted, and many of them found, a life that was good in material things. There was at first a housing shortage, but millions of new houses were built in the suburbs. For those most successful, there were "colonial" houses, or spreading "ranch" houses built a room or two deep across a building lot and looking more spacious and more expensive than they were. For the others there were F.H.A.- or G.I. Bill-financed boxes. Boxes were mass produced in the Levit-towns built by William J. Levitt's company. The first of the Levittowns was built on Long Island in the far suburbs of New York City. There were 17,500 houses in it, easily sold at $6,990 and up. They were sold before they were completed, even before they were started.

Part of the veterans' vision of the good life was quick marriage and several children. Early marriage became fashionable. In the 1950s, women married on the average two years earlier than before, and high school students' marriages were not unusual. To bear or sire three, four, or more children was also fashionable. For their rearing, Dr. Benjamin M. Spock, in best-selling manuals, advocated "permissiveness." The need for children to get to school, to Boy and Girl Scout meetings, and to piano lessons, and so forth, made suburban mothers chauffeurs for their children. The suburban "teenagers" (the term became popular then) had allowances or part-time jobs. In the 1950s, they spent on the average $550 a year, necessities not included. There was a teenage market for phonograph records, radios, cameras, and cosmetics. The biggest audience for movies was the teenagers. Teenagers made Elvis

Presley one of the greatest stars of radio and motion pictures. Eventually he was even allowed on television (from the waist up).

Television had been little more than experimental before the war. After the war, picture tubes were tiny, there were few television stations, and programs had to be produced locally. But after 1950, manufacturing television sets became a major industry; 2 million sets a year were sold. Color television appeared, triumphantly, in 1955. Watching television became an absorbing and time-consuming pastime. Those who were children then remember Howdy Doody and Buffalo Bob. Quite by accident they memorized a song: "Mickey Mouse: Mickey Mouse! . . . / M – I – C / – – See you real soon! /K – E – Y / – – Why? Because we like you! / M – O – U – S – E!" Teenagers and their parents could watch not only Elvis Presley, but also other performers on Ed Sullivan's variety show. One could also watch "lady" wrestlers and daily installments of the "soap operas." Disney's "Davy Crockett" was enormously popular television series. One of us remembers explaining in broken German to a new immigrant high school student that Crockett was "langzeit gestorben," long dead. The student was upset.

Middle- and upper-income parents, their younger children and affluent teenagers, watched television in their new suburban homes. Automobiles had made the new suburbs possible. The great American love affair, it was often said, was the Americans' love for their automobiles. Many, usually most, new automobiles were General Motors Chevrolets, Pontiacs, Oldsmobiles, Buicks, and Cadillacs. Year by year, automobiles increased in size, in power, in top speed, in ornateness. There were tail fins (perhaps suggested by those of the P-38 fighter plane) and engines that grew larger year by year (but gasoline was less than 25 cents a gallon) and numberless accessories. A few of those automobiles, such as the Ford Thunderbirds, are today "classics," beautiful sculpture in motion. Others now look like baking failures.

The automobile shaped the growth of American cities. Old downtown retail areas declined because there was too little parking space. New stores surrounded by acres of paved parking lots appeared in the suburbs. Korvettes, the first of the discount centers, appeared there. Drive-in theaters became common, in one sense or another. Outside the cities the interstate highways were being built. American soft-riding, bad-cornering cars and the interstate highways were built for each other.

If there had been a single key to the fifteen years between the end of the war and John F. Knnedy's presidency, it was prosperity. The value of goods produced—the gross national product—doubled and doubled again. There was a hesitancy at demobilization time and an uncomfortable lull after the war in Korea, but prosperity was the greatest America had ever known. It was prosperity earned and prosperity enjoyed. Money was to be made, even with moderate effort, and "big spender" was a complimentary term.

President Truman was elected in 1948 and proved to be more capable than most had expected. However, his "Fair Deal" plans, in the tradition of Roosevelt's New Deal, were largely blocked by conservative, and sometimes Republican, congress. In 1952, Democrats nominated Adlai E. Stevenson, governor of Illinois and to many the most appealing presidential candidate since William Jennings Bryan. Stevenson was badly defeated by General Dwight D. Eisenhower, running as a Republican. Stevenson attracted admiration because of his warmth and wit. Eisenhower, Second World War commander in Europe, inspired confidence and also votes. (The Republican vice-presidential nominee was Richard M. Nixon.) Eisenhower, in spite of a heart attack, easily defeated Stevenson again in 1956.

There were, of course, other political issues in those years, but looking back the most important of them were issues of foreign affairs, or arising from foreign affairs. The most pressing of all concerns was Russian communism. The Cold War came from the seeming possibility that Russian communists would overpower the free world. At the end of World War II, Russia had established control over Central Europe. The communist overrunning of Greece seemed likely unless blocked. Communists (though not Russian communists) did establish control of mainland China. American ally Chiang Kai-shek was driven to refuge on the offshore island of Formosa. Russian technology and Russian espionage were more effective than had been expected, and the explosion of the first Russian atom bomb in the summer of 1949 was much sooner than the United States expected. Fidel Castro, who had seemed to be an admirable opponent of a dictatorship, became the communist ruler of a communist state only eighty miles from southernmost Florida. In 1950, communist North Korea attempted to overrun South Korea. The United States came to the aid of South Korea on behalf of the United Nations; 32,629 Americans were killed in the Korean War.

It has often been argued that the origin of the Cold War was American efforts to surround and control Russia, and that it was generated by an American military-industrial alliance. This may have been true, at least partly, but the appearance was to the contrary, and the appearance determined events.

An indirect consequence to the United States was a long and hurtful campaign against those who seemed to have even the slightest reservations about the American way. Part of this started with charges of Russian espionage, in which there were some fragments of truth. Russian secret documents turned over to Canadian officials by a Russian code clerk seeking political asylum showed that Klaus Fuchs, a physicist at the atom bomb laboratories in Los Alamos, New Mexico, had regularly supplied information to the Russians.

In addition to Fuchs's, there were a few other cases in which espionage was, with or without reasonable doubt, apparent. But beyond these there were hundreds accused for unlikely or trivial reasons. The Truman administration "verified" the loyalty of all civil service workers. The attorney general drew up a list of "red front" organizations. Membership in any one of them was strong evidence of guilt. The motion picture industry's "black list" of suspected communists kept some individuals out of the industry for twenty years or more.

Senator Joseph R. McCarthy claimed again and again that he knew of hundreds of cases of disloyalty. His attack upon the army led to Congressional hearings that were nationally televised. McCarthy was humbled by attorney Joseph N. Welch. McCarthy was censured by the Senate and dropped from prominence.

The Supreme Court ruled, 9-0, in 1954, that separate, segregated schooling was in itself unequal and therefore unconstitutional. In 1955, the Reverend Martin Luther King led a boycott of buses in Montgomery, Alabama. The court decision and boycott were the beginnings of the black Civil Rights Movement.

The rights of Negroes (or, as they now prefer, Blacks) had been, seemingly, guaranteed by the radicals' Civil Rights law of 1866, and by the Fourteenth and Fifteenth Amendments, ratified in 1868 and 1870. Nevertheless, in the seventy years that followed they were eroded by court decisions and white supremacist politicians. The Supreme Court decision of 1954 reversed earlier decisions. The bus boycott was directed at segregation and discrimination.

There had been tentative steps toward racial equality by Roosevelt and the New Deal. The W.P.A. and C.C.C. had aided Blacks as well as Whites. Only months before Pearl Harbor, A. Philip Randolph, black head of the black union of sleeping car porters, had planned a black march on Washington to protest job discrimination against Blacks. To prevent it, Roosevelt issued an executive order requiring employees and unions "to provide for the full and equitable participation of all workers in defense industries, without discrimination because of race, creed, color, or national origin." By 1944, the National Association for the Advancement of Colored People (far more often called the "N double A CP") increased its membership ninefold, to nearly half a million. None of these seemed by itself very important, but there was enough power and strength for the next steps.

The NAACP had come from the "Niagara Movement." In 1905, W. E. B. DuBois and his followers met in Niagara Falls, Ontario, Canada (because the hotels in Niagara Falls, New York, were segregated). Following DuBois's argument, the Niagara Movement demanded that ". . . the laws be enforced against rich as well as poor . . . against white as as well as black. . . . We want the Fourteenth Amendment carried out to the letter. . . ." The NAACP had been organized in 1909, by Niagara Movement members and Progressive friends, including John Dewey. Its court strategy, designed by Roy Wilkins and later by NAACP counsel Thurgood Marshall, moved step by step to end discrimination. The 1954 triumph in *Brown v. Topeka* was probably their greatest success, but it was neither their first nor their last.

In Montgomery, Alabama ("the birthplace of the Confederacy"), in late 1955, Rosa Parks, a Black, refused to give up her seat in the front of a bus. She was arrested and fined ten dollars. Blacks organized a boycott of Montgomery buses. The Blacks' leader was Dr. Martin Luther King, Jr., pastor of a Montgomery Baptist church, twenty-six years old, a Boston University graduate. King (with whom one of us was briefly acquainted) was an intent, energetic man sometimes quiet and somewhat distant, but one of this country's most inspired orators. King did not believe in violence, though he did believe in equality for Blacks. It was to be won through passive resistance, which had been successfully employed by Mahatma Gandhi of India. The Montgomery bus boycott lasted for more than a year. King was arrested and found guilty, and he appealed. Then the Supreme Court declared "separate but equal"—that is, segregated—bus transportation unconstitutional, and the boycott was ended. King was famous. Black civil disobedience had begun.

The peak of King's influence was at the end of August, 1963, at the March on Washington. About 200,000 Blacks and sympathizers were there, singing their anthem-hymn, "We Shall Overcome." King spoke at the Lincoln Memorial. "I have a dream," he said, "of . . . equality . . . brotherhood . . . freedom and justice." King and other black leaders met with President Kennedy. The march aided the passage of the Civil Rights Act of 1964, ending discrimination in public places, allowing the attorney general to file suits to speed school desegregation, and prohibiting racism in hiring. The Voting Rights Act of 1965, following demonstrations in the South by King, guaranteed Blacks the right to register and vote.

WHEN EVERYTHING, ALMOST, WENT WRONG

At the end of Dwight Eisenhower's second term, in 1960, Republicans nominated Vice-President Richard Nixon as their candidate for President. The Democratic candidate was Senator John F. Kennedy. It was to Nixon's advantage that prosperity had made Americans more conservative, even though, paradoxically, they were more often Democrats. Kennedy's support came from the New Deal coalition of blue-collar workers, city political machines, and the solid South. Kennedy's victory in November was by a razor thin margin of 0.17 percent of the votes.

Kennedy was youthful, the youngest president ever elected, and youthfulness had become admirable. He was brave, witty, and compassionate. He recruited for government the ablest of minds. In his first three months in the presidency he asked Congress thirty-nine times for new legislation and appropriations, most of them to improve the quality of American life. There was a new and wholly successful agricultural policy. To aid schools—one of Kennedy's first concerns—there were appropriations for colleges and universities, public schools, and vocational education. There were programs for the jobless and to improve housing. The Russians were persuaded or forced to remove their ICBM missles from Cuba. Massive aid was provided for declining American "inner citites." It was a promising beginning, even though marred by a bungled CIA-directed attempt to land an invasion force at the Bay of Pigs in Cuba. Some conservatives and reactionaries, members of the John Birch Society, hated Kennedy for, they said, being "soft on communism" and for a dozen other cardinal sins.

At 12:30 PM, Friday, November 22, 1963, in Dallas, Texas, President Kennedy was killed by Lee Harvey Oswald. Those who remember say that Kennedy's death was nearly as great a shock as Pearl Harbor, a greater shock than Franklin Roosevelt's death by natural causes. Until after the president's funeral, Monday afternoon, television coverage was continuous. There was no time, attention, or spirit for any other matter. But in a suburb of Dallas, pupils in a fourth grade class had clapped when they had been told of Kennedy's death.

The new president, sworn in three hours after Kennedy was shot, was Lyndon B. Johnson, from the hill country of Texas north of San Antonio and west of Austin, the first president from the South in a hundred years. In style and manner he was nearly Kennedy's opposite. As symbolism we think of Kennedy's deft handling of a sailboat on the Atlantic contrasted with Johnson's nearly swamped motor cruiser barging through the dammed Pedernales River. Johnson had been born poor, Kennedy rich. Johnson had graduated fom Southwest State Teachers College in San Marcos, Texas, Kennedy from Harvard. Johnson had a Texas accent; Kennedy's had been Harvard and Boston.

Johnson was elected president less than a year after Kennedy's assasination, in 1964. The martyrdom of Kennedy helped. The Republican nomination of Barry Goldwater, honorable senator from Arizona and archconservative also helped.

Johnson secured the passage of Kennedy's New Frontier bills and then declared the "War on Poverty." The War on Poverty was intended to set free the one American in five or six caught in poverty, in which poverty resulted in poor health, poor schooling, hopelessness, and continued poverty. That Johnson had country manners and enormous conceit was probably unimportant, although journalists emphasized them. Johnson was magnificently successful in dealing with Congress.

Whites, Blacks, and Hispanics were the underculture. The War Against Poverty was to provide help for those who were trapped by poverty. Whites in the Appalachians were stranded by shifts in technology, or caught in city slums. Blacks, many of whom had moved to the North during the Depression, during the war boom years, and after, were isolated, more than ever before, in city "ghettos," where there were too few jobs and too much crime. Ghetto schools were much too unsuccessful in teaching rudiments, in preventing dropping out, and in inducting these members of the underculture into the common culture.

Those who did not speak English—especially those who spoke Spanish as a first language—were also at a disadvantage. Some of the Spanish-speaking ethnic communities were made up of Mexicans who had come to the United States legally or illegally—"wetbacks" was the scornful term for the latter—and their descendants. However, we must remember that the United States came to some who spoke Spanish, when Southwestern territories were annexed after the Mexican War. Mexican-American Hispanics in the Southwest—"Chicanos" was the popular name for them—lived in "barrios" in the Southwest, and made up most of the Spanish-speaking population there.

Puerto Ricans, citizens of the United States since 1917, came to the mainland as agricultural laborers, to cultivate and harvest vegetables and fruits. Many more Puerto Ricans came directly to cities in the Northeast, especially New York City, after the Second World War. Airline fares were low, jobs more plentiful and better-paying on the mainland, and welfare payments more generous.

The most recent wave of Spanish-speaking immigrants was of refugees from Castro's communist Cuba. In Miami's "Little Havana," one was served Cuban food, a creditable copy of Cuban beer (made in Newark), and heard Hispanic music: minor key, guitar accompaniment, with a throbbing beat. By the 1980s, Spanish was nearly as common a first language as English in Miami. A "Little Haiti," where the first language was French, would also appear there.

All these, Whites, Blacks, and members of ethnic minorities, were to be aided by the War Against Poverty. It was to provide jobs, better schooling, medical care, community development. Johnson wanted to be remembered as another Franklin Roosevelt. He might have, except for one fatal policy decision.

The old French "protectorate," then called Indo-China, had been occupied by the Japanese and had declared itself independent of France. After the Second World War, the French had reappeared, to be opposed by communists led by Ho Chi Minh, and to be finally defeated at the fortress of Dienbeinphu. French troops surrendered and were withdrawn. The northern half of Vietnam would be communist, the southern half, not. But Ho Chi Minh and his followers were determined to "liberate" South Vietnam at any cost: no matter how many lives lost, no matter what damage inflicted.

Eisenhower's administration had provided financial aid to the French. Eisenhower himself opposed and prevented military action by the United States. Kennedy's administration sent to Vietnam more weapons and money and military "advisers." President Kennedy's policy had been to continue the United State's plan for the containment of communism and, for that reason, continue to support South Vietnam against the communists of North Vietnam. Johnson inherited the policy, with which he agreed. In August 1964, on the pretext that U.S. ships had been attacked in the Gulf of Tonkin, Johnson asked for congressional endorsement of the use of force. No representative and only two senators voted against the joint resolution. At the time, involvement in Vietnam was favored by three out of four Americans. The first American bombings were in February 1965, "reprisals" by navy airplanes. The next month the first U.S. combatants, 3,500 marines, were sent ashore. Month by month, American military forces increased, until in 1968, there were 550,000 members of the armed forces there. The war was managed by Robert McNamara as he had managed Ford Motor Company. There were endless numbers: body counts, sorties flown, villages liberated—all the information needed for scientific management. The latest technology was employed: helicopters, gunships, defoliants, improved napalm. In some weeks, more bombs were dropped on the Vietnamese than on Germany in all of World War II. "Search and destroy" infantry ("grunts" in the Vietnam war) missions killed hundreds, probably thousands, of Vietnamese. None of this seemed to matter if Vietnam and those it supported were defeated. The South Vietnamese governments—there were several of them—were uninspiring, incompetent, dishonest, and vacillating, and never had the full loyalty of the South Vietnamese. Massive bombings did not disrupt a primitive technology. It was easier to make a road impassable for trucks than to make it impassible for bicycles (which many North Vietnamese used).

After Nixon's inauguration there were peace talks, but there was no peace. A cease fire did not come until 1973, and it was violated almost at once. The final solution was not reached until the spring of 1975, when the North Vietnamese overran South Vietnam.

Among the direct costs to the United States were the lives of 56,000 Americans and $150 billion in military aid. The United States was engaged in Vietnam longer than it had been in World War II.

The war in Vietnam had become overwhelmingly unpopular. First, there were antiwar petitions. On college and university campuses there were "teach-ins" on days set aside for presentations, discussions, and exhortations. Step by step, war protests became stronger and more violent. The demonstrations at colleges and universities were a part—sometimes a senseless and meaningless part—of efforts described in Chapter 13. Many students also demonstrated off campuses, of course. A Quaker American, who believed that war was immoral followed a Vietnamese precedent. In front of the White House he doused himself with gasoline and struck a match. The public effect was naturally hard to assess; the private effect was death. Other protesters against the war marched in Washington, D.C. They demonstrated on the anniversary of the Hiroshima bomb, and they also demonstrated against Dow Chemical Company, which had produced napalm. The demonstrations by students and others were primarily against the war, but they were also demonstrations against the technology that surrounded and threatened to enslave—if it had not already done so.

The years of the antiwar demonstrations were also the years of the "hot summers." As King's leadership became less effective, a number of new leaders, or spokesmen appeared. Malcolm X—with his memorable, cold, penetrating gray eyes— might have been the most effective of them, but he was murdered before King. Of course, there were others: Huey Newton, Stokeley Carmichael, LeRoi Jones, James Forman, H. Rap Brown. Some were separatists, wanting not one society but two, one black, the other white. Tom Wolfe, in *Radical Chic*, did a splendid parody of the popularity among fashionable Whites of violent and separatist black agitators.

Black agitators contributed in some minor ways to the "hot summers." Those summers were hottest in the big cities. The Harlem riots started when an off-duty policeman shot knife-armed James Powell, age fifteen. For three days, black fury smoldered. Then came the rioting lasting five nights, spreading to Brooklyn, and then to Rochester, 300 miles away. There was a kind of pattern to the riots. They were summer events, when the temperature was high. They took place where Blacks felt—and probably were—politically powerless, and where there was hostility by and toward the police. Perhaps television played a part. A visible riot is more provoking than one only heard or read about. They started from an incident, or rumors of an incident, of police mistreatment of a Black. Rumors spread; anger increased. Nearly all the riots were spontaneous, and only seldom was there an outside agitator. Black rioters burned and looted black property as well as that of Whites. Blacks much more often than Whites were killed or wounded.

Harlem in New York City in 1964, Watts in Los Angeles in 1965 and 1966, Roxbury in Boston in 1967—these were some of the worst. There were hundreds of others. The worst outburst was in 1968, on the night of Martin Luther King's death. There were 2,600 fires and 21,000 injuries in 168 cities.

The "youth culture" or "counterculture" was at its height in the late 1960s. The postwar baby boom had produced millions more youths than there had ever been before, more than there would be again—for some time, at least. Prosperity had made it possible for almost half of them to attend college. (Only a minority of them were "hippies." There were far more earnest students and career-minded young men and women. There were even football enthusiasts.) Prosperity, the greatest ever, made it seem plausible that not everyone would have to work, and

that those who did work would not need to work much. It was a time of romanticism, more than any other time since the Transcendentalists. Feelings rather than
thoughts were to govern behavior. A popular bumper sticker said "IF IT FEELS
GOOD, DO IT!" Drugs, particularly "pot," became popular. So did free, near-
indiscriminate sex, although one suspects that talk about it changed more than
behavior. Professors and other serious-minded people wrote about the "post-
industrial society" and the "greening of America."

Perhaps the high water mark of the counterculture was the Woodstock
Festival. Hundreds of thousands gathered to hear, and maybe even to see the
Jefferson Airplane, Joan Baez, Janis Joplin, and others. Their music was the symbol
of the counter culture, and for that reason alone unbearable to some others. After
Woodstock, there were other festivals, and for too short a time, the "flower children" of Haight-Ashbury in San Francisco, terribly vulnerable to pushers, pimps,
and muggers.

Johnson's handling of the war in Vietnam cost him his popularity, and in the
spring of 1968 he decided not to seek reelection. The Republican nominee was
Richard M. Nixon, who eight years before had been defeated by John F. Kennedy,
and was later also defeated as a candidate for the Senate and for the governorship
of California. The Democratic convention in Chicago was besieged by peace demonstrators. Hubert H. Humphrey was nominated there the night the police rioted, not
without provocation, and attached the demonstrators. Nixon had been unfortunate
when he had been defeated by Kennedy, but his fortunes had changed. The Democratic platform had a hawkish plank. Humphrey was too closely associated with
Johnson and too long in disassociating himself from Johnson's war policy. Nixon's
election plurality was seven-tenths of a percent, greater than Kennedy's had been,
but still tiny.

Looking back, Nixon's terms in office seem to have been generally disagreeable times, in nonpolitical as well as political ways. The war in Vietnam did not end
for more than four years, although Nixon had offered hope that he would end it
quickly. Court martial evidence demonstrated that at a village named My Lai, U.S.
soldiers at least once massacred Vietnamese civilians. Television news coverage
made the war in Vietnam visible to everyone and horrifying to many. Nixon at
times increased combat and bombings. Antidraft meetings became larger and more
frequent. Thousands of young men went to Canada rather than serve in an immoral
and dangerous war. An "incursion" into Cambodia set off demonstrations at
hundreds of colleges and universities. At Jackson State in Mississippi, two students
were killed by police. National Guardsmen at Kent State in Ohio shot to death four
students and injured nine others. It was miraculous that none of the other demonstrations resulted in deaths.

There were other hazards, as well. In New York City, Weathermen and other
radical groups set off bombs on an average of six times a week. One inept bomb-
maker killed himself and an accomplice and demolished a house when there was a
premature explosion. Actor Dustin Hoffman's adjacent home was damaged beyond
repair. (Hoffman was not at home at the time of the explosion.) Violent crimes of

more ordinary sorts were becoming more commonplace. In 1969, there were sixty-eight skyjackings.

Nixon and his secretary of state, Henry Kissinger, did succeed finally in bringing to an end American action in Vietnam. The peace was much too late, but it was peace. The long stand-off with communist mainland China was ended. The United States's manned rocket program finally fulfilled its goal when Apollo 11's landing module *Eagle* touched down on the moon on July 20, 1969. While the world watched on television, Neil A. Armstrong took mankind's first steps on the moon. President Nixon was on hand to greet Armstrong and the other Apollo 11 crew members when they landed in the Pacific. The landing was a moment of great and bloodless triumph, especially for scientists and technologists.

Nixon's election had been by a narrow margin. His reelection was by a landslide, won by a wider margin than any presidential election since 1936. The Democratic nominee, George S. McGovern, senator from South Dakota, had been opposed to war in Vietnam. That seemed unimportant, since Kissinger said the war was ending. McGovern struck voters as too radical, and untrustworthy. George Wallace, the white supremacy candidate, was shot and paralyzed and was unable to campaign.

Early in the presidential campaign, five men who had broken into the Democratic headquarters in the Watergate complex in Washington, D.C. were arrested. On the surface it was tawdry political espionage, but no more than that, and it did not much affect the election. The unravelling of Watergate cannot be told here. When Nixon resigned on August 8, 1974, it was clear that he had encouraged perjury and that, starting soon after the Watergate break-in, he had conspired to obstruct justice. Above all he had demeaned and disgraced the presidency.

Gerald R. Ford had become Vice-President in 1973, after Spiro Agnew, who had been elected to the office, had resigned to avoid prosecution for bribe-taking. Ford became president upon Nixon's resignation. "Our long national nightmare is over," he said. A month later he pardoned ex-president Nixon. Ford immediately became the target for every liberal satirist and editor. The pardon may have cost Ford the election in 1976, though inflation and a business slump put him at a disadvantage. It also had been shown that both the F.B.I. and the C.I.A. had often exceeded their authority. Nevertheless, Ford was renominated after a hot contest with Ronald Reagan. Jimmy Carter (a distant descendant of the Carter family that had employed Philip Fithian so long ago) won the nomination, partly because he was a determined and astute politician. It does not seem unfair to say that he was elected because he inspired the confidence of voters. Carter's presidency suffered from misfortune, and ineptness. In 1980, he was defeated by Ronald Reagan, one-time sports announcer, actor, union official, radio commentator, ex-governor of California, and Republican conservative. The increasing costs of energy, the rate of inflation, and the high rate of unemployment seemed to be the first and most general concerns of voters. The invasion of Afghanistan by the U.S.S.R. had chilled international relations. At the beginning of Reagan's term as President, it seemed unlikely that social benefit programs, including educational ones, would have high priority. The mood of conservatism seemed again to be upon America.

CONCLUSION

To summarize a summary of half a century's history is scarcely possible. Perhaps it is worth saying that, although there have been admirable accomplishments during that history, there are, as always, grave unresolved issues and absorbing problems. History, after all, is a continuing story.

CHAPTER ELEVEN
SEARCH FOR COMPETENCE

INTRODUCTION

In the despair of the early 1930s, bare survival took precedence over all other concerns. Even later in the 1930s, there were many more workers than jobs. The Second World War demanded all available resources, time, and energy. There were fewer teachers. There were wartime needs for schooling and a greater demand for knowledge and skills useful in wartime.

In the 1950s, curriculum builders and other educators formulated "life adjustment education." It appeared far too late and was completely vulnerable to the attack that ensued. The most conservative position was that great ideas from great classical authors were what students should learn, and would of course not learn in a child-centered school. Other opponents of educational Progressivism felt that society and culture, rather than the student's interests, were most important. As most critics saw it, schools certainly were not intended to change society, but were to support society as it was. After the Second World War, there was again a return to conservatism. To Senator Joseph R. McCarthy, whatever might be associated with leftist or even liberal sympathies was "communistic," "unpatriotic," wrongheaded, and criminal.

Research in university physics, and other, laboratories had consequences that President Gilman and the first faculty members at Johns Hopkins University could not have imagined. University research had created a new world, a world of A-bombs, H-bombs, intercontinental missiles—and color television. When science and scientific research seemed to have all answers to all questions, research in education again attracted attention and support.

The logical, rational world of crewcut scientists and businessmen in grey flannel suits seemed, particularly to those who were growing up in it, too binding, too dominating, and terribly dangerous and bloody. Dr. Strangelove was too possible, *1984* too close. The costs of new knowledge were too great. After the early 1960s, a stronger commitment would be made to equality in schooling, to righting the wrongs of 300 years of discrimination. Freedom for the individual, "self-actualization," would become more important. But there would be another turning, a new mood of caution and conservativeness. School administrators would again stress "basics," "mastery," and competence.

DEPRESSION

The Depression's effects upon some school systems and their teachers were much more severe than upon others. Schools and teachers in heavy industry cities such as Gary were especially hard hit. In rural areas, many of which were already poverty-stricken, schools were closed. In the South the already slender means of black teachers and black schools were reduced still further. In many schools class sizes were increased. High school teachers taught additional classes. Many classes in foreign languages, advanced mathematics, home economics, and physical education were dropped. In Chicago, junior high schools were closed, and the junior college discontinued. Teachers, child psychologists, and truant officers were laid off. In many school systems, the school year was shortened and many teachers were laid off. One former principal worked as a common laborer at Boulder Dam, and tens of thousands of teachers were employed by the W.P.A. Salaries were cut and pay-days were late. Some teachers were paid in "tax warrants," school board IOUs, which many stores refused to accept and others accepted only at a discount.

In Chicago, teachers' tax warrants were discounted 20 percent. For those who continued to teach, there were more pupils and more classes. It was true that teacher salaries fell more slowly than the cost of living, but teachers as well as others were baffled, threatened, and despairing at the Depression. Teachers contributed to emergency funds for pupils. When she wrote about it thirty-five years later, one Oklahoma teacher remembered that many of her pupils had had only one meal a day, or none. In the Great Plains states, droughts and dust storms came with the Depression. Pupils at one school brought their own drinking water from home in fruit jars. Schools were dismissed because of the dust storms; midafternoon was as dark as night. One teacher remembered crying when there was a payday without pay. Beatrice Stevens Nathan, by then married and teaching near San Francisco Bay, remembered teacher contributions and P.T.A. card parties and rummage sales to help pupils. Her school distributed used clothing to its neediest pupils. The fund provided free milk and paid for the repair of shoes and glasses and for emergency dental and medical care. Things were better, teachers remembered, after public relief was established, along with the W.P.A. In the mid-1930s, two Oklahoma teachers, man and wife, arranged a field trip for their students to Carlsbad Caverns in New Mexico. The cost was $5 per pupil.

In the early 1930s, the despair of the public was shared by writers, journalists, educators, and intellectuals. Most of them expected a revolution momentarily and felt that a new form of society and the redistribution of wealth were urgently needed. For Progressive followers of Dewey, the crisis was especially significant. Progressive school reform had begun in the Progressive (in another sense) era when social reform had been the most important goal. Dewey's intent in reforming schools had been, implicitly or explicitly, to reform society, and Dewey, as well as many other reformers of the Progressive era, had been inclined toward socialism. For many Progressive educators it was time for a change.

FIGURE 11-1   "Victim of Drought." Photograph by Lewis Hine. From *Coronet,* Vol. 5, February 1939, p. 155.

Counts put the argument more strongly and introduced the concept of social class, and, implicitly, the concept of social class struggle:

> If Progressive Education is to be genuinely progressive it must emancipate itself from the influences of this [middle] class, face squarely and courageously every social issue, come to grips with life in all its stark reality, establish an organic relation with the community, develop a realistic and comprehensive theory of welfare, and become somewhat less frightened than it is today at the bogeys of *imposition* and *indoctrination.*

Counts's proposal, put in the form of a rhetorical question, was "Dare the Schools Build a New Social Order?" The question was rhetorical and the expected answer was "yes." A few did answer "no." Journalist Agnew de Lima wrote that teachers were too "docile," too well protected by tenure, "unlikely to challenge the status quo." Teachers were too timid and too disinterested to effect a new social order. They could not.

Another *New Republic* writer said that

> [T]he word *progressive* in progressive education never carried political or sociological implications; that it is descriptive only of educational techniques which *progress* in keeping with psychological and other findings. . . .

Schools, then, should not affect the social order. Counts replied with disdain. There were objections, too, to use of the schools for "indoctrination." "Indoctrination" seemed on its face to be inappropriate if schools were dedicated to the development and perfection of democracy. For another reason, then, schools should not undertake the building of a new social order—the means were inappropriate for the end.

Looking back, one sees that the schools, that is, the teachers, could not build a new social order because that was an inappropriate task, and because the means seemed inappropriate and insufficient. It now seems remarkable that Counts raised the question. Why "dare" what apparently could not, perhaps should not, almost certainly would not, be done? But of course, we now have an additional half century of experience, some of it quite unpleasant.

The beginning of the road to recovery from the Depression seemed to come at Franklin D. Roosevelt's inauguration in 1933. However, Roosevelt, especially in his first term, was uninterested in social reform as such. When in his second term he did secure the passage of the Social Security Act and the establishment of the National Labor Relations Board, the Progressive reconstructionists, who had by then moved to radical liberalism and socialism, were unappeased. But the antipathy was mutual. Roosevelt and his New Dealers did not enlist schools or teachers to secure reforms.

Some educators' commitment to social reconstruction persisted, although the entry of the United States into war changed its purposes and made it less radical and less urgent. Social reconstruction and child-centered education contributed to "life adjustment" education, to which we will return.

THE SECOND WORLD WAR

Some effects of the Second World War upon schooling were immediate, others remote and indirect. As in the First World War, teachers—this time 350,000 of them—left classrooms to enter the armed forces or defense industries, or simply for better pay. A teacher shortage developed. High school students dropped out far more frequently, because wages were high and jobs were plentiful. College students, too, dropped out in anticipation of being drafted, or were drafted. The number of women enrolled in college also declined, partly because of the number of jobs available. When manpower needs allowed, there were draft deferments for pre-medical, engineering, and science students. (There were no general deferments for college students, as there would be in the Vietnam war.) As college enrollments declined, armed forces service schools—preflight and army intensive programs for translators, as examples—appeared on many college campuses.

Wartime needs magnified the importance of scientific research, particularly research in physics and in engineering. American physics researchers had become highly competent, both as experimenters and as theorists. The number of Ph.D.s awarded in physics had quadrupled in the 1920s, and the "intellectual migration" of German Jewish scientists had further strengthened university physics departments. Even in the later 1930s, the United States's research capability had been the greatest in the world. Research during the war, the development of radar and atom bombs, of shaped explosive charges and of other devices, made it plausible to claim that the Second World War was the "physicists' war." Postwar changes in industry and the economy would clearly make research even more valuable. Defense research would continue because Russia, with atomic bombs and inter-continental ballistic missiles, seemed threatening.

The Depression and the war produced as after-effects changes in ways of thinking and talking about schools. "Life adjustment," an approach to high school curriculum, was clearly a product of the Depression, although it did not reach its greatest prominence, or notoriety, until after 1950. A new mode of thinking and talking about school administration, of "democratic administration," became popular because of both the Depression and the war.

The business management justification for school administration was one of the lesser victims of the Depression. Administrative techniques (budgeting, account-ing, purchasing, building design and maintenance, and so on), which had been enormously developed and refined, remained, but a new justification emerged. Its most prominent advocate was Jesse H. Newlon, superintendent of schools in Denver and later professor at Teachers College. His *Educational Administration as Social Policy* (1934) had been the first influential argument against school administration patterned solely on business management justifications. In 1939, he wrote

Education should, of course, be efficiently and economically administered, but it should be kept in mind always that efficiency and economy must be defined in terms of purposes and responsibilities and that economy and

parsimony are not synonyms in the parlance of public affairs. The fundamental desideratum is that the schools be kept free if they are to serve the
primary purpose of social education.

If the purpose of the schools was to serve democracy, the logical first essential was
that the schools be democratically organized and controlled. Decisions were to be
made by all involved. The basis for school administration was expertise rather than
authority. After the war one spokesman for administrators wrote that

> Actual leadership, as judged by the contribution made or the solution arrived
> at, may come from a classroom teacher, a parent, or the administrator. The
> role of the administrator may or may not involve the introduction of the idea
> finally accepted. In many situations, the administrator's leadership role will
> be that of encouraging others to participate effectively.

"Group dynamics" became an important part of educational thought and research
about the time of World War II, as support for "democratic leadership" (and of
course as condemnation of "authoritarian" leadership and governments). The most
widely cited study was by Kurt Lewin. One of the academic refugees from Nazi
Germany, Lewin had been engaged there in systematic research that would result
in a social psychological "field theory." At Iowa State University in the last of the
1930s, he and his assistants conducted experiments to determine the effects of
"democratic," "laissez-faire" and "autocratic" leadership. Groups of boys were
subjected to each in turn. The boys showed greater satisfaction and less aggressive-
ness when the leader was "democratic," and activities continued even when the
democratic leader was absent. For years this was the experiment most widely cited
in education, for its implications both for teaching and school supervision, even
though most attempts to replicate it were unsuccessful. It was still mentioned in
some sociology of education texts forty years later. Further support for democratic
leadership and group dynamics came from earlier studies initiated by Elton Mayo
when educators became aware of them. The studies were carried out at the Western
Telephone factory at Hawthorne, Illinois (and are referred to as the "Western
Electric" or "Hawthorne" studies). One of them, the "bank wiring room" study,
showed that workers' behavior and productivity were less determined by official
quotas and supervision than by the "norms" of the workers themselves. To put it
generally, the group was more important than the bureaucracy. Lewin's and Mayo's
studies were not the origins of democratic convictions, but were used to argue the
virtues of democracy in the schools and the value of research and application of
group dynamics.

POSTWAR SCHOOLING AND ITS CRITICS

Some returning veterans enrolled in the junior colleges, the first of which President
William Rainey Harper of the University of Chicago had been instrumental in establishing in the early 1900s. The thirteenth and fourteenth grades were a part of

general, preuniversity schooling, he argued. A few junior colleges had once been four-year colleges. There were other private junior colleges, but most were publicly controlled and supported. Many offered vocational, as well as liberal arts, courses.

More veterans attended four-year colleges, by 1945 far removed from the colleges of the 1880s. Their denominational connections were less strong, and their presidents were no longer invariably ministers. Some of the early colleges were closed, but other early colleges had proved to be astonishingly hardy. Transylvania, onetime forerunner of the comprehensive university, then reduced to a college and even to an academy, had survived fires, wars, cholera, typhoid and influenza epidemics, internal strife, and financial crises. Its faculty members had been charged at one time or another with teaching Darwinism and other heresy, and as being wartime collaborators. It had been a men's college and then had admitted women. At the end of the war its enrollment quadrupled.

By 1945, some professors at small colleges and most professors at universities had Ph.D.s. They had been trained as specialists, as scholars who were to make a contribution to a narrow corner of an established field, to, perhaps, detailed knowledge of the works of Denis Diderot, or of the learning of planaria (water worms). They were specialists because they had been trained as research specialists, and because the scholarly knowledge that had accumulated was far too great for even the gifted mind to grasp. College and university professors had been organized into departments, which also multiplied as new disciplines emerged. One department of sociology became the department of sociology and anthropology, then two departments. The department of anthropology then spawned the department of linguistics. Research sometimes took precedence over teaching.

Because colleges still saw themselves as *in loco parentis*—in place of parents—and because faculty members became less interested, "deans of men" and "deans of women" had been created to satisfy colleges' obligations. College women were required to "check in" at dormitories before a given hour. Deadlines on weekends were later. (It was as if "sinfulness" could never occur before late evening.) The grades of even twenty-seven-year-old ex-air force majors were sent automatically to their parents.

Universities developed in the pattern of William Rainey Harper's University of Chicago, with an undergraduate college and several professional schools. The land grant colleges had traditions of service. College had, by 1945, become the way of entering nearly all professions and management positions. For some, it was only a tiresome means to an end and a place to live for four years, to make "gentleman's Cs," to cheer for football teams, and vote for campus queens. But the former GIs were not usually interested in becoming "College Joes" or "BMOCs" (Big Men on Campus).

The GIs' children attended elementary schools that soon became overcrowded. There were not enough classrooms and not enough teachers. Teacher salaries had been frozen near Depression levels during the war and remained there afterward, even though postwar inflation raised the cost of living or even of subsistence. It was difficult to replace the third of a million teachers who had quit in wartime. As a generalization, the elementary curriculum was based, as it had been for a century and a half at least, on the traditional school subjects, perhaps leavened by project method units. There were dozens of recommended curricula for the grade schools, none of which had any wide acceptance.

High schools, which the children of the ex-GIs would enter in the late 1950s, were at the center of education controversies. The high schools, as will be recalled, were of mixed ancestry, descended from the common schools, the academies, and more remotely from the Latin grammar schools. Because varying intents and customs had formed the high schools' curricula, they varied greatly. This had been a matter of special concern to the colleges, which saw high schools as preparatory schools, although only a small proportion of high school graduates went to college. In 1896, the Committee of Ten, chaired by President Charles W. Eliot of Harvard, had recommended preparatory courses. It argued on the basis of faculty psychology that mental discipline would strengthen the mind, that "every subject which is taught at all in a secondary school should be taught in the same way and to the same extent to every pupil so long as he pursues it, no matter . . . at what point his education is to cease."

By 1918, faculty psychology was in disrepute, high school enrollments had begun to grow, and the matter was reconsidered by the Commission on the Reorganization of Secondary Education. It formulated the "Seven Cardinal Principles," objectives, rather, for high schools: health, command of the fundamental processes, worthy home membership, vocation, citizenship, worthy use of leisure, and ethical character.*

In the Depression, secondary school enrollments were high and unemployment seemed likely to endure, and so the appropriateness of conventional high schooling seemed questionable. For some high school students, perhaps one fourth of them, conventional academic preparatory schooling seemed appropriate. Vocational education would prepare perhaps another one fourth of high school students for employment in the skilled trades. But what high school curriculum was appropriate for the remaining half? By 1934, Ernest W. Butterfield was recommending a new curriculum for them. It was not to be too difficult, nor was there to be too much homework. Students would, for instance, be prepared to read the *Saturday Evening Post*. They would learn about paying taxes, borrowing money, and buying insurance. That would "permit the individual to fit himself into" society. They would learn to drive cars and to operate vacuum cleaners. She would learn about "beauty culture," the application of cosmetics. In 1939, Charles Prosser, long influential, had refined and elaborated *life-education* subjects and added that they should be for all high school students. There the Second World War intervened.

After the war, the Commission on Life Adjustment education publicized and further elaborated life adjustment education proposals. By then, life-adjustment education was an idea whose time had passed. When the demand for skilled workers

---

*William F. French, in *American Secondary Education* (New York: Odessey, 1967), argues that the seven Cardinal Principles reflected Herbert Spencer's *What Knowledge Is of Most Worth?* (1860).

and college graduates seemed unlimited, training for being unskilled seemed utterly inappropriate. The name, *life adjustment* was fatally unfortunate, and adjustment *to*, rather than adjustment *of*, did seem to be the inappropriate intent.

Joseph Mayer Rice, in his series of articles in *Forum*, in 1892 and 1893, at the beginning of the Progressive era, had pictured the schools as reactionary and over-conventional. The critics of the schools in the 1940s and 1950s, as Cremin pointed out, attacked the schools on opposite grounds. They saw the schools as too liberal, too progressive.

Criticism of the schools between 1945 and 1960 was common, pointed, and often persuasive. It appeared in newspapers, in *Life* and other big circulation magazines, Congressional hearings, books, and motion pictures. In itself, it could be the subject of a book; only the most important ideas and representative spokespersons appear here. Critics argued, to put it in the most general terms, that changes in schooling after 1920 had not been improvements, that the school did not aid in the growth of the intellect, that they did not meet society's needs, that public schools had escaped the control of the public, and that they did not train the technologists needed for defense.

Some objections that had been raised before the war were repeated more strongly. One critic, the most important of the educational "perennialists," was Robert M. Hutchins. Hutchins was a prodigy who had been dean of Yale's law school at age twenty-three, even though he was not a lawyer, and president of the University of Chicago at age thirty. He argued that the schools should deal primarily with ideas and matters of the intellect, and should teach from sources that demonstrated intellectual processes. The intent of this schooling was to prepare for citizenship. This approach to schooling was, if not reactionary, surely very old, traceable to Aristotle and classical Greek thought. It was the basis of the University of Chicago's four-year undergraduate program in general education, beginning after two years of high school. It was also the basis of the great books course of study at St. John's College in Annapolis, Maryland.

Another criticism that was made again after the war was that schools should teach what the nature of society required. This was put in general terms by William C. Bagley, a dissident professor at Teachers College, who called himself an "essentialist." A specific case was argued by Rudolph Flesch in the widely read *Why Johnny Can't Read* in 1955. Girls and boys in the primary grades, he said, were taught only to memorize the shapes and patterns of words, beginning with the most common ones as determined by research on frequency of use. Primers and readers written on that basis had stories that were "meaningless, stupid, totally uninteresting to a six-year-old or anyone else." But of course many children who were taught that way with those primers learned to read well. At the end of the 1970s, it was generally agreed that pupils in the primary grades read better in 1955 than primary grade pupils had read earlier. Ailment or not, Flesch had a universal remedy—phonics, the sounding out of words. He ended his book with illustrated letters and seventy pages of phonics exercises that would have pleased Noah Webster: A good way of teaching was presented as the only legitimate way.

There were also attacks upon what would now be called the education "establishment," against "educationists'" claims of superior knowledge, against "quackery in the public schools," as Albert Lynd titled his book. Lynd searched for and found the most trivial educational research and its greatest elaborations. (Teaching load = SP [CP − 2 Dup/10 + (NP − 20 CP) / 100] × [PL + 55/100] + PC/2 [PL + 55/100].) He quoted the most overblown course descriptions. The grounding assumptions of Dewey's philosophy of pragmatism or instrumentalism, with which he disagreed, were carefully put, and the gaps between Dewey's philosophy of pragmatism and Kilpatrick's recommendations were carefully noted. The control of the schools, Lynd wrote, had been taken from parents and communities. Instruction and curriculum were based upon a philosophy that was not generally accepted.

(Nathan wrote that she had retired partly because of her dissatisfaction with progressive education. Instruction in basics, penmanship, spelling, reading by phonics, grammar, even arithmetic, had been deemphasized or abandoned. Homemaking, manual arts, and music lessons had taken time from basic instruction. Principals had become autocrats. Democracy in the schools had been destroyed. Exit Beatrice Stevens Nathan, grey haired, in great anger.)

Another criticism, much more intense than it had been before the war, was that the schools were not teaching patriotism. That criticism is understandable, although we do not excuse it. An American Legion committee, the Sons and Daughters of the American Revolution, and other arch-patriotic organizations investigated charges against the public schools. They charged that the "social studies" and history that were taught in the public schools were damaging because they were not patriotic, were often socialistic—sometimes even communistic. Harold Rugg's social study textbooks in particular were condemned, but many other textbooks were also seen as tainted with "Red" propaganda.

On October 4, 1957, the U.S.S.R. launched Sputnik I, the first manmade satellite. No bigger than a bushel basket and broadcasting only intermittent beeps, it became the symbol of Russian scientific and military superiority. If a satellite could be put into orbit, an atomic warhead could be fired at a target anywhere in the United States. The "missile gap" threatened the future of America, or at least it was felt that it did. Within a month, Russia launched Sputnik II, which weighed a half ton and carried a dog as passenger. President Eisenhower appointed an adviser on science, the first ever. Every resource, technical, financial, and educational, was to be employed to overtake the Russians.

John Gunther wrote, in his widely read *Inside Russia*, that Russian tenth graders were better educated in science than American college graduates. Ex-President Hoover emerged from oblivion long enough to say that Russia was turning out two or three times as many scientists as the United States. But the most important spokesperson was Admiral Hyman G. Rickover, naval engineer and atomic energy specialist. He had directed the design and construction of the first atomic-powered submarine, *U. S. S. Nautilus* and the first nuclear power plant. He is legendary as a hard-driving, demanding commander, satisfied only by perfection,

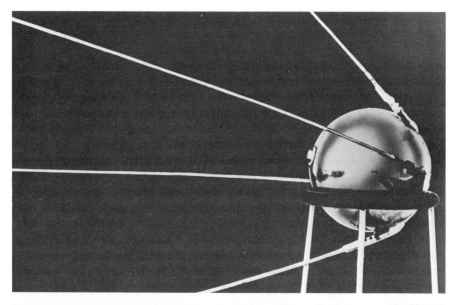

FIGURE 11-2   The Russian's Sputnik launched in late 1957 was the first man-made object to orbit the earth and marked the beginning of the space race and a new thrust in American education. Courtesy of United Press International.

if at all. At the risk of overstatement, it might be said that Rickover's world was often a world of things, of marvelous and magnificent machines that humans had brought into being, of which humans were to be servants.

Rickover said again and again that the schools' first concern should be intellectual training. That training should be speeded and intensified. American students should learn more and learn it more quickly. It was particularly important that the most capable students be the best trained ones. For them there should be special classes, or special schools as there were in England. Their university training should be assured, as it was in Europe, by scholarships and living allowances. Scientists should have greater prestige. For slower students he suggested "minimum competency tests" to guarantee the value of high school diplomas. Teachers' salaries should be increased, and teachers should be more carefully selected on the basis of their academic competence.

Congressman Clarence Cannon, chairman of the House of Representatives Committee on Appropriations, endorsed these views in the preface to one of Rickover's books. ". . . [T]oday a nation's position is largely determined by the respect accorded its science and technology. . . ."

There were perennialist critics, essentialist critics, antipragmatists, and those concerned for the future of science and technology. There were also all-purpose critics. One of these was Augustin G. Rudd, apparently a spokesperson for the Sons of the American Revolution. His *Bending the Twig*, subtitled "The Revolution in Education and its Effects on our Children," was a 300-page tirade against Progressive education. It was atheistic, socialistic, communistic, indoctrinating, and Marxist, he said. Rudd quoted every imaginable authority, including Cecil B. De Mille. Students from Progressive schools were said to be ignorant of or incapable in history, geography, mathematics, spelling, grammar, English, and punctuation. Rudd was one of those who were, to borrow a phrase, "mad as hell." There were many other critics, some of them capable and prominent, others scurrilous and as outrageous as outraged. The educator's natural impulse is to come to the defense of educators under attack. Having controlled that impulse, we conclude that some of the critics, including Hutchins, Lynd, and Rickover, capably presented arguments that were legitimate, sound, and logical, even if one did not accept the premises that were their starting point and did not accept their conclusions. But there were also unacceptable arguments, condemnation by innuendo, guilt by association, arguments ad hominem (against the arguer, rather than against the argument).

Of course there were defenders of the schools. They were at a disadvantage, because in ideological or rhetorical contests, defense is more difficult than attack. It is easier to accuse than to disprove accusation. Perhaps critics, rather than defenders, best caught the spirit of the time. That aside, the defense was in a number of ways ineffective. Educators tended to argue their cases before other educators when the need was to convince noneducators. In general, defenders wrote muddily, turgidly. Perhaps the most effective counterargument was by David Hurlburd in *It Happened in Pasadena*. Willard Goslin was superintendent of schools in Pasadena, California, a staunch Progressive, whose consultant was Kilpatrick. Goslin's opponents won an election and seats on the board of education, with the help of an obscure rightist, Arthur Zorn. While Goslin was at a meeting in Philadelphia, the board met and requested his resignation by telegram. Hurlburd maintained that Goslin had been the victim of extremists, and his argument seemed credible to many. Looking back, it is not entirely clear how important Zorn was in the campaign against Progressivism, or why Goslin was in Philadelphia while his hostile board was meeting 3,000 miles away—that was beyond all valor. Nevertheless, *It Happened in Pasadena* was convincing at the time. In other articles and speeches, defenders as well as attackers used arguments upon which logicians frown. As an example, it was asked what an admiral, no matter how capable an admiral, knew about education. In summary, defenders, in spite of a telling counterattack, in spite of a variety of arguments good and bad, lost in the debate far more than they preserved.

THE SCIENCE OF EDUCATION, CONTINUED

Unfortunately, there has been no comprehensive history of educational research, but it is possible to reach some tentative conclusions about it during the 1930s and 1940s, and, even more tentatively, during the 1950s and 1960s. (Estimating the value and usefulness of the most recent research is quite hazardous, like touring a battlefield while artillery is still in action.)

Educational research had decreased during the 1930s and 1940s, but had not ceased and in the 1950s, it would increase again. The educational researchers were probably most successful in measurement and evaluation, largely technical in nature. Achievement tests were refined, and aptitude tests improved. With carefully worked out and concrete objectives of learning, careful use of statistical techniques, and achievement testing, it was possible for evaluators to reach conclusions that were by no means infallible, but nevertheless highly informative. It is unfortunate that Ralph W. Tyler's evaluation of the Eight Year Study had so little impact. It showed that graduates of "Progressive," nonconventional high schools did as well in college as graduates who had conventional ones. Tyler's evaluation was completed in wartime when attention was on other matters, and its impact was blunted by obtuse and obscuring criticisms.

The borrowing or importation of concepts from other behavioral and social sciences probably had more substantial impact upon thought and planning. Studies of leadership and group dynamics came from social psychology and management engineering. Child development was the direct descendant of the Child Study Movement described in Chapter 8; Arnold Gesell, a ranking authority in the field, had been G. Stanley Hall's student. Concepts of personality had come from psychoanalytic sources that could be traced back to Sigmund Freud. Willard Waller, to whose work we have referred, was a sociologist. Studies of "Yankee City" and "Jonesville," which showed the subservience of schools and schooling, were by sociologists W. Lloyd Warner and P. S. Lunt. The "sociology of education," which described and explained, was usually the subject of sociologists, although educationist Robert J. Havinghurst did sociological research and George S. Counts had. As a rule, "educational sociologists" in teachers' colleges and departments of education prescribed, recommended, and exhorted. The distinction between "sociologist of education" and "educational sociologist" was maintained by some scholarly directories until recently.

SCHOOLING IN A NEW WORLD

In the 1950s and early 1960s, there was a nearly complete change in general concerns for schooling and education. Teacher shortages and teachers' low salaries, and classroom shortages had been the most immediate concerns in the years just after the war. Beginning before 1950, but especially after the launching of Sputnik in 1957, there was new concern for the quality of education, for the need for intellectual competence and excellence. These were seen as the needs of a changed society and culture for its progress and defense. The symbol of the need was the Russian satellite Sputnik. Sputnik as a symbol gained significance from a number of sources. The Second World War had speeded technological and social change. Fear of Russian intentions and the Cold War added significance to the symbol. In 1961,

President Kennedy approved the Apollo space program and moon explorations. In a way a symbolic response to the symbol of Sputnik, it created additional needs for technology and science, and additional opportunities for technologists and scientists. There were also nondefense opportunities for highly trained experts. As scientific research increased, knowledge increased exponentially, "exploded" as some said. There was much more to be learned. It has been suggested that, as postwar babies neared college age and colleges again became crowded, parents grew more anxious about their children being admitted to college. To an extent, all these factors changed schooling and the schools.

The National Citizens Commission for the Public Schools, chaired by Roy B. Larson of Time-Life Inc., expressed business people's concern. In 1951, the Ford Foundation established the Fund for the Advancement of Education, which would be a prestigious force for change. The National Science Foundation, a government agency, funded the first summer institute for science teachers in 1954, and by 1960, there would be sixty-seven N.I.E.-sponsored summer institutes. In 1956, N.S.F. underwrote the production of teaching films for science. That year the Course Content Improvement Program had a budget of $18,000. In 1957, N.S.F. granted it $450,000. Its intent was to write an entirely new physics course of study. It was headed by Professor Jerold Zacharias of the physics department of Massachusetts Institute of Technology. There would be many more grants for the preparation of new courses of study, new curricula. In 1956, Congress had made its first appropriation for educational research, $1 million.

Some of the new curricula and new methods of teaching were based on "teaching machines" and other technological developments, and upon operant conditioning. Others were developed from the structures and processes of academic disciplines—it was not apparent at the time how great the conflicts were between them. The output of educational research was greatly expanded. Researchers from several social and behavioral sciences were often involved, and concepts were introduced from a number of fields. Beginning in 1963, educational research and development ("R&D") centers were established. With the increased emphasis upon skill and intellectual learning, the role of the teacher was changed and in a way diminished. The changes that had begun before Sputnik were much greater in the ten years that followed it.

One development in curriculum was based upon the teaching machine, which had been reinvented, and operant conditioning, B. F. Skinner's modification of Thorndike's S-R psychology. As has been pointed out, that sort of curriculum was in the American tradition and in an American convention of educational thought that is familiar. In 1932, S. L. Pressey, the first inventor of the teaching machine, said it would lead to an industrial revolution in education, like the earlier one in factories. Skinner argued more than twenty years later that the teaching machine, which he had independently reinvented, with behavior modification would be the basis of a truly empirical science of education.

Teaching of this kind began with the careful and precise statement of pupil behavior to be learned. Thereafter, teaching was the control of pupil behavior, so that appropriate responses to appropriate stimuli would be rewarded and learned. What was to be learned was to be broken down into bits of behavior, which would add up to the behavior desired. Stimuli were to be presented and correct responses rewarded and reinforced by teaching machines, or in later, more advanced applications, by computers. This prospect enticed communications and high technology corporations, which expected that a huge and profitable market would develop for hardware (teaching machines) and software (programs). Teaching machines were not demonstrated to be generally superior to more conventional forms of instructional materials—such as books. However, in this frame of reference it was, and is, possible to see teaching as behavior modification and the teacher as behavior modifier, rewarding and reinforcing desired behaviors, perhaps by distributing M&Ms, or tokens.

Writing a revolutionary curriculum did not by itself ensure that students would learn the revolutionary "new science," or "new math." The curricula were difficult for teachers with conventional or less-than-conventional training; National Science Foundation summer workshops, intended to remedy that, were somewhat successful. Many parents were never convinced that the new ways were better than the old. It could be argued that principles and applications were far more important than process, that knowing was more important than knowing how to discover.

Emphasizing the importance of principles resulted in substantive changes. Emphasizing science as process led to emphasis upon discovery. *Discovery* became the basis for another alternative way of teaching. *Discovery learning* was based partly upon the psychology of cognition. To put it simply, the presumption was that people, including pupils, think. Thorndike's psychology had eliminated "mind." Now, under the synonomous name of "intellect," it reappeared. The most prominent spokesperson for the discovery method and its psychological basis was Jerome Bruner of Harvard, who maintained that "the foundations of any subject may be taught to anybody at any age in some form." It was for many a provocative, even an enticing, claim. Principles were to be discovered by pupils, not told to them. In discovery learning a pupil was given information and asked to solve a problem, and then the pupil was to make generalizations, to discover them. Discovered knowledge was of a special and important kind, better remembered, and more readily applied. Even its most enthusiastic supporters agreed that discovery teaching was difficult, time consuming, and not always appropriate.

Naturally, new curricula and new teaching methods had implications for the role of the teacher. The bureaucratization of the schools had overlaid the teacher's "calling" with the presumption that the teacher would be the faithful and obedient servant of the school administrator. In contrast, Progressives had seen the teacher as a fully participating colleague. Teaching "the whole child" had implied that the teacher's concern would be the whole child, the child's emotional well-being as well as the child's academic progress. Beyond that, the teacher was to be capable in test making and was to be a participant in the development of curriculum. But emphasis upon academic performance meant lessening emphasis upon emotional development and teacher's responsibility for it. At best, this was a matter to be referred to the counselor, one of the schools' increasing number of specialists. Further, since emphasis was upon academic achievement, especially in mathematics and the physical sciences, it seemed far more plausible for mathematicians and physical scientists to determine curriculum. The teacher was only to implement it. Specialists constructed standard and standardized tests. In many as yet unexplained ways, the role of the teacher seemed to have been diminished, at a time when teachers were better educated than ever before.

These teaching (and learning) models, especially when contrasted, raise philosophical as well as practical questions. The first philosophical question, one which has arisen before, is whether knowledge is indeed almost endlessly divisible. (Skinner might argue that behavior is, and that the question does not deserve further discussion.) Further, we might consider what model of humanity is implied by these views of learning and teaching. Our general conviction is probably clear. Our deepest conviction is that a method of instruction should not be accepted without considering its full implications.

EDUCATION "R&D"

The supporters of educational research in the 1950s would have agreed that much of what had passed for "research" was not research at all, but routine census taking, status study. There had been many—a hundred thousand, someone guessed—educational research studies. But compared with the volume of research in other fields, research in education had been a minor contribution by a few professors and school system directors of research, and many more doctoral candidates. The doctoral candidates were, naturally, beginners, and often carried out their research without knowledgeable advice or supervision. Research designs were often flawed, and too often led to no conclusion, or even to false conclusion. Doctoral candidates too often looked for easy nontheoretical problems (and sometimes still do). Mundane questions lead naturally to mundane answers. Educational research was not cumulative; research was not built upon research. With a few remarkable exceptions it had little effect generally upon classroom teaching and learning.

But science was seen as having been generally successful. In wartime, science had created new weapons that may have been crucial. It had led to computers and the perfection of television, even color television. Medical research had resulted in cures, of tuberculosis for instance, and Jonas Salk's polio vaccine offered children protection. If scientific research had been successful for the military, industry, and in medicine, research should be successful in improving schooling.

If research was to be successful in education it was necessary for it to resemble more closely research by engineers and medical researchers. It must, in the first place, rest upon a sound theoretical base, so that it would provide systematic knowledge. It must have been knowledgeably performed by professional researchers, not by inexperienced doctoral candidates. It must match the sophistication of research in other fields.

Beginning the upgrading of educational research was difficult. The U.S. Office of Education staff had experience only in gathering data of generally ordinary and routine sorts, data that was useful for describing or providing examples but that provided few insights. Only a few university schools of education had traditions of competent research and almost none of the teachers colleges did. A few scattered pockets of competence provided the first researchers for the new, improved theoretically oriented research.

A second difficulty was securing sufficient funding. University contributions were limited. One of the first sources of substantial funding was the W. W. Kellogg Foundation, which, starting in 1950, contributed $6 million to eight universities for the improvement of training of school administrators. The project, called the Cooperative Program in Educational Administration, did produce some changes in administrator training programs. Funds from the training programs were also channeled into research on administration: The project resulted in a new scientific line of approach to school administration. In 1955, Congress passed the Cooperative Research Act and in 1956, appropriated $1 million for research programs to be carried on outside the U. S. Office of Education.

From 1956 to 1960, appropriations for research increased tenfold, to $10 million, and research grants relevant to education were also being made by the National Institute of Mental Health, the Office of Naval Research, and the National Science Foundation. In 1966, appropriations for the U. S. Office of Education were more than $100 million.

At the beginning the U. S. Office of Education distributed most research funds by asking researchers to propose projects, to justify their questions and hypotheses, and to describe their research procedures. This was less than satisfactory for several reasons. Initially, most research proposals were for routine and familiar kinds of research. Proposed and funded projects were small and were not cumulative. Detailed history does not belong here, but the general change by the U. S. Office of Education was from "unsolicited proposals," by which researchers propose their own questions and hypotheses, to "requests for proposals," "RFPs," in which problems were outlined and researchers asked to describe methods of solving them. That seemed to make it more likely that solutions would be more useful in schools and that they would be cumulative. Admitting the advantages, critics felt that if problems and questions were dictated, answers would be dictated, and that the admittedly rare question of great merit would not be forthcoming. There were some later funds for unsolicited research; critics say they are too small.

After the first impulse the most influential precedent for educational research was private enterprise "R&D," research and development. R. Louis Bright of Westinghouse, who was in charge of U. S. Office of Education funded research, thought of educational research as educational development, R&D, to be conducted as the private enterprise R&D was. Outside review committees became less important, staff more important. There was more applied research, and theoretical research was more often undertaken by researchers from outside education. To disseminate findings, the Educational Resources Information Center, ERIC, was set up, computer-accessible indexes were developed, and reproductions of research reports were mass photoreproduced. In 1962, the first of ten "R&D centers" was established. Practical value of output was emphasized, and research programs were analyzed by Program Budgeting and Planning Systems. Researchers constructed elaborate PERT, program planning and review charts. All this was most businesslike and impressive. But it did not work very well.

There are at least two standards by which educational research and development can be judged. First, most concretely, it did not secure additional funding and was not even successful enough for funding levels to be maintained. Appropriations for the R&D centers fell from $12.4 million in 1968 to $7.2 million in 1971, because it did not capture the imagination or confidence of budget makers or the public. Second, although there has not been, and perhaps cannot be, a comprehensive evaluation of contributions of educational R&D, everyday life in a classroom—in a sense, the technology of schools—has not changed at all radically in the last twenty-five years.

Success or failure, like all else, is relative, and educational research and development has not been a complete failure. It is still funded, although less heavily, and has made conceptual and methodological contributions. Experimental designs in which statistics are employed are much tighter, less error prone, and there have been refinements in statistical treatments of data, and improved computer programs for statistical computations. Evaluations can certainly be more precise, although precision is expensive. There have been some applications and some new components of educational technology. The first Coleman Report did shed new light on school and teacher effectiveness, although some of its conclusions did provoke long debate. New courses of study and instructional materials have been improved by field evaluations before general introduction. New applications of audio-visual equipment have been developed, although much audio-visual material is underused.

There have been a number of conjectures about the relative failure (or, its supporters would say, limited success) of educational research and development. One early explanation was that information and techniques that were the products of research and development simply did not become known to school personnel. But the comment of Andrew Halperin a few years ago comes to mind: "... we have nothing to disseminate."

Perhaps the limits of educational research and development have been set by the limits of the basic science upon which they are supposedly based. But, as

Robert M. W. Travers argues, changes in technology generally have not necessarily rested upon scientific knowledge. That is certainly true. But more recent technological changes have often been based on basic or "pure" science, and the social sciences are certainly much less developed now than, say, physics was a hundred years ago.

Perhaps, more reasonably, it can be said that the chief lack has been one of patience. Research priorities have been redirected again and again because of political or social needs, or even because of a change of bureaucrats. Twenty-five years may not be long enough to develop a new technology, even supposing a reasonable freedom from interruptions, and the total resources that have been devoted to educational research and development have been relatively small, perhaps no more than the cost of designing and tooling up to make a new model automobile.

After twenty-five years of devotion to research and development, and reflection upon them, some of the intellectually most able of our colleagues still have faith in their enterprise. We hope they are not mistaken.

AMERICAN FEDERATION OF TEACHERS: TEACHER BARGAINING

The first recorded teachers' union was in San Antonio, Texas, in 1902, where teacher salaries were low, and where Franklin Bobbitt would conduct one of the first school surveys. But the Chicago Teachers Federation's (C.T.F.'s) affiliation with the American Federation of Labor (A.F.L.) that year was far more important because of the large membership and strong leadership of the C.T.F. In 1916 Chicago teacher organizations and those from four other cities formed the American Federation of Teachers (A.F.T.), a national component of the A.F.L. A court order forced the Chicago local to withdraw, but the A.F.T. continued.

A.F.T. membership increased rapidly at first, then lagged in the 1920s. Unions were not well thought of then and union membership generally declined. In New York City the A.F.T. local was active in leftist and communist causes—politics and "bread and butter" union goals seemed to be in conflict. A.F.T. policy prevented strikes and teachers generally opposed them. George Counts, who was opposed to communism in the A.F.T., was elected its president in 1939. In 1941 the A.F.T. locals in New York City and Philadelphia were expelled because of their communist links. A third of the A.F.T.'s members belonged to the expelled locals. Nevertheless, the A.F.T.'s membership had grown to forty-seven thousand by 1947.

That year members of an independent teacher organization in Buffalo, New York struck for a week. The strike was not supported by Buffalo A.F.T. unions and was opposed by the city government and the state superintendent of schools. Nevertheless, the strike closed all the Buffalo schools and the striking teachers won substantial pay raises. The Buffalo strike was an important precedent. A.F.T locals would strike in the future and the N.E.A. found it necessary to abandon its anti-strike policy. The teacher strike in New York City for recognition of the United

FIGURE 11-3　New York City teachers hold a strike rally outside of City Hall on April 11, 1964. Courtesy of United Press International.

Federation of Teachers there as bargaining agent in November 1960, was pivotal. Teacher strikes would be numerous in the 1960s and 1970s.

SUMMARY

Concern for academic performance, whether for competence or excellence, was muted in the later 1960s and earlier 1970s, but since then has been forcefully expressed. Paul Cooperman's *The Literary Hoax* (1980) repeated the charges of *Why Johnny Can't Read* (1955), which reappeared in a new edition. School systems and state legislatures made competence tests, to demonstrate minimal reading and other academic skills, a precondition for high school graduation. Critics noted the costs of remedial courses in colleges and universities. Some colleges and universities returned to older, more stringent admission standards and the number of required college courses was increased. Declining average scores on college admissions tests were matters of great concern nationally. Even that college admission scores had not on average declined in 1981 was important news. Demands for academic adequacy or excellence had not ceased twenty years before, but had only paused.

The Depression had been costly to schools and to teachers, as it had for most humans and most organizations. The Second World War had other and lethal costs. However, the Depression and war had transformed the American society and economy, and so transformed American schools. College attendance became as commonplace as high school attendance had been not many decades before. In some ways and in some times the transformed schools would be more liberal in that human rights and human freedom and dignity would be of greater concern; those developments will be the subjects of subsequent chapters. However, schooling became more technological, in that the production of technologists became more important, and in that content and method of instruction were influenced by technology, as for instance by Admiral Rickover's atomic submarines. Educational R&D centers applied technological models to research in education, without perfect success. One of the costs of technological pursuit of quality of student achievement seems to have been the changing and reducing of the teacher role. It also made some contribution to the rise of teacher bargaining organizations, A.F.T. or N.E.A., although of course there were other causes for that, quite possibly of greater importance.

CHAPTER TWELVE
QUEST FOR EQUALITY

Especially since the mid-1950s, equality of schooling has been the goal of many reformers. "Equality"of schooling means, in the minds of most, equal access to schooling of equal quality, or access to the same schools attended by others. *Equality* has been and is one of the most important goals of Blacks. It has been an important goal also for members of other racial and ethnic minorities: Hispanic-Americans, Native Americans, and smaller ethnic minorities. It has also become one of the aims of Women's Movement campaigners, and equality of access for the physically handicapped has been required by law.

In the 1960s and since, there have also been other arguments for reform. Since society had unjustly oppressed Blacks and members of other minority groups, they were entitled to compensation for injustice. That sometimes took the form of "compensatory education," schooling and learning to make up for wrong.

President Kennedy planned and President Johnson's administration largely carried out plans to create the "Great Society," a transformed society in which prosperity would be fully shared, in which the poor would be freed from generations-long entrapment in the "culture of poverty," and in which racial discrimination would be ended. If the poor were to share in prosperity, it would be necessary to provide for their children improved schooling. Thirty years earlier, George Counts had asked: "Dare the schools build a new social order?" Now onetime teacher Lyndon B. Johnson and his administration had decided that the schools would indeed be one of the chief ways of building a new social order. The opportunity had come.

REMEDIES AND DIAGNOSES

As school work is usually judged, "minority group members" (Blacks, Hispanic Americans, Native Americans) on the average do less well, poor pupils do less well, and poor minority members do least well. There have been many efforts to improve the school achievement of minority group members and the children of the poor. Laws and financial aid, court orders, organizational changes, revisions of curricula, and other remedies have been applied. These remedies have implied diagnoses. The nature of these make the attempted remedies more understandable.

Most simply, one could deny the evidence of differences in school performances, insisting that conventional tests and teachers were biased. But if it was agreed that the difference was real, then there were several possible causes, alone or in combination. It has been argued:

> The basic cause has been the racial segregation of schools.
>
> The "one best system," the organization of school systems and of schools, has been the root of the problem.
>
> Curricula and materials of instruction have been inappropriate for the poor and the Black, and obviously unsuited for pupils who did not speak English as their native language.
>
> Teachers have discriminated against minority group members and poor children, and have been poorly prepared to teach them.
>
> Pupils' shortcomings have led to their inferior performance, because of their social and cultural environment, or perhaps because of malnutrition and poor medical care, or because of genetic, hereditary, differences.
>
> Most radically, all schools, any schools, discriminate, and all schools should be abolished.

TEST BIAS: TEACHER BIAS

That minority group members and other low socioeconomic status individuals in general scored lower on the average on achievement and aptitude, IQ, tests was indisputable. Evidence on that point had been accumulating at least since World War I, when the Army tested draftees. These lower scores, it was argued, came from several flaws in testing. Most fundamentally, there was no clear theoretical definition of intelligence, of what IQ tests measured. The measurement of "aptitude" as distinguished from achievement was for most purposes impractical. The standard tests were culturally biased, designed on the assumption that the pupil had a conventional middle-class background—this was the most frequent criticism. Aside from that, it was said that some pupils scored low because they were not used to miltiple-choice items and did not understand that test scores might be important. However, to list these criticisms is not to necessarily accept them.

All agreed that on standard tests some minority group pupils scored higher than some Whites, and that many minority group members scored higher than most Whites. For whatever reasons, the average of minority group member pupils' scores was lower than that of white pupils. (Even that had an exception: Japanese-American pupils on the average scored higher than white pupils.) But making a "culture-free" aptitude test seemed nearly impossible. A careful, systematic effort by Alison Davis and Kenneth Eels in the early 1940s had not produced any item, much less a test, that was culture free, on which Blacks did not score lower. Test scores were heavily influenced by pupil socioeconomic status.

It was possible to build tests on which Blacks scored high and Whites scored low. Herbert Foster's study of black slang (technically, "cant") yielded such a test. Another test named the "BITCH," (Black Intelligence Test Culturally Homogenized), developed by Robert Williams demonstrated that point also. Of course, these were not conclusive demonstrations that conventional achievement or aptitude discriminated because of cultural differences.

Possibly there was a kernel of truth in the criticism that black pupils were unused to answering multiple-choice questions and did not realize the importance of test scores. However, as later, more systematic evaluations have demanded more testing, it has been harder to imagine a black elementary pupil who has not taken several multiple-choice tests. Nevertheless, black pupils' scores remain on the average lower than the scores of others. A theoretical definition of IQ has not appeared, but IQ tests continue to predict, better than any other single measure, school success. (IQ scores seem not to predict success out of school for anyone, but that may be a different matter.)

While there were conflicting conclusions to be drawn from research on testing, a number of studies showed that most white teachers shared prevailing anti-Black biases, and that their bias affected their evaluation of pupils' work. One study even showed that white teachers generally reacted negatively to the voice of a black pupil, and evaluated pupil compositions as less good in every way if the composition was read by a Black. This was dismayingly true even when, as was often the case, the teacher did not identify the voice as that of a Black.

DESEGREGATION: EQUALITY OF SCHOOLING

From before the Civil War until before the Second World War, most Blacks lived on plantations or farms in the South. Better opportunities pulled southern Blacks (and Whites as well) northward and westward, especially during both World Wars and the Korean War. Of course, there were visits "back down home" and memories of the South and home ways. But even by 1970, nearly half of all American Blacks (48 percent) lived outside the South, in the North, or on the Pacific Coast. Even in the

South, most Blacks (58 percent) by then lived in or near cities. Outside the South, nearly all Blacks (97 percent) lived in or near big cities, and four out of five (78 percent) lived in old central cities.

For a century and more, Blacks have had traditional faith in the value of schooling, even when schools for Blacks were in nearly every way inferior. In nearly every other way, too, Blacks have been and still are at a disadvantage. Their income, status, and housing have been far below those of Whites and, in spite of the greatest efforts, remain so. Blacks' efforts, and those of their sympathizers, have been to remove or reduce discrimination on the basis of race, whether in schools, jobs and labor unions, housing, or voting rights. The integration (or, later, ruefully, "desegregation") of the schools has not been an isolated, single issue, though at times it has been more prominent than any other issue.

White prejudice against Blacks began hundreds of years ago, as Winthrop Jordan has shown. Before 1500, at the time of Christopher Columbus, Portuguese explorers were sailing down the west coast of Africa, and returning with tales of black men and women not much different from the larger apes, although valuable as slaves for working in the fields. The first English-speaking colonists in America brought with them that picture of the Blacks. It was strengthened by slavery because to some, slavery showed that it was true. It was one of the best possible arguments for slavery.

Although they would not win out for nearly a hundred years, there were also antislavery traditions. The Declaration of Independence had after all said that ". . . all men are created equal." That, as has been seen, was in the tradition of John Locke, who had written more than a hundred years before the Revolution. More explicitly, as to what Blacks learned in school, before 1800, Anthony Benezet, Quaker of Philadelphia, had written that his black pupils learned as well as white pupils would have.

Although the Civil War freed the Blacks, freedom—not equality—was the abolitionists' goal, and after the war most of them turned to other matters, public or private. After the end of Reconstruction in 1877, white southerners again imposed upon the South a caste system. To be Black was to be under most circumstances untouchable, to live apart, to be, as Ralph Elison said, "invisible." Jim Crow laws and custom perpetuated the caste system. There were black—and white—churches, train coaches, waiting rooms, drinking fountains, hospital entrances, and even seats on the bus. There were also black schools.

In most of the South there was public schooling for black children, but of a terribly, unjustly inferior kind. Buildings were old, often rickety, unpainted, far too small, far too overcrowded. Black teacher salaries were less than white teachers', which were much lower than outside the South. Compared with schools for southern whites, schools for Blacks were no better supported in 1900 than they had been in 1875, and the relative level of support declined until 1930. Although there were exceptions, such as the "M" Street School in Washington, D.C., and Dunbar High School in Norfolk, Virginia, high schools for Blacks were slow to develop, and slower still to meet accreditation requirements. For every accredited black high school in the South in 1928-29, there were twenty-five accredited high schools for Whites. In Mississippi there were 335 accredited high schools for Whites, none for Blacks.

A thin scattering of Blacks attended college, although of course the vast majority did not. Of that scattering, a small fraction attended otherwise white colleges, such as Antioch in Yellow Springs, Ohio. Most attended black colleges. Private church-related black colleges had been established at the close of the Civil War and, although very poor, they provided scholarships and schooling for some applicants who were in need. Other Blacks attended black land grant "A&M" schools, or black normal schools. Only Howard University in Washington, D. C., was thought of by Whites as academically respectable.

NAACP AND THE COURT

Thurgood Marshall had been a part-time, and later full-time, counsel for the NAACP since his graduation with honors, in 1933, from Howard University's law school. Marshall's strategy was to bring before the Supreme Court school desegregation suits from scattered states at the same time, so that segregation would not be seen by the Court as a solely southern practice. The key decision was *Brown v. Board of Education of Topeka*. When the decision was read in 1954, Marshall was forty-six years old and already prominent. By 1961, he would have argued thirty-two cases before the Supreme Court (most attorneys never appear there) and won twenty-nine of them. He was appointed U. S. circuit court judge, in 1961, by President Kennedy. President Johnson appointed him solicitor general and, in 1967, the first black Supreme Court justice.

Before *Brown v. Board of Education* was decided, there had been, as Butts and Weinberg each point out, several suits in which the courts seemed to waver, rather than fully accepting the 1896 decision of *Plessy v. Ferguson*. The Supreme Court had decided then that "separate but equal" facilities satisfied the Bill of Rights and the Fourteenth Amendment.

In 1950, Oliver Brown of Topeka, Kansas, a black welder and part-time minister, had attempted to register his daughter in the all-white elementary school that was closest to her home. She was not admitted. The NAACP protested, and then a suit was filed even though the black teachers and P.T.A. of Topeka supported segregation of the schools.

The suit was appealed to the Supreme Court. The NAACP's case, directed by Marshall though argued by Robert Carter, was supported by a thirty-two-page brief from the U.S. solicitor general. The Supreme Court's decision was difficult to predict. Chief Justice Earl Warren had been appointed only six months before. He was thought of as a states' rights man, and had supported the internment of Japanese-Americans in World War II. The significance of the decision was clear, however. One justice came from his hospital bed for the occasion. Newsmen had not been given the usual printed copies of the decision, which was lengthy. Warren himself had written the decision and read it in the courtroom.

> To separate [Negro children] from others of similar age and qualifications solely because of their race generates a feeling of inferiority as to their status in the community that may affect their hearts and minds in a way never to be undone. . . . We conclude that in the field of public education the doctrine of "separate but equal" has no place. Separate educational facilities are inherently unequal. We hold that the plaintiffs . . . are, by reason of the segregation complained of, deprived of equal protection of the laws guaranteed by the Fourteenth Amendment.

Especially in the South there was public resentment of the court ruling. Many southern politicians voiced that resentment and some tried to use it for political gain. One of them was Arkansas Governor Orval Faubus, who was running for reelection in 1957. The Little Rock, Arkansas, Board of Education announced that it would begin desegregation that fall by enrolling nine black students with the 2,000 white students at Central High School. Faubus predicted violence, and called out the National Guard to prevent the black students from entering the school. In spite of personal pleas by President Eisenhower and federal officials, and in spite of a federal court injunction, Faubus refused to admit the black students. When they were admitted, a mob pushed through police barricades and it was necessary to send the black students home. Seeing no alternative, President Eisenhower sent regular combat soldiers from the 101st Airborne Division to Central High School. The soldiers, with bayonets fixed, broke up mobs. The nine Blacks returned to Central High School. Governor Faubus was reelected; the cost to the federal government was $4,051,000. Resistance to desegregation of the schools became a notorious cause. The "Bonnie Blue Flag" of the Confederacy, even the song "Dixie," became symbols not for a lost cause, but of militant and sometimes violent white supremacy.

In the years after *Brown v. Topeka*, schools in the big cities outside the South became more, rather than less, segregated. In Philadelphia, for example, the proportion of black children attending nonsegregated schools declined from 28 percent in 1953 to 15 percent in 1963. Increased segregation in the cities came from several sources. The racial segregation of housing was increasing, and white parents did not want to send their children to mostly black schools. Black neighborhoods resulted in black schools, but the reverse was also true. Some school boards changed attendance district boundaries to protect all-white schools. It was rumored that in some cities, sites for new schools were selected so that student bodies would be all White or all Black. The city schools for Blacks were, on the average, older than schools for Whites. Schools for Blacks were more crowded. The teachers of Blacks were less experienced. In many, though not in all, cities, teachers transferred out of black and poor schools as soon as possible. There was obviously prejudice, but "color blind" policy also had its cost. Nearly all school board members were white.

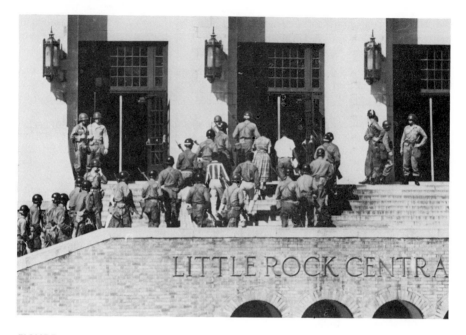

FIGURE 12-1   On September 25, 1957, Federal troops escorted nine black students into the previously all-white Little Rock Central High School. Courtesy of United Press International.

Some southern Whites also tried to prevent the desegregation of colleges and universities. In 1961, a black applicant, James A. Meredith, was denied admission to the University of Mississippi. With the help of the NAACP, Meredith won suits in federal courts, and again applied for admission. Governor Ross Barnett prevented his admission, on the grounds that states' rights took precedence over federal court orders. Attorney General Robert F. Kennedy tried unsuccessfully to arrange Meredith's admission. Barnett physically blocked Meredith's way. Four hundred federal marshals accompanied Meredith to campus. There was tear gas and Molotov cocktails—homemade fire bombs—and rifle fire. National Guardsmen came to the aid of the marshals. A reporter and an onlooker were killed. The marshalls and National Guardsmen did not return the rifle and shotgun fire, although nearly 200 of them were wounded or injured. When the regular army arrived, forty soldiers were injured, too. There were 200 arrests. The next morning Meredith was admitted to the University of Mississippi.

It seems to us that the best and conclusive argument against segregation is that it is morally wrong, as well as unconstitutional. It was widely thought in the 1950s, that integration would erase the differences in academic performances of white and black pupils. As late as 1977, Meyer Weinberg wrote that "Segregation, [in the North] as in the South, prepared the way for the wholesale deprivation of minority and poor children." The reality was more complex. When evaluators compared the performances of black pupils bused to otherwise white schools, it did seem to be true that their academic performance improved, although it might have improved because bused pupils were academically apt, or because their parents were especially concerned. An optimistic estimate is that bused Blacks' academic performances were improved by perhaps one third of a standard deviation, improving their relative standing by maybe 15 percent. It is of course possible that the performance of bused pupils would continue to improve from year to year, as one study has indicated. Still, the reality remained. Academically, black pupils did less well. No matter how great a moral evil segregation was, desegregation by itself did not end Blacks' academic shortcomings. Desegregation might be—we feel is—a moral requirement. A study of Craine that we find convincing shows that the lifestyle of Blacks profits from attending a desegregated school. Nonetheless, desegregation has been no panacea.

A few weeks after the *Brown v. Topeka* decision, psychologist Kenneth Clark pointed out theat there were segregated, all-black schools in New York City. Segregation was defacto, in fact but not by law. Efforts in New York City in the next ten years or so were watched nationally, and spread ideas for (and against) desegregation. They show some of the difficulties in school desegregation in the largest cities. Our account in general follows that of Diane Ravitch.

In 1955, 8 percent of New York City's schools were more than 90 percent Black and Puerto Rican. The New York City School Board had already named a "commission" to plan desegregation and had issued a policy statement condemning school segregation. There were at least three, interrelated, obstacles. First, many white parents opposed school integration, especially if it required "cross busing," busing white pupils into schools in black neighborhoods. Second, either as a rationalization against integration or sincerely, many favored the "neighborhood school," which was convenient, attuned to local needs and customs, and ideally the focus of the community. Third, the geography of simple numbers and distances had already made New York City desegregation nearly a physical impossibility. In the 1950s, the white population of New York City fell by 800,000, while 700,000 Blacks and Puerto Ricans arrived. Of course, this made school desegregation even harder to achieve.

The difficulty became even greater in 1961, when the board of education lost much of the public's confidence. Citywide averages of achievement scores had fallen below the national average. There was evidence of payoffs and other irregularities in school construction funds. Ravitch says that the responses of the superintendent—attempting to reassure at the same time neighborhood school supporters and members of minority groups—did postpone a crisis, but made it worse when it came. In 1961, the U.F.T. (United Federation of Teachers) became the teachers' official bargaining agent; the U.F.T. would very much affect New York City education policy.

"Open enrollment," allowing black students to transfer out of segregated schools into desegregated ones, was of only slight help. "Higher Horizons," a compensatory enrichment program, seemed successful at first, but when it was extended to all the pupils in thirty schools, its resources were spread too thin and it became ineffective. P.A.T. (Parents and Taxpayers) appeared, an organization opposed to transfers and favoring neighborhood schools. As early as 1959, Whites boycotted schools in two neighborhoods.

In 1963, New York Commissioner (Superintendent) of Schools James Allen, Jr., "compassionate, humane, and liberal," intending to speed desegregation, ordered New York State school systems to report their progress toward desegregation, a *segregated school* being defined as more than 50 percent "minority"—Black and Puerto Rican. By then more than 40 percent of the pupils in New York City schools were members of minority groups, and 400,000 white children attended parochial and private schools. Integration by Allen's standard was becoming almost impossible. Nevertheless, minority action groups continued to demand school integration. Ravitch feels that "confrontation politics," politics depending upon newspaper and television publicity, produced extremism, and extremism ruled out compromise. It also led to the studied neglect of reality, the reality that within a very few years the minority—Black and Puerto Rican—would be a majority in the city's schools.

The board and Superintendent Calvin Gross proposed desegregation without forced busing of pupils. The plan angered both integrationists and neighborhood supporters. Milton A. Galamison, then the most important integrationist leader, said that "anyone who talks about integration and is against busing is not serious about the matter." He demanded a schedule for desegregation and planned a school boycott. White liberals were becoming doubtful, but on February 4, 1963, schools were picketed. There were 3,500 demonstrators at the board of education building, and one third of a million children stayed home. The board asked Commissioner Allen to prepare an integration plan. The P.A.T. also picketed and planned a mass rally. Galamison planned a second boycott. The next spring his supporters attempted to block the opening of the New York World's Fair.

The Allen report pleased the integrationists, even though it admitted that the complete desegregation of New York City schools was no longer possible. The report called for neighborhood elementary(K-4) schools, new "middle" (5-8) schools that would be desegregated, and comprehensive high schools to replace vocational high schools and increase integration. Even at the time the plan seemed to some too simple minded, and as inadequate as treating a broken leg with aspirin. The new middle schools would cost $250 million, which the board could not realistically hope to get.

There were new participants in 1964. New York City had elected a Republican reform mayor, John V. Lindsay. He would not support the school board, which had been named by a Democratic mayor. President Johnson's "War on Poverty" funded community action organizations intended to give the poor greater power. Preston Wilcox, a community organizer and Columbia University faculty member, organized parents who were more concerned with quality of schooling for Blacks than with desegregation. In 1966, a new middle school, IS 201, was completed in East Harlem. Although school board officials had said it was to be integrated, it could not be. The leader of the IS 201 activists said before television cameras that "either they bring white children in to integrate 201 or they let the community run the school—let us pick the principal and the teachers, let us set the educational standards and make sure they are met." Local control was replacing integration as the issue. Parents planned to boycott the school.

Perhaps the obvious had been demonstrated. New York City schools could not be integrated. What would be at issue would be local control, a matter to which we will return.

UP AGAINST THE SYSTEM

We cannot view the "system" with anything like an open mind. It did not deserve it. In every big city there was a shorthand expression for the rules and regulations of the school system's central offices: "110 Livingston Street says" (New York City); "City Hall Says" (Buffalo); "911 Locust says" (Saint Louis); "Lindsey-Hopkins says" (Miami). A more general term was "downtown." All these meant systemwide regulations and the office of the superintendent of schools and his assistant and staff. On days when "downtown" prevented the obviously appropriate, the teacher, or for that matter the building principal, mentioned "downtown" only when the word was accompanied with expletives.

In some downtown central offices of the city systems, the "sup'inten't" was mentioned only with a tone of awe and fear. Some, of course not all, the city superintendents were egocentric, autocratic, and punitive. The feelings of power and prestige were important rewards for some of them. Even the superintendent, however, would join in the condemnation of "Albany" (New York) or "Jeff City" (Missouri) or "Tallahasee" (Florida) or wherever. Again, there were more general terms; "state department" (not the Department of State, but the much more immediate state department of education); or "state ed." In "state ed" there were references to "Washington" and the "feds."

Part of this was an escape, we are convinced—the moves of bureaucrats to avoid responsibility and so avoid blame. Although it was difficult to gauge the extent to which it was true, the risk-free if binding control by "downtown" attracted into school administration many men (and a few women) who by disposition preferred to avoid risks, to "keep their noses clean," and to obey "downtown."

If segregation was not the cause of poor academic performance, then the organization of the city systems was. This was the conviction, the hypothesis, of some reformers. There were legitimate reasons (though perhaps also others) for condemning "the one best system." With occasional exceptions, the "one best system" prevented dishonesty and favoritism, and it certainly made them far more difficult. It set careful procedures for purchasing and for hiring and firing, and eliminated personal favoritism. In the development of city school systems, efficiency had been the first goal, although the efficiency of the city school systems had been challenged. As a prerequisite of efficiency, there was uniformity in school systems, of curriculum, of instructional supplies, of personnel practices, of accounting, of record keeping. Elaborate organizational pyramids had been erected. Even in moderately large systems, a teacher might have been five levels away from the superintendent, via (1) the departmental chairman, (2) the building principal, (3) an assistant superintendent, (4) an associate superintendent, finally to (5) the superintendent. The path to the superintendent might also have been by way of supervisors and coordinators. Although it was to be said that, as an asset, the one best system did establish orderly procedures, it was not certain that the advantages of the one best system outweighed its costs.

The ranks and tiers of administrators in the city systems seemed to reach as high and as far as the eye could see. Above and beyond the administrators there were the city school boards. As they had been for fifty years and more, the city school boards were made up of professionals and other members of the middle class, almost without representation by members of the lower class, and with only an occasional black member. Reformers asked whether it was reasonable to expect such school boards to be sympathetic to the needs and wishes of the blue collar workers' families, or to the families of the unemployed.

The authority of state departments of education had been extended. A part of that had come from state legislatures. They had by law set responsibilities for teacher certification, for curriculum (in New York State, lessons on the evil of tobacco and alcohol, for instance). State legislatures had composed formulas for state aid. State aid had been intended to give additional state funds to the proper districts. (That aid may have outweighed the drawbacks, but the drawbacks were real.) In New York State, "state ed" insisted on a numeration, a carefully tabulated sum of school head counts, for every pupil every day in every school. While knowing where the individual pupil was had value, knowing where all the pupils were had its costs—in teacher time, in school clerk time, in administrator time. It is not at all difficult to find ridiculous examples of the outcomes of state aid formulas. In the early 1960s, in one North Carolina fishermen's community, an agriculture teacher was hired because the state would pay his salary, and in spite of the fact that the nearest farm was thirty-five miles away, by boat. He fertilized the sand with fish heads and entrails—the Pilgrims had known how—and indeed harvested the first home-grown tomatoes the fishermen had ever seen.

There was increasing pressure and influence, too, from Washington. It came from newly enacted laws about desegregation and other matters. For instance, Congress, as the law was interpreted, required that teaching staffs be desegregated, and sometimes that they be rotated. That there were advantages to having black teachers teach black pupils seemed not to matter. That teachers in all white schools near the city limits had never taught a black pupil and wanted very much not to, also seemed not to matter. There could be other examples. What is entirely clear is that the federal government also played a more important part in the day-to-day management of the schools.

DECENTRALIZATION OR LOCAL CONTROL

There were two remedies for the overcentralization of school administration, as critics saw it. One, which might have been called the insider approach, was to decentralize school administrative patterns, to have decisions made as near as was feasible to the pupil. It was generally agreed that there were some parts of administration—accounting, purchasing, and maybe personnel—that could best be managed by "downtown," the central office. Nevertheless, there would be advantages in local control of teacher assignment, choosing instructional materials, and supervision of teachers. Saint Louis, as an example, appointed "district superintendents" in the early 1960s, and at least the first results were encouraging.

The more extreme solution was local control. This required that the neighborhood school boards, which the superintendents had been to so much trouble to extinguish, be reestablished. The neighborhood boards were to have the power to set policy, to appoint principals and perhaps local superintendents, and even teachers. At least the local boards would express local preferences and have the power to put them into practice.

In New York City, the IS 201 activists saw local control as appropriate, since IS 201 could not be integrated. The idea of local control had wide appeal, not only to black activists, but also to white liberals. IS 201 activists called the city school board the "Board of Genocide" and, with supporters, took control of the board of

FIGURE 12-2   Students wait outside as non-striking teachers hold a press conference at the entrance of Junior High School 271 in the Ocean Hill-Brownsville district of Brooklyn, September 15, 1968. Courtesy of United Press International.

education meeting hall in December, 1966. They held it for three days, and elected their own sham board. If nothing else, it made the real board seem ridiculous and powerless.

The move to decentralize the New York City schools first gained Mayor Lindsay's support because state aid would be increased if there were several districts instead of one. He appointed a panel to be chaired by McGeorge Bundy, then president of the Ford Foundation. Mario Fantini and Marilyn Gittell were the panel's staff chief and chief consultant. They were avid supporters of local control. The panel recommended that at least thirty local, semiautonomous districts be established. With Fantini's help three "demonstration districts" were established, IS 201 and its elementary school "feeders," Ocean Hill-Brownsville, and Two Bridges.

Rhody McCoy was named the Ocean Hill-Brownsville administrator. Ravitch portrays him as a militant Black with "pent up rage." He nominated as a building principal Herman Ferguson, while Ferguson was under indictment for conspiracy to commit murder. Granted, the activists' intentions were good, but their timing was not. In April 1968, while the New York State legislature was considering the decentralization plans, McCoy, on the recommendation of the Ocean Hill-Brownsville personnel committee, "ended the employment" of nineteen tenured teachers and administrators. The board of education and the U.F.T., their union, came to their support, and 300 teachers walked out in sympathy.

When school opened in the fall, McCoy had employed replacements for the U.F.T. members who had struck the spring before. McCoy was directed to reinstate ten members, but did not. The U.F.T. voted to strike citywide, and did so for two days and, when an agreement collapsed, struck again for more than two weeks. Black and white racism and anti-Semitism added to tensions. Nevertheless, when the board decided to return eighty-three strikers to Ocean Hill-Brownsville (the others had accepted transfers), a thousand policemen were assigned to protect them. However, there were disruptions and schools were closed. The Ocean Hill-Brownsville governing board was suspended and McCoy and seven demonstration district principals were, in effect, suspended with pay. The U.F.T. prepared for a third strike, which began on October 14, and lasted for five weeks. The Ocean Hill-Brownsville governing board, which had claimed independence, was told by a judge that they were "no more than an unofficial body of citizen advisors without power to transfer or suspend ... [or] to countermand any orders of the Board of Education. ..." There were demonstrations and boycotts in Ocean Hill-Brownsville through the winter. After much more negotiation, the New York State Legislature did approve decentralization, following in broad outline the recommendations of the Bundy panel.

Ravitch, who is deeply concerned for "community," and believes in compromise as the practical way, sees what she calls the last "school war" as having been unproductive. But it had some beneficial byproducts. Some school jobs went to minority group members. Far sooner than they otherwise would have, some Blacks became school administrators.

There were two unfortunate outcomes. First the decentralization of the New York City school system did not result in genuine local control. Only a few residents voted in local board elections. Because of racial or other differences, resident's votes were often divided among their candidates, who then lost to candidates sponsored by the U.F.T. Second, the academic achievement of pupils in the New York City schools did not improve substantially. It could be argued that this was due to the failure to decentralize power, as well as to decentralize in form. The more general argument was that decentralization would not be, at least by itself, an adequate remedy for the poor academic performance of minority group members.

BOOKS, LESSONS, AND TEACHERS

As a more gentle hypothesis, it was argued that conventional courses of study ignored Blacks, and that Hispanic-Americans and Indians were, if not ignored, then belittled. Blacks, it was argued, had been robbed of their place in history. The typical preprimer, first reading book, neither pictured nor mentioned Blacks. "Dick and Jane" and their counterparts in other preprimers lived in suburbs. They played on neatly cut lawns, and their houses had white picket fences around them. It was as if there had been no Blacks at all, no slums, not even any cities. Upper grade readers and literature books were scarcely better.

The first and easiest step was to change the preprimer illustrations. Beyond that, new stories were written, first for use in Detroit schools. History texts had had casts that were nearly all white, except for an occasional Indian. Partly, this reflected America's own picture of its past—who had ever heard of black cowboys, even though there had been many of them? Perhaps it was also the result of publishers' interest in selling books in the South. Nevertheless, new editions and new texts pointedly mentioned black historical figures: Benjamin Bannecker, Nat Turner, Steven Douglass, George Washington Carver, and others. Later, when it was ponted out that reading books typecast, stereotyped, girls and women and showed them only in traditional roles and occupations, there were more changes. History books pointedly mentioned women: Dolly Madison, Harriet Tubman, Harriet Beecher Stowe, Frances Perkins, and Eleanor Roosevelt.

For black activists and their sympathizers, minor revisions of whites' lessons and whites' books and whites' history was not enough. It seemed to even moderates among them that there could only be true equality for Blacks after they came to have self-respect as Blacks for Blacks. As a motto, shorthand, "Black is beautiful!" Extremists, far more often outside schools than in them, talked about "Negritude," Black separatism, about "Black power" and, threateningly, of "the fire next time."

Presumably more important than books and curricula, teachers were said to be responsible for the poor performance of black and other minority group children. One of the teachers' shortcomings was that they were nearly all white in the northern cities, even in schools where pupils were nearly all black. Black children,

Oh, Jane.

I see something.

Look, Jane, look.

Look here.

FIGURE 12-3　The "Dick and Jane" readers of the 1950s and 1960s reflected life in a comfortable middle-class suburban setting. Courtesy of the New York Public Library Picture Collection.

it was said, needed black "role models." They needed teachers who would understand and not criticize black "nonstandard" speech.

Surely there were a number of reasons for the relatively few black teachers in northern cities. Historically, first-generation immigrants to the city had not gone to college and had not become teachers; that was the least dishonorable reason, though simply because things had been that way was not reason enough for their staying that way. The routine procedures of school personnel had in them institutionalized racism. One system recruited teachers, even when the teacher shortage was severe, only at nearby colleges, to save recruiter travel expenses. However, if nearby colleges admitted few Blacks, then new teachers would include few Blacks. Many school systems used the National Teacher Examination, with which it was said that black applicants had difficulty. As far as we know, there was no direct proof of it, but racism by white interviewers was alleged, and may well have occured. It almost certainly did, at least occasionally.

Some critics felt that teacher bias was not only a racism but also social-class bias. It was and is still true that most teachers come from middle-class families. If they carried into their classrooms with them middle-class concerns, then it seemed logical that they would discriminate against pupils from lower-class families. Certainly the teacher of the class that Ray Rist had observed had done that, and a more recent study by Constance Heavey, with a somewhat larger sample, confirms it, although both studies came long after the accusations.

For racism in teacher recruiting and selection, there were several remedies. Blacks could be encouraged to go to college, and in some places were, although that would not provide new teachers for several years. Teachers could be more widely recruited, recruited even from all-black teacher colleges in the South. The National Teacher Examination was used less often for selection, or its scores given less weight. The most capable of the nonprofessional teacher aides could be enrolled in special course sequences in teacher education.

That would also serve to provide more teachers who were not of middle-class origin. Beyond that, the matter of class origin was difficult to remedy. If teaching was a middle-class occupation—occupational status scales put it there—would not a person become a member of the middle class upon becoming a teacher? Aside from that, as radical critics have pointed out, the class and the bureaucracy seemed made for each other. The middle-class virtues—promptness, orderliness, obedience, tolerance for delayed gratification—were the same as the virtues of the ideal bureaucrat, and the bureaucratic nature of schools certainly reenforced them.

CONCLUSION

The attempt to integrate schools and to end racism in the United States continues. We believe that changed schooling has changed society in the last quarter century or more: We know that those changes have been slight. The answer to George Counts's question, "Dare the Schools build a new social order?" has been that it was dared, but that it was not done. The schools have not greatly changed society in this vital way. The opportunity arose, many made the effort, and the result, so far, has been nearer to complete failure than to complete success. The effort must and will continue, but having reflected upon the last quarter century of effort, we admit our disappointments.

CHAPTER THIRTEEN
PURSUIT OF FREEDOM

The 1960s were a period of cultural and political change unique in American history. The decade was defined and dominated by youth. Reacting to the conservatism and "sensibleness" of the 1950s, United States youth set in motion a cultural and political revolution of enormous magnitude. During the 1960s, a totally new set of social, political, and economic values was brought to the attention of the American people. Many of these ideas had their origin in or received important support from the youth culture. Radical politics altered the traditional role of the university; Eastern philosophies and drugs expanded the realm of consciousness; the introduction of birth control pills, with a radically changing set of social mores, set in motion a sexual revolution. Youth culture was at the center of most of the major events of the 1960s. It was male youths who served and often died in Vietnam. It was the same youths who prevented Lyndon Johnson from seeking reelection, and who laid the foundations for the United States' withdrawal from the war in Asia.

There were many voices in the '60s, often angry, almost always critical. Some of the most important were in the field of education. Such authors as Illich, Friedenberg, Holt, Goodman, Henry, Kozol, Fantini, Katz—from many disciplines and with many purposes in mind—asked what schools were about. Alternatives were often proposed and educational experiments were undertaken. While many of these experiments were dismal failures, others were important beginnings.

Traditional educators were faced from the beginnings of the 1960s with unprecdented problems. Those born in the post-World War II "baby boom" had reached adolescence. They placed unprecedented demands upon the support systems of schools and social service agencies. A teacher and classroom shortage made accommodating the youth population difficult enough. With the political assassinations that were one of the unfortunate hallmarks of the era, a confusing war in an isolated and obscure part of Asia, and a new set of values emerging in the culture, the schools were forced to contend with a set of problems unprecedented in difficulty.

For the schools, the '60s were a time of change and a time of innovation. Teaching machines, open classrooms, team teaching, and values education were all tried and tested. Often touted as the salvation of the schools, many of these innovations failed and were abandoned. New issues emerged, from elementary school to university. Questions of student rights grew logically out of the Civil Rights Movement. Sexism in education emerged as an issue, also undoubtedly inspired by the Civil Rights Movement. Tracking was seen as potentially prejudicial and infringing on the rights of minority students. Profound social changes were clearly underway, and there were expectations that schooling and American culture would be radically changed.

The issues of the youth culture, discussed earlier, were by no means unique to the 1960s. Many educational and social theorists at the turn of the century had been sensitive to the fact that roles of youth were being radically revised in American culture, as a result of the emergence of an increasingly complex technological system. John Dewey in *School and Society* (1899), and through his work at the Laboratory School of the University of Chicago, argued clearly for the need to develop an educational system that compensated youth for the loss of learning opportunities resulting from the reorganization of the industrial system. Dewey argued that the school must take the place of the farm and home that had formerly been educators.

The schools took the primary responsibility for providing the child with this new type of education, but other organizations played increasingly important roles. In 1907, the Boy Scout movement was organized in Britain by Sir Robert Baden-Powell. It quickly made its way to the United States, where it soon became popular. During the same period the Young Men's Christian Association and the Boys' Clubs spread rapidly. They provided alternative kinds of learning, nature lore, and crafts, as well as keeping boys and adolescents occupied.

By the end of the First World War, evidence of the importance of youth as consumer rather than as producer became apparent for the first time. In the 1920s, youth had an increasingly marginal role in the work force. A significant youth culture emerged then, identifying itself by new types of fashion, music, and social behavior. The values associated with the new "Jazz Age" and "Flapper" culture were seen by critics of the period as reflecting a decadence on the part of youth and America in general.

There is a certain irony in looking at the criticisms of the youth culture that emerged during the 1920s. In many respects the criticisms that were made during the 1960s paralleled them. Throughout the 1920s, critics maintained that youth was increasingly immoral. Drinking and petting and the lack of any visible meaning or purpose in the lives of many youths were discussed again and again. By the early 1960s, similar comments were being made, only this time about drugs instead of alcohol and premarital intercourse instead of petting.

The crisis for youth beginning in the early 1960s was part of a larger problem with origins at the beginning of the century or even earlier. Perhaps the only real difference in the 1960s was the problem's magnitude and the clear recognition by educational and social leaders that something must be done. Between 1890 and 1900, population between the ages of fourteen and twenty-four had increased from 14.2 million to 26.7 million. Between 1960 and 1970, this age group had expanded from 36.7 million to 40.5 million. This growth was greater than during the previous seventy-year period. If for no other reason than its sheer size and the subsequent pressures it placed on the large culture, the youth population had to be dealt with.

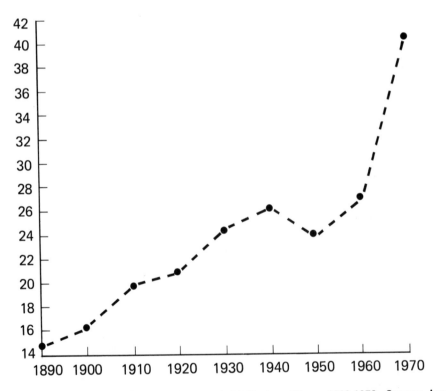

FIGURE 13-1   Size of population aged 14-24, in millions, 1890-1970. Source: James Coleman, *et al., Youth: Transition to Adulthood* (Chicago: University of Chicago Press, 1974), p. 46.

Economic issues clearly played an important role in setting in motion the youth crisis of the early 1960s. As Joel Spring has argued:

> Economic and social conditions were ripening in the mid-1950s for a repeat of the generation gap of the 1920s, although on a more massive scale. During and after World War II, productivity increased. By 1955 it had more than doubled the 1929 figure. Increased output per man-hour required increased consumption and displacement of portions of the population from production, but not from consumption. Locked in school, middle- and upper-middle-class youths could consume the excesses of technological production without contributing to its further increases.

Yet the alienation of youth was not rooted simply in economic issues. The "beat generation" of the 1950s, and its rejection of the "ideals" of American culture, anticipated in many respects the alienation of many youths in the 1960s. All was not well with American society and its youth. Perhaps because of its marginality youth provided vocal critics of a system that neither needed them, nor was particularly sensitive to their problem.

Although youth movements have been a widespread phenomenon in European history, until the 1960s their existence in the United States was limited by comparison. Perhaps Frederick Jackson Turner's thesis that the Western Frontier provided a safety valve for those who were dissatisfied explains in some way why a powerful youth movement had not developed in the United States. Student rebellions certainly occurred in American colleges during the nineteenth century, and the beginnings of a socialist student movement in the United States can be found in the early decades of the twentieth century. By the 1930s, Marxism was widely embraced by college students, who were to be humiliated by the hypocrisy and brutality of Stalin's regime. Yet by the 1950s, political activity on the part of college students was uncommon. Perhaps fearful of choosing a false ideology, as American students had in the 1930s, or perhaps fearing political reprisals, college students of the 1950s were by and large a "silent generation."

Student apathy was widely perceived throughout the '50s as a serious problem. While on the surface there was relative calm during the Eisenhower era, there were many deeply rooted problems. Youth rebellion manifested itself in popular culture figures—singer Elvis Presley and actor James Dean. Dinner tables in many homes became battlefields over which youths fought wars with their parents about the appropriateness of certain types of dress and hairstyles such as the infamous "D.A." or "Duck's Ass" haircut (for men) and toreador pants (for women).

Many symbols might be chosen for the period, but perhaps none reflected the spirit of the youth during the late 1950s better than the figure of *MAD Magazine*'s Alfred E. Newman. His philosophy was characterized by his motto, "What, me worry?" and personified the detachment that much of youth clearly felt toward the culture. *MAD*'s wide popularity among youth, and its overt criticism of the idealized suburban lifestyle sought by most Americans, was a telling indicator that all was not well in American culture and society during the late '50s and early '60s.

Clearly, profound changes were overtaking American society to which future historians will undoubtedly pay great attention. To begin with, the system of social values and traditions that had dominated American culture for the past 175 years were being challenged, perhaps as they had never been before. As described in Chapter 12, the social revolution set in motion by the 1954 *Brown v. Topeka* decision was profound. Other important changes as well were underway during this period. There was the threat of total destruction through nuclear war. A media revolution was underway. The introduction of commercial television in the late 1940s had precipitated a communications and educational revolution of unprecedented magnitude. In 1949, there had been 1 million television sets in the United States. By 1960, that figure had grown to 50 million.

The precise impact of television on education during this period cannot be determined. No one can be sure about how much televising of Civil Rights protests in the South radicalized many viewers. As during the Vietnam War, television literally brought war into the homes and the consciousnesses of the American people.

By the end of the 1950s, and the early 1960s, many educators and writers had become increasingly sensitive to the alienation of youth. In *The Lonely Crowd* (1950), sociologist David Reisman with Revel Denney and Nathan Glazer had examined the forces that motivated both youths and adults in American culture. In 1959, another sociologist, Edgar Z. Friedenberg, published his pioneering analysis of youth problems, entitled *The Vanishing Adolescent.* Friedenberg argued that the emphasis on conformity and group adjustment directly interfered with the adolescent's development of a sense of self. According to Friedenberg, rather than being given the opportunity to differentiate one's self from the culture and to establish an identity, the adolescent was homogenized and depersonalized by the schools and other institutions. Friedenberg called for a redirection of the schools, the recognition of a far wider range of competence in the students they taught:

> Schools ought to be a place where you can not only go to be a scholar, a fighter, a lover, a repairman, a writer, or a scientist, but learn that you are good at it, and in which your awareness and pride in being good at it becomes a part of your sense of being you. More emphasis on the sciences, higher standards, stricter discipline; these of themselves will not help at all. They may hinder. A school that while raising standards in certain academic areas, treats the students more than ever as an object or an instrument, simply becomes a more potent source of alienation.

Friedenberg was among the first critics to recognize that the schools were not only failing youths in helping them to realize a sense of self and purpose in their lives, but that, even worse, they were preventing many youths from achieving the autonomy and self-direction that would lead them to fully realize meaningful adult roles.

Later in the 1960s, there was more criticism of the schools for failing to meet the needs of the individual. Paul Goodman in *Growing Up Absurd* (1962) reiterated many of the same points as Friedenberg. In *Compulsory Mis-Education* (1964)

Goodman described the educational systems as a "compulsory trap" and proposed radical alternatives to the existing school system. Goodman proposed the use of the community as a classroom. Field trips to factories, museums, stores, parks, and movies would allow children to learn by immediate experiences from the culture and environment in which they lived. Both in school and outside of it, adults from the community—druggists, mechanics, storekeepers, and so on—would introduce children to the world of work and the experiences and responsibilities of adult life. School attendance would no longer be compulsory. Goodman, somewhat romantically, argued that if the teaching was good, students would naturally come to class. Further suggestions by Goodman included the decentralization of the schools: using available storefronts and youth clubs, decorating and furnishing them so that they would attract young people; or sending students to economically marginal farms for a few months to a year to live in the countryside and learn something about the rural environment.

Goodman's ideas were not new. John Dewey had argued in the 1890s for a curriculum that emphasized learning from the environment. Similarly, the inclusion of field trips and the opportunity to learn from people who worked in the child's community were ideas emphasized by Dewey. Yet, that Goodman, a sensitive thinker and social critic, would propose the reintroduction of these innovations suggests the limited degree to which they had become part of the educational system.

Other approaches were taken by other critics of the schools. Anthropologist Jules Henry, in *Culture Against Man*, began to systematically analyze classroom activities and their implications for the larger culture. Among Henry's most interesting observations was that the schools and their curricula served the function of making men vulnerable. Picking up on the idea of Rousseau's social contract, Henry argued that to make men obey the demands of the society or culture, they must be made to fear the consequences of deviating from accepted norms and values. According to Henry, society deliberately discouraged independence of the individual to insure its own security.

> The child's vulnerability is sustained and intensified by the elementary school, where he is at the teacher's mercy. The teacher, clearly through no fault of her own, is the agent of vulnerability; and she transmits the sense of vulnerability to the child through two weapons thrust into her hands, sometimes against her will—discipline and the power to fail the child.

Without fear of failure, according to Henry, the American educational system "would stop as if its heart had been cut out."

Henry, and others such as Lawrence Kohlberg, postulated that the schools might have a hidden agenda or "hidden curriculum." It was argued that the schools served to teach acceptable patterns of social behavior, racial and economic values, and specific moral points of view. Much of this instruction was unconscious but nonetheless an important part of the educational system. A second grader called to the board to do an arithmetic problem did not simply learn to add or subtract, but also learned how to stand straight, to respectfully address an adult or authority figure, and to deal with peers. Such lessons, according to Kohlberg and Henry, continued throughout one's schooling and provided the basis for expected behavior in the adult world.

The alienation of youth, so clearly recognized by Friedenberg and Goodman, increasingly manifested itself in the form of youth protest during the mid-1960s. Theodore Roszak in his work *The Making of the Counter Culture* (1969) argued that this youth movement represented

> ... a culture so radically disaffiliated from the mainstream assumptions of our society that it scarcely looks to many as a culture at all, but takes on the appearance of a barbaric intrusion.

The leadership of the youth movement came largely from the universities. Although, as mentioned earlier, examples of student activism at the college level can be found in the United States during the nineteenth and early twentieth centuries, the student movement that began during the early 1960s was of an unprecedented scope and magnitude. Undoubtedly, one catalyst of the student protests of the '60s was the southern Civil Rights Movement, and can be dated from February 1, 1960, when four black students sat down at a segregated coffee counter in Greensboro, North Carolina, and asked to be served. Refused service, the students in the area carried out a sit-in, picket, and boycott. Subsequently charged with trespassing, the Greensboro demonstrators immediately set off a series of similar protests throughout the South and beyond.

Support for the black student Civil Rights Movement grew quickly on campuses throughout the country. Southern black student leaders toured college campuses describing their experiences and seeking support. White and black students joined together to promote the movement. In the spring of 1960, the Student Nonviolent Coordinating Committee (S.N.C.C.) came into existence. Made up of both black and white students, S.N.C.C. operated independently from the main Civil Rights groups, NAACP, CORE, and S.C.L.C., and others. By the summer of 1964, approximately 650 students, largely white and from northern schools were going through areas of the deep South to help Blacks register to vote.

The 650 students who went South during the summer of 1964 were a small proportion of the 2 million students then attending college. Their impact, by directing national attention to the Civil Rights Movement was, however, enormous. Students murdered while working for the movement became martyrs of the Civil Rights cause.

The Civil Rights Movement was, as a cause, in many respects ideally suited for student protests. The oppression of Blacks was a clear-cut and obvious issue. Right and wrong were defined clearly and the hypocrisy that extolled democracy, but denied equal rights to a significant portion of the population, was readily

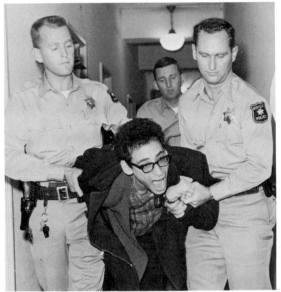

FIGURE 13-2   A University of California at Berkeley student chanting "Freedom Now" is carried to jail, December 3, 1964. Courtesy of United Press International.

evident. The Civil Rights Movement provided an ideal set of conditions for a generational conflict. The student movement had found a cause.*

Interest in political organization on college campuses began early in the 1960s. By 1962, the Students for a Democratic Society (S.D.S.) and other organizations were being founded and began to formulate coherent political points of view supporting Civil Rights, and opposing nuclear testing and arms proliferation. A coherent student political movement had come into being in American universities for the first time since the 1930s.

The most notable event at the beginning of the student protest movement was at the Berkeley campus of the University of California in September of 1964. The Berkeley Student Uprising grew from a minor incident on the campus concern-

*Attempting to define precisely what is meant by a student movement obviously presents a number of problems. Students are by no means the only participants in such movements. The objectives of those involved are often different. Lewis Feuer in his work *The Conflict of Generations* provides a useful definition:

> We may define a student movement as a combination of students inspired by aims which they try to explicate in a political ideology, and moved by an emotional rebellion in which there is always present a disillusionment with and rejection of the values of the older generation; moreover, the members of a student movement have the conviction that their generation has a special historical mission to fulfill where the older generation, other elites, and other classes have failed.

ing the rights of students to use university facilities to promote various political positions and candidates. During the summer of 1964, the Republican National Convention had met in San Francisco and complaints were made by the supporters of Barry Goldwater that the University was being unfairly used to organize support for Governor William Scranton's bid for the presidency. In September, the Berkeley administration, which had for some time overlooked existing regulations prohibiting solicitation of funds for political groups on the campus, as well as the organization of political drives there, once again began to enforce old regulations.

On September 29, 1964, members of the Student Nonviolent Coordinating Committee, the Congress of Racial Equality, Slate (a local student political party with Marxist leanings) and the Y.S.A. (Trotskyist Young Socialist Alliance) set up tables in front of Sather Gate to solicit funds and political support for their causes. A representative of the administration managed to identify a number of the students, but allowed the booths to remain. The students identified by the university administration were told to appear the following day before the university's dean of men. By 3:30 P.M. the next day, at least 400 students assembled outside of the dean's office. A petition circulated and signed by the students stated that they had manned political booths in conscious violation of the university's rules, and that they should be subject to the same disciplinary measures as the students who had been called to appear before the dean. The students also demanded that all disciplinary charges be dropped.

The university's chancellor, Edward Strong, refused to meet the students' demands. He asked that the five students who had been called to the dean of student's office, with the three student demonstration leaders, meet with him and discuss the disciplinary actions that should be taken for violating the unviersity's regulation against political solicitation. None of the students appeared at his office, and a strike was quickly organized.

Mario Savio, a sophomore and recent transfer student, quickly emerged as the leader of the strike. A sit-in was begun at Sproul Hall, the administration building. Money was collected for food, blankets, and bedding. The university *free speech movement* was underway. A rally was planned on the campus for the following noon. At the start of the rally, Deans George S. Murphy and Peter Van Houten and a university police lieutenant requested that Jack Weinberg, a former Berkeley student who was soliciting funds for the Congress on Racial Equality, leave the campus. Refusing to do so, Weinberg was arrested for trespassing and a police car was brought in to take him away.

Weinberg went limp when the police car arrived and had to be carried to it. Approximately 200 students at once lay down in front of and back of the car. Mario Savio climbed in the car with Weinberg. For the next thirty-two hours, Weinberg remained there. The university administration, Savio, and other student leaders negotiated.

Weinberg was an activist in CORE and a former Berkeley graduate student in mathematics, a vocal advocate of the use of drugs, and at the time of the Berkeley uprising on parole from jail. While ostensibly based upon a conflict over the rights of free speech, the Berkeley uprising was also clearly a conflict involving the aspirations of youth and its opposition to established authority. A classic generational conflict was underway.

On Friday, October 2, 1964, the university announced that it would take police action to stop the demonstration. Six hundred forty-three policemen assembled and prepared to come on campus. The demonstrators and the university administration negotiated to prevent the police from coming on campus; compromise was reached. The police and students dispersed. Weeks of negotiations followed, and the campus was relatively peaceful once again.

When four of the student leaders of the October demonstration were summoned before the Faculty Committe on Student Affairs in November, conflicts arose again. The university regents directed that they answer charges that they had committed violent acts against the university police. Specifically, Mario Savio was accused of having bitten a policeman. The four leaders, including Savio, faced the threat of being expelled. On December 1, student activist leaders presented an ultimatum. Unless the charges were dropped within twenty-four hours, there would be a general strike. The following day, Sproul Hall was once again occupied by the students. Folksinger Joan Baez, who had participated in earlier demonstrations, led nearly a thousand students to the administration building singing the Lord's Prayer and "We Shall Overcome." At 3:00 A.M. Chancellor Edward Strong pleaded with the students to leave Sproul Hall. They refused. At the orders of Governor Ronald Reagan, the police entered Sproul Hall and arrested 814 protestors, of whom 590 were students.

Thursday, December 3, students struck to close down the university and set up picket lines. Approximately half of the university's scheduled classes did not meet. On the following Monday, December 7, the president of the university, Clark Kerr, addressed 18,000 students and professors in the university's Greek Theater. Kerr accepted proposals that the university not press the prosecution of those involved in the demonstrations and that censorship not be imposed on the student protesters.

These concessions by the university administration were a remarkably liberal, if not in fact radical, approach to the demonstrations. Some would argue that they capitulated and surrendered, but the approach was consistent with the university's liberal policy. It is worth noting that the Berkeley campus, despite criticisms and protests of the students, had the reputation throughout the country of being the most liberal campus in the United States. In 1964, the university's administration had been awarded the Alexander Meiklejohn Prize by the American Association of University Professors for its consistent support of academic freedom.

On December 8, the Berkeley faculty senate passed an open-ended resolution, that the university should in no way restrict speech or any political advocacy. Defending academic and personal freedom, emphasizing absolute freedom of speech, the faculty's position protected the right of students to be involved in extralegal demonstrations, to engage in obscene speech, and to advocate acts of violence and terrorism.

Critic Lewis Feuer has argued that the Berkeley faculty "in effect created a moral and political vacuum in the heart of the university." He saw the situation at Berkeley as a denial of the adult generation's authority. The resolution of the faculty senate restrained the university's administration from taking action against the students who claimed to be exercising the right of free speech. Local civic authorities were reluctant to enter the university and take control—feeling that the problems with the students should be dealt with by the university's faculty and administration. The student activists in turn took full advantage of this indecision of the adult authorities.

Major protests continued at Berkeley during the mid-1960s. Within a short period of time, the university became a major center for political protest and generational conflict. As the student movement became stronger throughout 1964 and 1965, the ethics of activist student leaders clearly declined. A philosophy of the "end justifying the means," seems to have increasingly come into effect. Contradictions between philosophy and action were evident in the movement from the start. Individuals such as Mario Savio during the early demonstrations consistently maintained that they were part of a nonviolent movement. Yet, when questioned several months after the October demonstrations when he was accused of having bitten a policeman, Savio admitted to having committed the act. It is perhaps worth noting that at the conclusion of Kerr's speech in front of the students and faculty on December 7, Savio marched across the stage and attempted to seize the microphone and take control of the meeting, directly attacking the administration's right of free speech. The student activists demanded the right of free speech but denied it to others.

This phenomenon was by no means unique to Berkeley. One of the authors attending the University of Rochester in upstate New York during the 1960s recalls that nuclear armament specialist Herman Kahn was prevented from presenting a speech to the university community by a guerilla theater presentation by student radicals who marched with pigs' heads on top of stakes in order to protest Kahn's presentation. Only after a major confrontation between the members of the theater group and the audience attending the lecture was Kahn finally allowed to go on with the speech. In instances like this, the student protest movement was frighteningly reminiscent of the pro-Nazi youth protests that took place in Germany during the period immediately prior to the Second World War.

Berkeley became a national symbol for student militancy and generational conflict. Led ideally by a naive utopian vision, the student protests succeeded in undermining the university and many of the principles for which it stood. By 1967, the university and the surrounding town of Berkeley had gone through profound changes. The city was becoming a center for alternative life styles. People flocked there from everywhere. It quickly became the center of the hippie movement and the drug culture that was becoming a powerful force in America during the late 1960s.

If Berkeley was the model for the student protest movement during the 1960s, the sources of generational conflict were no less evident in other universities throughout the country. Protests at Cornell University, for example, focused on racial issues. At Columbia University in New York City, 300 students occupied Hamilton Hall on April 23, 1968, and held the dean of students as hostage. The issue of contention was the university's plan to build a gymnasium on a rocky slope of Morningside Park. The upper levels of the gymnasium would be used by the university and the lower levels by members of the adjacent Harlem community. Significantly, the Harlem community when first approached about the idea of building the gymnasium was in favor of it, since youths from the black community would have easy access to the facilities.

Despite local community interest in the project, members of the campus-based Student's Afro-American Society complained that the gym was encroaching on the black community. This was despite the fact that most of the land intended to be used by the university for the gymnasium was part of an escarpment or cliff that had no practical use. A cause had been found, and student activists with a wide range of purposes and intentions joined together to organize a major protest at the university.

James Simon Kunen in his book *The Strawberry Statement* (1968) has left a rather remarkable account of what it was like taking an active part in the student demonstrations at Columbia. Kunen, a graduate of Andover, was clearly part of a privileged elite attending Columbia. Describing himself and his fellow students, Kunen explained that

> We think how lucky we are to be able to go to school, to have nice clothes and fine things and to eat well and have money and be healthy. How lucky we are really. But we remain unhappy. . . . We're unhappy because of the war, and because of poverty and the hopelessness of politics, but also because we sometimes get put down by girls or boys, as the case may be, or feel lonely and alone and lost.

Kunen described how he and his friends became preoccupied with the notion that their college years were the best years of their lives. Yet something was very wrong. The reality of college being "exhausting, confusing, boring, troubled, frustrating and meaningless," was compounded by the realization that life would only become more difficult. Refusing to accept such a situation, Kunen explained that he and his friends ". . . took adaptive measures, which consisted chiefly of constructing an alternative world structure in which we felt a bit more comfortable." Kunen was one of approximately 200 students who on April 24, 1968, began the occupation of President Grayson Kirk's office in the Lowe Library building. With the arrival of the police, all but twenty-seven of the students remained, including Kunen. The students were not arrested and the occupation went on.

Kunen's account of the occupation took on comic elements. Professor Orest Ranum in his academic robes was described climbing through a window "like Batman" to warn the protesters that their action would set off a massive right-wing reaction among the faculty. After spending the night in the office, Kunen took

FIGURE 13-3 Columbia University students and others climb out of windows of the office of Columbia president Grayson Kirk, April 24, 1968. Courtesy of United Press International.

great pleasure in shaving with the president's razor and using his after-shave lotion and toothpaste. As on the previous day when he left the occupied offices to find out the baseball scores, Kunen slipped out of the president's office at four in the afternoon to attend crew practice. When practice was over he slipped back in to the sit-in.

Kunen described a debate that began on his return to the president's office. The students discussed piling in front of the windows paintings and sculptures on display in the building so that the police would have to destroy them if they entered the building. One student suggested that he use poles to push the police off the ledges of the building should they try to recapture it. When criticized for the violence of his suggestion, the student tried to explain that he would push the police off the ledges "in a nonviolent way." Kunen spent the night in the occupied offices and then left them the following morning to take a bus to Boston, where he rowed in a crew race for the university. Two days later he returned to the occupied campus, where he once again became actively involved in the student demonstrations.

Kunen described occupying the math building and writing home to his parents. He explained how he tried to justify in his letter spending his father's money while he was rebelling. Arguing that the danger of going to college is that you learn things, and that his present actions were strongly influenced by the reading he had done for Contemporary Civilization (C100ly) Kunen in the end admitted that

> After sealing the letter, I realize that my conception of the philosophy of law comes not so much from Rousseau as from Fess Parker as Davy Crockett. I

remember him saying you should decide what you think is right and then go ahead and do it. Walt Disney really bagged that one; the old fascist inadvertently created a whole generation of radicals.

Kunen continued his story, including his description of being arrested and booked for trespassing, and getting the names and addresses of various female students also involved in the demonstrations.

Campus upheavals went beyond Berkeley and Columbia to hundreds of other campuses, even to European universities, spread by common discontent and by instant and graphic television journalism. We cannot describe each of them here, but former students now in their thirties (nonetheless completely trustworthy) remember them. They remember the sounds of chanted mottoes ("Hell no, we won't go!") and of bull-horn-amplified exhortations, the crash and tinkle of breaking glass, the sounds of police sirens and police helicopters, and the flat pop of gas grenade launchers. They remember the smell of tear gas ("CS" was especially acrid) and of the smell of burning buildings, and books, and often the sweet lingering smell of pot.

There was endless variety in demands and negotiations, in police tactics and countertactics, marches, building occupations, police assaults and sometimes counterassaults, barricades, Molotov cocktails, and police clubbings. Former students remember stolid "peace officers" wearing battle visors, carrying "crowd control" clubs, and sometimes shields. Aging policemen and sheriff's deputies remember running, shouting "crazies," and showers of bricks, stones, and ice. More tragic, there are memories of the ragged volley of National Guard gunfire that killed students at Kent State University, and of gunfire that killed students at Jackson State. There was also the "protesters'" explosive blast in the computer laboratory at the University of Wisconsin, in which a student died.

At some point, this went beyond the search for freedom and dignity. Resistance to war in Vietnam and support for civil rights (less prominent on most campuses) are a part of our political history. The Chicago "police riot" at the Democratic convention in 1968, the "days of rage," and the Weathermen are also part of our political history. The youth culture, and its love for electronically produced, reproduced, and amplifed music of the Beatles and other rock groups, with accompanying garish lights and color, is a part of general cultural history, or perhaps of a history of fashions.

Kunen's opinions and comments, and subsequent events, have been analyzed by theorists, although the analysis seems pale compared with events. In *The Student Revolution: A Global Confrontation*, Joseph A. Califano, Jr., made five major points. He began by arguing that many students were undergoing a profound crisis of belief, one shared by many adults, and for which they were largely responsible. Califano felt this crisis went far beyond the university. The legitimacy of existing political and social systems were in question.

Califano further argued that students had to be given a greater measure of control over their own lives, and the things that affect their lives. Such feelings were particularly evident on the issue of the Vietnam War. Students were being drafted and sent to fight in the war, but had no part in starting it or determining how it would be conducted. Quoting Paul Goodman, Califano argued that students were caught in "the psychology of being powerless." The student activist movement provided youth with a sense that they were somehow affecting the course of their own lives.

According to Califano, the Democrats and the Republicans had done little to attract the attention and interest of college students. College students existed in a political vacuum and, because they were largely overlooked and ignored by the mainstream political groups, often adapted the romantic views of Mao, Guevara, and Marcuse. Califano concluded by asking the question of whether or not a college education was necessary or useful for many of those attending universities and colleges, and noting that the increase of the university population from 2.7 million in 1950 to 7 million when he was writing in 1970, placed unprecedented pressures on the system of higher education.

ALTERNATIVE SCHOOLS

Radical approaches to education were by no means limited to the universities. By the mid-1960s, alternative programs were being proposed and implemented at both the elementary and the secondary levels. Known as "free schools" or "alternative schools," these school experiments were diverse in philosophies and purposes. In general, the school experiments were unified by a belief that traditional schools were not meeting the needs of children, and that new types of schools needed to be established to provide alternatives to the traditional public school system.

Alternative schools were set up both privately and as parts of existing public school systems. Philosophically they drew on many different sources. By the mid-1960s, a great deal of interest had developed in the programs and curricula developed by many of the English primary schools. In these programs, an emphasis was placed on the need of children to learn from their environment, to learn to live with other people including both children and adults, to assume responsibility, and to enjoy learning. A strong emphasis was also placed upon children being carefully guided in their learning by their teachers. As the 1967 Plowden Committee, which reported on the schools to the English Parliament, explained: "From the start, there must be teaching as well as learning: Children are not 'free' to develop interests or skills of which they have no knowledge. They must have guidance from their teachers."

The philosophy of the English primary schools was by no means new, and reflected many of the basic themes found in Dewey's Laboratory School at the University of Chicago, as well as in the programs of the Progressive Education movement. Popular interest in the English primary schools was stimulated by a series of articles by Joseph Featherston published in *The New Republic* in August and September of 1967. At the same time, increasing interest developed in the work of the radical British educator A. S. Neill, whose book *Summerhill—A Radical*

Approach to Child Rearing, described his nontraditional approach to schooling. Neill argued that students will only learn if they have the need or desire to learn. Rote memorization, discipline, exams, and all of the traditional paraphernalia of most school systems destroy the spirit of many students, according to Neill, as well as the desire to learn. Neill ultimately argued for an approach to education that encouraged "freedom without license."

Neill's *Summerhill,* Jonathan Kozol's National Book Award-winning *Death at an Early Age* (1967), together with various works by John Holt such as *Why Children Fail* (1965), Nat Hentoff's *Our Children Are Dying* (1966) and Herbert Kohl's *36 Children* (1967), generated a widespread interest in what was believed to be a failure of the educational system to meet the needs of many children. Basing their ideas loosely upon the ideas of these and other authors, teachers, concerned private citizens, and parents began to promote altenative types of educational programs.

Criticisms of the schools were made not only by the popular authors listed above. For example, among historians of education, a significant revisionist movement began to emerge. The schools were no longer described as vehicles of personal freedom and economic advancement, but instead their potential for perpetuating existing social, political, and economic systems was emphasized. The "Great School Myth" was thrown into doubt by the careful research of Raymond Callahan, Lawrence Cremin, Michael Katz, and others.

Tremendous confusion has gathered around the definition of "free" or "alternative" schools. In general, the schools adopted themes that had been delineated by the counterculture revolution of the 1960s. Many of the founders of these schools believed that the public schools had become too large and impersonal and that children were not allowed to develop naturally in such settings. The idea of "freeing" children from the traditional schools became a theme underlying the development of many of the alternative schools.

The first alternative schools were private ventures. Others gradually appeared as parts of public school systems. A variety of free schools or alternative schools, begun as early as 1966, addressed the needs of specific groups within the culture. For Blacks and ethnic minorities, freedom schools, street corner and storefront schools, and academies were started. Middle-class Whites promoted various "free" schools: open classroom experiments, Montessori-type schools, and community-oriented schools. In a loose sense, all of these approaches were alternative types of education.

Many of the alternative schools founded then reflected the wider unrest and disaffection in American society. Educators and parents frequently felt inadequate to handle the problems that were so common among many of their students. The Philadelphia Parkway School, which was one of the first public alternative schools started in the United States, was consciously begun in

... a background of violence, increasing use of narcotics, under-achievement, dropouts, vandalism, and arson in the Philadelphia school system—these despite every effort at improvement by a blue-ribbon school board, its president, former mayor Richard Cilworth and his new school superintendent.

Terence Deal and Robert Nolan, in their article "Alternative Schools: A Conceptual Map," argued that while the alternative school movement drew much of its energy from the social critiques of the 1960s, the alternative school movement clearly drew upon themes from the Progressive Education movement. Among these were: 1) the needs and experiences of the student as a starting point for schooling; 2) the teacher assuming the role of an adviser; 3) the recognition of the school as a social community; 4) active instead of passive learning; 5) an emphasis upon drawing on a variety of learning resources, especially those found within the community; 6) recognizing skills as means of achieving something, rather than ends in themselves; 7) student participation in at least some of the important decision making for the school; and 8) an emphasis upon the individuality of students and teachers.

In 1975, there were approximately 5,000 public alternative schools operating in the United States. The number of private alternative schools then was much more difficult to determine, since many of the older private schools in the United States included elements consistent with the aims and ideals of the newer free schools or alternative schools. Too, records of these schools are often much more difficult to obtain.

In interviews conducted with alternative school teachers and administrators during the mid-1970s, an attempt was made to determine some of the reasons why people became involved in establishing alternative programs. An administrator responsible for establishing an alternative high school in suburban Saint Louis explained how

> We had in this district the two types of students. The affluent white students who were dissatisfied with the Vietnamese war, and the militant black students who were tired of being put down. These two forces coverged onto our high school about the Spring of 1970. It was pretty obvious we needed to rethink what we were doing at the high school.

The Vietnam War, the Kent State killings, and the general turmoil evident in the society were cited again and again by teachers and administrators when asked why they had become involved in setting up or teaching in an alternative school. One teacher, for example, explained how it became increasingly evident that:

> ... Students would not accept things because you told them to do it. If they couldn't see how it would apply to their practical life they wouldn't bother with it.... These kids were going off to the war after they graduated. With my first year in the alternative school there were the Kent State killings and the kids were questioning not only the school, but the government and the president. I was questioning them too. I saw the ridiculousness of my teaching sociology units when the kids were going to be shipped off to Vietnam in the next month.

The war and social crisis that seriously affected the adults of the United States were clearly affecting younger Americans as well.

The alternative school movement provided alternatives not only for students but also for teachers. Traditional approaches to schooling were seen as inadequate to meet the demands and needs of the young. Numerous attempts were made to formulate and understand the problem, and to find solutions. In 1972, the Panel on Youth of the President's Science Advisory Committee was established to address the problem of youth. Its chairman was James Coleman, the principal author of the 1964 report, *Equality of Educational Opportunity.* The Panel on Youth report, *Youth: Transition to Adulthood* was published in 1974.

Commonly known as "Coleman II," *Youth: Transition to Adulthood*, seriously questioned the extent to which schooling had come to be seen as the primary way in which the youths and adolescents had been introduced to adult life. As the labor of children had become less necessary for the culture and economy, schooling requirements had been increased. Schooling had come to be seen as the only means to prepare for and help make the transition to adulthood. The report went on to challenge the effectiveness of the schools in fulfilling this function:

> But schooling, as we know it, is not a complete environment giving all the necessary opportunities for becoming adult. School is a certain kind of environment: individualistic, oriented toward cognitive achievement, imposing dependency on and withholding authority and responsibility from those in the role of students.

According to the report, schools had expanded to fill the time that had formerly been taken up by other activities. These other activities, rather than emphasizing the development of cognitive skills, emphasized the development of opportunities for responsible action and leadership—skills crucial to the adolescent becoming an adult. The school provided no corresponding types of experience.

The Coleman II report framed seven major issues. It began by arguing that youth (aged 14 to 24), which in earlier periods had been in regular contact with many older individuals, knew among older individuals only parents and teachers. Age segregation had once served to protect youth from the harsh work of the adult world, and from adults who were unsuitable as associates. In addition, segregation of youths and children had served a custodial function, so that adults might get on with their own work. However, age segregation also separated youth from the world of adults, and from roles and activities they would soon have to become engaged in. The report strongly argued that benefits of integrating youth with the adult population clearly outweighed advantages of segregating the two groups. Age integration would benefit adults, lessening conflicts between youth and the adult population, as well as enlivening the environment of adults by the presence of youth.

Age segregation among the younger was the second issue raised by the report. Because of the ways schools had been organized, segregation by age had become universal. High school students had little contact with college students. The births of siblings were closely clustered in most families. Opportunities for cross-age associations had been seriously reduced. Age segregation made it easier for schools to teach groups of students of the same approximate age, level of physical maturation, and development. It also prevented older children from taking advantage of younger children. But by integrating children across age groups, a wider range of experience and perceptions would be opened to individuals, from which they could learn to grow and develop. The third point developed by the report was really derived from age segregation. Despite a nearly two-year difference between the age when boys and girls reached puberty, grouping in the schools continued to be based upon chronological age rather than physiological stages of development.

The fourth issue raised was failure to integrate work and education. Most youths had attended school and then gone to work. Once having left school, they received little further schooling. The report suggested alternative approaches of continuing education for individuals in the work force: recurrent education, in which the individual would work for a time and then return to school for further training; career education that focused on schooling for the individual, dealing with future occupations he or she might have; and work-study programs that combine youths with adults working in real occupations while also receiving formal schooling.

The fifth issue addressed by the report was the extent to which youth should have its time segmented. Should students, for example, be able to attend schools for only two or three days a week and with the rest of their time be allowed to engage in other activities, such as training for a job or instruction in an art or a craft? Logically extending the question, should a youth capable of learning the required school curriculum in half the normal time be required to attend school on a full-time basis instead of engaging in other activities?

The sixth issue dealt with the scope of formal schooling. Should nonacademic activities, such as driver's education, be made part of the curricula of the schools? The report argued that such activities were frequently distorted by the schools and were better dealt with outside of the schools.

The seventh and final issue addressed by the Coleman II report was the legal status and rights of youths. It argued that youths frequently found themselves constrained by laws that supposedly benefited them. Restrictive child labor laws and compulsory school attendance laws, while protecting many youths, restrained others and prevented them from entering activities and experiences from which they might ultimately benefit.

The report advocated several radical shifts in the approach taken toward youth. The possibility of establishing smaller, more personalized, schools; the alternation of work and schooling for many students; the inclusion of young people in work organizations where they could also learn; the expansion and establishment of youth organizations; and increased employment possibilities, including a lower minimum wage for youth workers that would encourage employers to hire them, were a few of the report's many suggestions.

The Coleman II report, perhaps more than any other work to emerge from the late 1960s and early 1970s, recognized the extraordinary problems faced by youth in the 1960s. At the same time, it realized the extraordinary ambiguity of their status:

> People below the age of majority are simultaneously the most indulged and oppressed part of the population. Both civil and criminal law accord minors special consideration and shield them from the full legal consequences of their acts. On the other hand, until reaching ages prescribed by law, children and young people are compelled to attend school, excluded from gainful employments, denied the right to drive automobiles, prohibited from buying alcoholic beverages, firearms and cigarettes, barred from the most interesting movies, and deprived of countless pleasures and liberties available to adults.

Undoubtedly, the issue that Coleman II addressed most clearly was the difficulty any modern culture faces in integrating its youth population into meaningful adult roles. As the report explained, ". . . the increase in the magnitude of the socialization task in the United States during the past decade was completely outside the bounds of previous and prospective experience."

The complexity of the socialization process for the youth during the 1960s has not been fully assessed historically. Perhaps the era is too close and painful, but the alienation and dissatisfaction of youth extended beyond the lack of opportunities and jobs. The threat of nuclear war, the assassination of John Kennedy, the Cuban missile crisis, the Vietnam War, the assassinations of Martin Luther King and Robert L. Kennedy undoubtedly had an effect on the nation and, in particular, upon its youth far more profound than has been fully realized. In fact, if the suicide, illegitimate birth, and drug statistics for youth of the late 1960s are any accurate indicator, youth went through an unprecedented social crisis during the late 1960s.

For example, illegitimate births among the 15- to 19-year-old age group increased from 40.5 per thousand live births in 1940 to 56.0 per thousand in 1950, to 87.1 per thousand in 1960 and, in 1968, to the extraordinary figure of 158.0 per thousand. In other words, between 1940 and 1968, the illegitimacy rate had increased in the 15- to 19-year-old population by nearly 400 percent.

Youth suicide figures over the course of the 1960s are particularly revealing. Among the white male population between the ages of 15 and 24, the suicide rate increased from 8.8 per hundred thousand in 1940, to 12.6 per hundred thousand in 1969. For black males in the same group, the increase was from 5.1 per hundred thousand in 1940, to 9.9 per hundred thousand in 1969. The suicide rate of other groups during the same period actually declined. In the case of the white male population between the ages of 45 and 55, the suicide rate decreased from 44.1 per hundred thousand in 1940, to 28.6 per hundred thousand in 1969. Other data of a

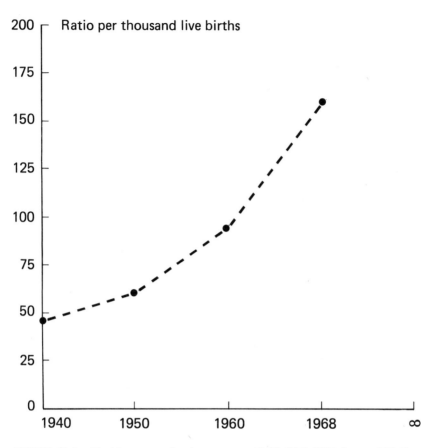

FIGURE 13-4   Illegitimacy rate for the age group 15-19, 1940-1968. Source: U.S. Bureau of the Census, *Statistical Abstracts of the United States, 1972* (Washington, D.C.: U.S. Government Printing Office, 1972), p. 51.

similar sort could be cited. What is clear is that youth was profoundly influenced and shaped by the social and political upheavals of the middle and late 1960s.

CONCLUSION

Future historians may well see the 1960s as a turning point for American culture. Few decades have brought with them as violent a series of social and political shifts as those witnessed then. Future historians will also probably look to youth as the principal source for understanding these events. Whether in the public schools, in the universities, or at the forefront of political demonstrations, it was youth that consistently experimented and pushed the system in ways that it had never been pushed before.

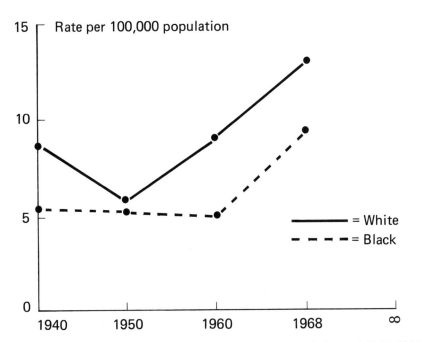

FIGURE 13-5   Suicides among the white and black male population aged 15-24, 1940-1969. Source: U.S. Bureau of the Census, *Statistical Abstracts of the United States, 1972* (Washington, D.C.: U.S. Government Printing Office, 1972), p. 63.

It was also youth that was most profoundly affected by the crisis of the culture. Alienation, rapid change, the redefinition of values made "coming of age" in America all the more difficult. Although at the beginning of the 1980s they have received less attention, we cannot imagine that youth's crisis and the search for freedom are at an end.

CONCLUSIONS

GENERALIZATIONS

We have described the developments in education in America that seemed most interesting and most important. What remains is to generalize, and to summarize.

Most clearly and most obviously, the educational importance of schools has grown as other institutions have ceded their responsibilities or failed them; or as the growing complexity of the economy, culture, and society have seemed to impose new needs for education. Schools have become more generally important in the teaching of cognitive or intellectual knowledge. Schooling has almost replaced apprenticeship as the entryway to occupations. At the same time, the clientele of the schools has greatly widened, to include younger children, late adolescents and youths, and members of black and other minority groups. In now includes more pupils and students who benefit less, or not at all.

There has been in the last century and a half an overwhelming trend toward public schooling. While public schools were providing schooling for all, or nearly all, the control of schooling was being more and more centralized. At the same time, there has been increasing standardization of schooling, the imposition of "the one best system."

It seems surely true that schooling and other organized education has steadily become less personal, less individualistic. Standardization of curriculum, method, teaching material, and even classrooms has limited individualism and constrained individuals. In schools and outside them, individuals seem less important at the end of the 1900s than they had seemed 200 years earlier.

It does seem, as Philip Jackson has observed, that there have been longtime changes in teaching and in learning. Corporal punishment is used less often as a teaching aid. Learning has become less a matter of memorizing, more a matter of understanding and doing. There has been a continuing, though not continuous, shifting of content, away from the classic toward the modern, toward the practical and away from the humanities.

The links between the schools and the larger society and culture have been more complex than might have been supposed. The school is not simply a smaller version of society, but it is not a small world of its own, sealed off from the real world. Social and cultural imperatives have shaped schooling, but in some ways schools have resisted and persisted in older ways. That times of school reform have come at times of national reform is not coincidental. The Common School Movement was a part of the general shift during the Jacksonian democratic era. Progressive reforms, philosophic and administrative, would not have come except for the more general Progressive movement near 1900. Johnson's Great Society attempted to change schools so that society would be changed. Even when Jefferson was president the "republican spirit" widened opportunities for schooling, especially in secondary schools and for women. Of political reform movements, the New Deal had the least influence upon the schools; but in some ways the New Deal was the least change minded of reform movements.

REALITY AND HOPE

Critics have said time and again that schooling in the United States has been and is in many ways futile—miseducating and disfiguring children. Defenders of the schools have responded that schooling is, all things considered, better than ever before. Compared with what they have been, they may be better, although there are limitations to objective measures supporting their improvement. Compared with hopes and expectations for them, schools are deficient and defective.

Both personal and public hopes for the benefits of schooling have far more often than not been largely unfilled—as hopes more generally often are. The diversity of pre-Revolutionary schooling precluded any general expression of hopes. Naturally there were personal hopes—sometimes, but often not, fulfilled. The common schools were not, of course, successful in meeting the expectations Mann and others set. The potentials of educational progressivism seemed far greater than the gains realized. The grandest, most optimistic hopes of the social reconstructions during the 1930s were, as it developed, no more than hopes. Plans for the Great Society called for the schools to be one of the most important agencies for achieving racial and social equality. Efforts to create the Great Society were not nonproductive, but the results were far short of aims. The "better tomorrow" was, when it became today, disappointingly like yesterday.

The past has not been simple, and much of it cannot be known to us. It would have been easier to demonstrate inevitable decline, just as fifty years ago, it would have been simpler and more fashionable to recount inevitable triumph. But the past has been complex, and a black-and-white representation would be too far from reality. Grays, tints, and colors, and light and shadow, come nearer to reality. The past and its history fascinate us, and we hope to leave the reader with some feeling for other times and other events. Knowledge of the past makes us less likely to be imprisoned by it. Knowledge makes it more useful to us.

BIBLIOGRAPHY, SOURCES, AND NOTES

Additional readings are suggested for each section, with brief descriptions.

The last three words of each quotation are given, followed by its source.

Other important sources, even though not mentioned in the text, are also cited.

INTRODUCTION

The pattern for most histories of American education written in the last half century was set by Ellwood P. Cubberley, in *Public Education in the United States* (Boston: Houghton-Mifflin, 1919, 1934). Cubberley concentrated on the organization and administration of the schools, seeing them as of greatest value and importance, and their history as leading inevitably toward their perfection. A current text in that tradition is Harry S. Good and James D. Teller, *A History of American Education* (New York: Macmillan, 1973, 3rd ed.). Criticisms of history of American education in Cubberley's tradition, with which we agree, are by Bernard Bailyn in *Education in the Forming of American Society* (New York: Vintage, 1960) and Lawrence A. Cremin in *The Wonderful World of Ellwood Patterson Cubberley* (New York: Teachers College, Columbia U., 1965). Of related interest is Colin Greer, *The Great School Legend* (New York: Basic Books, 1972).

A newer approach to history of American education has been to employ constructs which emphasize the function of the schools in the distribution of social rewards and power. This approach was employed by Michael B. Katz in *The Irony of Early School Reform: Educational Innovation in Mid-Nineteenth Century*

Massachusetts (Cambridge: Harvard, 1968), and subsequently by a number of others. This has been fruitful, but we have substantial reservations. First, this focus is quite narrow. Even if there were complete information on the distribution of rewards and power at a given time and place (which there most certainly is not), history should encompass a great deal more than that. There have been people and thoughts in history, as well as social forces. Second, by unfortunate parallel, the new social history of the schools has had the same air of inevitability as Cubberley's history did. Inevitable is the doom of our culture and society, largely brought on by our schools. There is not much in history, as far as we are concerned, that has dictated the inevitability of events in the past, or that does dictate them in the present or future. Third, some new social historians of education seem as certain of the evilness of schools as Cubberley was of their goodness. We are entitled to value judgments and, as historians, obligated to make them, but the history of our culture and our schools is far too complex for cosmic affirmation, or denial.

The most recent and comprehensive critique of the new educational history—one that we also do not entirely agree with—is found in Diane Ravitch's "The Revisionists Revised: Studies in the Historiography of American Education," *Proceedings of the National Academy of Education*, Vol. 4, 1977, pp. 1-84. An expanded version of this work was published under the title *The Revisionists Revised* (New York: Basic Books, 1978). A response to Ravitch's work can be found in Walter Feinberg, *et al.*, *Revisionists Respond to Ravitch* (Washington, D.C.: The National Academy of Education, 1980).

We have taken the general framework for values from Florence Kluckholn and Fred Strodtbeck, *Variations in Value Orientation* (Evanston, Ill.: Row Peterson, 1961).

General Source Materials: Throughout the section on *Bibliography, Sources and Notes*, there are references to general collections of source materials on the history of American education. The following are some of the more useful sources that can be found in most university and research libraries.

The most extensive collection of general documents on the history of American education is Sol Cohen (ed.), *Education in the United States* (New York: Random House, 1974, 5 vols.); approximately 3,500 pages in length, Cohen's documents are drawn from manuscripts, books, magazines, and other sources, from the sixteenth century to the present.

Numerous American and European sources are in the "Classics in Education" series published by Teachers College Press, Columbia University. Of related interest is Robert H. Bremmer, *et al.*, (eds.), *Children & Youth in America* (Cambridge: Harbard, 1970-71), 3 vols., over 2,000 pages in length. The editors attempted to include documents on all aspects of the welfare of children, including education.

The best general collection of documents of the history of education in the South is still Edgar W. Knight (ed.), *A Documentary History of Education in the South Before 1860* (Chapel Hill: U. N. Carolina, 1953, 5 vols.). No comparable source exists for the period since the Civil War.

Several reprint and microfilm collections are also of particular value to those interested in studying the history of American education. Lawrence A. Cremin, advisory editor, has provided an invaluable service by assembling the 161-volume reprint series titled *American Education: Its Men, Ideas, and Institutions* (New York: Arno/New York Times, 1970-71). Virtually every book published in the United States before 1800 can be obtained on either microprint, microfiche, or microfilm. Clifford K. Shipton, editor, has assembled the microprint collection *Early American Imprints, 1639-1800* (Worcester, Mass.: American Antiquarian Society). For nineteenth century educational sources the microfilm series *American Culture Series* (Ann Arbor, Mich.: University Microfilms) is also extremely useful.

PART ONE: BEGINNINGS

Readings: The most interesting single volume on pre-Revolutionary history is Daniel J. Boorstin, *The Americans: The Colonial Experience* (New York: Vintage, 1958). Pages 1-69, 97-143, on the beginnings of Massachusetts Bay Colony, Pennsylvania, and Virginia, are especially worth reading. We have read with pleasure J. C. Furnas, *The Americans* (New York: Putnam's, 1969). Pages 13-236 deal with pre-Revolutionary history. Samuel Eliot Morison, *The Puritan Pronaos* (New York: N.Y.U., 1936), republished as *The Intellectual Life of Early New England* (Ithaca, N.Y.: Cornell, 1967) may be overly favorable, but portrays intellectual life generally, rather than that of a few intellectuals exclusively. A general history may be helpful to provide an orderly and relatively succinct overview: Samuel Eliot Morison *et al., Growth of the American Republic*, (New York: Oxford, 1969, 2 vols.) serves that purpose well for this and later sections. Volume I, pages 3-226, covers these periods.

Pre-Revolutionary America has been the subject of some of the most interesting historical writing in the last quarter century; there is almost an overabundance of good scholarship. Among the most interesting works are David Hawke, *The Colonial Experience* (Indianapolis: Bobbs-Merrill, 1966); Max Saville, *Seeds of Liberty* (New York: Knopf, 1948); and Louis Wright, *The Cultural Life of the American Colonies* (New York: Harper and Row, 1957) which are more detailed intellectual histories. Harvey Wish, *Society and Thought in America,* (New York: D. McKay, 1964, 2 vols.) is still worth reading. The best single description of a prototypic New England town, if there was such a thing, is Kenneth A. Lockridge, *A New England Town: Dedham, Massachusetts, 1636-1737* (New York: Norton, 1970), but there are also other studies of individual towns. On education, Lawrence A. Cremin, *American Education: The Colonial Experience, 1607-1783* (New York: Harper & Row, 1970), with much detail, is the best single source. Some of what Robert Middlekauf wrote in *Ancients and Axioms: Secondary Education in the Eighteenth Century* (New Haven: Yale, 1963) also holds for the seventeenth century.

Concerning the distribution of wealth in the colonies, James A. Henretta, "Economic Development and Social Structure in Colonial Boston," *William and Mary Quarterly*, 3rd ser., vol. 22 (1965), pp. 75-92, showing that there was increasing concentration of wealth in Boston, is persuasive. However, Alice Hanson Jones's research, summarized in *Wealth of a Nation to Be: The American Colonies on the Eve of the Revolution* (New York: Columbia U., 1980) indicates that Boston was the exception, and that the rule was that wealth was not more greatly concentrated on the eve of the Revolution. Even so, the wealth of Boston would be important for the development of mercantilism, of shipping, and later of manufacturing. Although the matter can be argued endlessly, we are inclined to accept the argument that industrialization in its earlier stages strongly supported the concentration of wealth, but that in its later stages wealth has been, if anything, dispersed.

CHAPTER 1:
SOURCES, EUROPEAN AND COLONIAL

The main sources for our description of education in England at the end of the Renaissance were R. L. Clarke, *Classical Education in Britain* (Cambridge: Cambridge U., 1959) and Kenneth Charlton, *Education in Renaissance England* (London: Routledge and Kegan Paul, 1965). An earlier but still useful work is J. W.

Baldwin, *William Shakespeare's Small Latin and Lesse Greeke* (Urbana: U. of Ill., 1944), vol. 1. ". . . in the children": Colet quoted in Craig R. Thompson, *Schools in Tudor England* (Washington, D.C.: Folger Shakespeare Library, 1958), p. 11. Our most important source on pre-Revolutionary child rearing is Philip Greven, *The Protestant Temperament* (New York: Knopf, 1977). ". . . face lay hid": Anne Bradstreet quoted in Greven, p. 29. ". . . that doth appear": Adam Winthrop (1620) quoted in Greven, p. 156. ". . . responses for children": Greven, p. 32. "Certain established boundaries": *ibid.*, p. 151. ". . . of this Catechism": *Book of Common Prayer* (Oxford: Thomas Baskett, Printer to the University, 1757), not paginated. ". . . the Puritan creed": Edgar W. Knight, *Education in the United States* (Boston: Ginn, 1929), quoted in Morison, *Puritan Pronaos*, p. 55. ". . . a social obligation": *ibid.*, p. 66. ". . . assisting our endeavours": "Olde Deluder Satan" law, in many sources, including Theodore Rawson Crane (ed.), *Dimensions of Higher Education* (Reading, Mass.: Addison-Wesley, 1974), p. 8. ". . . or in commonwealth": quoted in Bernard C. Steiner, *History of Education in Connecticut* (Washington, D.C.: U. S. Government Printing Office, Bureau Circular of Information No. 2, 1893), p. 17. ". . . to our commonwealth": ". . . societies and republics": quoted in "History of Free Schools in Plymouth Colony. . . ," *Collections of the Massachusetts Historical Society*, 2nd ser., vol. IV (1816), p. 83.

Our information on Enoch Flower is from James Pyle Wickersham, *A History of Education in Pennsylvania* (Lancaster, Pa.: Inquirer, 1885), passim. Pastorius's biography is Marion Dexter Learned, *The Life of Francis Daniel Pastorius* (Philadelphia: Campbell, 1908). ". . . & Young Zealots": Francis Daniel Pastorius, *a New Primer. . .* (New York: William Bradford, 1693), p. 3. ". . . reduced to poverty": *Pennsylvania Gazette*, Nov. 29, 1733, quoted in Wickersham, p. 43. Corlet's biography comes primarily from George E. Littlefield, "Elijah Corlet and the 'Faire Grammar Schoole' at Cambridge," *Colonial Society of Massachusetts Publications*, XVIII (1913-14), pp. 131-40. ". . . youth under him": quoted by Littlefield, p. 134. There are several biographies of Cheever. We used Elizabeth Porter Gould, *Ezekiel Cheever and Some of His Descendants* (Boston: Clapp, 1879). Pauline Holmes, *A Tercentenary History of the Boston Latin School, 1635-1935* (Cambridge: Harvard, 1935) was useful. St. Paul's school, which Cheever had attended, had also been attended by John Milton a few years earlier. It is described in fascinating detail by Harris Francis Fletcher, *The Intellectual Life of John Milton . . . Through Grammar School* (Urbana: U. of Illinois, 1955). ". . . Sycthia [barbaric] grown": Cotton Mather, "An Elergy on Ezekiel Cheever," 1708. Repr. Carl H. Gross and Charles C. Chandler, eds., *History of American Education Through Readings* (Boston: Heath, 1964), p. 39. ". . . me with straw": Metcalf, quoted in Kenneth Lockridge, p. 57. ". . . in New England": Cremin, *Colonial Experience*, p. 212. See George Eliot Morison, *The Founding of Harvard College* (Cambridge: Harvard, 1935) for its beginnings.

Our information about New Netherland schools and Adam Roelansen is primarily from William Heard Kilpatrick, *The Dutch Schools of New Netherland and New York* (Washington, D.C.: U.S. Government Printing Office, 1912). There are many detailed sources, but Wickersham is the starting point in history of schools in Pennsylvania. ". . . worship of God" quoted in Gary B. Nash, *Red, White, and Black* (Prentice-Hall: Englewood Cliffs, N.J., 1974), p. 46.

CHAPTER TWO:
CULTURE AND SCHOOLING BEFORE THE REVOLUTION

The change in thought following the trans-Atlantic passage was noted but not described in Edward Eggleston, *The Transit of Civilization* (Repr. Boston: Beacon,

1959). Douglas Sloan, *The Great Awakening and American Education: A Documentary History* (New York: Teachers College, Columbia U., 1973) documents the Great Awakening well, although it leaves its effect upon schooling problematical.

Several books and articles by Robert Francis Seybolt on colonial and provincial masters and schools provide information. Among them are "The Evening Schools of Colonial New York City...," in Thomas E. Finegan, *Free Schools: A Documentary History ... Fifteenth Annual Report of the [New York State] Education Department* (Albany: The University of the State of New York, 1910), pp. 630-52; "New York Colonial Schoolmasters," *ibid.*, pp. 653-59; *Public Schools of Colonial Boston, 1635-1775* (Cambridge: Harvard, 1935); "Schoolmasters in Colonial Philadelphia," *Pennsylvania Magazine of History and Biography*, LII (1927-30) *(Transactions)*, pp. 130-156. For New York City immediately after the Revolution, see Carl F. Kaestle, *The Evolution of an Urban School System: New York City, 1750-1850* (Cambridge: Harvard, 1973). For Boston, see Stanley K. Schultz, *The Culture Factory: Boston Public Schools, 1789-1860* (New York: Oxford, 1973). Much recent history of education has concerned the cities. Aside from that, their importance is suggested by Richard C. Wade, *The Urban Frontier: The Rise of the Cities, 1790-1830* (Cambridge: Harvard, 1959).

There have been several book-length biographies of the venerated Christopher Dock. As far as we know, the most recent is Gerald C. Studer, *Christopher Dock: Colonial Schoolmaster* (Scottsdale, Pa.: Herald Press, 1967). The fate of Enoch Brown is from Wickersham, p. 109. Several sources remove it from pure legend. Our information on the schools and school masters of Dedham is from Carlos Slafter, *A Record of Education: The Schools and Teachers of Dedham, 1644-1904* (Dedham, Mass.: Dedham Transcript, 1905) "... troubling the master" "... coxcombs, chimney sweepers" quoted in Page Smith, *John Adams* (Garden City, N. Y.: Doubleday, 1962), p. 25. "... came by it" is from Devereux Jarratt, "Autobiography, 1732-63," ed. by Douglas Adair, *William and Mary Quarterly*, 3rd ser., 9 (1952), p. 367. Robertson's accounts were printed in part as "Donald Robertson's School," *Virginia Magazine of History and Biography,* XXIII (1935), pp. 194-98, 288-92; XXIV (1926), pp. 141-48, 232-36; XXV (1927), pp. 55-56. One of the most interesting documents in the history of education in Virginia in the 1700s is *The Journal of John Harrower,* Edward Miles Riley, ed. (Williamsburg, Va.: Colonial Williamsburg, 1963). "... know the letters"; *ibid.*, p. 42. *Journals & Letters of Philip Vickers Fithian,* ed. by Hunter Dickinson Farish (Charlottesville, Va.: U. of Va., 1957) is as interesting. "... man in Virginia": *ibid.*, p. 26. Boucher left an autobiography, *Reminiscences of an American Loyalist* (Boston: Houghton Mifflin, 1925). A recent biography, Anne Y. Zimmer, *Jonathan Boucher: Loyalist in Exile* (Detroit: Wayne State, 1978) adds little for our purposes. Carl Bridenbaugh, *The Colonial Craftsman* (Chicago: U. Chicago, 1971) is a good source. The relatively recent biography of Benezet is George S. Brookes, *Friend Anthony Benezet* (Philadelphia: U. of Pennsylvania, 1937).

For Franklin's papers on the academy, see Albert Henry Smith, ed., *The Writings of Benjamin Franklin* (New York: Macmillan, 1904-1907), III, pp. 395-421. "... they are intended": *ibid.*, p. 404. "... part of learning": *ibid.* "... useful practical knowledge": James Maury, "A Dissertation on Education in the form of a letter from James Maury to Robert Jackson, July 17, 1762," ed. by Helen Duprey Bullock, *Albemarle County [Va.] Historical Society Bulletin*, II (1941-42), p. 47. Dove was the subject of a biographical sketch, Joseph Jackson, "A Philadelphia Schoolmaster of the Eighteenth Century," *Pennsylvania Magazine of History and Biography*, XXXV (1911), pp. 315-32. "... upon his prey": Dove's contemporary, *ibid.*, p. 332. The by-now classical source for information on the development of the colleges is Frederick Rudolph, *The American University and College* (New

York: Random House, 1962), which, however, deals briefly, pp. 3-22, with the pre-Revolutionary colleges.

John Lovell appears in Clifford K. Shipton, ed., *Sibley's Harvard Graduates: Biographical Sketches*. . . (Boston: Mass. Historical Society, 1968), vol. viii, pp. 31-48. Other details are in James Speare Loring, *Hundred Boston Orators*. . . (Boston: Jewett, 1852), pp. 29-33. His estate inventory, dated 1781, is the better indicator of the time of his death. Lovell's estate inventory is in the office of the Registrar of Probate, Halifax County, Nova Scotia. James Lovell appears in Shipton, vol. xiv (1968), pp. 31-48, and in Loring, pp. 32-37. ". . . china punch bowls," ". . . tea kettle (old)" are from John Lovell's estate inventory.

PART TWO:
AGE OF THE COMMON MAN

Readings: Although many details are inaccurate, John Bach McMaster, *A History of the People of the United States* (New York: Appleton, 1883), Vol. I, pp. 1-102, catches the feeling of the times admirably. It served as one of the exemplars for this book. For a concise general account, see Samuel Eliot Morison, *et al., The Growth of the American Republic*, Vol I, pp. 262-818. George Rogers Taylor, *The Transportation Revolution, 1815-1860*, Vol. IV: *The Economic History of the United States* (New York: Harper & Row, 1951) describes the antecedents of industrialization. Maxine Seller, *To Seek America* (n.p.: Ozer, 1977), pp. 58-197, describes immigrants and immigration and this and subsequent periods.

Concerning education somewhat more narrowly, the best single treatment, though not reaching the excellence of the earlier volume, is Lawrence A. Cremin, *American Education: The National Experience: 1783-1876* (New York: Harper & Row, 1980). Michael B. Katz, *Class, Bureaucracy, and Schools*, 2nd ed. (New York: Praeger, 1975) is an effective and influential "revisionist" statement. As an example of academy education at its best, Julia Ann Hieronymous Tevis, *Sixty Years in a School-Room: An Autobiography*. . . (Cincinnati: Western Methodist, 1878) is informative. For parallel treatments, see David L. Tyack, *The One Best System*, (Cambridge: Harvard, 1974) pp. 13-125, and Robert L. Church and Michael W. Sedlak, *Education in the United States* (New York: Free Press, 1976), pp. 3-113, and David Madsen, *Early National Education: 1776-1830*, Studies in the History of American Education Series (New York: Wiley, 1974).

In fiction, Washington Irving, *The Legend of Sleepy Hollow* (many editions) is still a telling satire. D[aniel] P. Thompson, *Locke Amsden; or the Schoolmaster, a Tale* (Boston: Mussey, 1847, and later editions), although long out of print, was popular in its day, portraying the common school teacher as hero, the academy master as villain. Edward Eggleston, *The Hoosier Schoolmaster* (several editions), although not written until later, evokes earlier teaching and schooling experience. Ross Rranklin Lockridge, *Raintree County* (Boston: Houghton Mifflin, 1948) has a portrait of an academy master and students on the eve of the Civil War.

Notes: The Corliss engine was famous in its day. One convenient description is James D. McCabe, *The Illustrated History of the Centennial Exposition*, a Collectors Reprint (Philadelphia: National, 1976). The Exhibition is described at length there. Our more general source is Daniel J. Boorstin, *The Americans: The National Experience* (New York: Random House, 1965). An unpublished statistical analysis by Richard A. Zeller, Bowling Green University, shows that the inland port cities grew in a highly coherent collective pattern. Information on immigrants is from Seller, *To Seek America*. Economic and technological growth are described in Stuart Burchey, *The Roots of American Economic Growth* (New York: Harper &

Row, 1968), pp. 141-215. More specifically, these were informative: Zadok Cramer, *The Navigator, Containing Directions for Navigating the Monongehela, Ohio, and Mississippi Rivers* . . . (Pittsburgh, 1808, many later editions). Most of the 1814 edition was reprinted in Ethel C. Leahy, *Who's Who on the Ohio River* (Cincinnati: author, 1931). Carter Goodrich *et al., Canals and the American Economic Development* (New York: Columbia U. Press, 1961) was informative, as was Albert Fishlow, *American Railroads and the Transformation of the Antebellum Economy* (Cambridge: Harvard, 1965). Joseph A. Durrenberger, *Turnpikes* (Valdosta, Ga.: Southern Printing, 1931) was less satisfactory because the data available to him were more limited. For this and the following sections, Edward C. Kirtland, *A History of American Economic Life*, 4th ed. (New York: Appleton Century Crofts, 1969) was useful as part of the general background. ". . . will be heard": William Lloyd Garrison, *The Liberator*, Jan. 1, 1831, quoted in Morison *et al., Growth of the American Republic*, Vol. 1, pp. 500-501.

CHAPTER THREE:
SCHOOLING IN THE NEW REPUBLIC

John Davis, *Travels . . . in the United States* (1803, repr. New York: Holt, 1909) is partly description, partly unflattering satire. Abigail Mason's letters, ed. by Bessie M. Henry, appeared as "A Yankee Schoolmistress Discovers Virginia," *Essex Institute Historical Collections*, CI (1965), pp. 121-32. ". . . and domestic economy": Noah Webster, Jr., *American Spelling Book* (Boston: John West, 1810) p. vi.

The best biography of Thomas Jefferson is Dumas Malone, *Jefferson and His Times* (Boston: Little, Brown, 1948-1981, 6 vols.) Jefferson's ideas on education are collected in Gordon C. Lee, ed., *Crusade Against Ignorance: Thomas Jefferson on Education* (New York: Teachers College, Columbia U., 1962). ". . . and liberal mind": *ibid.*, p. xx. ". . . and Mary College": *ibid.*, p. xxx.

The role of education in the philosophies of various theorists is discussed by David Tyack, "Forming the National Character," *Harvard Educational Review*, 26 (1966), pp. 29-41; and Jonathan Messerli, "The Columbian Complex: The Impulse to National Consolidation," *History of Education Quarterly*, 7 (1967), pp. 417-31. For reference to original sources on educational theorists during the republican period, see Frederick Rudolph, ed., *Essays on Education in the Early Republic* (Cambridge: Harvard, 1965). Essays by Webster, Rush, Coram, and others are included. ". . . of our country", ". . . of a court": Rush, *ibid.*, pp. xxx, xxi. On the acquisition of national political symbols, see Provenzo, "Education and the Iconography of the Republic." *Teachers College Record*, Vol. 84, no. 2, Winter 1982.

Owen's educational ideas are discussed in John F. C. Harrison, *Quest for the New Moral World: Robert Owne & the Owenites in Britain and America* (New York: Scribner's, 1969), and A. I. Morton, *The Life and Ideas of Robert Owen* (New York: International, 1969). The most complete collection of Owen's ideas on education are included in Harold Silver's *English Education and the Radicals, 1780-1850* (London: Routledge & Kegan Paul, 1978). ". . . forces of nature": reprinted in Cohen, vol. 2, p. 823. Neef's and Maclure's educational ideas are discussed in detail in Gerald Gutek, *Joseph Neff: The Americanization of Pestalozzianism* (University: U. of Alabama, 1978). ". . . ending in death": Morton, p. 127.

One of the few available accounts of the Sunday schools is Edwin Wilbur Rice, *The Sunday-School Movement (1780-1917) and the American Sunday School Union* (Philadelphia: American Sunday School Union, 1917). Our most important source for biographical information on Andrew Bell is *Dictionary of National Biography* (London: Oxford, 1959-60), Leslie Stephen and Sidney Lee, eds., Vol.

II, pp. 149-52. The best biography of Lancaster is David Salmon, *Joseph Lancaster* (London: Longmans, Green, 1904). J. F. Reigart, *The Lancastrian System of Instruction in the Schools of New York City*, Teachers College Contributions to Education No. 81 (New York: Teachers College, Columbia University, 1916) is the best detailed study of the monitorial system in the United States. Most recently, Carl F. Kaestle, *Joseph Lancaster and the Monitorial School Movement: A Documentary History* (New York: Teachers College, Columbia University, 1973) is valuable for its documents and for its introductory essay. John M. Griscom, a monitorial school enthusiast who probably deserves more attention than he gets, wrote an auto-biography, *Memoirs. . .* (New York: Carter, 1859). ". . . of comfortable fortune" is quoted in Robert H. Potter, *The Stream of American Education* (New York: American, 1967), pp. 143-44. ". . . of his punishment" is from Nathan Hedges, "New Jersey Educational Biography," *American Journal of Education*, XVI (1866), p. 738.

The least unsatisfactory history of American schoolbooks is probably Charles Carpenter, *History of American Schoolbooks* (Philadelphia: U of Pennsylvania, 1963). Ruth Miller Elson, *Guardians of Tradition: American Schoolbooks in the Nineteenth Century*, (Omaha: U. Nebraska, 1964) struck us as simplistic. ". . . are they called?": Noah Webster, *American Spelling Book* (Concord, N.H.: Jacob Perkins, 1817), p. 56. ". . . more severe manner": *ibid.*, p. 52. ". . . virtue and morality": *Columbian Reader* (Cooperstown, N.Y.: H. & E. Phinney, 1815), p. 3. ". . . thy splendors unfold": Caleb Bingham, *American Reader* (Boston: Manning & Loring, 1799), p. 43. ". . . to his worth"is from *American Biographical and Historical Dictionary*, quoted in Asa Lyman, *American Reader* (Portland, Me.: Author, 1811), p. 65. ". . . name of Americans": Jedidiah Morse, *Geography Made Easy. . .* (Boston: Thomas and Andrews, 1798), p. 97. ". . . years and upwards" and ". . . people in Charleston": Jedidiah Morse, *Universal American Geography* (Charles-town, Mass.: Lincoln & Edmands, etc., 1819), vol. 1, pp. 285, 473. ". . . the latter severe": Josiah Quincy, *American Journal of Education*, XIII (1863), p. 740.

Miss Pierce's Academy is documented at length in Emily Noyes Vanderpol, *Chronicles of a Pioneer School* (Cambridge: University Press, 1903) and in her sub-sequent books. ". . . constituted the whole furniture" is by Catherine Beecher, quoted in Vanderpol, p. 79. ". . . in the Scriptures?" and ". . . of immortal beings" *ibid.*, pp. 230-31, 305, 318. ". . . youth was passed": S. H. Dickinson, *Addresses Delivered Before the New England Society in Charleston, S. C.* (Charleston, S.C.: Russell, 1855) quoted in John Hope Franklin, *A Southern Odyssey* (Baton Rouge, La.: State, 1976), pp. 70-71.

CHAPTER FOUR:
THE RISE OF THE COMMON SCHOOLS

Lawrence A. Cremin, *The American Common School, an Historic Conception* (New York: Teachers College, Columbia University, 1951) together with his more recent *American Education: The National Experience, 1783-1876* (New York: Harper & Row, 1980) provide an excellent overview of the Common School Move-ment and its history. Also useful is Frederick M. Binder's *The Age of the Common School, 1830-65* (New York: Wiley, 1974). Excellent primary sources are included in Rush Welter, ed., *American Writings on Popular Education: The Nineteenth Century* (Indianapolis: Bobbs-Merrill, 1971).

The relationship of economic development and the growth of the Common Schools is discussed at length in a number of studies. An interesting pioneer work is Frank Carlton's *Economic Influences upon Educational Progress in the United*

States, 1820-1850. First published in 1908, it was reissued in the "Classics in Education" Series (New York: Teachers College, Columbia U., 1965). Jay M. Pawa, "Workingmen and Free Schools in the Nineteenth Century: A Comment on the Labor Education Thesis," *History of Education Quarterly,* 11 (1971), pp. 287-302, specifically challenges Carlton's argument that labor played a significant role in the establishment of the common schools. Michael B. Katz's *The Irony of Early School Reform: Educational Innovation in Mid-Nineteenth Century Massachusetts* (Cambridge: Harvard, 1968), a key work in the revisionist movement in educational history, argues that the reform movement in Massachusetts was largely supported by—and for the benefit of—the middle class rather than labor. ". . . a reluctant community": *ibid.,* p. 218.

Recent studies of the connection between education and economic expansion include Maris Vinovskis's "Horace Mann on the Economic Productivity of Education," *New England Quarterly,* XLIII (1970), pp. 550-71. Data on the number of individuals attending the Common Schools is provided by Albert Fishlow, "The American Common School Revival: Fact or Fancy?" in Henry Rosovsky, ed., *Industrialization in Two Systems* (New York: Wiley, 1966), and Maris Vinovskis, "Trends in Massachusetts Education, 1826-1860," *History of Education Quarterly,* XII, (1972), pp. 501-30.

Arguments against the Common Schools Movement as a force promoting greater equality in American culture can be found in Samuel Bowles and Herbert Gintis, *Schooling in Capitalist America* (New York: Colophon Books, 1976). In particular see pages 23-29 and 164-79.

The history of the United States Office of Education is described in Donald R. Warren's *To Enforce Education* (Detroit: Wayne State, 1974). ". . . republic's first days": *ibid.,* p. 20.

The differences in role expectations for teachers and masters follows the logic of Peter L. Berger and Thomas Luckman, *The Social Construction of Reality* (Garden City, N.Y.: Doubleday, 1967) ". . . in this respect": quoted in Willard S Elsbree, *The American Teacher* (New York: American, 1939), p. 300.

William Manning's "The Key to Libberty," ed. by Samuel Eliot Morison, first appeared in print in *William and Mary Quarterly,* 3rd ser., XIII (1956), pp. 202-54. It has been reprinted in part several times. ". . . lucrative as possible": *ibid.,* p. 218. ". . . to hold plow": *ibid.,* p. 232.

Our discussion of the American child draws heavily on Bernard Wishy's *The Child and the Republic* (Philadelphia: University of Pennsylvania, 1972), and Robert Sunled's "Early Nineteenth-Century American Literature on Child Rearing," in Margaret Mead and Martha Wolfenstein, eds., *Childhood in Contemporary Cultures* (Chicago: University of Chicago, 1955), pp. 150-67. English views of American childhood are interestingly summarized in Richard L. Rapson's "The American Child as Seen by British Travelers, 1845-1935," *American Quarterly,* XVII (1965), pp. 520-34. The classic analysis of American society during this period by a European visitor is found in Alexis de Tocqueville's *Democracy in America* (1835), trans. Henry Reeve, ed. Phillips Bradley, (New York: Knopf, 1945, 2 vols.). Selections from de Tocqueville and Lydia Maria Child's *The Mother's Book* (1835), and Harriet Martineau's work *Society in* America (1837) are included in Robert H. Bremer *et al., Children & Youth in America: A Documentary History,* Vol. 1, 1600-1865. ". . . incontestable superiority warrents": *Democracy in America* (1835), reprinted in Bremer *et al., Children & Youth in America,* Vol. 1, p. 347. ". . . boy's resolute disobedience": *A Diary in America* (1839), quoted by Bremer *et al., Children & Youth in America,* Vol. 1, p. 344. A useful general bibliography on psychohistory that encompasses the history of childhood can be found in Faye Sinofsky *et al.,* "A Bibliography of Psychohistory," *History of Childhood*

Quarterly, 2, (1975), pp. 517-62. "... the sexual instinct": W. Dewees, *A Treatise on the Physical and Medical Treatment of Children* (Philadelphia: Carey and Lea, 1826), p. 251. "... the only good": Lydia Maria Child, *The Mother's Book* (1831), reprinted in Bremer *et al.*, *Children & Youth in America*, Vol. 1, p. 353. There are a number of interesting fictional and eyewitness accounts of district schools during the middle of the nineteenth century.

The South's failure to promote common schools prior to the Civil War is discussed by Irving Gershenberg, "Southern Values and Public Education," *History of Education Quarterly*, X, (1970). James G. Carter's *Essays Upon Popular Education* (Boston: Bowles and Dearborn, 1826; repr. Arno Press, 1970). "... become Anglo-Americans": *Transactions of the Fifth Meeting of the Western Literary Institute and College of Professional Teachers* (1836), reprinted in Cohen, *Education in the United States*, Vol. 2, p. 994.

Discussion of the workingman's movement in education is included in Rush Welter, *Popular Education and Democratic Thought in America* (New York: Columbia U., 1962). Sections from *The Working Man's Manual* (1831) are reprinted in Cohen, *Education in the United States*, Vol. 2, pp. 1054-56. "... part of government": *ibid.*, p. 1055.

The most convenient introduction to Horace Mann and his work is Lawrence A. Cremin, ed., *The Republic and the School: Horace Mann and the Education of Free Men* (New York: Teachers College, Columbia University, 1951). Additional selections of Mann's writings are included in Louis Filler, ed., *Horace Mann on the Crisis in Education* (Antioch, Ohio: Antioch, 1965). For our interpretation of Mann's life and work we have depended upon the excellent introductory essay by Lawrence Cremin included in *The Republic and the School*, and more specifically on Johnathan Messerli's *Horace Mann: A Biography* (New York: Knopf, 1972). "... of amassing property": *Fifth Annual Report* (1842), quoted by Bowles and Gintis, *Schooling in Capitalist America*, p. 164. "... distinctions in society": *Twelfth Annual Report* (1848), reprinted in Cremin, *The Republic and the School*, p. 87. "... and resistlessly onward": *ibid.*, p. 9.

Our discussion of the importance of phrenology to Horace Mann is based upon Cremin's discussion of the subject in the introduction to *The Republic and the School* and more specifically on John D. Davies, *Phrenology: Fad and Science* (New Haven: Yale, 1955). Also of interest, see Allen S. Horlick, "Phrenology and the Social Education of Young Men," *History of Education Quarterly*, XI (1971), pp. 23-38. "... affection is prone": *Seventh Annual Report* (1844), reprinted in Cohen, vol. 2, pp. 1091-92. "... fact and form": "Address, August 19, 1846," reprinted in Cohen, vol. 3, p. 1335. "... from grown men": *Ninth Annual Report* (1845), reprinted in Cremin, ed., *The Republic and the School: Horace Mann on the Education of Free Men*, p. 58. "... of the state": *Twelfth Annual Report* (1848), *ibid.*, p. 80.

A modern biography of Henry Barnard needs to be written. Early works on Barnard include Will S. Monroe, *The Educational Labors of Henry Barnard* (Syracuse: C. W. Bardeen, 1893); and Bernard C. Steiner, *Life of Henry Barnard* (Washington, D.C.: Department of the Interior, Bureau of Education, Bulletin No. 8, 1919). For our interpretation of Barnard we have depended upon the documents and introductory essay in Vincent P. Lannie's *Henry Barnard: American Educator* (New York: Teachers College, Columbia U., 1974). Also of use was the chapter on Barnard in Merle Curti, *The Social Ideas of American Educators* (New York: Scribner's, 1935). Most major libraries have bound or microfilm versions of Barnard's *American Journal of Education*. Among the richest sources on the history of American education, Barnard's journal is well worth careful perusal. A reprint of Barnard's *School Architecture* edited by Jean and Robert McClintock is available in the "Classics in Education" series (New York: Teachers College, Columbia U., 1970). "... their own grounds": *Connecticut Common School Journal* (August 1839), quoted by Rush Welter, *American Writings on Popular Education*, p. 70.

One biographical sketch of Partridge is Edward J. Durnall, "Alden P. Partridge," in John F. Ohles, ed. *Biographical Dictionary of American Educators* (Westport, Conn.: Greenwood, 1978), vol. ii, pp. 997-99. There is a record of a post-West Point march enjoyed by all in Alden Partridge, *A Record of a Journey Made by the Corps of Cadets of the American Literary, Scientific, and Military Academy... June 6, 1822* (Concord [N.H.?]: Hill & Morley, 1822). Henry L. Burr, *Education in the Early Navy* (Philadelphia: n.p., 1939) leaves much to be desired. The voyage of the *U. S. F. Potomac* is described in R. N. Reynolds, *Voyage...* (New York: Harper & Brothers, 1835).

There is considerable material on Ticknor, Bancroft and Cogswell, and Round Hill. Our source is James McLachlan, *American Boarding Schools: A Historical Study* (New York: Scribner's, 1970), pp. 71-101. Bruce Catton, *Waiting for the Morning Train: An American Boyhood* (Garden City, N.Y.: Doubleday, 1972) is strongly evocative.

Harriet Webster Marr, *The Old New England Academies* (New York: Comet, 1959) supplied information on Gardiner Academy and on Grant's former students. Orange Park is from a brief account in Arthur O. White, *One Hundred Years of State Leadership in Florida Public-Education* (Tallahassee: U. Florida, 1979), pp. 29-30. Coleman's log cabin academy appears in William Gordon McCabe, *Virginia Schools Before and After the Revolution...* (Charlottesville, Va.: Chronical Steam [sic], 1890). Fairfield Academy appears in an unpublished paper by Celia Erlich, "The Education of Asa Gray," SUNYAB. Enrollment figures are from Edgar W. Knight, *The Academy Movement in the South* (no publication data available) and Walter John Gifford, *Historical Development of the New York State High School System* (Albany: Lyon, 1922).

CHAPTER FIVE:
THE GROWTH OF THE COMMON SCHOOLS

For general histories of high schools, see Edward A. Krug, *The Shaping of the American High School 1880-1920* (New York: Harper & Row, 1964) and *The Shaping of the American High School 1920-1941* (Madison: University of Wisconsin, 1972); Krug's views were unfailingly positive. Elmer Ellsworth Brown, *Making of Our Middle Schools* (New York: Longmans, Green, 1902 and later editions) is still useful.

"... tuition and taxes": David Nassau, *Schooled to Order* (New York: Oxford, 1979), p. 83.

Most of the details concerning the Chicago public schools are from Mary J. Herrick, *The Chicago Schools: A Social and Political History* (Beverly Hills, Cal.: Sage, 1971). Chappell's teaching was briefly recounted in Mary H. Porter, *Eliza Chappell Porter: A Memoir* (Chicago: Revell, 1892). Joan K. Smith, *Ella Flagg Young: Portrait of a Leader* (Ames, Ia.: Educational Studies, 1979) is an account of Young's career. Information on the Buffalo schools is primarily from John G. Ramsay, a dissertation in progress, State U. of N. Y. at Buffalo. Jack K. Campbell, *Colonel Francis W. Parker, the Children's Crusader* (New York: Teachers College, Columbia U., 1967) is the best source of information on Parker.

There is an almost embarrassing mass of material on *McGuffey's* (or *McGuffey*; both spellings were used), either saccharine sweet or acerbic. The best source is Stanley W. Lindberg, *The Annotated McGuffey: Selections...* (New York: Van Nostrand Reinhold, 1976).

"... overseer, the superintendent": J. L. Pickard, *School Supervision* (New York: Appleton, 1890), pp. 1-2. "...and the poor": John Griscom, *A Year in Europe ... In 1818 and 1819* (New York: Collins, 1823), quoted in McLachlin, p. 58. McLachlin, *passim*, provided information about von Fellenberg's poor school. The American "manual academies" are described in Knight, *Academy Movement*; the Hawaiian ones, *passim*, in Hiram Bingham, *A Residence of Twenty-one Years in the Sandwich Islands* (Hartford, Conn.: Hezekiah Huntington, 1848). Goodale's "industrial school" for the Sioux was described by her in *Sister to the Sioux: The Memoirs of Elaine Goodale Eastman, 1885-91*, ed. by Kay Graber (Lincoln: U. Nebraska, 1978), pp. 30 ff.

The most nearly complete history of Catholic education in the United States is Harold A. Buetow, *Of Singular Benefit: The Story of U. S. Catholic Education* (New York: Macmillan, 1970). An excellent documentary source is Neil G. McCluskey, ed., *Catholic Education in America* (New York: Teachers College, Columbia U., 1964). "... the social order": "Report of the First Plenary Council of Baltimore," reprinted in Cohen, *Education in the United States,* Vol. 2, p. 1162.

The best source on Nativism and one of which we have made extensive use is Roy Allen Billington, *The Protestant Crusade, 1800-1860* (New York: Macmillan, 1938). A discussion of anti-Catholic sentiments in textbooks can be found in Marie Lenore Fell, *The Foundations of Nativism in American Textbooks* (Washington, D. C.: Catholic University of America, 1941).

The work of Bishop Hughes in New York is discussed in both Billington's *The Protestant Crusade* and in Diane Ravitch, *The Great School Wars* (New York: Basic Books, 1974) pp. 46-76. "... us with error": McCluskey, *Catholic Education in America*, p. 61. For background on the Protestant response to the Catholics' demands for school support in New York City, see Provenzo, "Thomas Nast and the Church/State Controversy in Education (1870-1876)," *Educational Studies,* Vol. 12, no. 4, Winter 1981-1982, pp. 359-379.

CHAPTER SIX:
COLONIALISM AND SCHOOLING

The concept of colonialism in education comes from Gail P. Kelly, "The Relation Between Colonial and Metropolitan Schools: A Structural Analysis," *Comparative Education*, 15 (1979), pp. 209-15. The best general introductions to education and colonialism are Philip G. Altbach and Gail P. Kelly, eds., *Education and Colonialism* (New York: Longman, 1978) and Martin Carnoy, *Education as Cultural Imperialism* (New York: D. McKay, 1974).

The standard but badly dated source of history of women's education in the United States is Thomas Woody, *A History of Women's Education in the United States*, 2 vols. (1929, repr. New York: Octagon, 1966). A new comprehensive history is long overdue. More general works on the women's movement are Ann Scott, *The American Woman* (Englewood Cliffs, N.J.: Prentice-Hall, 1971) and Nancy Cott, *Roots of Bitterness* (New York: Dutton, 1972). "... was by chance": John Ellis, ed., *The Works of Anne Bradstreet* (New York: Peter Smith, 1932), p. 101. A useful biography of Wollstonecraft is Emily Sunstein, *A Different Face: The Life of Mary Wollstonecraft* (New York: Harper & Row, 1975). "... fails to please": *An American Selection* (1804), reprinted in Cohen, vol. 3, p. 1572.

The best biography of Zilpah P. Grant (Bannister) is still Linda Thayer Guilford, *Use of a Life. Memorials* (New York: American Tract Society, 1885).

For background and documents on Mary Lyon and Emma Willard, see Willystine Goodsell, *Pioneers of Women's Education in the United States* (New York: McGraw-Hill, 1931).

A general perspective on the women's education movement is included in Jill Conway's "Perspectives on the History of Women's Education in the United States," *History of Education Quarterly*, XIV (1974), pp. 1-12. ". . . most excellent form": "An Address to the Public; Particularly to the Members of the State Legislature of New York, Proposing a Plan for Improving Female Education," (1819), reprinted in Cohen, *Education in the United States*, Vol. 3, p. 1575. ". . . do it cheaper": *ibid.*, p. 1580. ". . . tastes, and capabilities": Inaugural Address of President Charles W. Eliot (1869), reprinted in Cohen, *ibid.*, p. 1595.

Our analysis of black education has depended heavily on Henry Allen Bullock's *A History of Negro Education in the South: From 1619 to the Present* (Cambridge: Harvard, 1967). ". . . than twelve months": *A New Digest of the Statute Laws of Louisiana* (1844), reprinted in Cohen, *ibid.*, p. 1621.

Crandall's school in Canterbury has been a matter of intense and lasting interest. She has been portrayed as near-martyr and as agent provocateur. Our discussion is based on Leon Litwak, *North of Slavery: The Negro in the Free States, 1790-1860* (Chicago: U. Chicago, 1961).

For background on the history of Hampton Institute, see Francis Peabody, *Education for Life* (New York: Doubleday, 1904). Photographs of Hampton taken in 1900 for the Paris International Exposition were republished in Frances Benjamin Johnston, *The Hampton Album* (New York: Doubleday, 1966).

White Northern teachers in the South after the Civil War have received much attention, and the others little. One might suspect chauvinism; too, the Northern teachers, perhaps particularly the ones on Sea Islands, were prolific letter writers, which provided materials for historians. J. W. Alvard's semiannual reports, *Schools and Finances of Freedmen* (Washington, D.C.: Government Printing Office, 1868-70), reprinted as *Freedmen's Schools and Textbooks*, Vol. I (New York: AMS, 1980), Robert C. Morris, ed., show that more Blacks than Whites taught in Freedmen's schools, and that some White teachers were Southerners. Booker T. Washington's first schooling and first teaching is from Louis R. Harlan, *Booker T. Washington, The Making of a Black Leader, 1856-1901* (New York: Oxford, 1972), passim. ". . . of the Freedmen": "The Founding of the Hampton Institute," (1904), reprinted in Cohen, *Education in the United States*, Vol. 3, p. 1653. ". . . men and women": "Tuskegee and Its People," reprinted in Cohen, *ibid.*, p. 1674. Both Harlan's biography and Louis R. Harlan and Raymond W. Smock, eds., *The Booker T. Washington Papers* (Urbana: U. Illinois, 1972) demonstrate the complexities of Washington as an individual and his political talent.

The main biographies of W. E. B. DuBois include Francis Broderick, *W. E. B. DuBois, Negro Leader in a Time of Crisis* (Stanford: Stanford University Press, 1959); Alexander Lacy, *Cheer for Lonesome Traveler: The Life of W. E. B. DuBois* (New York: Dial Press, 1970); and Arnold Rampersad, *The Art and Imagination of W. E. B. DuBois* (Cambridge: Harvard, 1976). A general selection of his work is found in Meyer Weinberg, ed., *W. E. B. DuBois: A Reader* (New York: Harper & Row, 1970).

A collective noun for "Indians" is vexing. "Indians" is a misnomer, of course. But how could one have been a "Native American" before the invention of America, and "native" only in the sense that one's ancestors were the most remote immigrants? George Pierre Castile, in *North American Indians: An Introduction to the Chichimeca* (New York: McGraw-Hill, 1979), uses "Chichimeca," but a word used by the Aztecs is not an ideal solution. Castile's book is a readable and informative one.

General sources dealing with the history of Indian education include Estelle Fuchs and Robert J. Havinghurst, *To Live on This Earth: American Indian Education* (Garden City, N. Y.: Doubleday, 1972) and Margaret Szasz, *Education and the American Indian: The Road to Self-Determination, 1928-1973* (Albuquerque: University of New Mexico, 1974). Katherine Iverson develops an analysis of Indian education in a colonial context in her article, "Civilization and Assimilation in the Colonized Schooling of Native Americans" included in Altbach and Kelly, *Education and Colonialism*, pp. 149-75. ". . . model of colonialism": *ibid.*, p. 151. Also see Provenzo and Gary M. McCloskey, "Catholic and Federal Indian Education in the 19th Century: Opposed Colonial Models," *Journal of American Indian Education*, Vol. 21, no. 1, November 1981, pp. 10-18.

Background on Pratt and the Carlisle Indian Barracks School is provided in Richard Pratt, *Battlefield and Classroom: Four Decades with the American Indian 1867-1904* (New Haven: Yale, 1964). ". . . on their hearts": *ibid.*, p. 163.

CHAPTER SEVEN:
SCHOOLING AND INDUSTRIALIZATION

The importance and something of the spirit of the Centennial for Americans is well described by Dee Brown in *The Year of the Century* (New York: Scribner's, 1976). An interesting pictorial treatment of the same subject is Lally Weymouth's *America in 1876: The Way We Were* (New York: Vintage Books, 1976). Our discussion of Buisson is drawn from M. Ferdinand Buisson, *Rapport Sur l'instruction primaire à l'exposition univierselle de Philadelphia en 1876* (Paris: Imprimiree Nationale, 1878). Sections of this report were translated and reprinted as "American Education as Described by the French Commissioner to the International Exposition of 1876," *Circular of Information #5–1879, Bureau of Education* (Washington, D.C.: Government Printing Office, 1879). ". . . returned a hundredfold": *ibid.*, pp. 12-13.

Our discussion of the Land Grant College Act is largely based upon Frederick Rudolph's *The American College and University: A History* (New York: Vintage Books, 1962). Other secondary sources on the Land Grant College Act include Edward D. Eddy's *Colleges for Our Land and Time: The Land Grant Idea in American Education* (New York: Harper & Row, 1957), and John H. Florer, "Major Issues in the Congressional Debate of the Morrill Act of 1863," *History of Education Quarterly*, 8, (1968), pp. 459-78.

The history of early art instruction and its relationship to industrialization needs to be more carefully examined. Our source for the subject is I. Edwards Clarke, *Industrial and High Art Education in the United States, Part I, Drawing in the Public Schools* (Washington, D.C.: Government Printing Office, 1885). ". . . from such accomplishments": *ibid.*, p. 49.

Background on early industrial education in the United States is included in Bernice Fisher's *Industrial Education: American Ideals and Institutions* (Madison, Wis.: U. Wisconsin, 1967), and Charles A. Bennett's *History of Manual and Industrial Education up to 1870* (Peoria, Ill.: Manual Arts Press, 1926). Lawrence A. Cremin's *The Transformation of the Schools: Progressivism in American Education, 1876-1957* (New York: Vintage, 1961) provides an excellent introduction to manual training and vocational training during the last quarter of the nineteenth century.

Our discussion of the Della Vos method and Calvin Woodward is based upon several sources. Historical background and documents are included in Charles A. Bennett's *History of Manual and Industrial Education, 1870 to 1917* (Peoria, Ill.: Manual Arts Press, 1937). ". . . trade became apparent": *ibid.*, p. 320. Background on Calvin Woodward and the Manual Training School is included in Charles Dye's "Calvin Woodward and Manual Training: The Man, The Idea and the School, *The Bulletin* (Missouri Historical Society), XXXII, (1976), pp. 75-98. Of particular interest as a source is Calvin M. Woodward's *The Manual Training School* (New York: Arno, 1969, reprint of 1887 edition). A useful documentary collection is Marvin Larzerson and Norton Grubb's *American Education and Vocationalism: A Documentary History* (New York: Teachers College, Columbia U., 1974). "... a new tool": *The Manual Training School* (1887), reprinted in Cohen, *Education in the United States*, Vol. 3, p. 1865. "... of intellectual improvement": "Manual vs. Technical Training," reprinted in Cohen, *ibid.*, p. 1871.

William Torrey Harris is briefly discussed by Cremin in *The Transformation of the Schools*. A general biography of Harris, which needs to be revised, is Kurt F. Leidecker's, *Yankee Teacher: The Life of William Torrey Harris* (New York: Philosophical Library, 1946).

Lazerson's ideas concerning Manual Training are discussed in *Origins of the Urban School: Public Education in Massachusetts, 1870-1915* (Cambridge: Harvard, 1971). For background on the conditions of child labor and juvenile reform see Joseph M. Hawes, *Children in Urban Society: Juvenile Delinquency in Nineteenth-Century America* (New York: Oxford, 1971), and Walter Trattner, *Crusade for the Children* (Chicago: Quadrangle Books, 1970). The history of the New York Association for Improving the Condition of the Poor can be found in Roy Lubove's *The Progressives and the Slums* (Pittsburgh: U. of Pittsburgh, 1962). "... so at home": *A New England Girlhood* (1889), reprinted in Bremer, *et al.*, *Children & Youth in America*, Vol. I, p. 604. "... low-respecting community": *The Dangerous Classes of New York* (1880), reprinted in Bremer, *et al.*, *ibid.*, p. 742. "... afterwards to fill": Enoch C. Wines and Theodore W. Dwight, "Report on the Prisons and Reformatories in the United States and Canada," (1867). Reprinted in Bremer, *ibid.*, p. 752.

Durkheim's writings on education have been republished in recent years. See *Durkheim, Emile, Education and Sociology*, translated and with an introduction by Sherwood P. Fox (Glencoe, Ill.: Free Press, 1956).

The most complete treatment of the Lyceum Movement in America is found in Carl Bode, *The American Lyceum: Town Meeting of the Mind* (New York: Oxford, 1956).

Our interpretation of the history of libraries is drawn from the United States Bureau of Education's *Public Libraries in the United States* (Washington, D.C.: U.S. Government Printing Office, 1876), and Dee Carrison's *Apostles of Culture* (New York: Free Press, 1979). "... of public education": United States Bureau of Education, *Public Libraries in the United States*, p. xi. "... to something better": *ibid.*, p. 410. For the early history of libraries in the United States also see Jesse H. Shera, *Foundation of the Public Library: The Origins of the Public Library Movement in New England, 1629-1855* (Chicago: U. Chicago, 1949), and Seymour C. Thompson, *Evolution of the American Public Library, 1653-1876* (Metuchen, N.J.: Scarecrow, 1952).

Several general histories have been helpful in our interpretation of the kindergarten movement in America, including Evelyn Weber's *The Kindergarten: Its Encounter with Educational Thought in America* (New York: Teachers College, Columbia U., 1969) and Elizabeth Dale Ross, *The Kindergarten Crusade: The Establishment of Preschool Education in the United States* (Athens, Ohio: Ohio University, 1976). The kindergarten movement and its relationship to industrialization is dealt with most thoroughly by Marvin Lazerson, *Origins of the Urban School: Public Education in Massachusetts, 1870-1915* (Cambridge: Harvard, 1971), and Marvin Lazerson, "Urban Reform and the Schools: Kindergartens in

Massachusetts, 1870-1915," *History of Education Quarterly*, Vol. II (1971), pp. 115-42, and by Dominick Cavallo, "Kindergarten Pedagogy: A Review Essay," *History of Education Quarterly*, XVIII (1978), 365-68. ". . . use to create": Frank Lloyd Wright, *An Autobiography* (New York: Duell, Sloan and Pearce, 1943), p. 14. ". . . wanted to design": Frank Lloyd Wright, *A Testament* (New York: Brahmall House, 1957), p. 20. The impact of the Froebelian materials on Frank Lloyd Wright's work as an architect is discussed by Grant Carpenter Menson, *Frank Lloyd Wright to 1910* (New York: Reinhold, 1958), pp. 5-10. ". . . our Public schools": Letter to Susan Blow to William Torrey Harris, Manuscript Collection, Missouri Historical Society. ". . . as domestic markets": *Twenty First Annual Report, St. Louis Public Schools, 1876* (St. Louis, 1877), p. 11. ". . . place of society": *ibid.*, p. 81. ". . . citizens of them": "The Kindergarten: An Uplifting Social Influence in the Home and District," *NEA Proceedings* (1903), reprinted in Cohen, *Education in the United States*, Vol. 4, p. 2160.

PART THREE:
FROM FARM TO CITY

Readings: The most respected foreign commentator on the United States in the later 1800s was James Lord Bryce. In *The American Commonwealth* (2 vol., New York: Macmillan, 1888. Abridged ed., New York: Putnam, 1959) he condemned American politics and politicians, admired some other aspects of American life. A short but insightful treatment of urbanization is Blake McKelvey's *The City in American History* (New York: Barnes & Noble, 1969). There are informative histories of many individual cities. Frederick Lewis Allen, *Only Yesterday* (New York: Harpers, 1931) catches effectively the surface details of life in the 1920s. Seller, *To Seek America*, pp. 104-219, describes the immigrants of the time and their institutions. Morison *et al.*, Vol. 2, pp. 3-470, provides a general history narrative.

Concerning schooling, the best detailed narrative is Lawrence A. Cremin, *The Transformaton of the School* (New York: Knopf, 1957. Vintage, 1964). Written before *American Education*, it is a school-bound history of educational Progressivism broadly defined. The most important and most interesting monograph on the period is Raymond E. Callahan, *Education and the Cult of Efficiency* (Chicago: U. of Chicago, 1962). In other texts, see Church and Sedlak, *Education in the United States*, pp. 251-397; and David Tyack, *The One Best System*, pp. 126-268.

As one deals with the more recent past, writing historical accounts becomes more like constructing a mosaic, of fitting together disparate monographs, and disparate ways of life. There are many interesting details in Mark Sullivan's rambling *Our Times*, 6 vols. (New York: Scribner's, 1926-35). A few other details come from Furnas, *The Americans*. Ray Ginger, *Age of Excess: United States from 1877 to 1914* (New York: Macmillan, 1965) suggests a general view. Kirkland, *A History of American Economic Life*, provided information on economic change and growth. Ray Ginger, *Six Days or Forever?* (repr. Chicago: Quadrangle, 1969) is not only a vivid account of the Scopes "monkey" trial, but provides a background in the importance of Darwinism in early twentieth century thought. The conventional view of social Darwinism in the thought of American capitalists has, we hope, been finally quashed by Robert C. Bannister, *Social Darwinism: Science and Myth in Anglo-American Social Thought* (Philadelphia: Temple, 1979). Daniel J. Kevles, *The Physicists: The History of a Scientific Community in Modern America* (New York: Knopf, 1978) is in most ways exemplary, and a valuable guide in the development of science.

The material on Buffalo Polonia is from unpublished papers by Thomas Michalski, U. of Nevada-Reno. ". . . $1.50 a week": Seller, *To Seek America*, p. 120.

CHAPTER EIGHT:
PROGRESSIVE REFORM

Turner's work is available in a modern edition. See Frederick Jackson Turner, *The Frontier in American History* (New York: Henry Holt and Company, 1950). The idea of the West as an agrarian utopia is most clearly presented in Henry Nash Smith's *Virgin Land: The American West as Symbol and Myth* (Cambridge: Harvard, 1975).

Lawrence A. Cremin's *The Transformation of the School: Progressivism in American Education, 1876-1957* has been an invaluable source of our interpretation of American education during the late nineteenth and early twentieth centuries. Social Darwinism is discussed in a number of sources. Richard Hofstader's *Social Darwinism in American Thought* (Philadelphia: U. of Pennsylvania, 1945) has come under increasing criticism in recent years. Our interpretation has drawn heavily from Robert C. Bannister, *Social Darwinism*.

The myth of the "self-made man" is discussed in Irvin G. Wyley *The Self-Made Man in America* (New Brunswick, N.J.: Rutgers, 1954) and John G. Cawelti's *Apostle of the Self-Made Man* (Chicago: U. of Chicago, 1965). Background on Lester F. Ward and William Graham Sumner can be found in Clifford H. Scott, *Lester Frank Ward* (Boston: Twayne Publishers, 1976), and Robert G. McGloskey, *American Conservatism in the Age of Enterprise; a Study of William Graham Sumner, Stephen J. Field, and Andrew Carnegie* (Cambridge: Harvard, 1951).

Our discussion of the Settlement House Movement in the United States is based upon Cremin's *Transformation of the Schools* and Allen F. Davis's *Spearheads for Reform: The Social Settlements and the Progressive Movement, 1890-1914* (New York: Oxford, 1967). ". . . last analysis education": Cremin, *Transformation of the Schools*, p. 59.

For background on the origins of Jane Addams's idea as a reformer see Franklin Parker's "Jane Addams–Lady Who Cared," *Tradition*, 4 (1961), pp. 43-47. Also see John P. Rousmanière, "Cultural Hybrid in the Slums: The College Woman and the Settlement House, 1889-94," *American Quarterly*, 22, (1970), pp. 45-66. Biographical sources on Addams include Allen Freeman Davis's *American Heroine: The Life and Legend of Jane Addams* (New York: Oxford, 1973). Christopher Lasch's *The New Radicalism in America (1889-1963): The Intellectual As A Social Type* (New York: Vintage Books, 1965), combined with his anthology *The Social Thought of Jane Addams* (Indianapolis: Bobbs-Merrill, 1965) are an excellent introduction to Addams and her ideas. A critical and controversial interpretation of Addams is Paul Violas's "Jane Addams and the New Liberalism," in Clarence Karier *et al., Roots of Crisis* (Chicago: Rand McNally, 1973), pp. 66-83.

Our interpretation of Jacob Riis is based upon Alexander Alland's *Jacob A. Riis: Photographer and Citizen* (New York: Aperture, 1974) and James B. Lane's *Jacob A. Riis and the American City* (New York: Kennikat Press, 1974). Several reprints of Riis's work are particularly useful. See, for example, Jacob A. Riis *The Making of an American* (New York: Macmillan, 1970), edited by Jacob Riis Owre and Jacob Riis, *How the Other Half Lives* (Repr. New York: Dover Books, 1971). A limited but useful discussion of Riis is included in Sol Cohen's *Progressives and*

Urban Reform (New York: Teachers College, Columbia U., 1964). ". . . do not come": Jacob Riis, "The Making of Thieves in New York," *The Century*, Vol. XLIX (November 1894), pp. 115-16. ". . . one educational thought": Jacob. A. Riis, *The Peril and Preservation of the Home* (Philadelphia: George W. Jacobs and Co., 1903), p. 77.

Our interpretation of Rice is drawn in part from Cremin, *The Transformation of the School*. ". . . sensibilities, no soul": *The Public School System in the United States*, reprinted in Cohen, *Education in the United States*, Vol. 3, p. 1893.

Our interpretation of the work of the Committee of Ten is based upon Krug's *The Shaping of the American High School: 1880-1920*. The interpretation of the Committee of Fifteen is primarily that of Button, "Committee of Fifteen," *History of Education Quarterly*, V (1965), pp. 253-63. The Herbartian Movement in Europe and America is most thoroughly dealt with in Harold Dunekill, *Herbart and Education* (New York: Random House, 1969) and *Herbart and Herbartianism: An Educational Ghost Story* (Chicago: U. Chicago, 1970).

The foremost biography of G. Stanley Hall is Dorothy Ross's, *G. Stanley Hall: The Psychologist as Prophet* (Chicago: U. Chicago, 1972). Selections of Hall's work appear in Charles E. Strickland and Charles Burgess, eds., *Health, Growth, and Heredity: G. Stanley Hall on Natural Education* (New York: Teachers College, Columbia, 1965). Hall's autobiography, *Life and Confessions of a Psychologist* (New York: Appleton, 1925) is in some ways disarmingly frank and revealing. ". . . twentieth century totalitarianism": Strickland and Burgess, *Health, Growth, and Heredity*, introduction, pp. 25-26.

The sources available on Dewey are innumerable. An excellent starting point is George Dykhuizen's biography, *The Life and Mind of John Dewey* (Carbondale, Ill.: Southern Illinois U., 1973). Dewey's collected works are being republished by Southern Illinois U. Our description of Dewey's work at the Laboratory School is based upon Arthur Wirth, *John Dewey as Educator: His Design for Work in Education (1894-1904)* (New York: John Wiley and Sons, 1966); Katherine C. Mayhew and Anna C. Edward, *The Dewey School* (New York: Appleton Century Crofts, 1936); and Provenzo, "History as Experiment: The Role of the Laboratory School in the Development of John Dewey's Philosophy of History," *The History Teacher*, XII (1979), pp. 373-81. Dewey's place in intellectual history is discussed by Morton White in *Social Thought in America: The Revolt Against Formalism* (New York: Viking, 1949). A recent critical examination of Dewey is Clarence Karier's "Liberal Ideology and the Quest for Orderly Change," in Karier, *et al.*, *Roots of Crisis*, pp. 84-107. ". . . its special line": John Dewey, "The University School," *University Record* I (November 6, 1896), p. 417. ". . . and growing experience": John Dewey, *The Child and the Curriculum and The School and Society* (Chicago: U. Chicago, 1971), p. 23.

Unfortunately there is no really good history of the museum movement in the United States. Our interpretation of the Brooklyn Children's Museum is part of ongoing research concerning the origins of children's museums in the United States. For background on the Educational Museum of the St. Louis Public Schools, see Provenzo, "The Educational Museum of the St. Louis Public Schools," *The Bulletin* (Missouri Historical Society), XXXV, (April, 1979), pp. 147-53.

For an introduction to the role of the International Expositions and American education see Provenzo, "Education and the Louisiana Purchase Exposition," *The Bulletin* (Missouri Historical Society), XXXII, (January, 1976), pp. 99-109. ". . . the elementary schools": "The Children's Museum of the Brooklyn Institute," *Scientific American*, LXXXIX (1900), p. 296. ". . . on about them": *ibid*. ". . . soap are made": C. G. Rathmann, "Report of the First Year's Work of the Educational Museum, 1905-1906," manuscript included in the historical file of the Audio-Visual Department of the St. Louis Public Schools, p. 1.

Our interpretation of the Youth Movement in the United States has drawn heavily on Selwyn Troen's essay, "The Discovery of the Adolescent by American Educational Reformers, 1900-1920: An Economic Perspective," in Laurence Stone, ed., *Schooling and Society: Studies in the History of Education* (Baltimore: Johns Hopkins U., 1976), and Joel Spring's "Youth Culture in the United States," in Clarence Karier *et al., Roots of Crisis*. Spring's ideas on Youth Culture are also included in his book, *American Education: An Introduction to Social and Political Aspects* (New York: Longman, 1978). ". . . with its problems": *Adolescence* (1905), reprinted in Cohen, *Education in the United States*, Vol. 4, p. 2206.

Lewis Hine's background and significance as a documentary photographer is best described in Judith Mara Gutman's *Lewis Hine, Two Perspectives* (New York: Grossman Publishers, 1974). For background on National Child Labor Committee see Walter I. Trattner's *Crusade for the Children: A History of the National Child Labor Committee and Child Labor Reform in America* (Chicago: Quadrangle Books, 1970). ". . . for any child": Lewis W. Hine, "Baltimore to Biloxi and Back—The Children's Burden in Oyster and Shrimp Canneries," *The Survey*, 30 (May 3, 1913), p. 170. An analysis of Hine as a visual propagandist of education is included in Provenzo, "The Photographer as Educator: The Photo-Stories of Lewis Hine," *Teachers College Record*, Vol. 83, no. 4, Summer 1982.

CHAPTER NINE:
EFFICIENCY AND MANAGEMENT

This chapter is based on Callahan's *Cult of Efficiency*. Nearly twenty years after its publication, it is possible to add some contextual details from a new biography of Frederick Taylor, a biography of Louis Brandeis, and further historical research on production considerations and engineering history.

That centralization and standardization had begun before the school efficiency movement is stressed by Tyack, *The One Best System*, pp. 126-76. ". . . his entire service": Franklin Bobbitt, *Some General Principles of Management Applied to the Problems of City-School Systems*, Part I of the 12th Yearbook of the National Society for the Study of Education (Bloomington, Ill.: n.p., 1911), pp. 11, 79. Samuel Haber, *Efficiency and Uplift* (Chicago: U. Chicago, 1964), handles the efficiency movement generally as a rationale of social reform—by the efficiency experts. S. Chester Parker's "revisionist" view; "Free Schools and the Lancastrian System," *Elementary School Teacher*, 10 (1910), pp. 388-400.

Sudhir Kakar, *Frederick Taylor: A Study of Personality and Innovation* (Cambridge, Mass.: M.I.T., 1970) suggests that Taylor's eye strain was psychogenic. Taylor's employer at Midvale, William Sellers, had also started his career with an apprenticeship. That had not been unusual in Philadelphia, as Bruce Sinclair points out in "At the Turn of the Screw: William Sellers, the Franklin Institute, and a Standard American Thread," *Technology and Culture*, 10 (1969), p. 25. Sellers was more important for Taylor's success than previously thought.

". . . or monthly installments": Irving A. Berndt, "The Value of a Dollar's Worth of Labor," *Efficiency* (Sept., 1913), p. 13. "Schmidt" appeared in an example of Taylor's methods, in Frederick W. Taylor, *The Principles of Scientific Management* (New York: Harper & Brothers, 1913). The quoted passages appear in Callahan, pp. 37-38. Spaulding, with what strikes us as misplaced pride, wrote two autobiographical volumes: Frank E. Spaulding, *One School Administrator's*

Philosophy: Its Development (New York: Exposition, 1952) and *School Superintendent in Action in Five Cities* (Rindge, N.H.: Smith, 1955). Together, they are revealing of the man and his views. ". . . recitations in art", ". . . in something else": F. E. Spaulding, "The Applications of Principles of School Management," *NEA Proceedings*, 1913, p. 263. Information on early railroad management patterns is from Alfred D. Chandler, Jr., "The Railroads: Pioneers in Modern Corporate Management," *History of American Management* (Englewood Cliffs, N.J.: Prentice-Hall, 1969) ed. by James P. Paughman.

Most of our information on measurement in the physical sciences comes from Kevles, *The Physicists . . . passim.* ". . . business and industry": Sears, quoted in Callahan, p. 118. ". . . and field efficiency": Sara Helena Fahey, "Moral Education: What the School Can Do," *NEA Proceedings*, 1916, p. 641. ". . . as a monarch": A. W. Rankin, "Who Shall Administer Our Schools," *NEA Proceedings*, 1914, p. 915. ". . . the factory plan": W. C. Bagley, "The Status of the Classroom Teachers," *NEA Proceedings*, 1915, p. 1162. Dewey's misgivings were in "Professional Experience Among Teachers," *American Teacher*, IV (1913), pp. 115-16. Maxwell dissented in "On a Certain Arrogance in Educational Theorists," *Educational Review*, XLVII (1914), pp. 165-82.

CHAPTER TEN:
SCIENTIFIC PEDAGOGY:
TEACHERS AND CURRICULUM

There is a considerable literature on the Gary Plan. The essays of Randolph Bourne, liberal journalist, have been reprinted in *The Gary Schools* (Cambridge, Mass.: M.I.T., 1970), edited by Adeline and Murray Levine, who also supplied a helpful introduction. Some recent studies appear in Ronald D. Cohen and Raymond A. Mohl, *The Paradox of Progressive Education* (Port Washington, N.Y.: Kennikat, 1979).

For his formulation of the science of education, see Charles Hubbard Judd, *Introduction to the Scientific Study of Education* (New York: Ginn, 1918) pp. 299-307. Lawrence A. Cremin, David A. Shannon, and Mary Evelyn Townsend, *A History of Teachers College, Columbia University* is less than satisfactory. There are some additional details about the founding of Teachers College in Nicholas Murray Butler, *Across the Busy Years* (New York: Scribner's, 1939, 2 vols.) and about its early years in James Earl Russell, *Founding Teachers College* (New York: Teachers College, Columbia U., 1937).

Our impression of Galton comes from D. W. Forrest, *Francis Galton: The Life and Work of a Victorian Genius* (New York: Taplinger, 1974). Robert I. Watson, *The Great Psychologists* (Philadelphia: Lippincott, several editions) has brief sketches of the life and work of Galton, and also of Binet. ". . . she committed suicide": quoted in Guy Montrose Whipple, *Manual of Mental and Physical Tests* (Baltimore: Warwick & York, 1910), p. 508. Walter S. Monroe, *Ten Years of Educational Research*, U. of Illinois Bulletin No. 51 (Urbana: U. of Illinois, 1928) is a useful source on early educational research. ". . . Now, go ahead": quoted in Whipple, p. 500. ". . . Army and Navy": quoted in Robert M. Yerkes (ed.), *Psychological Examining in the United States Army*, Vol. XV, Memoirs of the National Academy of Science (Washington, D.C.: U. S. Government Printing Office, 1921), p. 7. Cremin's analysis of Thorndike's psychology is in *Transformation*, pp. 111-12. As part of his multivolume study of genius (that is, those with high IQ scores), Terman's colleagues estimated the IQs of famous men. George Washington as a boy had an estimated IQ of 125. Lewis B. Terman, ed., *Genetic Studies of Genius*, vol.

2 (Stanford: Stanford U., 1926), pp. 345-46. "Philoprogenitiveness," "vitative-ness," "consciententiousness," O. S. Fowler, *Self-Culture and Perfection of Charac-ter* (New York: Fowlers and Wells, 1854), *passim.* In other books Fowler assigned the faculties other names.

The Thorndike and Woodworth experiments were reported in E. L. Thorn-dike and R. S. Woodworth, "The Influence of Improvement in One Mental Func-tion Upon the Efficiency of Other Functions," *Psychological Review*, VII (1901), pp. 247-61, 384-95, 553-64. "... matter how similar" *ibid.*, p. 250. Lotus Delta Coffman's study, a doctoral dissertation, was *The Social Composition of the Teaching Population*, Teachers College, Columbia U. Contributions to Education No. 41 (New York: Teachers College, Columbia U., 1911). Beatrice Stephens Nathan, *Tales of a Teacher* (Chicago: Regnery, 1956) is one of the few recent volumes of teacher reminiscences. Francis R. Donovan, *The Schoolm'am* (New York: Stokes, 1938) provided information but did not attempt serious analysis. Willard Waller, *The Sociology of Teaching* (repr. New York: Wiley, 1967) is still seen as an important sociological work.

"... a Baptist accent": Donovan, p. 178. "... their social philosophies", "... regulation of authority", Figure 10-A, and "... comes to pass": George S. Counts, *School and Society in Chicago* (New York: Harcourt Brace, 1928), pp. 77, 79, 85. Coggin, Haley, and the Chicago Teachers Federation are a subject of William Edward Eaton, *The American Federation of Teachers, 1916-1941* (Carbon-dale, Ill.: Southern Illinois U., 1975), pp. 5 ff.

There is a brief critique of activity analysis in Cremin, *Transformation,* pp. 198-200. The *Commonwealth Teacher-Training Study* was W. W. Charters and Douglas Waples (Chicago: U. Chicago, 1929). Walter S. Monroe provides more specific information and a guarded criticism. "... and sometimes absurd" and "... ordinary good breeding": Abraham Flexner, *Universities, American, British, German* (repr. New York: Teachers College, Columbia U., 1967), pp. 97, 104. "... is concerned with": Bobbitt, quoted in Monroe, p. 126.

William H. Kilpatrick, "The Project Method," *Teachers College Record*, XIX (1918), pp. 319-25, is a succinct statement of his view. His *Foundations of Method* (New York: Macmillan, 1925) adds little. Julia Weber Gordon, *My Country School Diary* has been reprinted (New York: Dell, 1970) with an introduction by John Holt.

Alice Barrows' perpetuation of the Gary Plan is described in Cohen and Mohl, pp. 10-34. A shorter version by Mohl is "Urban Education in the Twentieth Cen-tury: Alice Barrows and the Platoon School Plan," *Urban Education*, IX (1974), pp. 213-37. "... meaning to them": Barrows, "A Brief Statement. ..." unpub-lished, quoted in Cohen and Mohl, p. 192.

PART FOUR:
FROM DEPRESSION UNTIL NOW

Readings: For feelings and concerns during the Depression, 1929-1939, perhaps the most appropriate and most readable source is Frederick Lewis Allen, *Since Yester-day* (New York: Harper & Row, 1940. Repr. New York: Harper & Row, 1972). Allen's *The Big Change: America Transforms Itself* (New York: Simon and Schuster, 1952) summarizes his earlier books, but may be most interesting as imply-ing the ways in which America saw itself in the early 1950s. John Brooks, *The Fate of the Edsel and Other Business Ventures* (New York: Harper & Row, 1963) is one of the most engaging of several books by business journalists. Of social and socio-logical treatments, perhaps the most interesting are Vance Packard, *The Status*

Seekers (New York: D. McKay, 1959); William H. Whyte, *The Organization Man* (New York: Simon and Schuster, 1956); and C. Wright Mills, *White Collar: The American Middle Class* (New York: Oxford, 1951). For an informal but informative history, see Eric F. Goldman, *The Crucial Decade—and After: America, 1945-1960* (New York: Vintage Books, 1960). Seller, pp. 172-97, 220-93, describes the most recent phases of immigration and ethnicism. For a brief general history, see Morison, *et al., Growth of the American Republic*, Vol. II, pp. 471-792.

For school history, see Cremin, *Transformation*, pp. 240-353. Martin Mayer, *The Schools* (New York: Harper, 1961) was enormously popular for nearly a decade. A. S. Neill, *Summerhill: A Radical Approach to Child Rearing* (New York: Hart, 1960) was nearly obligatory reading for aspiring educationists. James Simon Kunen, *The Strawberry Statement* (New York: Random House, 1969) is the most striking of student accounts of campus uprisings at the end of the '60s. Edgar Z. Friedenberg, *The Vanishing Adolescent* (Boston: Beacon, 1959) was the first—and in many ways the best—critique of schools and society.

In fiction, perhaps the most lasting impression of the Depression and the dust bowl is John Steinbeck, *Grapes of Wrath* (several editions). Among novels of the Second World War, Norman Mailer, *The Naked and the Dead* (New York: Rinehart, 1948), about infantry soldiers in the Pacific, and Herman Wouk, *Caine Mutiny* (several editions), an account of naval officers aboard a destroyer, were popular in their time and perhaps representative. Sloan Wilson, *The Man in the Gray Flannel Suit* (New York: Simon and Schuster, 1955) seemed to catch a mood of its time. Two novels, Evan Hunter, *The Blackboard Jungle* (several editions) and Bel Kaufman, *Up the Down Staircase* (Englewood Cliffs, N. J.: Prentice-Hall, 1964) now seem encumbered with faulty plots, but do catch the grim aspect of city schools. J. D. Salinger, *Catcher in the Rye* (several editions) was seen as the essence of the plight of the adolescent in the 1950s; reread, it is still of interest, but faulty in execution. John Knowles, *A Separate Peace* (several editions) caught the dilemma of the adolescent boy on the eve of hostilities.

Our additional important sources are Kelves, and William Manchester, *The Glory and the Dream: A Narrative History of America, 1932-1972* (Boston: Little, Brown, 1974, 2 vols.), rich in detail but in later passages perhaps overly irate.

CHAPTER ELEVEN:
SEARCH FOR COMPETENCE

Many details early in this chapter come from Cremin, *Transformation*. Information on Chicago in the Depression is from Herrick, pp. 209-28. Teachers in Oklahoma recalled their Depression experiences in James Smallwood (ed.), *And Gladly Teach: Reminiscences of Teachers from Frontier Dugout to Modern Module* (Norman, Okla.: U. Oklahoma, 1976), pp. 138-79.

". . . imposition and indoctrination": George S. Counts, "Dare Progressive Education be Progressive," quoted in Cremin, *Transformation*, p. 259. The political statements of Counts and other social reform educators come in large part from C. A. Bowers, *The Progressive Educator and the Depression: The Radical Years* (New York: Random House, 1969). ". . . the status quo": Agnes de Lima, "Education for What?" *New Republic*, LXXI (1932), p. 317, quoted in Bowers, p. 38. ". . . other relevant findings": Augusta Alpert, *New Republic*, LXXII (1932), p. 317, quoted in Cremin, *Transformation*, p. 259. I. L. Kandell, *The Impact of the War on American Education* (Charlotte: U. N. Carolina, 1949) provides some factual information on the immediate effects of the war.

"... purpose of social education": Jesse H. Newlon, *Education for Democracy in Our Time* (New York: McGraw-Hill, 1939), p. 129. "... to participate effectively": Grayson N. Kefauver, "Reorientation of Educational Administration," in *Changing Concepts in Educational Administration*, Part II, Forty-fifth Yearbook of the National Society for the Study of Education (Chicago: U. Chicago, 1946), p. 3. Lewin's study was published in several forms. Its first description was Kurt Lewin, Ronald Lippitt, and R. K. White, "Patterns of Aggressive Behavior in Experimentally Created Social Climates," *Journal of Social Psychology*, X (1939), pp. 271-99. The Western Electric study first appeared as F. J. Roethlisberger and W. J. Dickson, *Management and the Worker* (Cambridge: Harvard, 1939).

William F. French, in *American Secondary Education* (New York: Odyssey, 1967) argues that the Seven Cardinal Principles reflected Herbert Spencer, *What Knowledge is of Most Worth* (1860). Part of our information on the Life Adjustment Movement is from Bowers. "... + PC/2" appeared in Albert Lynd, *Quackery in the Public Schools* (Boston: Little, Brown, 1953), p. 74. Lynd might have consulted the further elaboration of the formula, which appeared in Harl R. Douglass, "The 1950 Revision of the Douglass High School Teaching Load Formula," *Bulletin of the National Association of Secondary-School Principals*, XXXV, No. 179 (May, 1951). We would agree with Lynd that it was a "prodigious triviality". As Callahan points out (p. 240), principals found it "extremely useful." "... its science and technology": Clarence Cannon, in H. G. Rickover, *American Education—A National Failure* (New York: Dutton, 1963), p. vii.

For brief discussions of the Eight Year Study, see Cremin, *Transformation*, pp. 251-56; Krug, *Shaping ... 1920-1941*, pp. 255-66. For a description of discovery learning research ca. 1973, see Graham Nuthall and Ivan Snook, "Contemporary Models of Teaching," in *Second Handbook of Research on Teaching* (Chicago: Rand McNally, 1973), Robert M. W. Travers, ed., pp. 59-65. Information on education R & D and subsequent funding of educational research, although not of substantive matters, appears in Richard A. Dershimer, *The Federal Government and Educational R & D* (Lexington, Mass.: Lexington Books, 1976). The Kellogg Foundation's contribution to training and research in educational administration is described in Hollis A. Moore, Jr., "The Ferment in School Administration," in *Behavioral Science and Educational Administration*, Sixty-Third Yearbook of the National Society for the Study of Education, Part II, Daniel E. Griffiths, ed. (Chicago, NSSE, 1964), pp. 11-32. The appearance of the first R & D Center is described in David F. Noble, *America by Design* (New York: Knopf, 1977). For the earlier history of teachers' unions we have relied primarily on Eaton, *The American Federation of Teachers*. For the development of the United Federation of Teachers in New York City, see Diane Ravitch, *The Great School Wars*. Diane Ravitch and Ronald K. Goodenow, eds., *Educating an Urban People* (New York: Teachers College, Columbia U., 1981) provides some additional information and a current bibliography, but was not available to us when we wrote.

CHAPTER TWELVE:
QUEST FOR EQUALITY

R. Freeman Butts, *Public Education in the United States* (New York: Holt, Rinehart and Winston, 1978), pp. 326-40 provides a brief resume of desegregation until 1976. Ravitch, pp. 251-454, is a history of the unsuccessful efforts to desegregate New York City schools, and of subsequent events there. Meyer Weinberg, *A Chance to Learn: The History of Race and Education in the United States* (London:

Cambridge U., 1977) was useful, although, as has been pointed out, it is a wholly pessimistic account. Richard Kluger, *Simple Justice* (New York: Knopf, 1975, 2 vol.) is a painstakingly detailed account of *Brown v. Board of Education* and related litigation and other events, and takes a somewhat more positive view. Some details of this chapter are from the back files of *Urban Education*.

Foster's first report of his research on the "cant"–slang–of black high school students was Herbert L. Foster, "A Pilot Study of the Cant of the Disadvantaged, Socially Maladjusted Secondary School Child," *Urban Education*, II (1966), pp. 99-114. The thesis of Winthrop D. Jordan, *White Over Black* (Chapel Hill: U. N. Carolina, 1968) seemed powerful. However, one has the impression that first impressions of Native Americans as "noble savages" did not result in much subsequent advantage for them. ". . . the Fourteenth Amendment": from Earl Warren, *Brown v. Board of Education of Topeka*, quoted in Kluger, vol. II, pp. 890, 893. ". . . and poor children": Meyer Weinberg, *A Chance to Learn*, p. 134.

CHAPTER THIRTEEN:
PURSUIT OF FREEDOM

Joel Spring provides a useful analysis of recent education in *American Education: An Introduction to Social and Political Aspects* (New York: Longman, 1978). There are numerous sources on the youth movement and education during the 1960s, such as Theodore Roszak, *The Making of the Counter Culture* (New York: Anchor Books, 1969). We have depended heavily on Spring, *American Education*, for our interpretation of the youth movement. ". . . its further increase" *ibid.*, p. 78. Spring also discusses the youth movement in his essay, "Youth Culture in the United States," included in Clarence Karier, *et al.*, *Roots of Crisis*.

Works concerned with the alienation of youth during the 1950s and 1960s include David Riesman, Reuel Denney, and Nathan Glazer, *The Lonely Crowd* (New Haven: Yale, 1950); Edgar Z. Friedenberg, *The Vanishing Adolescent*; and Paul Goodman, *Growing Up Absurd* (New York: Vintage Books, 1960). ". . . source of alienation": Friedenberg, *The Vanishing Adolescent*, pp. 218-19. Jules Henry, in works such as *Culture Against Man* (New York: Random House, 1963) and his essays, *On Education* (New York: Vintage Books, 1972), provides some of the most perceptive analysis of education in American society during the 1960s. ". . . jail the child": *ibid.*, p. 11. ". . . a barbaric intrusion": Roszak, *The Making of the Counter Culture*, p. 42.

Our discussions of the student movement are based primarily on Lewis Feuer, *The Conflict of Generations* (New York: Basic Books, 1969) and Joseph Califano, Jr., *The Student Revolution: A Global Confrontation* (New York: Norton, 1969). ". . . classes have failed": Feuer, *The Conflict of Generations*, p. 11. There are a number of good sources on the student movement at Columbia University, including Kunen, *The Strawberry Statement*, which provides a unique look at the protests at Columbia. ". . . alone and lost": *ibid.*, p. 11. ". . . generation of radicals": *ibid.*, p. 38.

Discussions of new approaches to education from the late 1960s are numerous. Among the most interesting texts are A. S. Neill, *Summerhill: A Radical Approach to Childrearing*; Joseph Featherstone's articles on schools published in *The New Republic* in August and September 1967; John Holt, *How Children Fail* (New York: Pittman, 1964); Herbert Kohl, *36 Children* (New York: New American Library, 1967); and Nat Hentoff, *Our Children Are Dying* (New York: Viking, 1966).

The history of Parkway School is described in John Bremer, *The School Without Walls* (New York: Holt, Rinehart and Winston, 1971). ". . . new school superintendent": *ibid.*, p. 131. Probably the best introduction to the alternative school movement is A. Graubard, *Free the Children: Radical Reform and the Free School Movement* (New York: Pantheon, 1972). ". . . the high school": interview conducted by Provenzo, during the fall of 1974. ". . . the next month": *ibid.*

Problems of youth during the 1960s and early 1970s are discussed in James Coleman, *et al.*, *Youth: Transition to Adulthood* (Chicago: U. of Chicago, 1974). ". . . role of students.": *ibid.*, p. vii. An analysis of Coleman's *Youth* is included in Spring, *American Education*, pp. 81-84. ". . . available to adults": Coleman, *Youth*, p. 29.

INDEX

INDEX